THE WORKS OF
SIR JOHN VANBRUGH

Sr John Vanbrugh.

Kneller S.R. Imp. et Mag. Brit. Baronet pinx.   Simon fecit   Sold by J. Tonson in the Strand.

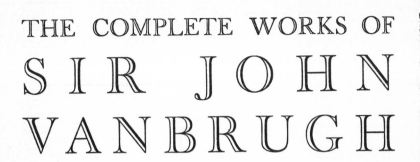

THE COMPLETE WORKS OF
SIR JOHN VANBRUGH

The plays edited by
BONAMY DOBRÉE

The letters edited by
GEOFFREY WEBB

THE FOURTH VOLUME *containing*
THE LETTERS

BLOOMSBURY

THE NONESUCH PRESS

16 Great James Street, W.C.

MCMXXVIII

AMS PRESS, INC. • NEW YORK • 1967

Reprinted with the permission of
THE BODLEY HEAD LTD.

AMS PRESS, INC.
New York, N.Y. 10003
1967

Manufactured in the United States of America

The Contents

PREFACE

THE text of the following letters has been taken as far as possible from the originals of Sir John Vanbrugh. The Note on Sources (p. xli) gives the whereabouts and some details as to the occasional publication of these. As the Note indicates, in certain instances it has not been possible to arrive at the originals, and these letters have perforce been taken from the best available sources, often the only one. With these exceptions, and one other especially notable, the letters have been reproduced with the spelling, punctuation, and use of capital letters of the originals.

Before going on to the question of the letters to the Duke and Duchess of Marlborough, the Editor feels that his grateful thanks must be expressed, in the first place, to the Hon. Geoffrey Howard, whose hospitality and kindness have made the Editor's visits to Castle Howard among the pleasantest of his duties in connection with this book. How greatly the book is indebted to the Castle Howard MSS., not only for the text of many letters, but for the material of many notes derived from unpublished letters of Hawksmoor and others, the reader will himself be able to judge. Special thanks are also due to the Hon. Mrs. Waters, of Arley Hall, Cheshire, who herself copied the letter to Lord Godolphin of November, 1704, and sent it to the Editor; to the Duke of Portland, and to his librarian at Welbeck Abbey for his kind help and for making copies of the two letters from among the Harley Papers; to Mr. H. Avray Tipping and the proprietors of *Country Life* for the loan of the photographs of the Bayforbury letters and for much kindly help and encouragement; and, lastly, to Mr. H. S. Vaughan for information as to Vanbrugh's brothers in the Royal Navy.

In conclusion, an apology is due to the reader for that the letters to the Duke and Duchess of Marlborough and some others connected with the building of Blenheim Palace can only be reproduced from the transcripts in the British Museum. Permission was asked of the present Duke of Marlborough to examine and copy such originals of Sir John Vanbrugh's MSS. as he might have in his possession, and the nature of this book was fully explained to him; but in the course of a short correspondence, his Grace not only refused his permission, but declared, with doubtful Historical sense, that Blenheim Palace was the private house of a private English gentleman, and went on to express a wish that there might be no discussion of the house or its building history either in the newspapers or in book form. The Editor and his publishers, while fully conscious,

vii

by reason of the great kindness they have experienced elsewhere, of the consideration that is due from them to the owners of the buildings and manuscripts which form the material of this book, yet feel themselves unable to defer to the Duke's wishes in this matter. In their opinion Blenheim Palace, as perhaps the most important architectural work of Sir John Vanbrugh, cannot be ignored in such a book as this, and they have not hesitated to reprint from the copies in the British Museum the text of the letters relative to its building, feeling that, after two hundred years, it cannot be held an unwarrantable invasion of family privacy to ventilate an incident of such importance to a personage of Sir John Vanbrugh's eminence in the history of English art and literature, and of such interest in regard to a great national monument as Blenheim Palace and a great public figure as the first Duchess of Marlborough.

GEOFFREY WEBB.

FOVANT,
August, 1927.

INTRODUCTION

A PASSAGE in Dryden's *Essay on Heroic Poetry* contains advice which has a peculiar relevance to Sir John Vanbrugh's architecture and indeed to that of his period as a whole. It runs as follows : " 'Tis true, there are limits to be set betwixt the boldness and the rashness of a poet : but he must understand these limits who pretends to judge as well as he who undertakes to write : and he who has not a liking to the whole ought in reason to be excluded from the censuring of the parts." The expression is uncompromising, but it is none the less true that neglect of this advice has been largely responsible for the ill-judged criticism and scamped unsympathetic treatment that Sir John Vanbrugh's period in architecture has often received from scholars and critics in the past. Educated taste in England has not really approved our " native " Baroque style, and only Sir Christopher Wren's immense popular reputation and the accessibility of many facts about his charming and many-sided personality have saved a man of even his genius from being ignored, with his contemporaries. The extant " lives of Wren," with but one all too slight exception, seem to indicate no really intelligent sympathy or attempt at understanding his buildings. And if Wren has suffered in this way, we cannot expect much in the way of critical appreciation of Sir John Vanbrugh as an architect whose highly-developed Baroque style was not universally admired even in his own day.

The cause of this neglect of the Baroque period in English architecture is not hard to find; hitherto, while there has been a reaction in some sort against the Gothic revival and John Ruskin, and people have brought themselves to appreciate the quiet country gentlemen's houses of the Queen Anne period and their urban counter-parts in Queen Anne's Gate or Bedford Row, it has always been what is called the " vernacular," not the monumental architecture of the period, that has been admired. Such buildings, as being the product of the influence of the new Renaissance theories on the traditional building methods of the country, are considered to be more " English " than the monumental works. Though whether a more significant gulf is fixed between the vernacular of the English brick-building districts and that of similar districts in France or the Low Countries, than there is between the Baroque monumental style as handled by English, Flemish and French architects, seems to the writer a question much too nice to be valuable. This preoccupation with the vernacular has been helped on by the circumstances of the working architects who have done so much of the initial propaganda work to revive public interest in Queen Anne and early Georgian architecture, and they, being in the main engaged in building small country or town houses, naturally turned to the study of the solutions of their own problems in the past. Another reason is that the associational charms of monumental architecture are, to say the least, recondite; the " literary overtones " of a building like Blenheim Palace are very subtle and complex, and require a very considerable historical sense of the position of the great Duke of Marlborough and of the whole course of develop-ment of Renaissance and Baroque art for their just appreciation; whereas the " ver-nacular " architecture fits readily into the picture with the Tory country gentleman

ix

and the beau about town who have between them captured all the historical sentiment-ality most people allow for this period. The great Whig magnates for whom Van-brugh worked were often romantic enough as personalities, but John Bull was a Tory country gentleman, and his taste in architecture is considered the only English and the only "gentlemanly" one. An extraordinary distortion of historical and critical perspective resulting from this modern approach to the English Baroque through the vernacular has been the exaltation of the "well-bred," "gentlemanly," "English," "traditional," etc. etc., qualities in the works of Sir Christopher Wren at the expense of his real and quite conscious contribution to architecture, which was the inauguration of the grand manner, the first essay in English (*pace* Inigo Jones) monumental Classic. A great deal of such criticism is based on sentiment, and ignores the fact that all the delightful qualities enumerated above were to be found in such houses as Tittenhanger and Coleshill before Wren's time, and it would be difficult indeed to prove Wren added anything considerable to that part of the English tradition. The foregoing must not be understood as a denial that these qualities exist in Wren's work, or that they contribute to its charm (for example, in Hampton Court), but as a corrective to a too-prevailing tendency to overrate their importance, which has gone far to obscure the real significance of his position and of his relation to succeeding architects, especially Vanbrugh. For in Vanbrugh none of these delightful qualities exist; people have had the impertinence to call St. Paul's the parish church of London or even of the Empire, but no one with any perception would ever dream of calling Blenheim Palace the Manor House of Woodstock, or even describing it as a country house of the Duke of Marlborough.

Present-day research is only now opening up the whole subject of the relations of the architects of this period to each other, their artistic pedigrees, their mutual influences and antagonisms: and for some time to come opinion on these points must be content to remain fluid. Even when the Wren Society shall have completed its great work there will still be more research to be done before any authoritative synthesis can be attempted. The latter part of this volume, where the Blenheim "business letters" are brought together in part, is justified only as it contributes to this work. In the mean-while an hypothesis is emerging of a School of Wren which flourished more and more as the great man grew older. The expression "School of Wren" may sound grandilo-quent, but it is the only term which really covers all the lesser related architects, though the gist of the matter may be put more briefly as follows: Nicholas Hawksmoor, born 1661, had been associated with Wren ever since 1679, and from that time onwards, in his own words, " I had the favour to serve under Sir Christopher Wren in the King's Works, in the rebuilding of the churches, the Cathedral Church of St. Paul's, London, and many other fabricks both Private and Publick, for which service Sir Christopher Wren appointed me Clerk of the Works at the King's House at Kensington, which small post I kept till his present Majesty (George I) came to the Throne."* By the time such works as Hampton Court and Kensington Palaces were undertaken, both begun 1690, Hawksmoor had grown to be Wren's right-hand man, and when Green-wich Hospital was taken in hand in 1695–6 it is suggested that he was associated with it in some special sense, again to quote his own words: " All knew that I had carried on and finished so much as was done of that Fabrick for little more than £100 per

* From an unpublished MS. at Castle Howard.

annum.''* It seems probable that it was in connection with Greenwich Hospital that Vanbrugh first came into touch with Wren and Hawksmoor. Evelyn mentions a Mr. Vanbrugh as Secretary to the Commission for Greenwich in 1696, though whether this is John or his cousin William, afterwards an official at the Treasury, is uncertain. But between this and his appointment as Comptroller of the Board of Works in June, 1702, in succession to Talman, John Vanbrugh must have been growing to a closer and closer association with the Board of Works: in July, 1699, he had been granted the site of the famous " Goose Pie " house amid the ruins of old Whitehall Palace, and Wren had to enquire into and report on the detail arrangements of the grant. The plans of Castle Howard were ready as early as the autumn of 1699 (see page 5), and Vanbrugh was recommending Hawksmoor in a letter to Lord Carlisle (page 6) that must date from 1700 or the early part of 1701, for in May of 1701 Hawksmoor is on the job and himself writing to Carlisle to report progress. By 1702 the " Goose Pie " must have been nearly finished, and we come to the appointment as Comptroller, and the lately opened question of the great Greenwich Hospital scheme. As to the appointment it is possible, even probable, that Lord Carlisle's tenure of the Treasury from November, 1701 to March, 1702, when Anne appointed Lord Goldolphin to that office, was the decisive factor: Vanbrugh was a Whig, and Wren, if anything, probably a moderate Tory, but it is unlikely that the appointment was anything but quite acceptable to Wren, who must have found the new Comptroller a happy change after Talman, with whom there had been considerable difficulties. It seems probable that there was no opposition from the Board of Works to the appointment; for if Wren was a moderate Tory he was of Godolphin's party, and the change of Ministry at Anne's accession was favourable to such: but, at any rate, the Whig setback made no difference, and in June Vanbrugh took up his position.

The next architectural landmark is the new scheme for completing Greenwich Hospital, of which Mr. Bolton, Curator of the Soane Museum and one of the Editors of the Wren Society, has recently published some most interesting details,† at the same time suggesting that the scheme dates from 1702, and shows the new influence of Vanbrugh at the Board of Works in the characteristic grandiosity of its conception. It is perhaps significant that at Castle Howard there is preserved a drawing for the central feature of the Greenwich scheme, made on the back of a sketch plan of Henderskelf (the original name of the site of Castle Howard) initialed N.H. and dated 1701. But until a great deal more work has been done on the Greenwich Hospital building history all theories as to the respective shares of Wren, Hawksmoor and Vanbrugh in these early works must be extremely tentative. What can be said with certainty is that about the turn of the century a new spirit appeared in the official architecture of the Board of Works. Three hypotheses may be suggested to account for it: first, the development of a late manner of Wren's own, foreshadowed perhaps in Chelsea Hospital with its colossal porticoes; secondly, the gradual and increasing influence of Hawksmoor in the work of the Office; and lastly, a new influence from outside in the personality of Vanbrugh. Mr. Bolton dismisses the " Hawksmoor sous clef " hypothesis altogether, and throws the whole weight of his authority on the side of Vanbrugh influence. The protagonist for Hawksmoor is Mr. Goodhart-Rendel,

* MS. at Castle Howard dated May 20th, 1726.
† *Architect's Journal*, June 23rd and 30th, 1926; *Builder*, January 7th, 1927.

and in an able and stimulating little essay* he has championed his man with great spirit. The hypothesis of a " later Wren manner " has not, as far as the writer knows, been advanced in this connection, but although Wren was born in 1632 and would thus be sixty-eight at the turn of the century, he was a genius, and such late second blossoming is not unknown in the history of art. Titian is an instance. Castle Howard and the Goose Pie are quite certainly Vanbrugh's. The Goose Pie may, it seems to the writer, be ignored as evidence of style. The nickname seems to have been extraordinarily apt, and the crenellations, the disproportionate height, and the scale of the rustications do indeed suggest what is known in the trade as a Raised Pie. But against this it must be said that our knowledge of its appearance is very imperfect, and that Vanbrugh was never at ease with small scale buildings even in later life, though he improved in this respect. Moreover, even Swift admitted " 'tis owned by all, thou art well contrived, tho' thou art small." Castle Howard is, however, quite another matter. The chronology of the building can be worked out in detail for the accounts are preserved, though unfortunately we have only one letter from Vanbrugh to Lord Carlisle and two of Hawksmoor's letters before 1720. It is quite certainly by Vanbrugh, though what share Wren and Hawksmoor, especially the latter, may have had in the original design, it is probably now impossible to determine. It has been supposed that without Hawksmoor the design could not have been made. Mr. Goodhart-Rendel says: " Neither in the general conception nor in the details of Castle Howard is there any faltering; everywhere in it there is evidence of the great technical skill and experience of its author. It was built under the supervision of Hawksmoor," and proceeds: "A few years later Vanbrugh again astonished his countrymen by a design for a still larger and more prodigious house, a design in which technical skill blossoms into extremes of bravura." (Blenheim Palace.) Further remarks at this juncture, some of which are open to question on points of fact, are not quoted in justice to Mr. Goodhart-Rendel, for in a short essay one cannot look for the same apparatus of supporting facts and authorities behind the generalizations, that a fuller treatment implies, but the above passages have a special importance because it is upon this feeling that such a design as Castle Howard implies a practically experienced architect, that the " Hawksmoor sous clef " hypothesis is based. But it is on precisely this point that the present Editor cannot agree with Mr. Goodhart-Rendel; relative to Vanbrugh's whole architectural achievement it seems to him that Castle Howard is definitely an immature and tentative work, a work in which many of the later characteristic " motifs " and qualities are indeed present, but only just—in embryo ; the word " faltering " is hardly appropriate to any work of an architect of such " gusto " as Vanbrugh, for " gusto " or high spirits is the most important quality shown alike by his writings, his architecture and his personality, but nevertheless the outstanding qualities of his later work do appear " falteringly," or at any rate rather uncertainly in Castle Howard. Something, however, must be said first of the style of this Wren School as a whole, its position in the course of English architecture and its characteristics as a Baroque variant and its origins in, and its relation to the Continental Baroque.

That Michael Angelo was the originator of the tendencies which distinguish the painting and sculpture of the later sixteenth and seventeenth centuries, not only in

* Prefixed to Hawksmoor in Messrs. Benn and Brother's small series, *The Masters of Architecture.*

Italy (the Baroque style), has long been recognised; and recently Mr. Geoffrey Scott has attributed to him a position of similar importance in the history of architecture. In a recent essay on St. Peter's Mr. Scott says: "He (Michael Angelo) has got away from the conception of architecture as a box of classical bricks, limited and fixed in shape, to be arranged, and treats his units of design as high-handedly as in the dome he treated his laws of structure. He conducts, as it were, an orchestra of forms. The window shape in the attic (at St. Peter's) must give out the note which is just then required of it, without regard to habits it may have acquired in classic solo or quartet. The motive of its upper frame is suddenly called upon to close the entire vertical progression. I have dwelt on this detail because it serves as well as another to illustrate the decisive change which Michael Angelo brought into architecture. These are the 'liberties' which constitute 'Baroque.' But they have, as here, a law and logic of their own." Elsewhere in the same essay Mr. Scott points out that "since properly considered, the whole of Renaissance architecture, culminating in Bramante, is humanised, it would be more exact to say that Michael Angelo sought to stress the energetic rather than the static physical implications in architectural form."* This also, as he says, is a Baroque quality: in other words, Baroque architecture gesticulates, though it may be that some critics would further distinguish between the gesticulations of Michael Angelo and the declamatory gestures of seventeenth-century Baroque. But however we may refine and distinguish between High Renaissance or "Proto-Baroque" and Baroque proper, assigning Michael Angelo to the one and Bernini to the other, Mr. Scott's analysis will hold, and this new conception of architecture, and this enlargement of the unit of design, are the fundamentals from which all other qualities which have been claimed as characteristics of the Baroque style, as "movement" and the new variety in planning, ultimately proceed. I have quoted these passages from Mr. Scott at length more for the sake of the admirable clarity with which those fundamental points are made than with any intention to trace the development of the style from Michael Angelo onwards till we come to its English variety in Wren, Hawksmoor and Vanbrugh. The outstanding monuments of the style in Italy are now well known, and such masterpieces as Cortona's façade at St. Maria della Pace and Bernini's colonades before St. Peter's are recognised as they deserve to be. There is no evidence, however, that any of the three English architects under discussion ever visited Italy, and it is probably that the only first-hand contact of any of them with Italian architecture was Wren's interview with Bernini in Paris in 1665, when "the old reserved Italian" gave him but a "five minutes' view" of the designs for the Louvre. Hawksmoor, it is true, in his later letters to Lord Carlisle† shows considerable familiarity with the names and the works and the positions of architects in Rome, but at the time he was engaged in contesting the changes in the Mausoleum design pressed on him by Sir Thomas Robinson and the Burlington Palladian party, and probably felt that a parade of Italian architectural learning was necessary to meet them on their own ground. Indeed, he says as much. And we need not assume, I think, that any of this knowledge was first-hand. In the absence, then, of first-hand knowledge of Italy, Wren and his fellows must have relied on engravings and illustrated editions of the architectural authorities as Serlio Vignola and, of course, Palladio. Mr. Bolton, in

---

* *The Vatican Basilica of St. Peter II.* Geoffrey Scott. *Country Life,* 1927.

† *Castle Howard :* unpublished MSS.

his recent examination of the Greenwich Hospital drawings, has endeavoured to trace some of these Italian authorities in detail from internal evidence of the original drawings: his results are necessarily inconclusive, but this much may be taken as certain, that Wren was continually and increasingly influenced by Italian architecture through the medium of engravings and illustrated books, and that it is in them that the sources of the " new manner " are to be sought in so far as they are Italian at all. How far they are Italian rather than French is a further question. Wren, as we have noted, was in France in 1665 and Vanbrugh possibly in 1683 and certainly in 1690–1692. But he spent a large part of this time in prison. We do not know how long he was at liberty before his arrest at Calais, and we have no evidence that this journey was in any special sense connected with his subsequent profession of architecture. The change in French architecture in the interval between the visits of the two men is, I think, significant. In 1665 when Wren was in France he mentions as architects after Bernini, François Mansart, Le Vau and Le Pautre, men who were soon to be broken or ignored by the cast-iron system of Colbert and supplanted by the triumphantly successful J. H. Mansart, who fitted so well into it. The works of these former men may be said, especially in the last instance, to have been moving towards, but not yet to have arrived at, a true Baroque, while J. H. Mansart and his works, though grandiose, were never adventurous enough to capture that spirit. Nevertheless, in many minor characteristics of J. H. Mansart's style and in the works of lesser and provincial architects, for example the fine Porte de Paris at Lille by Simon Volant (built 1682), affinities with the works in the " new manner," especially Vanbrugh's, are clear. By the time Vanbrugh was in France the buildings Wren examined and measured and the architects he admired were definitely out of fashion and favour as looking back to the style we may call Louis XIII, and the newer " Grand Manner " of Colbert and the Roi Soleil had begun and carried some way to completion many of its most notable monuments. Vanbrugh's indebtedness to Le Notre and his development of the French monumental garden style is more obvious and direct. As to Baroque in England, attempts have been made to label early seventeenth-century conceits, mostly derived from the German or Flemish ornamentalists, by this honourable name, but the Baroque style does not consist in a certain licentiousness of classically derived ornament, and even the mid-seventeenth century work at Oxford attributed to Inigo Jones, such as the Porch of St. Mary the Virgin and the central features of Canterbury Quadrangle at St. John's, beautiful as these are, must be considered as the ultimate and most perfect examples of that naïve Jacobean taste for Rennaissance sculptural conceits, rather than the adventures of an architect so absolutely at ease in the classical idiom as to attempt daring feats in his syntax. Of Inigo Jones himself it is dangerous to venture an opinion, but even should such works as the Castle Ashby screen be allowed him, and the strict Palladian chastity of the Banqueting Hall and the Queen's House at Greenwich be regarded only as one phase of a many-sided career, it would be hard to find any real Baroque quality in him. But with Wren the Baroque qualities are present, if not from the very beginning, at any rate in St. Paul's and many of the city churches. How far the Baroque qualities to be found in St. Paul's may have been increased or diminished in the process of modification of the design during construction, can hardly be determined here, but, whenever it may have come about, many of the most important features of the design are essentially Baroque, and this is now generally admitted.

This brings us to the beginning of the eighteenth century, the appearance of

Vanbrugh, and the new departures in architecture. This "new manner" is, in the first place, more massive, almost heavy-handed: instead of the "lightness and grace" for which Wren is so often praised, there is a feeling for mass, and a very conscious and much more thorough exploitation of it and, secondly, of those formal relations which Robert Adam termed "movement." This quality for which Adam so praised Vanbrugh is an example of those imaginative terms which are so really useful and so difficult of definition. Mr. Barman, by implication, equates it with "composition in three dimensions," describing how, as a man walks round the exterior of Blenheim Palace in widening or diminishing circles, new compositional effects are continually presenting themselves to him; but the term can imply something other than this, something which can apply equally to the new and characteristic bold compositional grouping and combination of principal masses and to the design of individual features and façades. If we take the orthodox classic orders, it will be seen that their elaboration is, in a sense, an "explaining away" of the transition from the vertical columns to the horizontal beam that rests upon them, and from these to the third dimensional member, the over-sailing roof. But in the disposition of the "enlarged units of design" (cf. Mr. Geoffrey Scott, quoted above) endless new transitions called for treatment, and it is by the exploitation and emphasis of these that the Baroque architects sought to attain their striking effects. It is perhaps in this aspect of Baroque design that the "quality of movement" consists. Moreover, this method of design is applied to individual features, as it were almost in lieu of sculptural ornament, and accounts sometimes for the curiously unnecessary elaboration of recessions and projections in their façades.

As an illustration of these qualities in what we have called the new manner at the Office of Works, no better example could be found than the Kensington Orangery. This building, designed in 1704, has been generally assumed to be by Wren, though it is known that Hawksmoor was specially appointed Clerk of the Works (see above), and Vanbrugh's intimate association with the building is indicated in the letter to Godolphin (page 11.) It is admittedly a masterpiece, but a masterpiece in the new manner. For apart from detail resemblances to later works of the School (the ringed Doric columns, for example, are found at Blenheim, Eastbury, Seaton Delaval, Grimsthorpe, and the façade of Hawksmoor's St. Mary Woolnoth, and there are other resemblances), the centre and end feature compositions, especially in their upper parts, with their elaborate play of square-advancing masses and receding curves, are typical of this quality of movement. Detail ornament has been reduced to a minimum, and variety is given almost entirely by such compositional devices. The Orangery is in red brick and Portland stone, the only example of the new style in this material. A comparison of these features with, say, Wren's gateway to Christ's Hospital (1672), shows the change very clearly. The Orangery is a masterpiece that stands with Cortona's façade of St. Maria della Pace as the ultimate but perfectly logical development of the tradition initiated by Michael Angelo, whereby the formal part of architecture, released from the tyranny of construction, and the unit of design enlarged from the confines of the orders, proceeded to new and surprising effects.

The illustration of Castle Howard here given represents the whole group of buildings as Vanbrugh would like to have finished them; and as there are no real discrepancies between the illustrations in the first and third volumes of Vitruvius we can say that this was at any rate his conception in 1715, when the first great period of work upon the house came to an end, and attention began to turn to the gardens. Various modifications were suggested (see p. 164). These only applied to that system of gates and terrace walks to be seen in the foreground of the picture. Briefly, the chronology of the building was as follows: Plans were approved by the end of 1699 and work was certainly begun in 1701 and possibly the year before. From that time till 1714–15 the building went on steadily, beginning from the east (the reader's left in illustration), and when in 1715 attention was diverted elsewhere to gardens and outworks, everything was complete except the north-west wing and the stable courts and detached block on the west side. These were indeed never built, in spite of Vanbrugh's suggestion towards the end of his life, reiterated by Hawksmoor some years after. Vanbrugh was peculiarly unfortunate in this respect and did not live to see any of his designs carried to completion, with the possible exception of Claremont and Blenheim, and in the latter instance he was not personally associated with the later stages of the actual building operations. As regards design, that is, planning and elevations and the general conception of the scheme as a whole, Castle Howard and Blenheim must be taken together. Their relations to each other, to the Greenwich scheme, and as a group to Vanbrugh's later work, are of supreme importance in the understanding of his architecture. The design of Blenheim was made some time in the early months of 1705, for the Duke of Marlborough returned from the Blenheim campaign in January of that year and the foundation-stone was laid in the June following: and the building was in much the same stage of completion as Castle Howard in 1716 when Vanbrugh ceased to be personally associated with it. So the two houses, allowing for a difference of over four years in the date of the designs, progressed very nearly parallel to each other. This is due to the great efforts that were made to press on the work at Blenheim, which, moreover, was being paid for with public money and therefore did not need, or should not have needed, to wait upon the exigencies of a private fortune.

It is first necessary to make clear Vanbrugh's conception of his task in building houses for such men as the Earl of Carlisle and the Duke of Marlborough. Both Blenheim and Castle Howard have been criticised as inconvenient, as too large, as not being " homes " (!), as sacrificing every interest of the client to the " megalomania " of the architect, quite apart from detailed criticisms of the designs. The most celebrated remarks of this kind are the lines on Blenheim:

> " Thanks, sir," cried I, " 'tis very fine
> But where d'ye sleep or where d'ye dine?
> I find by all that you've been telling,
> That 'tis a house, but not a dwelling."

Criticism of this kind is based, however, on a fundamental misconception of what Vanbrugh conceived to be the requirements of such personages as the Earl of Carlisle and the Duke of Marlborough, of whom the former was a personage in England and an institution in Yorkshire, the latter a personage in Europe and an institution in England, and their houses to be conceived accordingly. Nowadays in designing houses we divide the accommodation required into entertaining rooms or sitting-rooms, bedrooms and offices, and convenience for service is the first consideration. Vanbrugh once defined the qualities he aimed at in his houses as " State, Beauty and Convenience," and his houses are made up as regards accommodation of one or two great halls and saloons (Hawksmoor called them the " ceremonies "), two or three more state suites, consisting of an antechamber, a drawing-room on to which the antechamber gave,

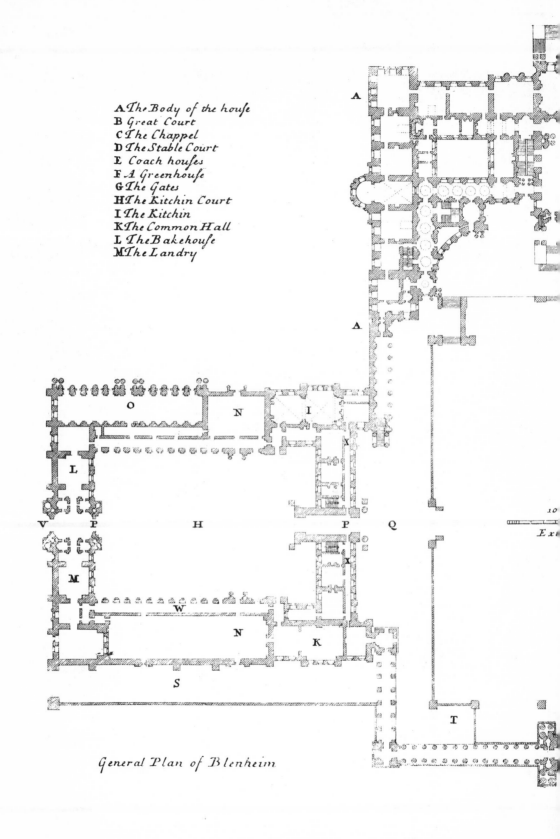

A The Body of the house
B Great Court
C The Chappel
D The Stable Court
E Coach houses
F A Greenhouse
G The Gates
H The Kitchin Court
I The Kitchin
K The Common Hall
L The Bakehouse
M The Landry

General Plan of Blenheim

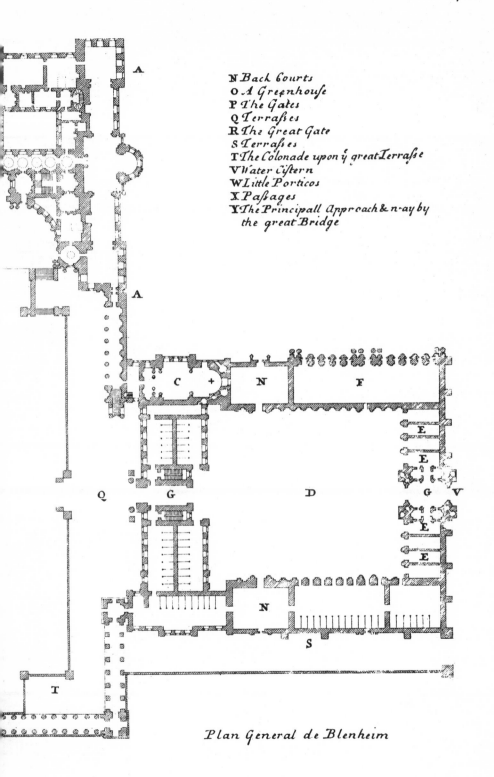

N Back Courts
O A Greenhouse
P The Gates
Q Terrasses
R The Great Gate
S Terrasses
T The Colonade upon ÿ great Terrasse
V Water Cistern
W Little Porticos
X Passages
Y The Principall Approach & n-ay by
   the great Bridge

Plan General de Blenheim

a bedroom, dressing-rooms and a cabinet, or study to each suite. In these suites the owners and principal guests could live and hold their levees independently; each suite was a self-contained unit. Besides these, there was a small "eating parlour," a certain amount of extra bedroom accommodation, a chapel and offices and servants' accommodation. This organisation in suites is the kernel of the whole matter, once it is understood: the criticism levelled against the State rooms at Blenheim and Castle Howard, that they are so divided up, that though they extend for 300 to 400 feet, yet the size and the grandeur of the individual rooms is not worthy of the scale of the houses, falls to the ground. Vanbrugh himself claimed that his houses were the most convenient ever yet planned, and this is not unreasonable. In his plans this peculiar method of internal arrangement is worked out most conscientiously and logically, great care being taken, almost invariably, to provide a way out of each suite independently of the others, and without the necessity of passing through the anteroom. It is quite clear that the planning is specially adapted to a special type of daily life, quite as carefully as the most up-to-date modern villa residence is modelled on the requirements of the social and intimate life of the middle-class household that will inhabit it. Vanbrugh's patrons required something quite different; in the first place a stately setting for magnificent ceremonial occasions, and secondly and more importantly, an arrangement suited to the ritual of their daily lives, a ritual devised to protect the great man from the importunities of his clients and increase his dignity by elaborating the processes whereby he could be approached. Again, Vanbrugh's houses have been criticised because the kitchen is often placed at a very considerable distance from the family lodgings. This again rests on a lack of imaginative insight into the conditions of a household such as Blenheim. The kitchen at Blenheim must have had to provide food for a whole army of servants when the house was in full commission, for in addition to the staff of the house the important guests would all bring several more, and the noise, smell and business of such a place would be necessarily inconsistent with State, Beauty or Convenience. Indeed, the placing of the kitchen in Vanbrugh's plans is always as near as may be to the main part of the house, but never, of course, actually in it.

Vanbrugh's plan of Castle Howard consists in the first place of a main central block or nucleus from which radiate wings; in this block are the great hall, open to the dome above, and a fine saloon above which is another saloon with two relatively small state suites leading off it, one either side of the lower saloon, and opening from it are two antechambers; on either side of the hall, the staircases and two small rooms, one a bedroom and the other the "private eating parlour." On the south, that is the saloon side of this block, two wings extend to the east and west, each of which contains the drawing-room, bedroom, dressing-rooms, and cabinet or study, of the two great state suites. These rooms all communicate with each other, and alternative access is provided by two corridors running down the north sides of the wings. On the north, or entrance side of the central block, two more corridors curve outwards from the angles and join two advanced wings in which are the chapel and more bedroom accommodation and the kitchen and several rooms distinguished on the plan as the "hunting apartment." The wings on the south side are low, having no floor above the state suites, but those to the north have an upper story providing further bedroom accommodation. To the east and west of the two northern wings are great courts, for offices and stables respectively, and closing these over against the house two more large blocks to accommodate, above the offices and stables themselves, the domestic servants and stable hands. At Blenheim, the same arrangement of a nucleus containing the hall and staircases, the great saloon, etc., and having wings radiating from it, has been united into one great block by east and west ranges joining the ends of the north and south wings on each side, and making the re-entrant spaces between the wings into internal courts: apart from the extra accommodation provided by these ranges, additional state suites to the east and a long gallery to the west, and some less important differences noted below, the arrangement of the hall and staircases, the small "eating parlour" and the little bedroom, the great saloon with its antechambers leading off it on each side to the great suites along the south front, etc., is precisely the same as at Castle Howard. Of the minor differences made to the plan by the addition of the east and west ranges, the chief has been that the northern corridors no longer needed to be carried out to the advanced wings, but could run straight out to the new ranges, that on the east turning at right angles northwards to provide alternative access to the north-east suite. Another important change is the provision of a second story over almost all this new part of the building, greatly increasing the number of bedrooms. Of necessity the offices and stable courts at Blenheim have been placed well forward of the house on the north or entrance side, in order to clear the fronts of the east and west ranges (which did not exist at Castle Howard), and thus form a much more deeply recessed entrance court between their inner walls. Stress has been laid hitherto on the essential resemblances between the Castle Howard and Blenheim plans, as this is not apparent at first sight; but the importance of the modifications in the plan as used at Blenheim can hardly be exaggerated. The uniting of the relatively diffuse Castle Howard arrangement of central nucleus and spreading wings into one great block with strongly marked corner pavilions and a recessed north side, and the advancing of the offices and stable courts with their subordinate masses of building to positions on each side of the deeply recessed entrance court, mark the evolution of the typical Vanbrugh plan and composition, which he afterwards developed with such mastery at Eastbury and Seaton Delaval. Blenheim is the essential link between plans of Castle Howard and of later houses. The disposition of the main and subsidiary groups of buildings evolved at Blenheim on an immense and complicated scale was, as we shall have occasion to note later, simplified and cut down to essentials in the designs of Eastbury and still more of Seaton Delaval: but those essentials whereby, in the words of Sir Joshua Reynolds, "To support his principal object he produces his second and third group of masses," remain the same. At Castle Howard these essentials are present, but the planning being, as we have said, more diffuse, the silhouette, for instance, has become rather a picturesque and immensely varied skyline of towers, cupolas and domes—not to speak of statues, urns and chimney-stacks—than a great piling up of related masses to a magnificent cumulative effect as at Blenheim, or a subtly graduated and selected disposition of forms to contrast and compare with one another, as at Seaton.

In the detail treatment of the designs, that is the use of orders, walling treatments, ornament, etc., all of which is as much the resultant of plan and elevation considered together as the large questions of composition and silhouette we have been discussing, a similar evolution to that in plan and composition can be observed. And Blenheim again forms a link between Castle Howard and the later designs. In Castle Howard the large discrepancies of scale, especially of height between the central "nucleus" block and the wings, another aspect of which has already been described as the diffuse character of the design, and, moreover, the weakness of the termination to the southern wings as compared with the great corner pavilions at Blenheim, all these things tend to differentiate the various parts making up the building so considerably that a unity of basement, order and wall-treatment has perforce been insisted on, especially along the south front, in order to knit the design together. This is the explanation of the scholastic solecism of employing a single Corinthian order throughout the length of the south front, as well in the high central block as in the wings, though in the former it is necessarily twice the height in the latter, while the distance apart from centre to centre remains the same. At Blenheim, where the general disposition of the design is so much more closely knit together of itself, exactly the reverse treatment has been followed and each component part differentiated by the treatment of the basement, walling or order. To take the south front again in this building, while it forms a single block, as we have said, the articulation of the various parts, of which this block is made up, the central nucleus, the wings and the great corner pavilions which have been added to them, to make returns to the east and west fronts, are all treated differently. A colossal Corinthian order of great magnificence emphasises the central nucleus: in the wings is a severely plain ashlar walling with very simple treatment of the window dressings, and a heavy and severe rusticated treatment of the two terminal pavilions closes the composition at each end. Thus in both houses the articulation of the parts in an essential unity of composition is clearly expressed. It cannot be denied that the solution at Blenheim is sounder, more satisfactory and more complete as well as more daring in effect than that of the south front at Castle Howard, gracious, even charming in a magnificent way, as that composition is. This principle or method of design which we have been tracing out in these two buildings, the principle of expressing the articulation of the parts within a compositional unity, is a perfect example of what is meant by the " enlargement of the unit of design " in Vanbrugh's works and those of other Baroque architects, and it is also in this way a link with the great Greenwich Hospital scheme of 1702, and seems to be a development in practice of those aphorisms on the æsthetics of architecture by Sir Christopher Wren contained in a fragmentary document published in the *Parentalia* : " Views contrary to Beauty are Deformity, or a Defect of Uniformity, and Plainness, which is the Excess of Uniformity; Variety makes the Mean. Varieties of Uniformities make compleat Beauty: Uniformities are best tempered, as Rhimes in Poetry, alternately, or sometimes with more Variety, as in Stanzas." The Greenwich Scheme forms a link between the Castle Howard and Blenheim schemes; in it the principle of expressing the articulation of the parts within a compositional unity is very marked, especially in the buildings grouped round the ends of the great elliptical arcaded court which forms the most striking feature of the scheme. This is so much the case as to appear in certain parts of the design almost capricious, or at any rate exaggerated, notably in the returns from the broken ends of the elliptical arcade in an extraordinary series of angular and curved blocks set radial to the ellipse and therefore skew to the main side. Mr. Bolton, the discoverer of this magnificent project, calls attention to the " general analogy of the grouping of the long lines of the oval court, and the central raised mass of the portico of the ante-chapel with the general lines of Castle Howard. . . ." To the present editor, it seems that, while there is almost undoubtedly a general analogy to the compositional lines of Castle Howard, there is a closer analogy with Blenheim in the general treatment of the elevations, both as to differentiation of block units and in the character of the details which both here and at Blenheim are more definitely in accordance with what we have called the " new manner " than is the case at Castle Howard. Another name for this aspect of the " new manner " has been the " high Roman fashion " as opposed to the " French frippery " of representational sculptural ornament in low relief, which is a characteristic of Talman's designs and plays a considerable part, and not a very successful one, in the fronts at Castle Howard, but is notably absent in Blenheim and this Greenwich design.

Mr. Bolton attributes the Greenwich scheme in the main to Vanbrugh, on the general grounds of these resemblances and considerations such as the imaginative magnificence and scale of the scheme, and certainly, in view of these and the date of the scheme (1702, the year Vanbrugh was appointed to the Board of Works) we may assume his association with it. It is only when Mr. Bolton proceeds in his examination of the actual sketches of the Greenwich scheme " The rough and incomplete state of the half-drawings we have suggests that Vanbrugh abandoned the project at an early stage. Never having been through the drill of the professed architectural student, he seems to have been incapable of the sustained effort that the full development of such a great design must demand. Technically the draughtsmanship is crude in the extreme. The impetuosity of his temperament is suggested by the haste to convert elevation into perspective, a dramatic touch which gives a special character to the drawing . . ." that we would venture to qualify his judgments. This passage, it would seem, needs to be read with two considerations in mind. There are several indications in the letters that Vanbrugh often left the making of his drawings other than preliminary sketches to others. Even Hawksmoor, that model of the architect who " has been through the mill," was forced to do so in later life by reason of his gout, and it is quite probable that in many cases Wren did so too. And, secondly, as to the " haste to convert elevation into perspective." If Vanbrugh always endeavoured to conceive his designs in the round and therefore made his first draft sketches in perspective (and the present editor is inclined to agree that this is probably the case), the source of this characteristic is surely to be found in these words of Sir Christopher Wren from the Tract already quoted: " The Architect ought above all things to be well skilled in Perspective: for, everything that appears well in the Orthography, may not be good in the Model, especially where there are many Angles and Projectures; and everything that is good in Model, may not be so when built; because a Model is seen from other Stations and Distances than the eye sees the Building: but this will hold universally true, that whatsoever is good in Perspective, and will hold so in all the Principal Views, whether direct or oblique, will be as good in great, if only this Caution be observed, that Regard be had to the Distance of the eye in the principal Stations." This doctrine of the importance of perspective in making architectural designs would seem to have been one of the tenets of the School of Wren, for in 1707 we find the names of Wren, Vanbrugh and Hawksmoor subscribed to a short letter of commendation prefixed to a book teaching perspective drawings for architectural purposes. This characteristic of the School seems to the present writer of the deepest significance in connection with the remarkable " three-dimensional quality " in the works in the " New Manner."

The foregoing tentative analysis of the relations of Vanbrugh's two most important works to other buildings of the School and to each other has been attempted to support the contention stated earlier in the essay that the Castle Howard design is immature as compared with Blenheim, and that even Blenheim itself is not the final blossoming of Vanbrugh's style, the ultimate example of his peculiar contribution of English architecture. With this contention goes the corollary that it is unnecessary to suppose that any man of much greater technical experience than Vanbrugh, e.g. Hawksmoor, must needs have had a dominating influence on the designs. That both buildings have in them a strong element of technical bravura, especially Blenheim, is admitted, but the present writer has yet to be convinced that the quality of " displayed technique " is a hall-mark of maturity in an artist. That the case is incomplete, at this juncture, without the detailed examination of the later works which follows in due course, is also true, and further the writer agrees that without such skilled assistance as that of Hawksmoor Vanbrugh probably could not have seen his conceptions as satisfactorily realised. There are also letters of Hawksmoor in existence which show that in details he often exercised a large discretion, certainly as regards interiors at Castle Howard and probably exteriors also. But then it is not for refinements of details that one goes out to seek in Vanbrugh's houses. Further, that Vanbrugh was a fellow-member of the same school or group of architects with Hawksmoor and Wren is certain, but as to the respective contributions of each to the common style it seems impossible to be at all certain as yet.

In the interval between the designs of Castle Howard and Blenheim, and quite apart from any official connection with Greenwich, Vanbrugh was engaged architecturally on two smaller enterprises. The first was the modification or rebuilding of a house for Sir Godfrey Kneller near Twickenham (Hounslow). This was a very moderate-sized house built of brick, a new material with Vanbrugh, and may possibly have been in a semi-mediæval style; the existing building has been so much altered by P. Hardwick and others as to be hardly recognisable. The other building was the New Opera House in the Haymarket—an ill-fated personal enterprise. Of this we know very little, architecturally speaking, except that its acoustics were defective, at any rate for plays, though possibly better for music, that it had a dome internally and was very gorgeous; Defoe described it as like a French church. Up to this time Vanbrugh's architectural career had been a series of unqualified successes, at any rate from a worldly point of view, and to secure the Blenheim commission was a triumph of the first order. But with the inception of the Blenheim and Opera House enterprises, he opened up for himself sources of continual worry and trouble both financial and personal which were to last almost for the rest of his life. The Opera House gave trouble from the start; but before any serious difficulties had arisen at Blenheim, Vanbrugh was commissioned to complete the rebuilding of Kimbolton Castle for the Earl, afterwards Duke, of Manchester, evidently from the letters of an old-standing friend.

The reconstruction of this early Tudor house (built 1525) had been begun in the latter part of the seventeenth century, when the courtyard was finished in a typical and very charming style in red brick with stone dressings. By 1707 the rest of the building seems to have become so ruinous that Vanbrugh was called in to complete the work of rebuilding. It is difficult to determine exactly what Vanbrugh did to the interior of the house, in the matter of general dispositions, but there are several individual rooms such as the Saloon (Vanbrugh's " stately room of Parade ") and the Chapel which are very characteristic of his interior style. Otherwise the four external fronts are his: these are plain and severe to the point of bareness and yet, though Vanbrugh was greatly hampered by the confines of the old plan and by the need for economy, there is still a very characteristic quality in the greatness of the scale and the boldness of the detail treatment. The outstanding quality of the design is the extraordinary " sense of mass " and the success of the grim, overpowering, fortress-like effect achieved with the greatest economy of formal devices. In his letter of July 18th, 1707, to the Earl of Manchester, Vanbrugh discusses this " Castle " air as he calls it which he has given to the building, and defends it, citing Hugh May's building at Windsor as his model. This passage and its fulfilment at Kimbolton are of unusual interest in connection with Vanbrugh's romantic and " mediævalising " tendencies.

This aspect of his work was remarked as early as Gwyn (*London and Westminster Improved*, 1767) who says: " As an architect he was generally a Romantic Castle. builder," and constitutes one of the most curious bypaths of the history of taste in the eighteenth century. The Romantic revival in architecture has often, quite inaccurately, been fathered on Horace Walpole, by reason of his Strawberry Hill aberrations, but Horace Walpole was not born till ten years after Kimbolton was begun, and we must now recognise Vanbrugh in that capacity, with Hawksmoor perhaps, as the more specifically " Gothic " enthusiast under Wren. [i.e. for pointed arches, lanterns and what not.] Wren's attitude to mediæval architecture is explained in several reports and tracts printed in the *Parentalia ;* he considered it as definitely inferior to the classical, of course, but there is a marked absence of that intolerance which is to be found in Evelyn. He shows some critical appreciation of its constructional aspect, and was ready to build in a Gothic style to harmonise with existing work as at Christ Church, Oxford, and in the now-disappeared works on the north transept of Westminster Abbey. In one of the letters to Dr. Fell in the matter of the Christ Church gateway, he explains a theory of Gothic composition being based on the pyramid, as opposed to the horizontal and vertical lines of classic, an idea that is echoed in his dictum from the Tract already quoted: " Pyramids are Gothick; pots Modern French." In contradiction to his practice, which derives rather from the perpendicular, Wren praises the early Gothic of Salisbury Cathedral " beyond what I find in divers Gothic Fabricks of later date, which tho' more elaborated with nice and small Works, yet want the natural Beauty which arises from the Proportions of the first Dimensions . . . the Mouldings are decently mixed with large planes without an affectation of filling every Corner with Ornaments, which, unless they are admirably good, glut the Eye, as much as in Musick, too much Division the Ears."* Hawksmoor, in his Gothic, with his preoccupation with the motif of the Ely lantern, shows the same derivation from the later rather than earlier mediæval styles.

Vanbrugh as a member of the same group as Wren and Hawksmoor and working in the closest association with them, would find little to discourage any Romantic leanings he had to the mediæval. We may, I think, distinguish two sides to his Romanticism; the one, of which Kimbolton is the most pronounced example, affecting his compositions in a general way and only slightly in detail, and allied to the " emotional " aspect of Baroque architecture, only that in Vanbrugh's case the emotional effects he sought were those of the romantic towering fortress. This is, I think, noticeable in the sites of his houses as Castle Howard and Eastbury, and dictated his choice of Nottingham Castle, which he persuaded the Duke of Newcastle to take as his northern seat, and also in the actual compositions of Blenheim, Seaton, etc. The other is the

* *Report on Salisbury Cathedral*, 1669, printed in *Parentalia*.

actual production of quasi-mediæval designs for comparatively trivial occasions, such as garden buildings at Castle Howard and Claremont and small suburban villas as at Greenwich. This is a point to which we shall have to return in discussing Vanbrugh as a garden-designer, but here it must be mentioned as an aspect of the return to mediævalism that was destined to survive; Kent built a Gothic villa for Newcastle's brother, Henry Pelham, and even in Strawberry Hill the revival was not yet freed from the taint of " garden decoration "—a distinction that was reserved for Wyatt at Fonthill. But Vanbrugh even in his garden buildings never adopted the ogee and the pointed arch, and except for a use of corbel-tables the detail is all classic and the mediævalism only appears in the main lines of the building, enough to make a definite suggestion at Kimbolton and rather more nearly imitation in the smaller works. His Romanticism, it would seem, was literary; he tried to catch the likeness of the sensational effects of the Mediæval Castle, and it is a strong testimony to his real architectural gifts that he saw that this could be done better by an adjustment of proportions and a special disposition of masses than by imitation of detail. Critics have seen in this aspect of his work a reflection of his interest in the stage, especially opera, and certainly a comparison with the literary developments of the Restoration suggests that in some respects much of Vanbrugh's work stands in the same relation to orthodox classical architecture as the Heroic drama of Dryden stands to Classical tragedy. Indeed, Heroic architecture is as good a description of his style as could be found. It may be just this quality that provoked the charmingly naïve comment of a nineteenth-century critic of Castle Howard and Blenheim: " (These buildings) infinitely more fittingly attest the nature, grandeur and majesty of our nobility than the baronial castles and fortified strongholds of their ancestors."* In this castellated manner of building Vanbrugh and Hawksmoor found no successors until Robert Adam at Calzean Castle, a building with more detailed reminiscences of Vanbrugh than this. But then Robert Adam's admiration of Vanbrugh and sympathetic understanding of his achievement is well established.

In the letters we can follow the discussions on the rebuilding of the south side only of Kimbolton in some detail; the rest of the house was completed by Vanbrugh in subsequent years, but the Earl of Manchester being returned from Venice and on the spot himself, there is no correspondence preserved. Kimbolton is the first occasion, to our knowledge, when Vanbrugh was commissioned to reconstruct an older house. For this kind of work he achieved a great reputation and there are several references in the letters to such commission as alterations to Newcastle House, Lincoln's Inn Fields, and Nottingham Castle for the Duke of Newcastle, and Lumley Castle, in which he again exploited to the full the romantic possibilities of the mediæval character of the place, possibly at Gilling House in Yorkshire also. Grimsthorpe was to be a similar reconstruction, which was in fact only partially carried out. As we shall see, it was his reputation for skill in this kind of work which obtained for Vanbrugh the commission to work for Admiral Delaval, who did not originally intend to do more than reconstruct his existing house.

Meanwhile, from 1705 onwards, the building of Blenheim had been pressed on with all possible speed, and a great deal faster than the money was issued from the Treasury. Whether this haste was due to the desire of Marlborough to get his house built for him by the Queen while he maintained his influence over her, or whether Vanbrugh wished to get the whole scheme so far advanced that there should be no

* *The Builder*, 1860.

question of its being left unfinished, or whether again neither Vanbrugh nor the Duke saw any reason for delay, since neither of them were paying the bill, can never be determined. But it was this haste to press on the work in the early years, involving as it did the accumulation of immense debts due to the contractors, that was at the root of all the subsequent troubles. The quarrels with the Duchess of Marlborough in which Vanbrugh was involved, and the bitter enmity which eventually developed between them, has attracted more attention than any other aspect of his career. And undoubtedly the constant worry and the circumstance of being owed and not paid the sum of £1660, added to the financial embarrassments consequent upon the failure of the Haymarket Opera scheme, were of the greatest importance in his life; but for all that Blenheim is not his only building, and picturesque as the character of the great Duchess is, too much importance can be given to this part of the correspondence. Vanbrugh deserves to be remembered for more important things than having been the victim even of the greatest and most celebrated shrew in history. In the letters themselves Vanbrugh's own point of view is sufficiently stated; it is therefore the endeavour of the writer in the following account of the affair to give as much weight as possible to the point of view of the Duchess.

It appears that from the very outset Lord Godolphin and the Duchess were in favour of a more modest house, it is said a design by Wren. Marlborough himself was not only Vanbrugh's friend, but had also set his heart on Vanbrugh's design as we know it. This is well attested by the Duchess, who declares in letters written long after the Duke and Vanbrugh were both dead that she had spent money on improving Blenheim because the Duke had had the scheme so much at heart. In addition to this first consideration, that the Blenheim scheme was the Duke's favourite and not the Duchess's, it must be remembered that during the period of the early quarrels (1706 to 1711) the Duchess was in a position which grew increasingly unpleasant. While the Duke still had his victories and his hopes of a march on Paris to console him for the increasing difficulties of the political situation at home, the Duchess was in the very midst of those difficulties, and how nerve-racking they could be is amply suggested by the descriptions that have come down to us of the terrible scenes between the Duchess and the Queen in the later stages of their estrangement. That the Duchess was a violent and dominating character hardly needs to be insisted upon here. And it must be remembered to her credit that for all the violence of her temper in these earlier quarrels she seems to have borne no malice, and was on the best of terms with Vanbrugh in the years 1711 to 1714 when he, in common with herself and her great husband, were suffering hard times. But then, Vanbrugh had lost his official positions through loyalty to the Duke of Marlborough and that would atone for much in the Duchess's eyes.

The first trouble with the Duchess seems to have arisen as early as 1706, for Godolphin was moved to write to the Duke asking him to restrain her a little. Then, in 1708, a new difficulty arose over the price of the carriage of stone from the quarries; the Duchess firmly refused to pay more than a certain rate and Vanbrugh, who was in low water financially at that time and had hopes of obtaining some lucrative appointment by the Marlborough influence, was in no position to insist. The position was the more difficult in that the year before the Duke himself had been vexed at the stone not coming through quickly enough. In 1709 the wet season increased the difficulty of carrying stone over the country roads, and arising from these difficulties two wholly

A. The Great Hall
a. The two principall Apartments
   making a line of 300 feet.
b. The Corridores
c. The private Eating parlour.
d. The Chappell.
e. The Kitchin.
f. The hunting Apartment.

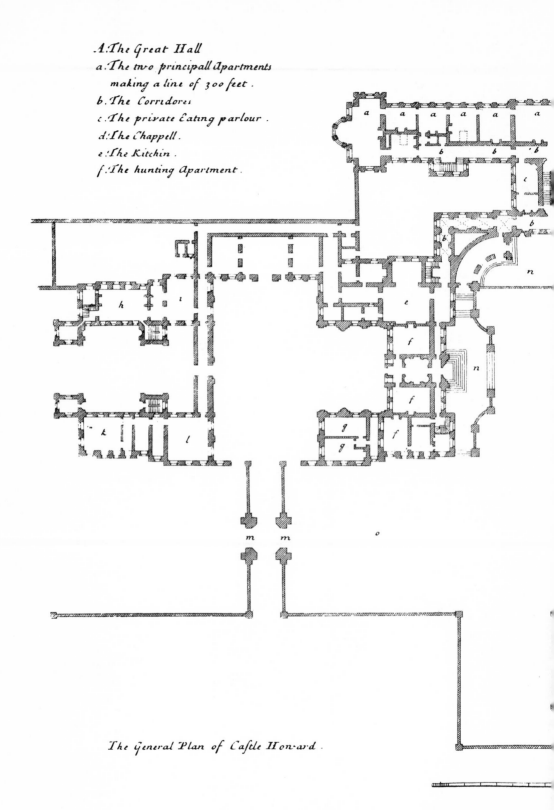

The General Plan of Castle Howard.

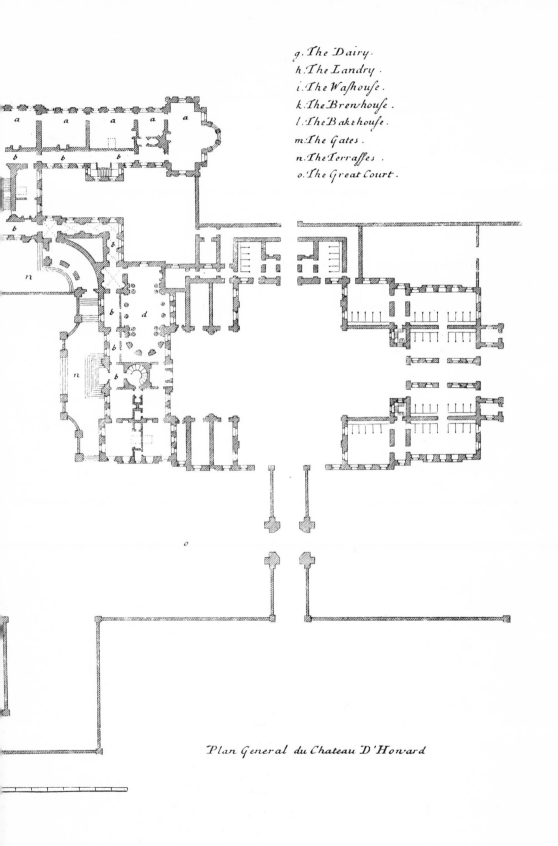

g. The Dairy.
h. The Landry.
i. The Washouse.
k. The Brewhouse.
l. The Bakehouse.
m. The Gates.
n. The Terrasses.
o. The Great Court.

Plan General du Chateau D'Howard

INTRODUCTION

new issues appear—the question of the preservation of the old Manor House at Woodstock as a picturesque monument in the park, and the Duchess calling in question important parts of the design—the western Orangery, for example. This is by far the most interesting and important of the quarrels hitherto, for in it Vanbrugh is contending for things he had very much at heart, the romantic value of an historical building and the integrity of his own design. This quarrel died down in due course, but the suspicions aroused by it in the Duchess's mind smouldered, and as early as March, 1710, she is making trouble over smith's work. At last, with the fall of Godolphin, she was thoroughly alarmed and stopped the works under circumstances as humiliating for Vanbrugh as possible. That is a brief record of the early quarrels, and behind them we must try and realise not only the Court intrigues and great issues of high politics in London, but endless repercussions in Oxfordshire, where there were Tories enough, in and about Oxford, to take advantage of every difficulty at Blenheim for political purposes. Vanbrugh, who lived much at Woodstock during this time and had become quite a figure in Oxford and the county, seems to have been considerably involved in local politics. All this side of the Blenheim affair is very obscure; there are plenty of hints, about combinations among the workmen and people who wished no good to the work, and there is the curious question of the paving of Woodstock town in 1712–13. It is readily understandable that the large sums of money accruing to Oxfordshire builders and the uncertainty of wages or employment among the workmen could be exploited very easily by Tory enemies of the Duke's political interests in Oxfordshire. It is said that great scenes of excitement took place in Oxford after the Duchess stopped the works in 1710, and there is some comment upon this in a letter preserved among the Harley MSS. Further, it was a letter to the Mayor of Woodstock that procured Vanbrugh's dismissal from the Office of Works, and it seems most probable that it is to his taking a too active part in Oxfordshire politics as some sort of unofficial agent in the Duke of Marlborough's interest that his troubles under the Tory administration of Queen Anne's last years are due.

After the accession of George I, all appeared well: Vanbrugh was knighted and restored to his position as Comptroller at the Board of Works, and it was decided to proceed with Blenheim. The financial position of that scheme appears to have been much as follows. A very large sum (well over £200,000) had already been issued by the Crown, and the buildings had been pressed on even beyond this vast expenditure, so that a great sum was still owing to the contractors. After the work had been stopped in 1712 the workmen had set on foot proceedings to obtain their debts, and at that time Vanbrugh had been active in reminding the Treasury that it was the Queen's business to find the money to satisfy these creditors. After the Queen's death a sum of £500,000 was voted in settlement of her debts, and the debt on Blenheim was acknowledged at £60,000. Beyond this the Duke of Marlborough accepted responsibility. But for one reason or another no more than £16,000 was issued immediately, and in due course the contractors instituted proceedings against the Duke of Marlborough. The difficulty of Vanbrugh's position was this: he, acting on a warrant issued in Marlborough's name by Godolphin, had made these agreements with the contractors, and the money had all been issued as to the Duke of Marlborough, the contractors never dealing immediately in law with the Crown. At length in 1719 the case came before the Barons of the Exchequer. The Court found that the Duke was responsible mainly on the ground of Vanbrugh's warrant, and certain of the Duke's letters to Vanbrugh about detail points in the building. It was for his evidence at this trial that the Duchess of Marlborough became so bitter against him: in two letters to Lord Carlisle she puts her case with her usual vehemence, her argument being that Vanbrugh perjured himself in saying that the Duke of Marlborough recognised the contracts as being made in his name, and she proceeds to hint at peculation on the score of prices being fixed too high. "The most material witnesses," she says, "were plainly perjured under their own hands, but most flamingly Sir J. V." And in the second letter, "because Sir John, by agreeing with any of the works people upon an old dirty piece of paper may yet make whatever contracts he pleases." And finally, "I have good reason to believe that Bury and Price (Barons of the Exchequer) were gained by the influence of a very artful man who is a great friend to Sir John"—meaning, probably, the younger Craggs. The Duchess had every reason to be angry; for why did not Vanbrugh insist at this trial as he had done before that the debt was the Crown's? The answer is, in the writer's opinion, twofold. Firstly, the question of the Crown's responsibility had been settled at the beginning of the reign once and for all, and Vanbrugh had borne his part in this settlement on the Duke's behalf. That was not the question now at issue. Secondly, if he had made any such attempt to turn the contractors' onset from the Duke on to the Crown, it would probably have been more than his Crown appointments were worth, especially in view of the unsettled state of the Board of Works at that time. And so, though he had jeopardised his career for the sake of the Duke of Marlborough in 1713, he could hardly be expected to do so again in 1719 for the Duchess, who had quarrelled with him for the last time three years before, and dismissed him from his position at Blenheim. This last quarrel of 1716 has not been referred to before, but it is unnecessary to dwell on it here; in the letters themselves it is the clearest and best documented of all the episodes of the Blenheim affair. It took place not long after the Duke of Marlborough's paralytic seizure, when his mollifying influence was removed, and as it appears in the letters seems a recapitulation of all the previous differences: the old Manor House again, and similar charges on the part of the Duchess of excessive prices for works done and extravagant expenditure on out-buildings, such as the Bridge and Causeway, which in their later quarrel have taken the place of the Orangery and Office Court. After her failure before the Barons of the Exchequer, the Duchess took the case to the House of Lords, the occasion (see page 133) of Vanbrugh's writing his *Justification* (page 177). Being again defeated there, she marshalled all the forces of the Court of Chancery to hinder the pressing of the contractors' claims, and obtained a declaration from Lord Chancellor Macclesfield to the effect that Vanbrugh had never been employed by the Duke of Marlborough. The object of this was to deprive him of his claim for some £1600 due to him in fees. Shortly before his death, however, he triumphed signally over the Duchess by persuading Sir Robert Walpole to use his all-powerful influence to have the money paid directly to him from the Treasury out of one of the sums that, from time to time, were at last forthcoming to make up the £60,000 agreed upon in the first years of the reign, but this was not until 1725. This was the last stroke in the great quarrel, and nothing was now left the Duchess except the satisfaction of having insulted her architect on the occasion of his visit to Blenheim earlier in the same year.

The human interest of the quarrel with the Duchess of Marlborough has always diverted attention from the design and building history of the Palace itself. As in the case of Castle Howard and to a less degree the Duke of Newcastle's buildings, these

INTRODUCTION

are extremely well documented. Indeed, with the St. Paul's accounts and others of Wren's works at Hampton Court, Kensington Palace, and so on, it is possible to collect the names and works of a large company of craftsmen, masons, joiners, carvers, etc., who passed from one great enterprise to another; thus a carver from Chatsworth is employed at Castle Howard, and Smallwell the joiner who was also engaged at St. Paul's and Chelsea Hospital appears in connection with the Duke of Newcastle's buildings. The Blenheim contractors are, many of them, Wren's men from St. Paul's, and include Strong himself. The system of building is the same at Blenheim and Castle Howard: the houses are built in the main from east to west and in both cases in the western parts the finishing work is not Vanbrugh's. Blenheim adheres more closely to the architect's intention, and we can safely assume that it is not very materially different, except perhaps inside the long gallery. At Castle Howard, as we shall see, a radical alteration was made in the whole character of the house, even more radical at the time than is now apparent, for nineteenth-century modifications have softened in some degree the selfishness of the later western façade.

Vanbrugh's professional connection as an architect was of a snowball character. That is to say, his practice did not consist of a series of undertakings, each of which was finished off in turn. Once having been engaged to build or modify a house for one of his friends among the Great, Vanbrugh seems never to have ceased to be employed except in the case of Blenheim and possibly of Kimbolton. Rather he accumulated building commissions which went on concurrently, one of them might lie dormant for a year or two only to start again, and last to the end of his life. Thus, in his last years, after 1720, he was engaged on Castle Howard, his first employment, Claremont, still under modification, Eastbury in Dorset, dating from 1716, Seaton Delaval and Grimsthorpe, possibly still King's Weston, begun 1711, and probably the Gardens of Stowe. This reflects a certain light on the character of the Duchess of Marlborough, the only client with whom he quarrelled and with whom he was still at odds over the payment of his account.

Kimbolton, begun in 1707, must have continued building for some years after 1708 when the surviving correspondence on the subject ceases. That correspondence (pages 13, 15, 19, 25) only refers to one side of the building, the south-western, and the remaining sides were completed in succeeding years, according to the *Historical Monuments Commission* volume, *Huntingdonshire*. They are in the same massive embattled manner as the south-western façade, except for a great projecting portico with columns on the south-eastern side—a very characteristic piece of Vanbrugh's later work. The plan of Kimbolton, a four-sided block having a central courtyard, dictated by the character of the earlier work, does not lend itself to Vanbrugh's usual "cumulative" treatment, and this places it somewhat outside the main current of his work; the only other example of this type of plan is at Grimsthorpe, which was also a reconstruction upon old foundations, and never completely carried out, so that only one was ever completed. Grimsthorpe was almost the last commission Vanbrugh got and, in the published designs for the unbuilt fronts, shows tendencies which can only be treated properly at a later stage of this essay. Moreover, its connection with the Kimbolton design is not close enough to warrant its being taken out of due order.

After Kimbolton the next enterprises were Claremont and King's Weston. Vanbrugh is said to have begun a small house at Claremont for himself about 1710, and afterwards to have sold the house and land to Pelham—soon to become the celebrated

Duke of Newcastle. The early history of the house is rather obscure, and it seems probable that the scheme did not develop until 1714 or 1716. The illustration shows the peculiar disposition of the house, the two enormous wing blocks linked together by a relatively insignificant central building. This rather confirms the suggestion that Claremont was a modification and enlargement of a much smaller house. If this is the case the design is most ingenious and, with its exaggerated receding forecourt and successive towers, very characteristic of Vanbrugh. It is, however, altogether too unusual in plan to be explained except by some special circumstances as that of a gradually growing scheme of enlargement and addition. King's Weston, begun for Edward Southwell, in 1711, is another design which does not at first sight link up with the logical chain of development that we have indicated as joining Castle Howard and Blenheim to the later Eastbury and Seaton designs. It is a single block without outlying wings or courts; its silhouette only diversified by the original expedient of linking the chimney-stacks together with an arcade. This device and the colossal order of the central front are enough to give it a very characteristic air, but the absence of any spectacular effects of grouping is remarkable in Vanbrugh. It is true that among the drawings discovered by Mr. Hussey at King's Weston is a project for an elaborate forecourt dating from February, 1716 to 1717. The project is described by Mr. Hussey as follows: " Apparently the forecourt was to have been surmounted by a 2 foot 6 inch wall with a ' fossee ' on the outside and below it. Opposite the front entrance was a Cyclopean archway surmounted by a pyramid. . . . The whole would have been some forty feet in height." All this would, no doubt, have brought the whole effect much more into line with what we expect from Vanbrugh. The description of the archway is interesting and fits one extant at Castle Howard. In one way King's Weston forms a connecting link between Blenheim and the George I designs, for in it the process whereby the sprawling Castle Howard plan was enclosed into one block at Blenheim is complete. King's Weston is the first single-block plan conceived as such and the ancestor of the unified central blocks of Eastbury and Seaton. In all these houses the disposition of the staircases differs from the Blenheim and Castle Howard arrangement whereby these were placed on each side of the entrance hall, ascending parallel to its length, as it were in side aisles, and a new solution is attempted in each case. At King's Weston, where there is no great saloon, the entrance hall gives on to an inner staircase hall of great magnificence relative to the scale of the house. The existing staircase, according to Mr. Hussey, dates from 1719, and differs considerably from the original design in *Vitruvius Britannicus*. It is a handsome feature in the house and with its decoration of the well is characteristic of Vanbrugh, though hardly so much so as the original design with a cloister arcade surrounding it on three sides. This is the only design in which Vanbrugh has made a leading feature of the staircase.

After King's Weston we come to a group of three designs in the last of which, Seaton Delaval, Vanbrugh's architecture may be said to have reached its finest and most complete achievement. The precursors of Seaton Delaval are Eastbury, Bubb Doddington's house in Dorset, and the " New Design for a person of quality in Dorsetshire," also given as Somersetshire in the description of the plates in the second volume of *Vitruvius Britannicus*. This last is dated 1716 and was possibly a preliminary sketch or alternative design for Eastbury, which is dated 1718 in *Vitruvius*, third volume. The " New Design " is on an even grander scale than Eastbury, but the general dispositions are similar, and it is doubtful whether Bubb Doddington would have gained by adopting the larger scheme, supposing it to have been intended for him. The general arrangement of the plan is the same in all the three designs under discussion: two relatively small square pavilions stand at either side of the entrance to a deep forecourt, arcaded walks running down each side of the court connecting at the farther end with the main block. These arcades form the ground floor to the wing buildings. At Eastbury these wing buildings rise up as square towers to a considerable height; at Seaton, though quite high, they would seem to emphasise their length and horizontal lines, only advancing out into the court a pedimented centre feature (not included in the plan reproduced). We have no evidence as to the elevations of the wing blocks of the "New Design." Behind each wing block are the office and stable courts respectively: at the end of the court comes the house itself, a unified block standing quite free of its wings except for the arcaded walks. In this scheme of composition everything depends on the climax, this central block, to which the whole arrangement of the forecourt is intended as an introduction or setting. In treating of Blenheim we have already referred to the genesis of this typical Vanbrugh composition scheme, and it is possible that the primary conception originates in certain French designs, such as Richelieu, where there is a similar leading up to the central block through a deeply recessed forecourt flanked by towers as at Eastbury. It is curious to notice that the quadrant colonnades linking the house and wings—a peculiarly Palladian feature— are not found in these later designs, though in other respects there are evidences that Vanbrugh was influenced by the Palladianism of his rivals during his last years.

These later block plan designs are very interesting internally. The two earlier, Eastbury and the "New Design"—of one only a fragment of the office wing and court and the entrance court arcade remains, while the other only exists on paper— are both conceived on a more lavish scale than the surviving Seaton Delaval. At Eastbury the great Doric rusticated portico towards the entrance court (i.e. the west side) led to an entrance hall which extended some 55 feet north and south and had a breadth of 28 feet; on the further side (east) of this the two staircases were each approached through two arches, and between the staircases was a lobby (24 by 12) entered by a most elaborate doorway in the form of a Venetian arch. This lobby led to a great saloon (25 by 26) on the east or garden side of the house. On the north side was a state suite of three rooms on the usual system, and to the south an anteroom giving off the saloon, the "great eating-room," and some smaller service rooms to the west of it. Four towers at the corners of the building provide cabinets 14 feet square in three instances and a service stair hard by the great eating-room. The accommodation is further enlarged by the provision of two octagonal rooms placed away from the central block of the house in the centres of the walls dividing the stable and office courts from the gardens—the position of the greenhouses at Blenheim. These were reached by external corridors and formed the "small eating parlour" and the chapel respectively, of which the former survives in part at Eastbury. The projected "New Design" is very similar, the chief difference being that the greater breadth of the front towards the court has made it possible to place the entrance hall with its major "axis" running from the entrance door to that of the saloon, leaving the staircase wells in approximately the same relative position as at Eastbury but absorbing the lobby into itself, and leaving room for two additional rooms along the entrance front on each side of it. Correspondingly the saloon which, except for ante-rooms to the state suites at each end of it, occupies the whole of the garden front, is on a far vaster and more magnificent scale than at Eastbury; its suggested dimensions are given as 84 feet by 30 feet. A threefold division is marked by columns in this vast apartment, corresponding to the breadth of the hall and the two flanking chambers on the other front. The remaining two sides have each state suites of three rooms corresponding to that on the north side of Eastbury. The plan of Seaton is a much smaller and simplified variant of the " New Design." The hall is placed similarly to that of the " New Design " and on each side of it towards the entrance front are two chambers as before. But there are no state suites beyond these, and the saloon (68 by 22) runs the entire length of the garden front; between the two chambers on the entrance side and the saloon, two fine corridors lead from the hall on each side to the staircases, which are placed in towers which stand out flanking the whole block; these corridors are repeated on the floor above, being carried across the hall on a wrought-iron railed gallery, as at Blenheim and Castle Howard. The genesis of this plan with the central corridors leading to tower staircases is partly, of course, the Castle Howard and Blenheim plans, but more directly the plan of Vanbrugh's house at Blackheath—a curious and not very successful small house, since destroyed. This building forms one of a group erected by Vanbrugh in the early years of George I (the date is said to be 1717, but some of his work there may be older), including the celebrated Bastile House built for himself as a country house. Vanbrugh House was not a very successful building, but it has other interesting features linking it with the Seaton Delaval design.

In the elevation treatment Seaton Delaval recalls Blenheim, rather than the two designs I have grouped with it, in the differentiation of parts by varying surface treatment. On the forecourt side there is the elaborate treatment of the basement with a plain plinth and the heavy " cushioned " masonry above it; a terrific rusticated Doric front to the entrance hall is flanked by ringed columns recalling St. Mary Woolnoth and Blenheim forecourt (see above), and the plain ashlar of the walling at each side, and of the octagonal corner towers, contrasts with the large scale horizontal rustications of the staircase towers, the tops of which are again in plain ashlar in common with the attic story above the hall. On the garden front, though there is no rustication of the central portion, the large Ionic portico amply carries out the idea of the threefold division of the entrance front and the curious basement is carried right round the building. In many respects Seaton Delaval is more closely connected with Eastbury as regards elevation treatment than with the " New Design," to which we have shown its relation as regards plan. At Eastbury there was the same rustication of the hall combined there with a great hexastyle portico of the ringed Doric columns, and a similar treatment of the tops of the two flanking towers with Venetian windows. The main block of Eastbury being now destroyed, there seems to be no evidence of the treatment of the towers in the general side elevations. But the basement, though slightly differentiated by rustication at Eastbury, is not nearly so much emphasised as at Seaton. The " New Design " shows no differentiation of parts by surface variations, and in this resembles King's Weston. Seaton Delaval is the logical conclusion of a series of experiments; the line of development was laid down in the transition from the Castle Howard to the Blenheim design. King's Weston, Eastbury, the " New Design " and the Greenwich houses all contribute something, until we have a building that seems the quintessence of Vanbrugh. The extent of the great entrance façade is a bare 100 feet, not much more than King's Weston, as compared with 180 at Eastbury and 320 at Blenheim, but in it is expressed all that peculiar quality of romantic magnificence, of "noble and masculine show," or "magnanimity," to use a favourite word of seventeenth-century criticism, that theatrical quality in Vanbrugh's architecture which seems to ally it with the Heroic drama of Dryden and Congreve; the façade of Seaton, admirably set off by the splendid yet comparatively sober fronts of the wing blocks, even more than Blenheim, is the final expression of what we may call "Heroic" architecture in England.

Admiral Delaval called in Vanbrugh in about 1718, for in February of that year he writes: " I intend to persuade Sir John Vanbrugh to see Seaton if possible and to give me a plan of a house, or to alter the old one, which he is most excellent at; and if he cannot come, he'll recommend a man at Yorke who understands these matters. So something may be done by degrees and be the entertainment of our old age, as long as we can live. I am much out of order with the scurvy." The date 1720 is given in *Vitruvius Britannicus*. Before this time Vanbrugh had undertaken the remodelling of Nottingham Castle for the Duke of Newcastle, and is said to have designed Fleurs for the Duke of Roxburghe. (1719.) On this last house information is hard to come by, but it is said to have been so much altered by a nineteenth-century architect as to be quite unrecognisable. In the early 'twenties Vanbrugh was again employed to alter Lumley Castle, and here his alterations remain. A garden front with two fine towers recalls Kimbolton, but these are linked by a comparatively modest and gracious front rather in the early Restoration manner. The other alterations are in the way of interior accommodation, and do not relate to his methods of monumental design under discussion here. Vanbrugh's last great commission was Grimsthorpe, dated by Campbell 1723 (see also page 151). Only one range of this great scheme was carried out, but a plan and elevations of the other three sides are given by Campbell. (*Vit. Brit.*, Vol. 3.) The plan is in four ranges about an internal court as at Kimbolton, and may have been determined as in that instance by the pre-existing building. The plan is, however, remarkably convenient, and given the inherent difficulty of the internal court plan really a great achievement, amply fulfilling the requirements of State, Beauty and Convenience, as Vanbrugh understood them. The entrance front, the only range actually completed, is a fine composition carried out with a characteristic elevation treatment. It consists of two boldly projecting three-storied towers, linked to a lower range containing the entrance hall carried up two stories in height. (Compare Lumley Castle above.) The towers are of plain ashlar walling with rusticated quoins, and window-dressings of a strict Palladian propriety; the middle window of the three is a Venetian; the towers are surmounted with a balustrade and urns. The elevation of the hall, however, is more characteristic. Next the towers are on each story single round-headed windows at each side, of the familiar type, having the imposts heavily stressed, then couple-ringed Doric columns, as at Seaton, the elaborate Doric entablature being returned over the columns and carried across the centre of the elevation. Between the columns are the two storys of arched windows, the arches being of two orders with a good but relatively unimportant doorway feature in the middle, the whole crowned with a balustrade, figures on pedestals above the columns, urns, etc. Internally the hall is a magnificent and typical design, having staircases behind handsome two-storied arcades as at Blenheim. This entrance elevation was approached through a fine forecourt having square detached pavilions advanced before the towers and making the outer corners of the square court. The strict Palladian principles of the flanking towers of his range are more than maintained in the other elevations shown in *Vitruvius Britannicus*. Here are façades which, though they are bolder and more varied in point of silhouette and relief than the general run of Burlingtonian designs, are yet more closely allied to them than to any of Vanbrugh's previous work. The contrast is very marked and incites to some interesting speculations which cannot, however, be fully exploited until we have digressed a little into general contemporary architectural history and the influence of opposed schools on the personnel of the Board of Works.

On the accession of George I, when Vanbrugh was reinstated as Comptroller of the Works, schemes were on foot for the reformation of the whole constitution and routine of the office. The letter of 1704 referring to the difficulties with Sir Christopher Wren in the matter of the Kensington Palace Orangery and the Memorial to Ld. Halifax (Appendix) give some indication of the need for, and the nature of, these reforms. In 1718 Sir Christopher Wren was superseded at the Board of Works and William Benson appointed Surveyor. It is possible that the appointment was offered on this occasion to Vanbrugh and refused, as he says in his letter to Tonson; "out of tenderness to Sir Christopher Wren." Or it may be that this offer was made before Wren's dismissal; but whatever the circumstances on this occasion there is no doubt that Vanbrugh had every reason to be dissatisfied with the change. Hawksmoor lost his appointment, the old triumvirate was broken up, and Benson brought into the office his nephew (of whom very hard things are said), and one Colin Campbell, the compiler of *Vitruvius Britannicus*. Benson only retained the office for about a year, and then was dismissed for incompetence; this time Vanbrugh seems to have really hoped for the Surveyorship; his claims were strong, and a Duke of Newcastle a powerful friend. But these things were very much a matter of delicate adjustment of the respective claims, not only of the candidates, but of their great patrons, and in circumstances which are obscure Vanbrugh was induced to withdraw his pretensions in favour of Sir Thomas Hewet, formerly Surveyor of Woods and Forests and apparently a protégé of the Duke of Kingston. In withdrawing in favour of Hewet, Vanbrugh seems to have been in a position to demand compensations, a promise of reinstatement for Hawksmoor from Hewet and a new additional office for himself from Newcastle and the authorities. Hewet never redeemed this promise as to Hawksmoor, who was compelled to wait for reinstatement until the surveyor's death shortly before that of Vanbrugh himself. Thus the two were never associated together at the Board of Works again.

Of the two surveyors thus placed at the head of Vanbrugh's department, Benson and Hewet, the latter seems to have been quite negligible as an architect; his only recorded building, the stables at Thoresby, may not have deserved the scathing comments of Hawksmoor, who was naturally prejudiced, but was at any rate insignificant. Benson, however, was of more importance. While at the Board of Works, and apart from his blunders in regard to the House of Lords, which occasioned his dismissal, he designed some fountains for George I at Herrenhausen, and he imported Colin Campbell into the office. Before this he had designed and built a house for himself, Wilberry in Wiltshire, thus described by his protégé Campbell in the first volume of *Vitruvius Britannicus*: "Wilberry in Wiltshire is the seat of William Benson Esq., invented and built by himself in the Stile of Inigo Jones, who, by his excellent choice, discovered the Politeness of his Taste: and as he is Master of the most refined parts of Literature, has here expressed a particular regard to the noblest manner of architecture, in this beautiful and regular design, which was executed Anno 1710." The wording of this is highly significant, for Inigo Jones and Palladio were the twin Gods of the new school among the pioneers, of which it would seem we are to count William Benson. This new tendency was in some degree a reaction from the style we have described in the earlier part of this study and called the " New Manner of the Office of Works." Instead of the " Romantic " exploitation of mass and the all-important quality of " movement," the ideals of Vanbrugh and Hawksmoor and to a less extent of their follower, James of Greenwich, the builder of St. George's, Hanover Square, and the celebrated Cannons for the Duke of Chandos, and of that mysterious figure Thomas Archer, of whom more below, instead of what has been called the " high Roman fashion " with its grandiosities and "terribilita," the new men set up the works of Palladio as an infallible authority, and Inigo Jones as his prophet. Palladio, who had always been regarded as a good guide to the orders, as an authority indeed, among others, perhaps even the first, but nothing more, was now to be exalted to a position in which his formulæ for proportion took on the character of unalterable dogmas, and his buildings however unsuited to English conditions, the final authority of perfect models which his humble worshippers must strive to imitate. Inigo Jones, as we have said, shared also in this apotheosis; devotees referred to him as " the Master," and in the hey-dey of the New School (1724 to 1735) Lord Burlington and his staff of architects devoted themselves with enthusiasm to collecting and editing his designs and publishing them. In some respects this new tendency may be looked on as the first of that series of self-conscious semi-antiquarian revivals which, continuing with the " true Roman " style of Adams and the Gothic, Etruscan, and Greek revivals, characterised the artistic history of the eighteenth century. It is the firstfruits of the introduction of scholarship into architecture, an introduction which dates back at least to John Evelyn and the very beginning of English Renaissance architecture. The practice of the Palladianists was far from being as contemptible as the pedantry of their theories. Gibb, if he may be counted among them, in his London churches, St. Martin's in the Fields and St. Marys-le-Strand, and at Cambridge, the Earl of Pembroke at Marble Hill and later Kent, certainly at Holkham and to a less degree at the Horse Guards, produced buildings which rank only after the very greatest. Even Colin Campbell himself, though rarely inspired, produced some worthy designs. But it was impossible in the eighteenth century to recapture that first lyrical rapture which saves almost all Inigo Jones's works even at their most Palladian from frigidity. This enslavement to Palladio, of course, effectually excluded that quality of " movement " that we noticed as the hall-mark of the School of Wren, from the compositions of the strict followers of the sect; their buildings have more than a tendency to approximate to the perfectly proportioned box adorned with porticoes and window-dressings, rusticks and what not, all of an unimpeachable refinement, and in the best instances often attaining to great merit, but after the heady wine of Vanbrugh and Hawksmoor, rather insipid. Gibbs and Kent are exceptions to this, and in them the quality of movement is to be found and still a certain robustness of manner, but then Gibbs was never accepted as a Burlingtonian of the true faith and can in some ways be regarded as deriving from Wren, though from an earlier Wren than Vanbrugh's master. But Gibbs had been to Italy, and the Palladianist School is before all things the school of men who have studied in Italy. It is the architecture of the Grand Tour. Wren, Vanbrugh and Hawksmoor had never, as far as we know, visited that country, and been shocked by the vagaries of the later Baroque masters, but Lords Burlington and Pembroke, Sir Thomas Robinson and the small fry (from a social rather than architectural standpoint) had all visited Rome and turned from what Campbell calls " the affected and licentious works of Bernini and Fontana " and the " wildly Extravagant Designs of Borromini who has endeavoured to debauch Mankind with his odd and chimaerical beauties " to the chaste cities of the north, Verona and Vicenza, wherein Palladio, " this excellent Architect, seems to have arrived at the *ne plus ultra* of his art." To these Italianate gentlemen, and the architectural students they had picked up in Rome, it seemed that Vanbrugh and Hawksmoor were heading straight for those horrors that had so appalled them in Rome. And these Italianate gentlemen were the rising generation of patrons. If we compare Henry Bell's Custom House at King's Lynn with, say, the Kensington Orangery, it seems as if English architecture had passed through all the stages from Brunelleschi to Cortona in a single generation. The plant that had flowered too quickly, withered as quickly away.

The Grimsthorpe design shows the influence of the Palladianists far more markedly than the immediately preceding designs, but this may be more or less the effect of the square block appearance dictated by the plan round a four-sided internal court; for in these elevations much depends on the character of the detail, as window-dressings, etc., and all these had been growing increasingly nearer the Palladian standards in the later buildings. The window-dressings on the garden front of Seaton, with their little pediments and pillowed friezes, are good examples, and in Eastbury there are again Palladian details. Though the dates only just coincide, it is perhaps warrantable to suggest that the appearance of these Palladian details in the Eastbury elevation (dated by Campbell 1718, the same year that Hawksmoor left the Board of Works) may be due to some new assistant employed to work out the detail drawings of Vanbrugh's buildings much as Hawksmoor seems to have done in his early days. This is not to say that these Palladianisms were forced on Vanbrugh from outside; no doubt he was himself sufficiently affected by the general tendency of the times—by, for instance, the rise of a man such as Gibbs—to welcome, or at any rate not to object to them. In such a design as Seaton there is little but details of window-dressings to indicate any new influence, unless the great Ionic portico on the garden front should be considered another sign, for the present writer cannot recollect another instance of Vanbrugh's use of this order. It may be added as perhaps significant that Nicholas Dubois, with whom Vanbrugh was associated at the Board of Works, had published an edition of Palladio in French in 1715–16. It is generally known as Leoni's first edition, and is without plates.

That Vanbrugh was not on good terms with the personnel of the rising School is suggested by the story in Walpole's letters that he and Sir Thomas Robinson spat and swore at one another at Castle Howard. Sir Thomas Robinson, who afterward married one of Lord Carlisle's daughters, was destined to complete Vanbrugh's first great design in a manner much more unsympathetic to the intention of the original designer than certain nineteenth-century modifications allow us to realise now. And this lends a pathetic interest to the vain appeals made by Vanbrugh in the later letters to Lord Carlisle to suspend the outworks and devote himself to finishing the north-western wing. Hawksmoor, who succeeded to some extent to Vanbrugh's place in Lord Carlisle's regard, had to submit to constant interference on the part of Sir Thomas, with his design of the great mausoleum which he built at Castle Howard from 1729 to 1736. The history of this building is extremely well documented with letters from all the parties concerned, and affords an illustration of extraordinary interest of the conflict of styles at a period of changing taste. The mausoleum is the last monument of the " School of Wren," and in it are embodied several changes in the original design forced upon the architect by the enthusiastic apostles of the new school. Poor Hawksmoor's career was to some extent ruined by the change of taste, for after a long period, from 1677 to about 1710, during which he was overshadowed by Wren and Vanbrugh, his chances of independent architectural creation were curtailed by this revolution, which may be said to have lost him the opportunities of building King's College and the Radcliffe Camera, for both of which he made designs, but both of which were ultimately built by Gibbs.

In describing the plans of Vanbrugh's houses, certain aspects of his interior style have been noticed, as the arches and the columns with which he adorned his halls and his use of corridors, etc., there remains his manner of actual decoration. In this he may be said to be the precursor of Kent and the Palladians rather than the follower of the Wren of Hampton Court. The elaborate woodwork of Gibbons and his following which, in the generation before Vanbrugh, was considered the proper means of decoration for the state rooms of such a very consciously Italianate house as Chatsworth, even apart from its use in the more English style buildings as Belton, is used very much more sparingly by Vanbrugh. At Castle Howard and Blenheim there are friezes in the state apartments and an occasional overmantel with fruit and game and so on, but in the main the walls are to be lined with tapestry and damask, witness the Duchess of Marlborough's monstrous commission to the Earl of Manchester when Ambassador to Venice for green and red damasks, running into thousands of yards,* the celebrated set of tapestries at Blenheim and a letter of Hawksmoor's carefully prescribing the arrangement of the shadows on the tapestries to be woven for Castle Howard so that they should correspond to the direction of the light.† It is probable that Hawksmoor exercised an even more controlling discretion in the decoration of what we may call the secondary interiors, ante-rooms, drawing-rooms, state bedrooms, etc., than in the details of the exteriors, and we find him writing to Lord Carlisle as to the main proportions of the rooms. It is, however, in the great halls, the staircases and corridors and the great saloons that we find a style which is almost certainly Vanbrugh's own, and corresponds to the peculiar characteristics of his external architecture. Here the treatment is definitely architectural; arches and columns are used with great freedom and elaborate architectural ornament, mainly of the Corinthian order, lavishly displayed in carved stone or stucco. Painting by such men as Pelegrini or Thornhill is used on ceilings and in strictly limited areas on walls, but it is always, with the exception of the saloon at Blenheim, subordinate to the grandiose architectural effects in naked stone. It is in this that Vanbrugh anticipates the Italianate interiors of his successors, the lavishness of whose interior designs is in strange contrast to their restrained exteriors. Moreover, and this is the aspect of his interior designs that is most characteristic, they are planned in a fine heroical Romantic style; great play is made with fine vistas down superbly vaulted corridors at Castle Howard and Blenheim, and in the great halls themselves no staircase is allowed to break up and diminish the immense unbroken space. At both Blenheim and Castle Howard the placing of the stairs behind arches at each side of the hall attains this effect, while giving a fine effect of additional spaciousness by the glimpses through the arches to the staircase wells beyond. While discussing Vanbrugh's staircases, mention must be made of his fondness for the elaborate ironwork of

---

* See *Court and Society*. Elizabeth to Anne. The Duke of Manchester.
† See *Country Life*, June 1927.

his time which he used, not only for stair-cases, but especially for rails to the galleries which carried the first floor corridors across the ends of his great halls, which themselves rose two stories in height. These rails are among the most beautiful features of the Castle Howard, Blenheim and Seaton interiors. Reference has been made to Vanbrugh's use of columns for interior effect. A good example of this exists in that " Noble room of Parade " which he persuaded the Earl of Manchester to introduce into the south range of Kimbolton (see page 13.) The room is a rectangle, having its longest sides facing the garden. On the internal side, in the centre of which is an elaborate mantel-piece, two columns have been introduced at the corners but standing out well into the room about equidistant from both the long and the end walls. Thus an effect is obtained of recessing the long internal wall in the middle, greatly adding to the interest and dignity of the room.

The treatment accorded Vanbrugh's interior designs here may seem scarcely adequate in scale after the fuller discussion of his plans and exterior compositions, but due allow-ance must be made for the relative scarcity of material; while enough remains to in-dicate a definite and consistent style, yet the destruction of Eastbury and of the interior of Seaton and the incomplete state of Grimsthorpe make any attempt to trace the growth and variations of his manner of extreme difficulty. In garden design, as in his interior treatments, Vanbrugh occupies an intermediate position, and forms in some sense a connecting-link between the designs of the Restoration period, with their experi-mental uncertainty wavering between the Classic grand manner of Le Notre on the one hand, as yet but partially understood, and certain traditions and influences from Holland on the other, and the mid-eighteenth century aberrations of Pope, Kent and their landscape-gardening followers. It is difficult nowadays for us to appreciate the intensity and seriousness with which the men of those times seem to have regarded garden design. It was of all other artistic activities, hardly excluding architecture, the battle-ground of tastes and theories of æsthetic. The explanation is to be found perhaps in that gardening was, even more than architecture, the career open to the talents of the cultivated amateur who, enjoying a wider outlook than the more rigidly, technically educated professional artist, is naturally more inclined to speculation, and also perhaps in that here the contrasting elements of art and nature are brought into a more direct contact. The general Renaissance theory of gardening, stated briefly, is that there are two aspects of the art: firstly, the garden should provide an organised formal setting for the architecture of the house, as it were mediating between the pure artificiality of the architecture and the unmitigated savagery of nature, and secondly, provide a place of recreation where all kinds of conceits, surprises, jokes, wonders, might provide diversion for the visitors. The larger ideas of garden planning which Le Notre introduced into France, and of which Versailles and Chantilly are the great examples, were slowly gaining ground in England throughout the Restoration period, though it must be admitted that London's layout of Longleat, with its endless and tiresome adding of parterre to parterre out of all proportion to the size of the house, immense though that was, seems very old-fashioned as compared with the majority of designs shown in such compilations as Kilp's Nouveau Theâtre de la Grande Bretagne. But by the time Vanbrugh appears as a garden designer, the victory of Le Notre's ideas was assured, even in spite of the vogue of topiary work which is supposed to have had a great reinforcement from the Dutch influences imported by William III. Vanbrugh was a thorough-going disciple of Le Notre, but it was the later ideas of that master in which much more importance was given to " boscages," or organised woodlands and great vistas, and less to the elaborate parterres " de gazon " or " de broderie," which played such a preponderant part in his earlier designs. Castle Howard, Claremont and Stowe are the three most important of Vanbrugh's garden designs. At Blenheim he was associated with Wise, the royal gardener of Hampton Court and Kensington Palace, and alterations and the small scale of the extant plan have left us little to go upon in this case. At Claremont and Stowe the name of Bridgeman is met with. Bridgeman is a somewhat obscure figure whom that fanatical landscape enthusiast, Horace Walpole, praises highly as the inventor of the ha-ha and the precursor of Kent; he is said to have been a pupil of London and Wise in his early days. Both Claremont and Castle Howard gardens show Vanbrugh's style admirably both in detail and general layout, though in neither case has much of the latter survived. Both are situated on hills and at least partially wooded ground. At Claremont, where the house was placed with its back to a considerable hill (see Plate VII), the garden consists of two main parts: a system of two main avenue vistas crossing at right angles, the one purely ornamental, leading straight from the front of the house, and the other, the carriage approach, crossing the forecourt and leading on the walled gardens—the nearest approach to a parterre in the scheme; and the wooded hill itself, which was elaborately organised with winding paths, an amphitheatre and pond, temples (see Plate VII), and crowning all a splendid system of terraces embellished by a castellated structure (see Plate VII) which still survives. Castle Howard was more diversified. The house stands on the crown of the north-facing slope of a ridge, having a magnificent view across country; Vanbrugh's intentions with regard to this slope were never carried out, but apparently a main approach was to be made that way (see p. 164). To the west of the house two great avenues intersect at right angles, with an obelisk in honour of the great John Churchill erected at that point. The main avenue running north and south has been elaborately treated at the edge of the southern slope of the ridge, where is a great archway with a pyramid on the top, and at the foot of the slope a lesser but still elaborate gateway has been made. From the great upper archway, and running along a considerable distance, out of sight on each side, an immense embattled wall, with towers round and polygonal, crowns the ridge. The east and west avenue continues from the obelisk, past the fore-court of the house, past the office courts to a gateway leading into the Wray Wood, a large wooded hill to the east of the house. This Wray Wood was the *pièce de résistance* of the whole work, and was organised with winding paths, temples, statues and fountains as at Claremont. On the south side of the house, the garden proper, there were a system of walled gardens to the westwards, the gates of these are embellished with urns, grotesque masks and splendid wrought-iron work, the great " parterre of the Obelisks " (see pp. 131, 143, etc.), probably immediately opposite the south front of the house, and below, to the east where the ground slopes to a little combe, an extensive system of pools and cascades finishing with a large ornamental bridge. A fine walk starts from the western end of the walled gardens, where there are elaborate wrought-iron gates, passes between the house and the parterre, and then divides, one way going up into the Wray Wood and the other turning south-east as a terrace walk along the side of the slope of the wood and finishing in the temple (see pp. 156 to 160.)

At Claremont, in addition to the " castle " on the hill, the walled garden is also adorned with battlements. But the most remarkable of these mediævalising monuments is certainly the great wall at Castle Howard; this would seem to be definitely Vanbrugh's own idea (see p. 173), but otherwise there is indication at times that Hawksmoor was more given to these Gothic conceits than Vanbrugh. Colonel Tyrrel's garden (p. 167) at Shotover was probably laid out by Hawksmoor and there is a Gothic temple closely allied to his All Souls' work, closing the vista at the end of the long canal. This affair has pointed arches, cusps and ogees and even a rose window. Vanbrugh never went as far as this even in garden buildings where Renaissance theory allowed or rather encouraged fantasy beyond what even the most licentious Baroque architects would dare to do in the house proper. It is in these walls and castles, always designed with a nicely calculating eye upon the dramatic effect, as well as in his love for wide prospects and romantic vistas, that Vanbrugh appears as the precursor of the landscape gardeners, as much as in his sparing use of the intricate pattern parterres of the earlier fashion.

There are a number of miscellaneous works with which Vanbrugh's name is associated but which lie outside the main current of his work. Chief among these is Oulton Hall, Cheshire, 1716. There is, as far as the present writer's knowledge goes, no documentary proof of this ascription; but a very enduring tradition is reinforced by some characteristic passages in the interior and by a certain massive grandeur of the exterior which otherwise does not resemble very closely any of the better authenticated designs. Vanbrugh's name has also been associated with another great house in Cheshire, Cholmondeley (1715), now replaced with a building in the Gothic taste. The elevations in *Vitruvius Britannicus* show a certain resemblance to his style in one instance, but this is not very convincing in view of the omission of his name by Campbell, for though Campbell is by no means infallible Vanbrugh was too important a figure for that sort of slight. As regards both these Cheshire houses, it may be added that Vanbrugh had family connections with Chester, and he and Hawksmoor are said to have carried out some work upon the walls there (p. 163). In Yorkshire there are two more houses ascribed to him, Duncombe and Gilling, the first a complete scheme, the second an entrance front added to an earlier house; both houses are in the neighbourhood of Castle Howard. Duncombe is attributed by Campbell to Wakefield, an architect of some eminence in the north and patronised by Vanbrugh's enemy, Sir Thomas Robinson. This would seem to be final, were it not for some stylistic resemblance, especially in the entrance hall. There are also distinct reminiscences of his manner at Gilling. The explanation of these may possibly be contained in Vanbrugh's remark to Brigadier Watkins (p. 137) as to Hawksmoor's popularity in the north. Another building in the north attributed to Vanbrugh is Morpeth Town Hall, now destoyed. There is a drawing of this in the library of the R.I.B.A.; it is very much in Vanbrugh's manner and Morpeth was a stronghold of Lord Carlisle's influence, but there is something unconvincing about the design which suggests an imitation rather than a first-hand work. To these must be added Compton Verney, a house much altered by Robert Adam, but still showing traces of Vanbrugh's style on one front.

Round London a number of fragmentary works are recorded, Addiscombe House, Croydon, later the Cadet School of the East India Company, some work at Woolwich Arsenal, and some obscure waterworks in Kensington gardens. Vanbrugh, as Surveyor of the Royal Gardens and Water Works, would naturally be involved in such schemes. His assistant Bridgeman is said to have laid out the Serpentine. And lastly, there are the existing parts of Greenwich Hospital ascribed to him. These are probably authentic, and consist of one front of King William's block and the centre feature of another.

Vanbrugh succeeded Wren as surveyor to the hospital in 1715 and Hawksmoor was closely associated with the work there under both men. But the whole question of their shares in the designs is still very obscure, and will remain so, at any rate until the Wren Society publish their volume of Greenwich drawings.

Two architects are often termed Vanbrugh's pupils or followers, Hawksmoor and Thomas Archer. Hawksmoor's only large domestic building of which we know him to be the independent author is Easton Neston. The main block of this house survives, less the wings, and shows very great originality in its internal arrangement; it is quite unlike any plan of Vanbrugh's, and of far greater technical virtuosity. The whole scheme, including the wings, as shown in Campbell's plates, does indeed resemble Vanbrugh very closely with its Romantic piling up of the masses of the wing buildings about the central pile. It is a fine and most interesting design, and appears to date from after Hawksmoor's association with Vanbrugh. The date given as that of the completion of the house is 1713. The date on the exterior of the main block is 1702, but a wooden model is preserved in the house and shows an earlier scheme, identical in plan but treated in elevation with two superimposed orders and panels between the windows instead of the colossal composite order actually built. The model suggests some of Wren's designs for Hampton Court and the changes which are all in the direction of Vanbrugh's style and what we have called the " new manner " seem very suggestive of the relations of the two men. Thomas Archer was a man of considerable social position and enjoyed the office of Groom Porter at Court. His special patron was the Duke of Shrewsbury, for whom he built Heythrop (1705), and whose letter to Harley asking for the reversion of Vanbrugh's position as Comptroller of the Works on Archer's behalf, written in 1712, is at Welbeck Abbey. Archer also built the Garden Pavilion at Wrest for the Duke of Kent, a house at Roehampton and the church of St. Philip at Birmingham (now the Cathedral), all of which are illustrated by Campbell. St. John's, Westminster, and St. Paul's, Deptford, with the Rectory adjoining (now destroyed), are also his. At the end of his life he designed Umberslade in Warwickshire (see Gandon's volumes of *Vitruvius Britannicus*), and to these it would seem that we must add Chettle House in Dorset, 1710. Chettle has a long and most circumstantial tradition of Vanbrugh's authorship, but while there is no resemblance to any work of his except in the staircase, which recalls King's Weston, there are very marked resemblances to Archer's manner both in plan and elevation. The main entablature recalls Heythrop, and the lobed or apsed planning, both of the whole block and of the entrance hall itself, seems to have affinities with the Wrest Pavilion and the many-apsed entrance hall at Umberslade. There are also striking resemblances both in general effect and details to the Deptford Rectory. The whole work is of very great charm and originality even in its present state lacking the appropriate cupola, and should this attribution be correct it would greatly enhance Archer's reputation. Archer's relation to Vanbrugh can hardly have been close and personal in view of the fact that he is never mentioned in these letters, though there are two references to Heythrop. Several of his works have been persistently attributed to Vanbrugh, and there are definite resemblances in his churches to Hawksmoor's church designs. He is, in brief, just another and honourable name to be added to the short list of English Baroque architects.

The best peroration to an essay on Vanbrugh is perhaps Sir Reginald Blomfield's words from an account which is not on the whole very sympathetic to him.

Vanbrugh's "passionate appreciation of the abstract qualities of architecture gives him a place by himself among the architects of a country in which the very existence of those qualities has almost ceased to be recognised." This is the kernel of the matter, it explains Vanbrugh's peculiar claim on our attention nowadays, and it was this quality in him, that, while all others of his successors derided him, yet drew forth tributes from such a succession of men as Sir Joshua Reynolds, Robert Adam, and Sir John Soane.

Note on Sources

And previous publications of the letters

TO the Duke or Duchess of Marlborough, Arthur Mainwaring, etc. From the Coxe MSS. transcripts in the British Museum. Extracts from these have appeared in such works as Ward, Introduction to his edition of Vanbrugh's plays; Dobrée, *Essays in Biography*, etc.

To the Duke of Newcastle, Brigadier Watkins, etc. From British Museum Add. MSS. 33064 *et seq*. Many of these were published in the *Athenæum* of 1861, also extracts quoted by Dobrée (see above).

To the Earl of Carlisle. From the collection of MS. letters preserved at Castle Howard. Extracts from some of these were published in the Historical MSS. Commission's report on Castle Howard.

To Jacob Tonson. From photographs of the original letters in the collection at Bayfordbury, Hertfordshire, now dispersed. All these, including two of which I have been unable to trace the originals, and the letters to Edward Southwell and to the Mayor of Woodstock, appeared in the *Gentleman's Magazine* for 1804, 1836–37–39. That to the Mayor of Woodstock was first published in the *Post Boy* of 1713.

To an unknown, dated 27th December, 1711, and the malignant letter of J. S. with the enclosed copy of Vanbrugh's " Letter to a relation," from the Harley Papers in the collection at Welbeck Abbey. These appeared in the Historical MSS. Commission's report on the Portland MSS., Vol. II.

To the Earl of Manchester. From the Duke of Manchester's collection deposited at the Record Office. These have appeared in the *Athenæum* of 1861, and the late Duke of Manchester's *Court and Society* from Elizabeth to Anne.

To Lord Treasurer Godolphin, dated 9th November, 1704. From the original in the collection at Arley Hall, Cheshire.

To Sir Robert Walpole. From the notes to Dallaway's edition of Walpole's *Anecdotes of Painting*, Vol. II.

To an unknown, dated 29th November, 1713. From the original in the possession of Messrs. Tregaskis, of London.

THE
LETTERS

Blenheim House.

Erected for John Duke of Marlborough
and the victory of Blenheim
settled on the great Duke of Marlborough and the Posterity for ever.

Le Château de Blenheim.
Erigé au depens Public en Commemoration de la Victoire a Blenheim,
& concédée au longue Duc de Marlborough et sa Posterieur à jamais.

London. printed for Robt. Sayer and Son, at the Black Moon in Fleetstreet.

THE
LETTERS

A.D. 1699 TO 1726

I

[*To the Earl of Manchester*]

London. December ye 25th 1699.

My Lord

If I cou'd think of any way to make my Letters either usefull or entertaining to yr Ldship, I wou'd write to you oftener ; but as to all Parliamentary Affairs, or anything that Relates to business no doubt but you have a more exaĉt Correspondent than I can be, & for Towne Affairs, my Lady to be sure has 'em from hers; So that there's very little left for me to say to you: However, I think I shou'd be to blame if I did not write something or other, that yr Ldship mayn't suspeĉt I have forgot I am oblig'd to you.

The heat of this Session seems much abated, since the battle Jack How and his admirers have had, in the attack upon the Commission against Pyrates; It has opened the Eyes of a great many well meaning Gentlemen of the Country Party, who by this infamous prosecution are convinĉt they ought to look upon him more as a discontented Courtier than a Patriot; and as in this Vote they left him, so abundance of 'em Own they are asham'd of him; As he declares he is of them, swearing there never was before such a Crew of Rogues as this Parliament. He had great hopes of 'em last Sessions he says, but now he gives 'em over. Twas very happy that in this Queĉtion the majority was so great, it left no room to pretend the Court brought off the Courtiers; but evidently appear'd the juĉtice of their Cause preserved 'em, and made a great many Vote 'em Innocent, who wou'd have been heartily glad they cou'd have found 'em guilty. The Irish Grants have gone smoothly hitherto; The Report the Comrs: gave in, was the clearest and most exact thing of the kind that had been done, and all Partys in the House seem'd wonderfully pleas'd wth it; Mr Montagu spoak very frankly for this Bill, and said his concern in the matter shou'd be far from influencing him, and that nobody shou'd be more for the passing it than he. Several of these Grants are found prodigious great. My Ld Portland's is a hundred and forty thousand acres and my Ld Albemarles as much. There was in the Article that related to my Ld Romney several Items that brought in Mrs Unick, and lay'd open her Interest with him; Three of the Comrs: refus'd to sign to this part of the reports as an unnecessary personall Reflection; but the rest wou'd have it in for the jests sake to put the House of Commons into good humour; wch it did, for everybody laught very heartily. Poor Sir John Phillips was sent for out of the House tother day into Westminster Hall, and Cudgell'd, wch he took with the patience of an Appostle, went again into the House, tould 'em how he had been serv'd, declar'd his Conscience wou'd not let him fight and desir'd they'd take the Quarrel upon them, wch they did, and have order'd the Assailant into Custody. Twas one Harcourt did it upon a Lawsuit between 'em, not as a Champion for Immorality & Prophaness, as yr Ldship wou'd be apt to Imagine, if I did not tell you the contrary.

Neal's dead; the last word he mutter'd was Salesbury. They say he has made her Sole Executrix. I don't know whether it be true. Mr Newton is like to have his place in the Mint. Miss: Evans the dancer at the New Playhouse is dead too; a feaver Slew her in eight and forty hours. She's much lamented by the Towne as well as the House, who can't well bare her loss; Matters running very low with 'em this Winter; if Congreve's Play don't help 'em they are undone. 'tis a Comedy and will be play'd about Six weeks hence. nobody has seen it yet.

Liveridge is in Ireland, he Owes so much money he dare not come over, so for want of him we han't had one Opera play'd this Winter; tho' Purcell has set one New One and Fingar another. We have got the Woman from the Cheshire Cheese upon the Stage, who has the best Voyce for't by much that has been there at any time. We have the Emperors Crooked Eunuch here, Francisco. They give him a hundred and twenty Guineas for five times. he has sung Once and was well likt. Dogget was here last Week, they gave him thirty pound to act Six times, which he did and fill'd the house every time.

My Lady Arglass, having been for some time under strong Suspicions for pocketing some small goods by the by in shops was tother day catcht stealing four or five fans at Mrs Tooms, who made her refund just as she was getting into her Coach. the mob presently gather'd about and made noise enough. My Lady Dartmouth was with her, and Lady Betty Cromwell who's sick upon't and keeps house; this thing is seriously true.

I have been this Summer at my Ld Carlisle's, and Seen most of the great houses in the North, as Ld Nottings: Duke of Leeds Chattesworth &c. I stay'd at Chattesworth four or five days the Duke being there. I shew'd him all my Ld Carlisle's designs, which he said was quite another thing, than what he imagin'd from the Character yr Ldship gave him on't; He absolutely approved the whole design, perticularly the low Wings, which he said wou'd have an admirable effect without doors as well as within, being adorn'd with those Ornaments of Pillasters and Urns, wch he never thought of, but concluded 'twas to be a plain low building like an orange house. There has been a great many Criticks consulted upon it since, and no objection being made to't, the Stone is raising, and the Foundations will be laid in the Spring. The Modell is preparing in wood, wch when done, is to travel to Kensington where the King's thoughts upon't are to be had.

I don't find the D. of Leeds thinks of giving Mr Mt any trouble about his Place; at least he talks as if he wou'd not, laying it upon the small desert of his Son, who he says do's not merrit his help in it. The Dutchess was overturn'd sometime ago coming from Wimbleton by torchlight and so desparately bruis'd, she has been at the brink of death with't; but is beyond expectation recover'd to plague her husband, her son, and many others some time longer.

Before I end my Letter, I must congratulate yr Ldship upon yr Success, in wonderfully oblidging all the English who have been at Paris since yr Coming there, wch upon my word I take to be no easy matter. But you have done it effectually, for one and all speak of it, and everybody here is glad to hear on't. I remember you us'd to speak of it, but I thought it easilyer intended than executed; I am heartily glad however it succeeds. Nobody wishing more heartily your Ldship may come off with reputation upon all accounts, than your much Oblig'd and very faithfull humble Servant

J. VANBROOK.

Shrimpton is wedded to Mrs Saunders, and Henly is near the matter with the Vice's Couzin Old Peregrines youngest Daughter, a Mettled Jade.

Pray my Lord my humble Service to my Lady, who I am heartily glad to hear has her health better than at first. My Ld Carberry toasts her with an Exemplary Constancy.

Since I ended my Letter I supt wth Mr Montague, who tells me, Mr. Newton is Master of the Mint & Sir Jo. Stanley, Warden. Pour moy, je suis tout comme j'etois.

2

To the R^t Honble : the Earl of Carlisle
at Henderskelf Near York

Tadcaster.   Sunday noon

My Lord

I am got no farther than Tadcaster yet, My Lord Burlington carrying me away with him to Lanesborough.   I wish't I cou'd possibly have stay'd there 'till tuesday, that I might have seen yr Ldship, and known whether you are come to an agreement with the Mason & Carpenter.   I talk't a great deal to 'em both, the morning I came away; but found 'em very unwilling to come to any abatement.   They made a world of protestations of its being impossible, without letting the work pay for't: they say'd they believ'd yr Ldship might expect some abatement from their proposall as a thing of course; but that Mr Hawksmoor had persuaded 'em to make no provision for that, but to make the lowest offer they cou'd possibly work for, and do it well.   I ask't Mr Hawksmoor alone, what he really thought on't;   He said they were indeed come as low, as he ever expected to bring 'em; and yet perhaps it was not impossible for 'em to work lower. but the danger he apprehended in reducing 'em was this; that since they so positivly declar'd, they cou'd not do the best work lower, and that if they lessen'd their rates, they must save themselves in the performance, it was to be fear'd (unless they have more honesty than is reasonable to expect) they might take this pretence, to performe the work ten per Cent: worse for five per Cent: they were reduc't. since there was no direct form of Workmanship cou'd be agreed on, when once they had got loose from being oblig'd to the best.   So that this wou'd give 'em a loophole to play the Rogue very much, and one cou'd not tell how to redress it: wheras, if they have the rates they have propos'd, they own themselves engag'd to do as good work as that they receive twice as much for, at London, and by consequence they have no room left for evasion.   This I own seem'd a strong reason to me, not to insist upon much abatement; especially since all those Articles yr Ldship desir'd it in, would mount to no great matter. However, I advis'd him to persist in it with 'em, 'till he had privately spoak again wth your Ldship, and known your thought on't.   I fancy my Lord if you have stuck to it, they have comply'd with y^o: rather than make a fruitless Journey; but yet I own I shall be glad to hear you have agreed to such a bargain as they own themselves sattisfy'd with; for 'twere a pitty there shoud be any miscarriage in the Work for a small matter.

I spoak to Mr Hawksmoor about his perticular concern and found him as he us'd to be.   so he intended to ask yr Ldship fourty pound a year Sallary & fifty each journey wch mounts to £100 clear.   I hope he'll deserve it, and that all will go to yr Ldships sattisfaction. for I shou'd be very sorry to have meddled in anything shou'd do otherwise. being very much yr Ldships humble Servant

J. VANBROOK

I shall be about Chester at least a Week. if yr Ldship has any service for me, please to direct to me at Mr Samuell Taylors in Chester.

3

To Mr Tonson, at Mr Vatcks,
*   on the Dam near The Stadthouse*
*   in Amsterdam*

London, June ye 15th, 1703

Your letter I had from Amsterdam. My brother bids me tell you he is extremely obliged to you, and desires you will let him be a little more so, by improving (as it may ly in your way) the friendship he has begun with the gentleman at Rotterdam; tho' my hopes are, you'll be spueing at sea before this gets halfway to the Brill. In short, the Kit-Cat wants you, much more than you ever can do them. Those who remain in towne, are in great desire of waiting on you at Barne-Elmes; not that they have finished their pictures neither; tho' to excuse them (as well as myself), Sr Godfrey has been most in fault. The fool has got a country house near Hampton Court, and is so busy about fitting it up (to receive nobody), that there is no getting him to work. Carpenter Johns, too is almost as bad. I went up yesterday under a tylt (as everybody has done that has gone by water these three weeks, for the Devils in the sky): there's all in disorder still; every room is chips—up to your chin! They ha'n't been at work, you must know, this fortnight: there's a great deal done however —one week's sticking to't will fit it for the reception of a King: my room is finish'd and a bed in it. The compas window, below and above, is made, but the shashes [*sic*] are not yet up; both the rooms are ten times the better for't. Neighbour Burgess has been too honest; the pease and beans ly all languishing upon the earth; not a cod has been gathered. There will be a hundred thousand apricocks ripe in ten days; they are now fairer and forwarder than what I saw at the Queens table at Windsor on Sunday— and such strawberrys as never were tasted: currants red as blood to; and gooseberrys, peaches, pairs, apples, and plumbs to gripe the gutts (?) of a nation.

The Duke of Somerset has had had several letters from you; but do you know that the Torys (even the wisest of 'em) have been very grave upon your going to Holland;—they often say (with a nod) that Caezar's CommTs might have been carry'd through without a voyage to Holland;

there were meanings in that subscription, and that lift of names may serve for farther engagements than paying three guineas apiece for a book; in short I could win a hundred pounds, if I were sure you had not made a trip to Hanover, which you may possibly hear sworn when you come home again; so I'd advise you to bring a very exact Journal, well attefted.

Lord Carlisle went homeward yefterday, with wife and children, and has made Ld Essex Deputy Earl Marshall; to crown that, Harry St George Garter, and me Herald Extraordinary (if the Queen pleases), in order to be Clarencieux at his return to towne; but whether we shall carry either point at Court, is not yet sure, tho' it ftands home preft at this moment, and will I believe be known tonight.

I have finished my purchase for the Playhouse, and all the tenants will be out by Midsummer-day; so then I lay the corner ftone; and tho' the season be thus far advanced, have pretty good assurance I shall be ready for business at Chriftmas.

I saw Captn Saunders juft now, he sails tomorrow for Holland; that he may bring you back with him in health and good humour, is my moft hearty prayer.

J. V.

4

To Mr Tonson at Mr Vatcks
near the Stadthouse Amfterdam

London.   July ye 13th 1703

I had a Letter from you yefterday which I rec'd juft as I was sitting downe to dinner with my Lord Hallifax and Congreve. I shew'd it 'em, and we drank your health, and quick return, but gave some hard words to your Book, since it robs us so long of your Company. We remember'd you too the Night before at Hampton Court, as we were sopping our Arses in the Fountain for you muft know we have got some warm weather at laft, a Week ago I was in furs ftill, and so were moft Folks; but the Farmers are like to be all undone for all that; for in spight of this bantring ill Season, they are likely to have a Swinging Crop at laft; terrible complaints they make about it; they don't say 'twill produce a Famine, but they say 'twill ruin the Nation. I have not seen Neighbour Burges lately, but I intend to go suddenly and condole with him upon't. I have spoak with Carpenter Johns, and when you come over, all will be ready for business in a few days. Sr Godfrey has got a house near Hampton Court, and is eternally there; he has reduc'd that in Towne to a Lodging to save Charges. We shall get nothing finish'd there 'till you come; the Kit Catt too, will never meet without you, so you see here's a generall Stagnation for want of you.

My Lord Hallifax bids me tell you, he sets out the firft of Augt: for his Northern Progress; I shall move after him in ten days, Ld Kingston is lately gone. Ld Marshall has been there with his Family these three weeks, and writes me word he has near 200 men at Work; there's a new Quarry found, much better than the Old one, so all go's on smooth. He stay'd in Towne a good while about our Heralds business; there was a great deal of Saucy Opposition, but my Ld Treasurer set the Queen right, and I have accordingly been Souc'd a Herald Extraordinary, in order to be a King at Winter. Ld Essex was left Deputy to do the feat which he did with a whole Bowle of wine about my ears instead of half a Spoon-full. He at the same time crown'd Old Sr Harry, Garter. and King was on the Spot Suspended which the rest seeing, renounc'd him, Own'd he drew 'em into Rebellion, and declar'd him a Son of a Whore.

The Coats of Arms you mention I'll send you.

Ld Essex has been at Cashiobury this fortnight, with Lady Harriot Vere, Di: Kirk and Dormer. what if he shou'd but into the Candle too at last, as Dunch and others have done before him. Other folks wou'd wonder at it, but I shou'd not. His hangings are up, and the whole furniture of his house, comes to above £1200.

Mr Wms has finish'd all the writings for the ground for the Playhouse they will be engross'd and I believe Sign'd on friday or Satterday; wch done, I have all things ready to fall to work on Munday. The ground is the second Stable Yard going up the Haymarket. I give 2000. for it, but have lay'd such a Scheme of matters, that I shall be reimburs'd every penny of it, by the Spare ground; but this is a Secret lest they shou'd lay hold on't, to lower the Rent. I have drawn a design for the whole disposition of the inside, very different from any Other House in being. but I have the good fortune to have it absolutly approv'd by all that have seen it. However I'll willingly be at the expence of a draught of that where you are. if you'll give your self the trouble to order it. The book you mention wch I wanted, you'll oblige me to get. Tis Palladio in French, wth the Plans of most of the Houses he built. there is one without the Plans, but 'tis that with 'em I would have. My Lord Hallifax desires you will bespeak him a Set of all kinds of Mathematicall Instruments, of the largest sort in Ivory, but adorn'd as curiously as you please, they being more for furniture than any use he's like to put 'em to; He designs to hang 'em up in his Library. He's tould the best in the world are made at Ams. he expects they shou'd cost a good deal of money. All I can tell you of Mrs Baynton is, that I han't heard her hanging Speech cry'd, so I hope all will be well. Lord Grantham is dangerously ill of the Small Pox. Garth is his Physitian, and there's hopes of a great recovery. Beau Pheasant is in the same way. Sr Roger Mostyn is marrying (or married to) Lord Nottinghams Daughter. You see my Paper will hold no more but my most hearty Services to you.

V.

(9)

5

To Mr Tonson at Mr Vatcks house
near the Stadt House in Amsterdam

London July ye 30th 1703

I writ to you about a fortnight Since, and have since spoak more than once to Ld Essex for his Arms. which he said he wou'd not fail to send you, and has don't for ought I know: he's allways at Cashiobury, and Jack Dormer has kept him Company there this month, by the help of Di: Kirk, who has been there as long, but she's come away at laſt, and so is he. I said something to you of that matter in my laſt; my Opinion is ſtrengthen'd upon it since, by his ſtaying there so long, and that in the sobereſt way in the world, playing at Brag with the Women every night inſtead of drinking, and even my Lord Essex chim'd into this way of living very contentedly. Dunch is overjoy'd to see Dormer buzzing about the Candle, and is in great hopes he'll bob into't at laſt as he did. Sr Roger Moſthyn is wedded to Ld Nottinghams Daughter; and you have heard no doubt that that Old Prig Sr Steven Fox has tack'd himself to a Young wench of Twenty. She was a Parsons Daughter and a Parson managed the match, a Young dog, a Smirk, who I suppose has agreed with her how matters are to be when Widdowhood comes; but I hope she'll reward him with her Abigaill. Mr Fox and his Wife have been Sower upon this match. My Lord Northampton and his Folks were wiser, put on a Gay Air, and came immediatly up to Towne to congratulate. I wish my Lord Cornwallis had done so too: but I don't yet hear what turn he gives it. I hear there is something on foot towards a match between Ld Hartford & Laᵈ Mary Churchill tho' that between her and Lord Mounthermon *[sic]* was thought fix'd. My Lord Wharton was got to Holme Pierpoint in his way to York, and there fell very Ill; His Law business was however so much in his head, that he would fain have gone on, but with much ado they prevail'd with him to go back to Winchington, where he writ to Dr Garth to meet him; Dr Sloan too went downe, and extream ill they found him on Satterday laſt; on Munday he was so much worse, that they had very little hopes of him, and he none at all of himself. He acted the Hero however, took formal leave of 'em all; Talk'd to his Son a good deal, and charg'd him with a great deal of Duty and respect to his Mother; said a great deal to Ld Vasseur about his Education, and shew'd a World of tenderness and regard to Madam, telling her, he beg'd she would forgive him, that he left the Guardianship of his Son to her only during her Widdowhood, he being fearfull, that if she marry'd again it might prove to his prejudice. She melted downe with all this, threw herself upon the ground, and was not to be Comforted. Then came all the Principall

(10)

Burgesses of Ailsbury to enquire after him, and he order'd 'em to be brought into his room. Shook 'em every one by the hand, and by his usual Treatment of Honeſt Tom, Dick and so forth bid 'em farewell, and Stick firm to their Principles. Then recommended himself heartily to the Kitcat and Dyed——Bite (?). He got a little Sleep that Night, By Gods help and the Doctors, was better next day; and on Wensday Garth left him (he says) out of Danger. He go's downe to him again tomorrow, and is positive he will recover, but has as long a Hill to climb up to Health and Strength again, as he had before.

I have sent you my Own Coat of Arms, and have written to Ld Carlisle for his; but if you spend much more of your time about 'em in Holland, we all resolve never to subscribe to another Book that muſt carry you beyond Sea.

I have nothing to say about Publick affairs, but that Our Favourite Portugall Treaty when we were in great haſt for it from Vienna, was left in a Land Waiters hands at Harwich about a Week. the Fellow swore 'twas no Treaty, but a bundle of Flanders Lace, and so broak it open upon which the Gentleman that brought it refus'd to take it again, and came away without it. An Order has been sent downe for it since & we have it at laſt. I had like to have forgot what I am to say to you from poor Mrs Roach. She's in great fear you shou'd forget her Flanders Lace, You may draw a Bill for the money she says when you please. I am moſt heartily yours

J. V.

6

[*To Lord Godolphin.*]   *November ye 9th* 1704
Ord^d *20th Nov.* 1704
to be brought in tomorrow night

My Lord

Before I acquainted yr L'dship this Summer wth that shamefull abuse in the Board of Works; of those very officers doing the Work themselves, who rec'd Sallarys from the Queen to prevent her being imposed on by Others; I made severall attempts upon Sr Chr. Wren to perswade him to redress it himself without troubling yr Lordship; putting him in mind; that besides its being utterly againſt common Sense, it was contrary to an Express Direction to the Board upon the Eſtablishment after the Reſtoration. He always own'd what I urg'd him to was right and often promis'd to join with me in Overruling so bad a practice; but when I press'd him to the Execution, he ſtill evaded it, and that so many times, that at laſt I saw he never intended it, and so I gave your L'dship the trouble of a Complaint.

Your Lordship was pleas'd upon it to send us a Letter, in as express

Terms as it could be penn'd, that no such thing for the future should be Suffer'd directly or indirectly—

Upon this Order I desir'd Sr Chr. there might immediately be another mason got to work at Kensington upon the New Greenhouse; but wou'd recommend none to him, leaving that entirely to himself. He at laſt nam'd One Hill, and gave me leave to send for him and give him Directions; which I presently did, and he promis'd me to go to Work. But a few days after finding he had not begun, and enquiring into the reason; I found he had been frighten'd with some hints of what shou'd befall him if he durſt meddle with the Maſter Masons business. And this had been put so home to him that he sent to me to desire I would excuse him. I went to Sr. Chr: Wren and tould him what had paſt. He said the Man was a Whimsicall Man, and a piece of an Aſtrologer, and would Venture upon nothing till he had consulted the Starrs, which probably he had not found favourably enclin'd upon this Occasion and therefore had refus'd the Work. I desir'd he would employ Somebody that was less Superſtitious which he said he wou'd and the next day I went out of Town for the North; but when I return'd I found Mr Jacksons man at Work. I ask'd one of his foremen who they work'd for; he tould me One Palmer whom his Maſter had made his Deputy.

I was very much surpris'd at this, and went to Sr Chr. Wren but was much more so when he confessed to me that he had allow'd Jackson to go on, only oblig'd him to enter his Bills in Palmers Name. I ask'd him if he had forgot your Lordships Letter and all that had paſt on this Subject. He said no; but Jackson wou'd not be quiet without he let him do the Work.

This Story is so very improbable I'm afraid yr L'dship will scarce give me credit for it; yet it is a plain and literal truth in every Article. As for Sr Chr. Wren I dont in the leaſt believe he has any Intereſt in his part of it; but yr L'dship will see by this Decisive proof the power those Fellows have over him wch they never made so effectual a use of as when they prevail'd with him (againſt your L'dships Directions) to let 'em have a Clerk of the Works of Whitehall, whom he himself own'd but a Week before he cou'd put no truſt in: one who by nature is a very poor Wretch; and by a many years regular Course of morning Drunckenesses, has made himself a dos'd Sott. Yet this man my Lord is by his Place entruſted with the whole measurements; and he is our Sole Voucher for the Quantity of all Works done at St James's Whitehall and Weſtminſter So that tis very probable the Workmen put into their Bills what Quantitys they pleased, for he's One that (by all appearances) they can either perswade or deceive. And for the Prices when they come to our Board yr L'dship may judg how roughly we are like to handle 'em.

As for Jackson my Lord, Besides this Crime the higheſt the nature of his Office will admit of I muſt acquaint your L'dship He is so Villainous a Fellow and so Scandalous in every part of his Character; and that in the unanimous opinion of all Sorts of People he is known to; that he is indeed a disgrace to the Queens Service and to everybody that is oblig'd to be concern'd with him;

Your L'dship will pardon the freedoms of my Expressions, and I hope believe I have no Other end in what I acquaint you with; than to do what I think I am bound to in Duty to the Queen and in Gratitude to yr L'dship. Which I think I can never so effectually express as by endeavouring to be Serviceable to the Treasury whilst yr L'dship is at the head of it; which for the good of Mankind I hope will continue as long as your Life.

I am
Your Lordships most faithfull
and most obedt humble Servant

JOHN VANBRUGH

I apply to yr L'dship on these Occasions rather by writing than Speaking because I think a long Letter may easilyor find a Convenient time of being read; than a Long Speech of being heard, and I wou'd willingly be as little troublesome as I can.

7

[*To the Earl of Manchester*]

*London, July y*ᵉ 18ᵗʰ 1707

My Lord
If I had had my Ladys leave, I had sooner writ to your Lᵈship About Kimbolton. She has given you an Account by What means the whole Garden Front has come downe: and she did me the honour (when she saw it must do so) to, ask my Advice in carrying it up Again: I cou'd not go downe just then, but did soon after, and got Mr Hawksmoor downe with me: where having consider'd every thing, we all Agreed Upon the enclos'd Design; which Differs very much from what Coleman had drawn, And particularly in that he had not brought the Door of the House into the Middle of the Front; Many other great Exceptions there were to it, both within and without. the Chief of which are in this Design avoided.

Your Lᵈship will here See something, that differs in the Cast of the Rooms, from the Common mode; which is, to go immediately out of the Drawing Room into the Bedchamber. But the Drawing room here, falling in the begining of the Line, had the Bed Chamber been next, there cou'd have been no regular nor propper way out of this Front into the Garden, which wou'd have been an Unpardonable want. There was therfore a necessity for some new Contrivance. And I thought, there cou'd nothing in reason be Objected to being Surpris'd with a large Noble Room of Parade between the Drawing room and Bedchamber; especially since it falls so right to the Garden, that the Door is in the Middle of the Room, and takes exactly the Middle Walk and Canall. For my part; I cannot but hope, 'twill prove in the generall Opinion An Agreable (tho' Unusuall) Accident in the Appartment; And this I am Sure, that consider the Room in it's Self, and 'twill be beyond all contest the most pleasant in the House. I wish it cou'd have been made a reall Salon, by carrying it up into the Next Story, but that wou'd have destroy'd one of the three Bedchambers Above, which My Lady thinks cannot be Spar'd. 'Twill however be eighteen foot high, which is no contemptible thing, tho' not what in Strictness One wou'd wish. Y^r L^{d}ship will See its' length and breadth, (with that of the Other rooms) by the figures. As to the Outside, I thought 'twas absolutly best, to give it Something of the Castle Air, tho' at the Same time to make it regular. And by this means too, all the Old Stone is Serviceable again; which to have had new wou'd have run to a very great Expence; This method was practic'd at Windsor in King Charles's time, And has been universally Approv'd, So I hope your L^{d}ship won't be discourag'd, if any Italians you may Shew it to, shou'd find fault that 'tis not Roman, for to have built a Front with Pillasters, and what the Orders require cou'd never have been born with the Rest of the Castle: I'm sure this will make a very Noble and Masculine Shew; and is of as Warrantable a kind of building as Any. I hope I need say no more, to gain your L^{d}ships Approbation of it, than what I have done; and I shall be very glad, if when you return, You are pleas'd with it, I intend to call there again about a fortnight hence, and See how they go on. There is So much money requir'd for Publick good this Year, that My Ld Treasurer can't Afford us at Blenheim half what we want; however, there will a great deal be done; And two Summers more will finish it. My Lady Dutchess was there lately, And return'd to Windsor, so entirely pleas'd, that She tould me, she found She shou'd live to Ask my pardon, for ever having Quarrell'd with me, And I find she declares the same to My Lord Treasurer and every body. So I hope I shall come Off in her good graces at last. My Ld Carlisle has been a good while in Towne, won Two thousand pounds of the Sharpers, and is gone downe again to lay it Out in his Building; but they are following him to Henderskelf to have their Revenge, And ten to One they get it.

We are here in Vast Expectations about the Thoulon expedition Sure if it Succeeds, it must bring things to a Speedy Issue. I wish it may; And that we may See your L^{d}ship quickly here Again in peace and Plenty. I most heartily wish your L^{d}ship all Success and satisfaction whilst you are Abroad, Nobody being more,

Your humble & Obedient
Servant
J. VANBRUGH

8

[*To The Earl of Manchester*]

London. Sep^t: *y*^e 9th 1707

My Lord

I find your L^dship is not without some fears, things shou'd not go quite right at Kimbolton; but if you have no greater Objections than those you mention, I don't doubt but I shall See you entirely Sattisfy'd, tho' one can't perhaps do it fully by Letters, I don't deny but the Hall might be sufficient in such an Appartment, without an Other very great Room; but it do's not follow that the Appartment is the worse for a Second; And in this Case it so fell Out, that there was no way of Avoiding it, without (in my judgment) utterly Spoiling the Appartment within, or the Front without; both which are this way Sav'd; And that only by Adding One Room of State (or in truth only making it a little bigger) than was Absolutly Necessary. An Other thing to be Observ'd, is; That there was no way of disposing the Space there was to be divided, with less Expence than this may; for two Small Rooms ·cost more in finishing than One Great One. As to the Height, Your L^dship says true. that they Ought all to be 18 f^t: And So they will. We consider'd how to dispose the Stairs down into the Garden, so as not to break too much into the Terrace; And all that matter will be very well. Y^r L^dship says you wou'd have the Ceilings Cov'd for Painting, as the Hall is; I am afraid they are Two low for painting, nor will they Admitt of a Coving very deep. but if y^r L^dship returns before this time twelve month, you'll be time enough to consider that matter upon the Place; for I reckon the House won't be Cover'd before Midsummer, I was there about Six weeks Since; 'twas then but 6 or 7 f^t high. I lik'd mighty well what was done, And Coleman Own'd he begun to discover a Gusto in it, that he had no Notion of before. I shall be much deceiv'd if People don't See a Manly Beauty in it when tis up, that they did not conceive cou'd be produced out of such rough Materialls; But tis certainly the Figure and Proportions that make the most pleasing Fabrick, And not the delicacy of the Ornaments: A proof of wch I am in great hopes to Shew y^r L^dship at Kimbolton. I am now going back to Blenheim for a Fortnight, but next Month I'll make an Other Step downe,

I was at Windsor Yesterday, where the Duke of Devonshire was sworn into his Fathers Place of Steward, And a Great Dinner Was prepar'd for him at the Greencloath. His Father left but a Small Debt after All. Not Above ten thousand pounds as Sr James Forbes tells me. He says the Estate comes to the Present Duke, charg'd with but 36000£. his Sisters Portion and All things included; And there is due from Tenants this Michaelmas 22000£ besides 5 or 6000. in ready money And a Personall

Estate in Jewells, Plate and Pictures &c, to a Very great Vallew; So that he is left in a very good Condition, and I fancy will keep himself so.

I hear yʳ Lᵈship is Offer'd the Place you formerly had, and that the Duke of Richmond is to have it, if you refuse it.

We have been a Little Dull here upon the dissappointment at Toulon. I was with My Lᵈ Dorchester and Lᵈ Carlisle to make Mons: Tallard a Visit about 3 weeks Since; who told us juſt how 'twou'd end, tho' we did not then believe him. I am Oblig'd to yʳ Lᵈship for your good wishes to me; I hope I shall rub through my Difficultys at laſt, and be Able to wait upon you sometimes in Peace and Quietness in the Country. I moſt heartily wish yʳ Lᵈship a Speedy return into England, and All Happyness when you are here, being with a great deal of Sincerity

Yʳ Lordships Oblig'd &
Moſt Obedient humble Servant
J VANBRUGH

9

[*To The Earl of Manchester*]

London. Feb: yᵉ 24ᵗʰ 1707/8

My Lord

I intended to trouble yʳ Lᵈship with a Long Letter About Our Opera Affaire, But I have not time to Night, and yet I am engag'd by promise not to let Slip this Poſt. I'll therfore only Acquaint yʳ Lᵈship, that at laſt I got the Duke of Marlboʳ: to put an end to the Playhouse Factions, by engaging the Queen to exert her Authority, by the means of which, the Actors are all put under the Patent at Coventgarden House, And the Operas are Eſtablish'd at the Haymarket, to the generall likeing of the whole Towne; And both go on in a very Successfull manner; without diſturbing one an Other. This Settlement pleases so well, that people are now eager to See Operas carry'd to a greater perfection, And in Order to it the Towne crys out for A Man and Woman of the Firſt Rate to be got againſt Next Winter from Italy. But at the Same time they declare for the future againſt Subscriptions, and have not come into any this Winter. I have therfore (with Severall to back me) laid before my Lᵈ Marlborough the Necessity there is for the Queen to be at Some Expence, And have such an Answer both from him and my Lᵈ Treasurer, as makes me write this Letter to yʳ Lᵈship, to Acquaint you, that if Nicolini and Santini will come Over (my Lᵈ Hallifax telling me this morning yʳ Lᵈship very much desired they shou'd) I'll venture as far as A Thousand Pounds between 'em, to be either divided equally, or More to One and less to tother as yʳ Lᵈship shall think fitt to adjuſt it with 'em, if you please to give your

(16)

Self the trouble of making the Agreement. This Money I propose to give 'em for Singing during the Next Season, which as things are now Regulated begins the Tenth of September, and ends the Tenth of June. The Opera is very rarely perform'd above twice a Week, and in the begining and latter part of the Season, not above Once, so that their Labour won't be great. If yr Ldship cou'd engage 'em for Piſtolls or Louis d'ores inſtead of Pounds, 'twou'd be so much Saved to two of your humble Servants, Mr Bertie and my Self, We being now the Sole Adventurers and Undertakers of the Opera, for I have Bought Mr Swiney quite out: Only pay him as Manager. My Affairs are all thank God in a much more prosperous ſtate than When yr Ldship left London. I heartily long to see Your Ldship here again; My Lady comes to Towne to Morrow in her Way to Kimbolton where I design to wait upon her Soon. Coleman is now with me in Towne And by Midsummer I hope all will be cover'd in. I muſt leave a great deal more I wou'd write both of Building Musick and Other Matters 'till an Other Poſt for this will be gone in half an hour. I am

Your Lordships moſt
faithfull & Obedient Servt

J VANBRUGH

Valentini is mighty earneſt with me to get Nicolini over tho' he knows he so much exceeds him; but he wou'd fain See Opera flourish here, and is mightely pleas'd with the Civill Treatment he meets with.

10

[To The Earl of Manchester]

London. March ye 16th 1707/8

My Lord

I have rec'd a Letter from yr Ldship of ye 24th: Feb: And I shall with pleasure do you all the Service I am Capable of at Kimbolton. My Lady has fix'd upon Saturday to go down for a few days, to Set Coleman at Work, and I have promis'd to wait upon her: I shall come back on Tuesday, and will if I can by that Poſt give your Ldship an Acct: what we have done.

This Attempt of the French has been a great Surprise upon people, Nobody believing they Wou'd persiſt in the Enterprise after our Fleet had Appear'd before Dunkirk much Superiour to 'em. The News of their Slipping out, and getting 14 or 15 hours Start of Sr George Bing, came the day the Annuity Bill was to be pass'd; People Seem'd a good deal disorder'd at it: however, Nobody withdrew what they had Subscrib'd, but Appear'd as eager as before to truſt their Money with the Government. Mr Churchill &c of the Tory part of the Admiralty, have talk'd lowd againſt Sr G. Bing for Letting the Ennemy Slip him; but Others who have a great Opinion both of his Skill, Care and Integrity, have judg'd better of him, and don't doubt but he'll be Able to make it Appear, he cou'd do no more than he did: All however have Seem'd on this Occasion to Allow, that a Fleet alone is not a Sufficient Security in Time of Warr, And that had there been 5000 Men in Scotland as there Us'd to be, Such an Attempt had been impracticable. But at present there is not 1500. wch are only Sufficient to Garrison in a very Indifferent Manner, Edinborough Caſtle, Sterling and one or two Small things more. So that the Whole Kingdome are quite at Liberty to chuse wch Side they think beſt, But the Kirk Party have proclaim'd a Faſt, and renounce the French: However, whenever they Land, there's nothing to Oppose them, but they'll be in Quiet Possession Till Our Army Marches into Scotland, in Order to wch (besides the Troops now embarking at Oſtend) the Horse & foot Guards, with what other Small forces we have Are on their way to York wch is the Rendezvous. Severall Regimts: from Ireland are likewise Order'd away for Scotland; So that Unless they meet with more Friends than 'tis thought here they will, their Attempt can turn to no great Account, more than the present Interruption it gives to Other Affairs, And the Uneasyness it puts People Under. But the News that came to the Houses today at Weſtminſter, of Sr George Bings being in Sight of the Enemy Off of Edinborough I observ'd gave a very sudden change to Peoples faces. I'm Sure the News of the Battle of Blenheim was not receiv'd with more joy: Especially by the North Britons who were cruelly downe upon this business. It is now held for impossible they shou'd be Able to Land, And very good luck they muſt have to Escape An Engagement. So I hope this Attempt will shut the door for Our time againſt any Other, for to be sure propper Measures will be taken to prevent 'em for the future. I heard My Ld Marlb: say this morning, that by the laſt Letters from Paris, he had an Account this project was Opiniatr'd by the King of France, againſt the Opinion of Others; wch wou'd incline One to think if it did not Succeed, One way, he wish'd it wou'd an Other, by getting rid of the Pretender, which is likely enough to happen; And Since there is hopes of being quiet at home, I may think again of Operas. I had written to your Ldship a little before I rec'd your Letter, to desire you wou'd engage Nicolini & Santini for Next Winter, if a Thousand Piſtols, (or Pounds if Piſtols wou'd not do) between them wou'd be Sufficient, wch My Ld Dorset tells me will plentifully do. But they muſt perform the Whole Season wch is from the 10th of Sept: to the 10th of June. So that they muſt if Possible be here in Auguſt, Unless to have the Advantage of coming wth yr Ldship, they shou'd ſtay something longer, wch in that Case, to encourage 'em, one wou'd dispence with. Now cou'd there be a Third, some Young Agreable Person of a Woman, who not yet in great Vogue, yet promis'd fair to grow to it. who wou'd come for an Allowance of 80. or 100 pounds a Year, it might be of great Service to bring downe the Pride & Charge of Our Present Singing Ladys, who Cost the House four hundred pounds a Year apeice. Stanhope tells me of Such a One at Leghorn, that he believes wou'd Come. her Name is Redjana. He commends her extreamly.

Blenheim is much Advanc'd, and to My Ld Dukes entire satisfaction, nor have I any Quarrells with my Lady Dutchess About it. There will be a great deal done this Summer, And one Summer more I hope will Cover it all, I'm Oblig'd to Y^r Lordship for your kind Wishes in that Affair, And am Your most Obed^t: humble Servt

J VANBRUGH

11

[To The Earl of Manchester]

Stevenage. March ye 22th 1707/8

My Lord

I writ to your L^dship last Week; and acquainted you, that I had promis'd to wait upon my Lady to Kimbolton to Settle things for going on with the Building. I have accordingly been there, and am got thus far to Night in my way back: My Lady (wth Lady Ann & Lady Doddee [?] stays there a fortnight longer. We have Adjusted every thing to be done this Summer, except the Bow Window; wch is a Nice point, that will require a good deal of Consideration, with regard to the Outside of the House as well as the inside: I have taken all Necessary Memorand^s: About it, and will think of the best way I can tho' I am yet of Opinion it must be a projecting Window of some kind or Other; but it may be so Order'd, that it shall have nothing to do with the Proportion of the Room, wch may have its due dimensions without it, and yet be very much beauti-fyed by it; the Other New Rooms beyond, are almost up to the Ceiling, and will be perfectly as one wou'd wish 'em, and big enough of all Con-cience; the first of 'em wch is in the Place of the Old Drawing Room, is rather bigger than the Bowwindow Room, And the Salon beyond it, is Almost as big as the Hall, and looks mighty pleasantly Up the Middle of the Garden and Canall, wch is now brim full of Water, and looks mighty well: The Espalier Hedges will be in great perfection this Year, and the Fruit Trees are now Strong enough to produce abundance: So that I hope y^r L^dship will find it Altogether, much improv'd & to your Satisfaction: I do Assure you the old Stone of the Priory has done Speciall Service; and turns to a much better Account here, than it wou'd have done in the Office wch I'll engage may be done without one foot of freestone And yet be made handsomer than Any Gentlemans house in Huntingdon Shire. I think y^r L^dship need not fear the New Upper Rooms being too low; they'll be full as High as your Own Bedchamber is, and that's enough in Concience, for this pretends but to an Attick Story and has it's full height as such: there will be four very good Bedchambers in it, and a very handsome and Convenient coming to 'em: There is one Ugly thing remov'd wch is the way under the half s(?)pace of the Stairs to the Chappel, wch was so low, one knocked one's head but I have found it possible to Alter the Stairs for the Better, and at the Same time to make that as high as the rest of the Gallery: Severall Other small Amendments to the House we have thought on; And I Apprehend but One thing from the Whole, wch is, That your L^dship will two or three years hence find your self under a violent Temptation to take downe and rebuild (suitable to this New front) all the Outside Walls round the Castle, But I'll say no more of that, 'till I see you at home and Secretary of State again; I write this Letter here, being Alone; and likely to want time for it to morrow Night. Y^r L^dship will have the Publick News from better hands, So I'll Send my Letter and go to Bed. I am

Y^r Lordships most
Obed^t: humble Servant
J VANBRUGH

I must do Coleman the Justice, that he has manag'd the Old Materials to Admirable Advantage, And executed the Directions he has had, extreamly well.

12

[*To The Earl of Manchester*]

London. May ye 11th 1708

My Lord

I have Two Letters from y^r L^dship, of ye 16th of March & the 20th of Aprill. And am (as well as the Towne) oblig'd to you, for the endeavours you use to improve the Opera here. What y^r L^dship says of having one or two of the Top Voices, is most certainly right; As to my Self; I have parted with my whole concern to Mr Swiney; only reserving my Rent: So that he is entire Possessor of the Opera And most People think, will manage it better than any body. He has a good deal of money in his Pocket; that he got before by the Acting Company; And is willing to Venture it upon the Singers. I have been severall times wth him lately in Consultation wth the Vice Chamberlain Coke, (who being a great Lover of Musique And promoter of Operas; My Ld Cham^b: leaves that Matter almost entirely to him. I have Acquainted him wth what y^r L^dship writes; And Mr Swiney has engag'd before him, to Allow a Thousand pounds for Nicolini, to stay here two Winters; That is, to be here in Sep^t: And at Liberty to go away again the May come twelve month after. A Thousand pounds, I think makes about 1200 Pistols; which undoubtedly he may Carry away clear in his Pocket; for he can't fail of Advantages otherways Sufficient to defray his Expences over and over. As for Santini Mr Swiney offers the Same Conditions to Her, if y^r L^dship can prevail with her to come; Or if She won't, and you think Rejiana wou'd do as well, he leaves it to y^r Judgment, and will Allow her the Same, If neither of these Women will come He wou'd venture at half this Allowance, Viz^t: 600 Pistolls for Something more, as y^r L^dship shall think reasonable) for the two Winters, if a Young, improving Woman cou'd be found that had a good Person and Action, and that might be esteem'd as good a Singer as Margarita. If y^r L^dship can get any of these People over, on the Terms here Mention'd, Mr Swiney desires me to Assure you of punctuall performance on his Part; Nor is there any reason to doubt him; for he has behav'd himself so as to get great Credit in his dealings with the Actors And I know the Vice-Cham^b: do's not the least Question his making good all he Offers on this Occasion; Besides, he has Power Sufficient to Oblige him to it, the License being only during the Queens Pleasure. I have not yet had an Oportunity to discourse My Lady Marlborough, about y^r L^dships proposition to her for Manza. But I find no Disposition at all in Other People. to promote his Coming at any great Expence; And by a Letter Mr Dayrolls has sent me from him, I find he expects 600. Guin^s: a Year, wch is not to be thought on. 'Tis Voices are the things at present to be got: And if these Top ones come over, 'twill facilitate bringing the Queen into a Scheme, now preparing by my Ld Cham^b: and Others, to have Concerts of Musick in the Summer at Windsor, twice a Week in the Appartment. There is no doubt, but by some such way as this, if the best Singers come, they will tast of the Queens bounty: for every body will Solicite for 'em that they may go away Content, and encourage Others to come over hereafter: So that I hope upon the Whole, y^r L^dship will be of Opinion, you may Safely perswade a Couple of 'em to Undertake the Voyage: for 'tis most Certain the People of Quality will find some means or Other, to send 'em home in good humour. I must give y^r L^dship one Caution by the Way: which is; That I have good reason to believe that Valentini (tho' he pretends to wish for Nicolini's Coming) will underhand do all he can to discourage him for he has link'd himself with Mrs Tofts (who is wonderfully improv'd) And in order to make a great bargain for themselves for next Winter, will certainly play some trick, to hinder both Nicolini and a Woman from coming over; if y^r L^dship don't Apprise 'em ont. Coleman is going on at Kimbolton. I shall send him this Post the

Design for the Upper Story in which there will be four Bedchambers, and good Accommodations to 'em, with a Corridore that runs the Whole Length behind 'em, and will be very pretty & very well Lighted. I hope yr Ldship will see what we have done by Sept: wch if it pleases you, will much rejoyce

Your Lordships

moſt Obedient humble

Servant

J VANBRUGH

My Lady Marlborough go's now very often to Court, & is in perfect good humour. I hope all will keep right.

13

[*To ——? possibly Arthur Mainwaring.*]

July 8. 1708

I thought to have Seen you again before I came out of Town but coud not. I am now at Blenheim, but under such uneasyness, that I'm scarce fit for Service now, having only a Short Reprieve from what I expected woud have immediatly fallen upon me. I muſt therfore before it bee too late, make One Application, more. Which I hope My Lady Dutchess will think so Moderate, that she will desire My Lord Treasurer to Allow it: Which is: that for the time paſt. and to come, (till something can be had by way of a place, which she has been pleas'd to promise me her Assiſtance in) My Lord wou'd order me upon the Queens Account, but what he did to Mr. Boulter. Without this, (of which my very Expences come to much more than half) There is no means left for me to prevent the Mischiefs that attend me And with it, I muſt Still go through Extream Difficultys to Spare My Lady Dutchess the trouble of a Letter. I beg the favour of you to Speak of this to her. Tis impossible it can be refused me If it be; Tis purely from the Misfortune, of my Sort of Service in this Business, not being rightly Underſtood, which is indeed what I have always Apprehended, since I saw so much Stress laid upon an Officer in Mr Boulters Poſt. But in this. My Lord Treasurer is so very wrong Apprised, That tis moſt certain the good Husbandry of the Money in the Moſt Essential and Significant part, lys as entirely upon the Surveyor, as the Designing of the Building: All that comes in the way of a Comptroller or a Clark of the Works is to See, That the Prices are right, And that there is no more work allowd for than is done: And with the firſt of these, the Surveyor is chiefly intruſted, the Comptroller being only an

(22)

Assistant to him writ So that in this part of the good Husbandry I am at least of Equall Service with those joind with me, But in the great Article of Management, they have no sort of Concern Which is in so casting things in the Execution of the Building, And disposing the Materialls that nothing may be Superfluous, or Improperly Apply'd; But that the Appearance of every thing may exceed the Cost: Tis upon this that a Surveyor is to be reckond frugall or Lavish, And tis upon this Article depends the Work at Blenheim costing fourty thousand pound more or less. The Case is exactly Paralell to that of keeping a Frugall and yet a Creditable Table, Which I suppose nobody will say depends in any measure so much upon the Cheap buying in of the Provisions, as in a Right Management and Distribution of em Afterwards. This is therfore the Saving Services, I either am of, or ought to be of: I confess there must Pass two Years more, before it can be clearly Seen, whether I have done right, in this great Point or no. But this may be known at present. That I take ten times the Pains to Succeed in it, that Others in this kind of Business usually do, This Custome is, to give themselves very little trouble, after they have once found the Generall Scheme, Wheras there is not one part of it, that I don't weight and Consider a hundred times, before tis put in Execution, And this with two ends, one of trying to do it better, And tother of giving it Some other turn that may be as well and yet Come *Cheaper*. And tis this that makes me when I am here. Avoid all Company, And haunt the Building like a Ghost, from the Time the Workmen leave off at Six a Clock, till tis quite Dark And in a Word whereon I am, tis very Seldom that I am not Earnestly Employ'd, in Studdying how to make this the Cheapest, as well as (it possibly) the best Hous in Europe, *which I think my Ld Dukes Services, highly deserve*. And I do assure you, that this more than Common thought About it, has plentifully had the Saving Effect I have propos'd For I have daily by it, hit upon things, that have Spar'd great Sums of Money which wou'd otherways have been Unnecessarily consumèd And I woud upon the Whole pawn my Life. that when this thing is finishd twill by all the World be judgd to have Cost Double what it really has. I hope at least I have done nothing hitherto to make it So much doubted of, that my Ld. Treasurer shoud refuse me a small Support; to enable me attend it, till the Experiment is gone through with But I am run on to a long Unnecessary Letter.

Pray Excuse Yours

most Faithfully

JV.

14

[*To the Earl of Manchester*]

London July ye 27th 1708

My Lord

I have rec'd your L^dships Letter of the 22th of June. I loſt so Much Money by the Opera this Laſt Winter, that I was glad to get quit of it; And yet I don't doubt but Operas will Settle and thrive in London. The Occaſion of the Loss was three things, One; that half the Season was paſt, before the Eſtablishm^t: was made. And then, My Ld Cham^b: Upon a Supposition that there wou'd be Immence gain, Oblig'd us to Extravagant Allowances; An Other thing was, That the Towne having the Same Notion of the Proffits, wou'd not come into Any Subscription; And the 3^d was, That tho' the Pitt and Boxes did very near as well as usuall the Gallery People (who hitherto had only throng'd out of Curiosity, not Taſt) were weary of the Entertainment: so that Upon the Whole, there was barely Money to Pay the Performers & Other daily Charges; And for the Cloaths & Scenes they fell upon the Undertakers. I might Add a Fourth Reason which is, That I never cou'd look after it my Self, but was forc'd to Leave it to Managers. Mr Swiney has now Undertaken it himself, And I believe will go through with it very well Nor will he want Subscriptions to help him; I don't doubt but Nicolini will be mighty well rec'd, And find his Account, And if once a Peace Comes, there will be many things to Support Musick which Are wanting Now. This laſt Stroke in Flanders I hope will procure One. We are in great Expeƈtation of what will become of the French Army People taking it for graunted here, they cannot possibly get off without fighting again, wch is not likely to recover their Affairs. I have not yet been at Kimbolton Since My Lady came there from Lees, but design to Wait on her on Saturday next, where I believe I shall find all right, & as I hear very much Advanc'd; I have a Conſtant Correspondence with Coleman, and am in moſt things very well sattisfy'd wth him: If we had Such a Man at Blenheim, he'd Save us a Thousand pounds a Year. We have made a Vaſt Progress there, but it will Still take up two Seasons More to finish I met John Coniers there on thursday laſt, with Severall Virtuoso's with him; He made mighty fine Speeches Upon the Building, And took it for graunted No Subjeƈts house in Europe wou'd Approach it: which will be true, if the Duke of Shrewsbury judges right in Saying there is not in Italy so fine a House as Chattesworth, for this of Blenheim is beyond all Comparison more Magnificent than that, My Ld Carlisle has got his whole Garden Front up And is fonder of his Work every day than Other. The Duke of Shrewsbury's house will be About half up this Season; My Ld Bindon is busy to the Utmoſt of his Force in New Moulding Audley end, And All the World are running Mad after Building, as far as they can reach. I heartily wish to See your Lᵈship at Kimbolton; where I earneſtly desire nothing may be done to the Bow Window till you come; for there are many things to be Consider'd on, wᶜʰ may depend on that Alteration. The Vice has been lay'd up of a Severe fitt of the Gout at Grimsthorp ever Since his Election; but is now juſt got to Towne, & pretty well. Things are in an odd way at Court. Not all the Intreſt of Lᵈ Tre & Lady Marlᵇ: back'd and press'd warmly by every Man of the Cabinet, can prevail wᵗʰ the Queen to Admit My Lᵈ Sommers into any thing; nor so much as to make an Attorney Generall: She Answers little to 'em, but Stands firm againſt all they say. My Lᵈ Chamᵇ: is in a Tottering way, I know he expects to be out which he has not a mind to. He has in a Triviall thing dissoblig'd My Lady Marlborough to a great degree. She is very much at Court, and mighty well there, but the Qˢ: fondness of tother Lady, is not to be express'd.

I'll give your Lᵈship an Account of things at Kimbolton Next Week; I hope to your Sattisfaction being moſt Sincerely

Your Lordships
Oblig'd & moſt
Obedᵗ humble Servant
J VANBRUGH

Old Sʳ Walter Sᵗ Johns is dead at laſt; I hear One of the Old Gentlemen who ſtood in yʳ Lᵈships way at the Cuſtoms house, is so too: The Other I am Acquainted with, He lives juſt by Blenheim; is hearty; but Drunk every day at leaſt Once.

15

[*To the Earl of Manchester*]
Bickleswade. Augᵗ: yᵉ 17ᵗʰ 1708

My Lord

I writ to your Lᵈship near three Weeks since from London, that I shou'd go to Kimbolton in few days, which I did Accordingly. I have been there again a Second time, And left My Lady and all the Family very well about three hours ago. I'm glad to hear yʳ Lᵈship is order'd home. I hope you'll find the Shell of your Building Compleat, The Eaſt end is up to the Battlements, and the Weſt is not much behind it the Timbers of the Roof are rais'd upon 'em both. The Middle Part of the Front waited for some New Stone, so is not quite So forward as the reſt, but will very Soon overtake 'em: it looks extreamly well from the farther end of the Canall, and will make a Shew one wou'd not expect from a Building compos'd of Such very Indifferent Materiall: I hope yʳ Lᵈship

(25)

will find the Appartment within, worthy of the good furniture you have provided for it. The Velvet is to be downe on friday, and great expectation there is of it. This has been a most miserable Year for fruit; but there is much more and better at Kimbolton, than in any Other place I have Seen: And in perticular a Mighty prospect of Grapes, which have fail'd almost every where.

If the Painter yr Ldship brings over be a good one, he may find work enough; but the New Room at Kimbolton can't be ready for him this Winter. So I Suppose you'll Set him Upon the Hall. I most heartily wish your Ldship a Quick and Pleasant Voyage And am

Your Lordships
most Obedt & humble
Servant
J VANBRUGH

I doubt the Composer yr Ldship Speaks of bringing won't turn to Acct: neither to the Opera nor himself For People will never believe him good, unless they had heard of him, as a most Famous Man; besides. there are So many Operas now in being, wch are translated ready to be performed, that there will be no want of New Compositions in Many Years. But if yr Ldship brought a perfect good Violin to Lead & Govern the Orcastre, 'twou'd be of great Service. Nicolini that belong'd to the Duke of Bedford & is now at Rome, is thought by the Skilfull here, to be as good as any in Europe for that perticular Service.

I hope Nicolini the Singer continues his Resolution, for they have cast all their Affairs depending on his Coming And 'tis absolutely Necessary he shou'd be here as soon as possible or the best part of the Season will be lost.

16

[*To the Duchess of Marlborough.*]

*Blenheim Sep*t 14th 1708

Madam

I have your Graces commission about the Carriage of the Stone; but hope we have hit upon an expedient that may prevent the making use of it. this execrable Weather is the Chief difficulty we have to Struggle with at this time, but if the Latter end of the Month proves fair, I hope October will be as it uses to be, which five or Six weeks will do very great Service yet. I wish Mr Travers had held his Tongue when he Allarm'd your Grace About the Carriages in the beginning of the Season: there never was a worse piece of Officious Service; But your Grace fir'd so much at it, that I saw 'twas in Vain to Struggle, and so it went But there really was no such thing as a Combination amongst the Carters; nor is a

Combination practicable Amongst Such a Multitude, I thought it was right to refuse an Advance for Stone in generall, and Accordingly Stood it; But for the Great Stones, the Carters had plainly reason on their Side, and the Sum twould have mounted to was a trifle: It has been an Unlucky hindrance to the carrying up the middle part of the House. But however *I dare Answer* for it, that all shall be coverd in Two Summers more, and every thing finish'd both in the House and in the Offices, except the Great Appartment towards the Valley the great Gallery, the Chappell, and some of the Lodging Rooms at the end of the House; for the Walls of these Parts I mention, won't be dry enough to Venture the Wainscoat up so Soon. This I am positive y^r. Grace may depend upon in point of time; And as to the Expence it will Appear at last, That there has been such Husbandry in the design (which is the Chief Concern) as well as in the Execution, That the Whole will by all People be judg'd to have Cost full twice as much as will be paid for't.

I am
Your Graces most humble & most
Obedient Servant
J VANBRUGH

17

[*To Lord Godolphin* (?).]

Blenheim May 31. 1709

My Lord

I writ to M^r. Travers about a week ago to desire he would move your Lordship, that if possible there might be one payment extraordinary Issued at this time, My troubling Your Lordship with a repetition of what I writ to him, is from my being every day more sensible of the great service it would be of, towards compassing what my Lord Duke has so earnestly press'd me to get done this summer. The wet weather held so long, that a great part of the season has been useless: so that 'twill require the utmost effort to do what is intended, And tho' the generallity of the workmen do go on with what they reckon a great deal of vigour and is really So in comparison to their usual method: Yet I can assure your Lordship I could take such measures, as would put quite another spirit into the whole work, *Cou'd there be but an immediate advance of* 6000 *lb more, out of Course.*

Your Lordship will, I hope, pardon me if I take this occasion to mention one word of the old manner, I have heard your Lordship has been told there has been 3000 lb. laid out upon it, But upon examining into that account I find I was not mistaken in what I believed the charge had been; which does not yet amount to 1100. nor did there want above two more to compleat all that was intended to be done the planting & levelling

(27)

included, And I believe it will be found that this was by 1000 lb. the cheapeſt way that could be thought on, to manage that hill so as not to be a fault in the approach, I am very doubtfull whether Your Lordship (or indeed My Lord Duke) has yet rightly taken the design of forming that side of the Valley; where several irregular things are to have such a regard to one another, that I much fear the effeƈts of so quick a sentence as has happen'd to pass Upon the remain of the Manour I have however taken a good deal of it down, but before tis gone too far I will desire your Lordship will give yourself the trouble of looking upon a piƈture, I have made of it, which will at one view explain the whole design, much better than A thousand words I'll wait upon your Lordship with it as soon as I come to town, & hope in the mean time it wou'd be possible that the pains I take in this particular shou'd be thought to proceed only from a desire of providing my self an agreable Lodging; I do assure your Lordship that I have aƈted in this whole business upon a much more generous principle and am much discourag'd to find I can be Suspeƈted of so poor a contrivance for so worthless a thing, But I hope the close of this work will set me right in the opinion of those that have been pleased to employ me in it.

I am
Your Lordship &c
J VANBRUGH

[Endorsed by The Duchess of M.]

All that Sir J. V. says in this lettr is false. The Manor house had coſt near £3000. & was ordered to be pulled down & the materials made use of for things that were necessary to be don. The piƈture he drew to prevent this, was false. My lord treasurer went to Blenheim, to see the Work: all he had represented of it, was false, & is now ordered to be pulled down.

18

[To The Duchess of Marlborough.]

Thursday. June yᵉ. 9ᵗʰ. 1709

Madam

Whilſt I was laſt at Blenheim I set Men on to take downe the Ruins at the Old Manour as was direƈted, but bid them take downe the Chappel laſt, because I was preparing a little Piƈture of what had been in general propos'd to be done with the Descent from the Avenue to the Bridge, and the Reſt of the Ground on that Side. which I feard was not perfeƈtly Underſtood by any explanation I had been Able to make of it by words, This Piƈture is now done; And if your Grace will give me leave, I shou'd be glad to wait upon you with it either this morning, or some time before

The Old Palace in Woodstock Park

the Poſt go's to Night, for if you shou'd be of Opinion to Suspend any part of what they are now executing, I doubt the order woud be too late, if deferred till Saturday.

I hope your Grace won't be Angry with me for giving you this one (and laſt) moments trouble more, About this Unlucky thing, Since I have no designe by it, to press or Teaze you with a word: but only in Silent Paint to lay before, and explain to you, what I fear I have not done by other Means, And so assigne it to your owne Judgment and Determination, without your ever hearing one word more about it from

Your Graces
Moſt Obedient humble
Servant

J VANBRUGH

19

[*Reasons Offer'd for Preserving some Part of the Old Manor.*]

June 11*th.*—1709

There is perhaps no one thing, which the moſt Polite part of Mankind have more universally agreed in; than the Vallue they have ever set upon the Remains of diſtant Times Nor amongſt the Severall kinds of those Antiquitys, are there any so much regarded, as those of Buildings; Some for their Magnificence, or Curious Workmanship; And others; as they move more lively and pleasing Reflections (than Hiſtory without their Aid can do) On the Persons who have Inhabited them; On the Remarkable things which have been transaƈted in them, Or the extraordinary Occasions of Ereƈting them. *As I believe it cannot be doubted, but if Travellers many Ages hence, shall be shewn The Very House in which so great a Man Dwelt, as they will then read the Duke of Marlborough in Story; And that they Shall be told, it was not only his Favourite Habitation, but was Ereƈted for him by the Bounty of the Queen And with the Approbation of the People, As a Monument of the Greateſt Services and Honours, that any Subjeƈt had ever done his Country: I believe, tho' they may not find Art enough in the* Builder, to make them *Admire the Beauty of the Fabrick* they will find Wonder enough in the Story, to make 'em pleas'd with the Sight of it.

I hope I may be forgiven, if I make some faint Application of what I say of Blenheim, to the Small Remains of ancient Woodſtock Manour.

It can't indeed be said, it was Ereƈted on so Noble nor on So juſtifiable an Occasion, But it was rais'd by One of the Braveſt and moſt Warlike of the English Kings; And tho' it has not been Fam'd, as a Monument of his Arms, *it has been tenderly regarded* as the Scene of his Affeƈtions. Nor amongſt the *Multitude of People who come daily to View what is raising to*

(29)

*the Memory of the Great Battle of Blenheim; Are there any that do not run
eagerly to See what Ancient Remains are to be found. of Rosamonds Bower.
It may perhaps be worth some Little Reflection Upon what may be said, if the
Very footsteps of it Are no more to be found.*

But if the Historicall Argument Stands in need of Assistance; there is
Still much to be said on Other Considerations.

That Part of the Park which is Seen from the North Front of the New
Building, has Little Variety of Objects Nor dos the Country beyond it
Afford any of Vallue, It therefore Stands in Need of all the helps that can
be given, which are only Five; Buildings, And Plantations These rightly
dispos'd will indeed Supply all the wants of Nature in that Place. And
the Most Agreable Disposition is to Mix them: in which this Old Manour
gives so happy an Occasion for; that were the inclosure filld with Trees
(principally Fine Yews and Hollys) Promiscuously Set to grow up in a
Wild Thicket. So that all the Building left, (which is only the Habitable
Part and the Chappel) might Appear in Two Risings amongst 'em, it
wou'd make One of the Most Agreable Objects that the best of Landskip
Painters can invent. And if on the Contrary this Building is taken away;
there then remains nothing but an Irregular, Ragged Ungovernable Hill,
the deformitys of which are not to be cured *but by a Vast Expence; And
that at last will only remove an Ill Object* but not produce a good One,
whereas to finish the present Wall for the Inclosures, to forme the Sloops
and make the Plantation (which is all that is now wanting to Compleat
the Whole Designe) wou'd not Cost Two Hundred pounds.

I take the Liberty to offer this Paper with a Picture to Explain what I
endeavour to Describe, That if the Present Direction for destroying the
Building, shou'd happen hereafter to be Repented of, I may not be blam'd
for Neglecting to set in the truest Light I cou'd, a Thing that Seem'd at
least to me so very Matteriall,

J VANBRUGH

[Endorsed by Duchess of M., tho' not in her hand.]

This paper has something ridiculous in it to preserve the house for
himself, ordered to be pulled down; but I think there is something
material in it concerning the occasion of building Blenheim.

20

[To The Duchess of Marlborough.]

Madam   *June 11. 1709*

In Speaking of y^r Graces uneasyness about the New Building, I meant
the whole in general, not the new Court in particular; But since you
mention that, as one Instance amongst Others, where money might have

been Spar'd, I desire leave to acquaint you; That in so great and regular a Building as Blenheim is, it cannot be avoided, but there will be a great Quantity of Stone, which neither for the Size nor Quality is capable of being used in the Principle parts of the House There being an Absolute Necessity in that, of using Stones of particular Sizes, and which will Square and Range with one another. This, Madam, we consider'd in the beginning of the Worke; And concluded to lay those waſt Stones by to be used in the out Offices and Court Walls: Which has Accordingly been executed laſt Summer in this Kitchen Court. This is the reason of its being Built with Freeſtone, And for the Manner of disposing that Materiall, I can't See where the Objeċtion lyes. Tis perfeċtly plain, and only Ax'd, not Smooth'd and Cleanṣd as in other places: And if upon this whole it makes a better Appearance than such Courts do in other Houses; tis only owing to its Forme, not its Workmanship or Ornaments I'm under some disappointment in this, for I was in hopes to have been thank'd for it, As to the Cover'd ways which lead dry to the Inferior Offices; 'tis no more than what has been very much praċtis'd in Ancient buildings, And is I think very much wanting in the New: They are not made out of respeċt to the Offices they lead to, but for the Shelter of the people who are so perpetually oblig'd to frequent 'em. My Lord Carlisle was so far from thinking it an extravagance, when I propos'd it to him, that he very readily put it in praċtice. And here I muſt desire yʳ Grace to observe, That if any thing gives that back Court at Blenheim a more than Ordinary Appearance, 'tis those Corridores being open'd to it with Arches, which has been much less expensive, than if the Wall had been quite close. And tis by such kind of things as these, that for the same expence, One house may be made to look incomparably better than Another. I don't know how your Grace comes to charge me, however, with building this Court without shewing the plan to my Lord Duke; for I do positively Affirme I did shew it him; And can bring I believe those people to Swear they saw me do it. I have now by me the very paper I layd before him; And I remember no Objeċtion he made but that there was not provision on the Stable Side, for a Sufficient Number of Coach houses. But for the future if any new work is begun, I'll desire the favour the Plan may be Sign'd.

As to the Main concerne of all Madam, which is the Expence of the Whole, I will (as I writ your Grace Yeſterday) prepare in a very little time a Paper to lay before you, that I hope will give you a great deal of ease on that Subjeċt Notwithſtanding there is £134000. already paid. But I beg leave to Set your Grace right in One thing, which I find you are missinform'd in The Eſtimate given in was between Ninety and a hundred thousand; And it was only for the House and two Office Wings next the great Court; For the Back Courts, Garden Walls Court Walls, Bridge, Gardens, Plantations & Avenues were not in it, which I Suppose nobody cou'd Immagine cou'd come to less than as much more. Then there happen'd One great disappointment. The Freestone in the Park Quarry not proving good, which if it had wou'd have sav'd 50 p^r. Cent in that Article, And besides this, the House was (since the Estimate) resolv'd to be rais'd About Six feet higher in the principal parts of it. And yet after all, I don't question but to see your Grace Satisfy'd at last: for tho' the expence shou'd something exceed my hopes, I am most fully Assur'd it will fall vastly short, of the least of your fears, *And* I believe when the whole is done *Both the Queen*, Yourself and everybody (except your personall Enemys) will easilyer forgive me, laying out fifty thousand pounds too Much; than if I had lay'd out a hundred thousand too little. I am

Your Graces most humble & obedient

Servant

J VANBRUGH

[*Memorandum.*]   21

July 8th 1709

When my Lord Duke was at Blenheim last winter was twelve month, I shew'd him a Generall Plan of the Whole Building I proposed, In which appeared two back Courts, one for the out Offices necessary to the house; and the other to the Stables.

 1 A small private Yard, just close to the Kitchen to lay coales & wood in, and to set the Cistern, and other things necessary to be at hand for the Immediate use of the Kitchen & Scullery.

 2 A Covered Store place for Billets and other wood necessary to be kept dry for the use of the Apartments and Lodging rooms.

 3 A Bolting house, Bake house, Storeroom for meal &c and Lodgings of eight foot high for Inferiour Servants over them.

 4 A Wash house, Landry, Drying room, Lodgings for the Servants belonging to the Landry; and a large drying Yard with space for fewell.

 5 A Tower to raise the Great Cistern upon, which receives the Water from the Engine, And from whence the pipes go into the Gardens, Offices, and other Places in the East end of the house, This Tower is at the same time a Gateway for an entrance to the House from the East Avenue: which will be the constant way of approach from London and Oxford. And therefore 'twas necessary the Inside of this Court should be Regular, Descent and clean, which is all it pretends to; it being impossible to make any thing in nature plainer. There are likwise two Covered ways on each Side the Court (only of eight foot wide) for a dry communication of all the Offices with the Kitchen.

This covered way may make some little shew, being opened towards the Court in Arches; But when 'tis considered, that the making it close would have cost much more money, I hope it won't be reckond a fault, but otherwise.

As to the back Stable Court. It contains Inferiour Stables, Coach houses, Store places for Hay, Straw and Corn, with two little private Yards to lay the dung in out of sight till it can be carryed off. There is likewise a Gateway to answer that on the East side with a Cistern on the top of it for the Service of the Stable, and other uses on the West side of the house and Gardens.

There are besides what has been already mentioned (Comprized within the Walls of the Office Courts) Two Green houses, which Answer one another in the Gen^{ll}. view of the South Front of the whole Building.

That which joins the Kitchen Court (which is the least pleasant Situation) is intended purely to preserve the trees in Winter.

That on the Stable side, having a very beautiful Situation (the West end of it coming to the very brow of the Hill and so looking directly down the Valley and River) may perhaps be thought proper for a distinct retired room of Pleasure, furnished with only some of the best Greens, mixd with pictures, Busts, Statues, Books and other things of ornament and entertainment. These kind of Detached Buildings have ever been extremely valued, where there has happened any thing particularly fine for their Situation, And I believe there is not in Europe a finer than this.

The Plan of these Designs being shew'd My Lord Duke when he was at Blenheim, He objected against a little kind of Salon which was drawn at the end of the Greenhouses, and ordered me to throw it into the rest of the room. He talked a great deal both with Mr Wise and me about adjusting both the Breadth and Height of the Green: houses: And thought in the Stable Court there was not provision enough for Coach houses. I remember no other objection he made. And in the Memorandum that was taken upon the Instructions for the Works to be done the following summer (of which M^r. Travers kept a Copy), there are these words Viz^t. If *the Sum for this Year may be increased to forty thousand pounds*, the over plus, to be employed in carrying on the Out walls of the East Court and Fountain Court, with the Inferior Offices belonging to the Kitchen.

22

[*To the Dutchess of Marlborough.*]

*London July ye 14th—*1709

Madam,

Your Grace will receive by my Lord Herveys Servant to morrow the Designe you desired to See of the Manner intended for finishing the Salon, The Pannells at the bottom are to be of Wainscote, and run even without any breaks so that there will be room for above Twenty Chairs besides Tables The Pillaſters and Don Moldings are to be of Marble, with the Moldings About the Niches where the Figures Stand. The Figures intended for these Niches are now in the Palace of a Gentleman in Italy. The Late King had given Orders to buy them a little before he dy'd, And My Lord Duke has sent Directions to Florence to purchase them. All Above the Pillaſters is to be of Wainscote enrich'd.

I have likwise sent Your Grace Some Drawings for My Lord Duke, which when Your Grace has viewed I beg you'll please to let Mr Hodges put them up Safe, and Send them. I am going to Blenheim to Morrow. having taken Care of every thing your Grace directed me here in Towne & I don't at all doubt but I shall soon be Able to give you a very Certain Account, that the Work intended will be done this Year. And I hope when I return, to bring your Grace And My Lord Treasurer, Such a State of the Whole Blenheim business, as will convince you, You need not be Uneasy either as to the Time or Money that will be required to finish the whole Designe. I am

Your Graces moſt humble

& moſt Obedient Servant

VANBRUGH

I muſt beg a Moment of your Grace's time, to read over the inclosed Account of the Office Courts. I do assure your Grace I had my Lord Dukes Approbation, which I don't doubt he'll remember as Soon as he Sees the General Plan I now Send him. But I believe when yr Grace has read this Account of the Offices, you will plainly See there is no one Room of 'em to be dispencd with.

23

[*To Lord Ryalton?*]

Blenheim July ye 18. 1709

My Lord—

I am very Sorry it did not happen I was here when your Lordship was laſt downe: because I think I cou'd have explain'd severall things upon the Spot, much better, than by writing, And perhaps have given you some Satisfaction in moſt of those things I find you have Some Objection to.—As to the Height of the Salon, they inform'd you quite wrong, The eight foot they Mention'd was never design'd to be in it And I think there cannot be a juſter height given to a Room of that sort, than that will have.

As to the Offices in the Out Courts, I here inclose a Copy of a Paper I sent my Lady Dutchess, And to My Lord Duke. I hope it will Satisfy both them And your Lordship, that there is nothing more than this is

(34)

Necessary to all Houses of *much a less rank than this* And if your Ldship will Observe other Houses where you go, You will find hundreds that have more out buildings a great deal. All the Difference is, That they are generally ill favour'd by Scrambling about, And look like a Ragged Village Wheras these being all Compriz'd within One regular Handsome Wall, (And being likwise regularly dispos'd within) Form a Court, which by this means Adds to the Magnificence of the Dwelling, but not to the Quantity of it. Tis impossible this can be thought a fault, if seriously thought of at all. I am sure I had much other expectations from it; And I still believe they will not be disappointed at last.

I find your Ldship Seems to think the Greenhouse on the West Side, will take off too much of the View from the Gallery.—Tis impossible I believe so to dispose a great Building, with all that must Attend it, but Some things worth Seeing in the prospect will be hid, but I believe there is as little of that misfortune here, as ever happen'd in any Situation. All the most Valluable parts of the Views, lying to the most Significant Rooms in the Building. Nor is there any thing hid by this Greenhouse; from the Bow window in the Gallery, but the bleak naked part of the Park, And that to One of the Worst points of the Compass, which is the North West, from whence the Winds blow three quarters of the Year All the beautifull Wood upon the High Lodge hill is seen; And in Such a point of View, as if it had been planted on purpose. The Water (where it will Appear to the best Advantage, whether Lake or River) is full in View, And in a Word, nothing is cover'd, but what in my opinion is not worth being nam'd in the beauty one wou'd describe of the Galery prospect. But Such as it is however, the Pavillion at the South end Commands it, And one Window in the North Pavillion looks full up the Great Avenue. So that this Gallery from one part or other of it. Shews every thing worth seeing about the Seat, but tis impossible to See all things from all places. There is another thing, I think worth yr Ldships remark too in this Case, which is, that this Greenhouse will keep off the Westerly Sun from that end Garden, And Grott under the Gallery. at a time in the Summer evenings when the West Side of a house is intollerable. And there will not be so Agreable a place in the Whole Garden, as that will be towards six o Clock, provided the Sun be schreen'd a little off; Nor will there be so pleasant a Room for View Nor so cool (yet all the Same Gay and light) in the Whole house, as that Greenhouse or Detach'd Gallery, for that indeed is what I take it to be, And not a Magazine for a parcell of foolish Plants. I don't see why this shou'd not be the Room for the Tytian hangings which it will just hold. And Since there is no Library in the House. that may be the business (or pretended business at least) of this Gallery The Books dispos'd in Presses made handsome like Cabinets, And plac'd Regularly along with the Chairs, tables And Couches, This, my Lord has allways been my Notion of this Room: And I shou'd be mighty glad to find your Lordship come into it, for it Seems clearly to me the moſt Valluable Room in the Whole Building, And I never saw any one of this kind Abroad (which scarce any fine Place is without) that cou'd compare with it, for the Extreame pleasantness of its Situation.   I am

Your Lordships

moſt Obed^t. humble

Servant

J VANBRUGH

I desire your Lordship will please to let my Lady Dutchess and my Lord Treasurer know, what I observe to your Lordship about this Detach'd Gallery.

[*Endorsed by Duchess of M.*]

The second green house, or a detached gallery I thank God I prevented being built; nothing, I think can be more mad than the proposal, nor a falser description of the prospeƈt.

24

[*To the Duchess of Marlborough.*]

July 25. 1709

Madam

I am extreamly glad to find by your Graces Letter, there is hopes of My Lord Dukes quick return by a renewall of the Treaty: And I hope his House here will be ready to receive him, as soon as the Glorious end he is making of this long liv'd Warr. will give him leave to enjoy it in Peace.

The Middle Part of the Building has advanced so wonderfully faſt, that it wou'd have been cover'd much Sooner than I believe your Grace ever cou'd expeƈt, had not this Cruell Wett Season ſtopt the Stone, as it ſtill dos, for yeſterday there fell a great deal of Rain   Tis scarce possible How-ever there can be a Disappointment at laſt, only if this Weather continues till Harveſt begins (which will be about three weeks hence, there will no Stone come in more (without some extraordinary means) till 'tis over, which will be very late in the Year, But we shall get the Roof on Upon the Salon, the Room next to it on either Side.   And the Supping Room, in three Weeks at fartheſt, 'tis the North Front only that we want Stone for.   And tho' the Weather shou'd mend, I am very Apprehensive it will not come in (at leaſt in time) without a Small Allowance more for Carriage, For the Stone that now lyes nearly rais'd, is at the Quarys three miles farther than the reſt, And we have had Sufficient experience, that the Carts don't find it worth theire while to go thither at the prices now allow'd 'em, but sometimes when the ways are perfectly good, And that they have nothing at all else to do, as it may possibly fall out in October. There lys Madam at those Quarrys about a Thousand Tun ready, and of the best & most necessary Stone, for this Years Work, And an Advance only of Two Shillings a Tun (perhaps less) wou'd fetch it all in, in three Weeks time, if the ways are but barely passable. Which comes to at Most, but a hundred pounds.

The Height of the Salon will be just *forty feet* the eight foot they told my Ld. Ryalton was to be in it, was only a Space between the Ceiling and the Roof as there is in the Towers. but even that space won't be there now, the Roof being otherways fram'd tho' in the Towers there was a necessity for it The Upright I sent your Grace of the Out front of the Kitchen Court was right drawn, it being nothing but a High Wall, such a One as was first to Appear about Such a House, (*had there been no Occasion for Offices within it. Those Offices are* fourteen ft. high, And the Rooms over eight which are contained within the height of this Wall And only Appear to be Offices within the Court Nothing rising higher Without than the Wall, except the Gate, which is carry'd up to the height Necessary for raising the Water to the place where the Pipes are to go—the Windows of these Low Offices open into the Court, as your Grace guess'd except three or four which look outwards.

I must beg your Graces pardon for a short Visit I can't avoid making to my Ld. Carlisle, which I find I may do just now much better than a Month hence I shall come directly back hither without coming to London, And that before I can be wanted either by the Workmen, or your Graces coming downe for Your Grace won't find it worth your coming these Three weeks at Soonest, About which time I hope here will be a great deal to entertain you, And that you will be of Opinion to give some farther orders, towards Advancing the Work in Generall which it will not be too late to execute. I am   Your Graces
most humble & obedient Servant
J VANBRUGH

25

[*To the Duchess of Marlborough.*]

Madam   *Blenheim Novr. ye. 1st: 1709*

The Weather being come fair againe, And that with Frosts, which dry the ground almost as much as the Sun at Midsummer, I hope we may yet get in this Stone; which if we do, I am almost Confident, we shall cover the Great Gallery next Summer.

I desire your Grace will plase to let the Smith you employ, talk with Sr. Charles Hopson about Hinges Bolts &c. for they must Adjust those things together And Suit 'em to the Severall doors, According to their Scantlings And Manner of hanging—As to Mr Kays(?), I shan't engage myself to be his Advocate; I'll only Acquaint your Grace, that about four Months ago, I remember he told me he had been to wait upon you, and that by something he had heard Since, he fear'd he was Misunderstood about his Rates, which he said must be by your Graces mistaking him in the Sizes he put those Rates to; for that his Demands for the Same Size with My Lady Sunderlands was five and thirty shillings apeice for which he said, She gave but half a Crown less. And for the Great Size of all, for the Large Doors, he said he demanded three pound—He then desir'd I wou'd Speak to your Grace to Set you right in this Mistake, but I told him, I did not care to meddle in it, So he said when you sent for him again, he wou'd put his Rates & Sizes in Writing, to prevent any misunderstanding for the future. And that he wou'd engage himself, to keep all his Locks in repair at his own Charge during his Life.

The Duke and Dutchess of Shrewsbury give their humble Service to your Grace. I was there on Sunday; there is more of the Roof yet upon their house, And twil be with great Difficulty if they get it on this Season I wish your Grace joy at the Out side of yours at S^t. James's being quite compleated, which I hear it is

I hope my Lord Duke is in England by this time. But unless the fairness of the Weather engages him to come down I hope he'll defer it a Month. I beg the favour however, that your Grace will please to let me know his Resolution, because if he do's not come Now, there will be no necessity for my staying above a few days more. I am

Your Graces

most humble & Obed^t

Servant

J VANBRUGH

The Locks for the best floor shou'd not be less than between ten and eleven Inches long, And those in the Attick story between eight and Nine. I mean for the Chamber doors. those for the back Closets need not be more than between Seven and eight. If your Grace pleases to bespeak ten of Each of these Sorts, that may be enough for the Present. but they shou'd be half for one hand and half for the other.

[*To Mr Travers.*]   26

Sir

I find there is so cruell a Reflection lys upon my Lord Duke at Florence upon the Agreement not being in any measure perform'd, which by his Graces Directions D^r. Newton made with Seig^s. Soldani and Barrata, that any one who has a concern for his Hon^r. cant bear to hear it. I have repeated Letters upon it from Dr Newton and M^r. Cardonall, And am daily Spoak to by the Envoy here. For Gods sake Speak to my L^d. Ryalton of it, that a Remittance of £300 more may inſtantly be made out of the mony now lying in M^r. Taylors hands with Assurances that the third Payment shall Soon follow, The giving leave from the Great Duke to make these Statues, was a very great Compliment meant to Lord M. And obtain'd by Application from the Envoy here, so that you may judg how it muſt sound in the Court at Florence, to hear the Statuarys who are employ'd can't get their money Pray get directions about this Remittance without waiting my Lord Dukes Arrival, which is not at all necessary. For my Part; till tis done, I resolve never to Answer any Letter I receive from D^r. Newton one thing I shou'd farther observe to you, that Dr Newton being upon coming away, muſt make the thing Appear Ten times worse, he having made the agreement. I leave this matter to your care and am

Sir

Your moſt faithfull

humble Servant

J VANBRUGH

M^r. Tailer [*probably an endorsement*]
I think this Should be done forthwith.

27

[*To the Duke of Marlborough.*]

London April 28. 1710

[After mentioning that ſtone should be speedily provided for the Year's work, he proceeds:]

(*Note by Coxe MSS. Copyist*)

I believe your Grace laſt poſt may have received a letter from my Lady Dutchess about the Statues which the Duke of Florence has given leave to Signor Soldani to caſt in brass, for your Grace she having put a ſtop to any farther proceedings upon them for the present. I have received two letters from Dr Newton in answer to what I wrote to him by Your Grace's direction He tells me that having obtained the great Dukes leave to caſt the figures he immediately set Soldani to work and that there having been moulds newly taken for the Elector Palatine, the Duke had consented the figures should be formed upon those moulds which would give a very great dispatch to the work. He likwise acquainted me what Soldani was to have, and desired a Credit might immediately be lodged with some

(39)

Merchant at Leghorn from whence he might draw money from time to time as the work went on, according, to agreement. Which is that one third shall be paid down (because of buying the metal) one third when the work is half done, and the reſt when the figures are delivered. The whole for these four figures comes to near a thousand pounds. But Mr Travers speaking to my Lady Dutchess about this Credit she is not willing any thing should be done in it till Your Graces further direƈtion

Dr Newton writes likewise, that Barrata (whom Your Grace had direƈted laſt year to make two figures but could not being engaged by the King of Denmark) now offers to do something for Your Grace. He is in very great Eſteem; and if Your Grace thinks fit beforehand to make a couple of figures for a trial, I believe it would be beſt to leave them to his own fancy. Dr Newton will take care about the prices The figures Your Grace gave orders to buy (designed for the Niches in the Saloon) are ſtill held at double what they are judged worth. But if the owner sees your Grace begins to employ Barrata, it is probable, he may come to reason.

All the marbles that were at the Tower I had well packed up in cases which (with the two Black Figures Mr Churchill gave Your Grace, and the Tables from my Lord Cardigan) I have sent to Blenheim. And I am glad that I can now assure Your Grace, the Model of the Fountain of piazza Navona, is of Bernini's doing. I shewed it before it went to Blenheim to Mr Gibbons, and the beſt connoisseurs here who at firſt sight owned it to be what was pretended, and think it scarce to be valued The four figures make the moſt valuable part of it and there is but one of them that has received any damage worth naming. I was in hopes by the return of the yachts, Your Grace would have sent the buſt of the King of France.

I have not yet returned Your Grace my humble thanks for the kind letter you were pleased to write me from Harwich. My Lord Treasurer has not yet done what Your Grace recommended in my behalf; but has promised he now will.

28

[*To the Dutchess of Marlborough.*]

London June ye 6th—1710

Madam

By a Letter from Mr Bobart, which has follow'd me to Towne. I find Your Grace expeƈted I shou'd send the Draught of the Stone Gallery to you But I thought you had direƈted me to Send it to my Ld Duke, which I accordingly did, With explanations Upon the niches I have however kept a Copy of it, which if you please you may See.

He likewise mentions your Graces desire that Mr Bancks might go on with the Colonade Which is over against your own; that so, the Great Court might be Compleat this Year.

The Chief Part of this Colonade consists of Particular Stones which probably will be sent in from the Quarrys this Summer whether they are us'd or not: so that provided Mr Banks do's not drive on too fast, but only puts on such a Number of men, as may still work up that Stone which is design'd for the Colonade; tis certain that it may go on without any material hindrances to Mr Strong: *But the Chappel shou'd be entirely let Alone.*

I left things in such a Way Madam when I came from Blen^h. that I believe I may assure you the Whole House will be cover'd in this Year The Bridge got quite up, And the Great Court in a manner finisht: I mean as to, Leveling, paving & enclosing. And I think I may now Venture almost to Assure your Grace likwise (As I have already done my Lord Treasurer) That the whole Expence, of House, Offices, Bridge, Avenues & Gardens will not *exceed, Two* Hundred And Fifty Thousand Pounds. Tho' I find I shall have the Satisfaction of Peoples thinking it has Cost Double that Summ. I troubled y^r Grace last Week with a Long Remonstrance which I must beg leave to follow with one more which being the last, I hope they will both be forgiven

Your Graces

Most Obedient humble

Servant

J VANBRUGH

29

[*To the Duchess of Marlborough.*]

London June 24th 1710

Madam

Your Grace will not wonder that some of the People at Blenheim, who trusts the works with very great sums (some of them more than they are really worth in the world) *should be a little frightned with the news of my Lord Sunderland,* and other things they daily hear. And this apprehension I find is like to prove a great hindrance to the very hopefull progress this summer, unless something be done to encourage 'em; which I believe a Letter from your Grace would do, either to Mr Travers or to me, by which you shou'd give us commission to declare to them that whatever happen'd, you wou'd take care they shou'd not suffer. I believe such a Letter would be sufficient; and I suppose your Grace will have no objections to it, since Tis only what you have on your own accord often said. If your Grace pleases to do something of this kind, the sooner the better; because there is such a quantity of Materials got in, and such a number of men at present engag'd, that the work of this summer will be surprising, if no unlucky cheque be put to it

I am
Your Graces
most obedient humble Servant
J VANBRUGH

[*Endorsed by Duchess of M.*]

Instead of complying with him I stoped the Works in 1710, till the crown should direct Money for it.

30

[*To the Duke of Marlborough.*]

Blenheim Aug^t: 1. 1710

I have the Honour of a letter from your Grace in which you are pleased to say you writ some time since to My Lady Dutchess and Lord Treasurer upon the letter I was forced to trouble you with. I humbly thank your Grace for it, and hope when I return to Town I may find the effects of it which indeed I extremely stand in need of.

I am heartily touched with the thoughts your Grace should (after the great Services this barbarous nation is indebted to you for) meet with any sort of trouble that may allay the satisfaction, I flatter myself you else would find, in the great progress we have and shall make here this Summer. The rest of the House to the westward is now out of all danger of being uncovered. I have been here about a month in which it has advanced above ten feet, and does not now want above eight more to the roof So that by the end of this month I hope to see the Plumbers at work upon the Gallery: that Gallery which my Lady Dutchess has so often laught to hear talkt of as a thing in the air. This part of the work being advanced so much beyond what was hoped for, has prevailed with my Lady Duchess, to let the Colonnade go on which leads to the Chapel; where they have been working the Stone for some time: and are this day beginning to set. There is no doubt but it will be up and covered by Michaelmas. The great arch of the Bridge rises apace. It will be very near turned by the end of the month, so that I don't doubt, but the centres may be struck before Your Grace sees it; and I hope you may be able to ride over it. I have a large drawing of it almost finished to send your Grace. The north front is doing likwise. I'll hasten them all that is possible and send them away as soon as ever they are ready

I am &c

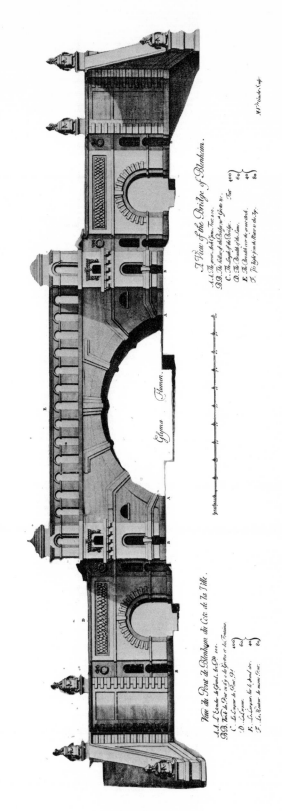

Pons Blenhemicus.

Pontis Blenhemicus Latus, ab Oppido Conspectum.

A.A. *Distantia inter adversas pilas, sivum maximum...*
B.B. *Planum Pontis in pari Congestu, 3, Turres.*
C. *Pontis Longitudo Tot.*
D. *Maxima Latitudo.*
E. *Eiusdem pars angustior.*
F. *Pontis Altitudo.*

Veüe du Pont de Blenheim du Côte de la Ville.

A.A. *L'Eendue du Grand Arc Dr.*
B.B. *Toute le Pont avec les y, et les Voûtes et les Fontaines.*
C. *La Longeur du Pont Tot.*
D. *La Lageur.*
E. *Le Largeur plus le Grand Arc.*
F. *La Hauteur du même Pont.*

Gigms Flumen.

Veduta del Ponte di Blenheim dalla parte della Villa.

A.A. *Il Vano del Arco maggiore, da Pira Pira Pot. 202.*
B.B. *Tuvum col Ponte con le Grotte e Fontanelle incluni.*
C.C. *La Longhezza del Ponte Tot. Piedi.*
D. *La Larghezza.*
E. *La Larghezza nella parte minore.*
F. *L'Altezza del Ponte.*

A View of the Bridge of Blenheim.

A.A. *The great Arch Open. Feet 202.*
B.B. *The hollow of the Bridge w. Grots &c.*
C. *The Length of the Bridge.*
D. *The Breadth of the Same.*
E. *The Breadth over the great Arch.*
F. *The hight from the Water to the top.*

M.r Vander Sculp.

31

[*To the Duchess of Marlborough.*]

London August 31st 1710

Madam

Mr Mainwaring shew'd your Grace the copy of a letter I was forc'd to trouble my Lord Duke with in May last; with the answer he was since pleased to write me to it. Tis only for the performance of what he there promises shall immediately be done that I am now troubling your Grace. Tis easy to imagine the change of my Lord Treasurer must bring some people very hard upon me, who with great difficulty were prevaild upon to wait before. But now seeing me totally disappointed on all sides there is nothing but money will satisfy 'em; of which I have none to give 'em. A condition I believe few people wou'd have been in, after having had the direction of such a business as Blenheim for Six years together; but I relied on what my Lord Treasurer at first declar'd, that he wou'd have no perquisites made; because twas intended there shou'd be such considerations, that they shou'd not be stood in need of. I hope he will at least for the present, give Mr Travers directions to comply with what my Lord Duke has consented to; and that it may be done out of the first money which shall come into his hands for the use of Blenheim. This favour I must earnestly press your Grace for, who am

Your most obedient humble Servant
J VANBRUGH

[*Probably early endorsement.*]

Mr Vanbrugh's letter about the money after Lord Godolphin was out.

32

[*To the Duke of Marlborough.*]

London Sept 22 1710

My Lord Duke

Lieut. Genl. Withers has done me the favour to charge himself with a little Bag for your Grace in which are the designs of the Bridge and the whole North front of the Building, the utmost extent of the offices included which is altogether about 800 feet The drawings are true but in no measure prepared for an Engraver to work after. I therefore desire Your Grace will please not to let them go out of your hands so as any body can take a copy, lest they should be published (as it often happens) to great disadvantage

(43)

I have got the East Front already engraved here, and the South is doing. I propose to adjust all the prints to a scale that they may form a book as is usually practised abroad in such cases.

I thought to have gone to Blenheim ten days ago but have deferred it in daily hopes I might be able to say something to the workmen about money who have by my threatenings as well as persuasions exerted this year to a great degree making an inconceivable progress with the Building. Such that had the Queen cleared what is now due, I don't believe but thirty thousand pounds more would complete all to Your Grace's Satis-faction. I am glad to find at last, there is a likelihood of this present Treasury's ordering money as usual. I have on this occasion informed them of one thing, which perhaps Your Grace may have forgot, that as soon as the model was made, I had it carried up into the Gallery at Ken-sington where the Queen and Prince considered it, asking all the questions needful to understand it thoroughly. But so far from making any excep-tions that the queen entirely approved of it and was particularly pleased with the magnificent part, and expressed a great desire of having it finished soon. I have acquainted them that this model still remains in Kensington House: and that it has been followed in everything material. I think this ought to have a very great weight with them, and undoubtedly must unless it be for reasons your Grace can better judge of than I. I shall however upon the hopes they give go for Blenheim tomorrow morning to do your Grace what service lies in the power of

Your Grace's &c.

33

[*Early Copy.*]

An Acc^t. of what has passd with the Treasury relating to the Building at Blenheim, since my Lord Godolphin was remov'd. Being at Blenheim the 30th. of Sept. 1710 I writ to the Duke Marlborough then in Flanders, as follows.

My Lord Duke

I acquainted your Grace before I came out of Towne that there was a liklyhood of mony being Order'd for your Grace's Service here, but it not being yet down, and Mr Travers desiring me to joyne in the Solicitation for it, I have writ a Letter this post to my Lord Poulet, of which I here inclose a Coppy, I hope Your Grace will Approve of what I have said to him, I am sure at least, tis most heartily mean't for your Service

I am &c

Coppy of y^e*. Letter to my Lord Poulet.*

Blenheim Sept. 30th. 1710

My Lord

It not having been my part in carrying on this Building at Blenheim, to Solicite the late Lord Treasurer for the mony, but only as Survey^r. to design and direct it, I do not now think it proper for me to lay any Memoriall, before the Treasury board, leaving that to the care of M^r. Travers as formerly, But finding things here on the point of falling into a Distraction not to be Express'd, from the Great Arrears due to a vast Number of poor familys, and not hearing any thing certain of mony being imediatly Order'd in some measure to releive them I thought it might not be Amis to Acquaint your Lordship in particular with something relating to this Worke, which very probably you may not have heard, Your Lordship will make what use of it you think proper.

When the Queen had declared she would build a House in Woodstock parke for the Duke of Marlborough, and that she Mean't it in Memory of the Great Services he had done her and the Nation, I found it the Opinion of all people & of all partys I convers'd with, that altho the Building was to be calculat'd for, and Adapted to, a private Habitation, Yet it ought at ye same time, to be consider'd as both a Royall and a National Monument, and care taken in the Design, and the Execution, that it might have y^e. Qualitys proper to such a Monument, Viz^t. Beauty Magnificence, and Duration, I must own I was very glad, to find the General Notion, so entirely to my owne, and was encourag'd by it, to do all I cou'd, sometimes Obstinatly, and sometimes Artificially, to get such a Fabrick Agreed to, as I thought the happy Occasion and the Queens Glory requir'd, However that the Queen herself might not be deceiv'd in what she Directed and be Afterwards dissatisfy'd with it, A very large, Exact, And intelligible Model of the Building, was made in Wood and when it was compleatd it was set in the Gallery at Kensington by her Order, and there left sometime, that she might Consider it at her leisure, both Alone and with other people, she was pleasd to View it thoroughly with the PRINCE, and to Ask all Questions Necessary, for the Understanding it Perfectly, She Expressd her Self extreamly Pleasd with it. Shew'd a desire of having it dispatch'd with all Aplication, and requird no sort of Alteration in it, this Model I have carefully preserv'd at Kensington that it may Appear I have exactly follow'd it, As to the Management in the Expence my Lord I shou'd be very glad to have Occasion to answer to Every Article of it, but perhaps the whole will be pretty well justify'd by one Observation, I am glad I have every Day Occasion to make, which is, That the Expence is by all People Judg'd to be twice what I know it will be, I wou'd not have given your Lordship the trouble of this Letter, but that I thought it might not be disagreeable to you, to be Appris'd of what I here aquaint you, has pasd on this Subject

I am &c:

By the same poſt, I writ the following Letter to M^r. Harley then Chancell^r. of the Exchequer

(b)

Blenheim Sept 30 1710

S^r

Altho', in the carrying on this Building of Blenheim it has not been properly my business to Solicite the Mony for it, but to take care of the Designe, the Execution & ye Contracts I hope you will not blame me, if looking upon it, much more as an intended Monument of the Queens Glory, than a private Habitation for the Duke Marlborough, I am so much concern'd for it on the former Account, as to represent to you, the Extream Necessity there is, for some immediate Supply, purely to Close and terminate what has been carry'd on this Summer in such manner as may secure it, from receiving vaſt injurys by the Winter Rains and Froſts, For it is so long since any Mony has been Issu'd for this Worke that the Credit is exſtend'd beyond even the power of getting in a little Lime & Bricks to compleat some things at the very point of finishing, And boards to cover other parts that could not be quite got up this Season, I cannot help looking on this Building wth. y^e. tenderness of a sort of Child of my Owne, and therefore hope you will forgive my troubling you for its Preservation

I am. &c.

J VANBRUGH

The same poſt I sent Another Letter to Mr Travers to lay before ye Treasury.

Three Days After I had sent these 3. Letters, there came an Express Order from the Dutchess of Marlborough to put a general Stop to the Building till mony should be Order'd from the Treasury to go on with it, and a Stop was put Accordingly

I then came Away to London, and found at my house the following Letter from Mr Taylour of the Treasury

(c)

S^r

The Lord Commission^{rs}. of her Majeſties Treasury, command me (in the Absence of M^r. Lowndes) to Aquaint you that their Lordships having represented to her Majeſty, the condition that the Building is in at Blenheim, as Statd in Your Letter to Mr Travers the 30th. paſt, and the great want there is, of an Imediate Supply of mony for it, that so you may not be forced to leave of, uncoverd & Expos'd to the Injurys of the Winter, what is so near a Close, Her Majeſty was pleas'd to Say, That Altho'. the condition of her Revenues, and the Arrears due to her Servants & Family are such, as will not at present Allow of what may be Necessary for carrying on that Worke so faſt as she could Wish, Yet that her Majeſty wou'd by no means, have what is so far Advanc'd left in a Condition to be injur'd by the Approaching Winter, and therefore Direĉts, that you do Imediately send their Lordships an Acc^t. of what Mony is Absolutly necessary for covering in, so much of the said Worke, as you propose to finish before Winter, that Direĉtions may be Given for Supplying the Same in the beſt Manner that may be.

I am &c
J. TAYLOUR

Treasury Chamber Oĉt. 6. 1710.

Four days After I Deliver'd into the Treasury the following Memoriall,

(d) Oĉt. 10th. 1710

May it please your Lordships
    In Obedience to her Majeſtys pleasure signifyd to me by your Lordships commands, That I Should lay before you what sum of Mony may be Absolutly necessary, for Covering in so much of the Building at Blenheim, as was proposd to be finisht before Winter, I beg leave to represent to your Lordships, that this whole Summer Season, happening so much more favourable than Usual, for Carriage of Materials, and raising the Shell of the house, I thought it would be exſtreamly for the Service of the Building to make an Extrordinary Effort for Covering in (if possible) the whole at once, that therfore I us'd my Endeavour to prevail with the Workmen and those who furnish Materials, to give what credit was possible for them to do—which having Occasion'd a much greater Arrear, than on the Close of Other Years, has caus'd the Difficultys your Lordships have been Aquainted with, and which are now so great (the whole Worke having been at a Stand) that I do not see it will be possible to perform what is Absolutly Necessary for securing it from the gr^t. mischiefs of the Approaching Winter, wth. less than an Imediate Supply of .8000£, which is humbly Submitted to your Lordships by &c

J VANBRUGH

Upon this Memorial 7000£ was Issu'd, and the Building was Cover'd up till next Summer, when waiting upon my Lord Treasurer. by the Duke of Marlboroughs Direĉtions to know the Queens farther pleasure, his

(47)

Lordship was pleas'd to Order I Should lay before him, a State of y^e. Debt, an Estimate of the Future Charge, And an Account of what the Duke desir'd might be carry'd on this Season, I waitd upon him at the Treasury Accordingly and gave him in Writting what he had requir'd of me, upon which he Ask'd me, if I had well consider'd the Estimate, so as to leave nothing out, I said there were many things left out, that I beleived the Duke might think fit, to do in time at his Own Expence, but I hop'd the sum I had mention'd might carry on the Dessign as far as I understood the Queen intended Should be done, my Lord was pleas'd to say he wou'd receive the Queens Order upon what I had represented, and sometime After he Obtain'd her Sign Manual for .20,000£, telling me, that he would look for a farther Supply as soon as possible,

I acquaintd the Chief Workmen & undertakers with the Queens resolution to go on with the Building upon which encouragment they went on with the Worke, without Insisting that all the mony then Issu'd Should go on to Discharge the Debt, which Otherwise they would have done,

J VANBRUGH

34

[*To the Duke of Marlborough.*]

Oxford Octr. 3, 1710

My Lord Duke

By last Post I gave your Grace an Account from Blenheim in what condition the Building was, how near a close of this years Work, And how happy it was, that after being carry'd up in so very dry a Season it was like to be cover'd before any Wet fell upon it to Soak the Walls. My Intention was to stay there, till I saw it effectually done; the great Arch of the Bridge likwise compleated and safe coverd, And the Centers struck from under it, But this morning Joynes and Bobart told me, they had recd a Letter from the Dutchess of Marlborough to put a Stop at once to all sorts of Work till your Grace came over, not suffering one Man to be employ'd a day longer. I told them there was nothing more now to do in effect, but just what was Necessary towards Covering and Securing the Work which wou'd be done in a Week or ten days: And that there was so absolute a Necessity for it, that to leave off without it wou'd expose the whole Summers Work to unspeakable mischiefs: That there was likewise an other reason not to Discharge all the People thus at one Stroke together, Which was That Altho' the principall Workmen who work by the great, Such as Masons, Carpenters &c wou'd perhaps have regard to the Promises made them that they shou'd lose nothing, and so not be disorderly; Yet the Labourers, Carters, and other Country People, who

us'd to be regularly paid, but were now in arrear, finding themselves dis-
banded in so Surprising a Manner without a farthing wou'd certainly
conclude their Money lost; And finding themselves distress'd by what
they ow'd to the People where they lodg'd &c. And numbers of them
having their Familys and Homes at great distances in other Countys, twas
very much to be fear'd such a general Meeting might happen, that the
Building might feel the Effects of it; which I told them I the more Apprehended, knowing there were people not far off who wou'd be glad to put
'em about it: And that they themselves as well as I, had for some days
past observed 'em grown very Insolent, and in Appearance kept from
Meeting only by the Assurances we gave them from one day to another,
that money was coming. But all I had to say was cut short by Mr. Joynes's
Shewing me a Postscript my Lady Dutchess had added to her Letter, forbidding any regard to whatever I might say or do.

Your Grace won't blame me, if asham'd to continue there any Longer
on such a foot; as well as seeing it was not in my power to do your grace
any farther Service; I immediately came away, I send this Letter from
hence, not to lose a Post that your Grace may have as early notice as I
can give you, of this matter; *which I am little otherwise concern'd at, than
as I fear it must give you some uneasyness*, I shall be very glad to hear no
mischief do's happen on this Method of Proceeding; but tis certain so
small a Sum as Six or Seven hundred pounds, to have paid off the Poor
Labourers &c. woud have prevented it; And I had prevail'd with the
Undertakers, not to give over, till the whole Work was cover'd Safe, I
shall notwithstanding all this cruel usage from the Dutchess of Marlborough receive and with pleasure Obey Any Commands Your Grace will
please to lay upon me being with the Utmost Defference I ever was

Your Graces most humble
And most Obedient Servant
J VANBRUGH

[*Endorsed by Duchess of M.*]

Sir J— V— his letter Oct. 1710 when I stopped the building

35

[*To the Duke of Marlborough.*]

London Octr. 10. 1710.

My Lord Duke,

I was forced to write your Grace a disagreeable Letter from Oxford
the 3rd Inst. upon my Lady Duchess's putting a sudden Stop to the Works
at Blenheim. And I had given Your Grace an Account before of the

Application I had made to the Treasury for money to finish this Year's work which upon my arrival in town, I found had some effect, for I received a letter from the Treasury of which I here inclose a Copy to Your Grace with the Answer I have this Evening delivered in to the Board. I have likewise Spoken to some of the Lords this morning and am encouraged to hope for an immediate good success.

Mr Travers arrived at Blenheim just upon the execution of my Lady Duchess's Order and immediately got 500£ upon his own Credit to satisfy the poorer and most distressed labourers, so that all passed quietly and no farther mischief happened to the Building than what happened in the night, which was not very considerable. I have upon this order from the queen writ down, that they may proceed to complete what was so near up and to cover in with all possible speed

I find by Mr Maynwaring my Lady Duchess is in great uneasiness from the arrear the Clerks of the Works at Blenheim have given her an account there is due and the vast expence she fancies there still must be to complete the Building. But lest any mistakes she may fall into on this subject, should give your Grace an unnecessary disturbance I will acquaint you in two or three lines with the real state of this Matter.

If the Treasury should order the money I have now asked for (which is the remainder of what was intended for this Year's service) there will then have been received in all two hundred thousand pounds and when this year's amounts are made up, there will remain due to the workmen &c about 30000£ more which is about 5000£ more than has usually been behind at the close of the preceding years. The completing of all the rest of the House Offices and Bridge I durst almost undertake for 30000£ But if an Estimate of the future charge should be demanded of me by the Commissioners of the Treasury (as I am informed it will) I shall be sure to delay giving it in till Your Grace's return that I may have your directions in it.

36

[*To Mr. Mainwaring.*]

(*Chargate ?*)
Margate October 25th 1710

I writ to Mr Travers at the Bath, that his deputy Mr Tayler was gone out of Town without taking any measures that I cou'd hear of for receiving the Blenheim money. I have an answer from him by which I find the neglect has been in Taylers wife. However, he has sent me up what is necessary under his hand, to have it received by the Person who has the Letter of Attorney, and has desir'd I wou'd see him immediately pay it into the hands of Mr Warner the Goldsmith as usual, to be afterwards paid at Blenheim as he has directed. I shall do as he desires me as soon as I come to Town; I only tell you what he has writ me of this matter that if you think fit you may acquaint the Duchess of Marlborough with it, she having, I suppose heard before, that the Money lay ready without any body to take care of it

I am faithfully
Your Servant
J VANBRUGH

37

[*To the Duke of Marlborough.*]

London Augt. 10 1711

My Lord Duke

I am glad I can at laſt acquaint Your Grace, there is a weekly payment begun for Blenheim at 1000£ a week to continue twenty weeks; and my Lord Treasurer told me this morning he would think of a further supply. This money will however be a great deal more than sufficient to compass what the remainder of the Season will allow. I am afraid there cannot be a great deal done without doors, though all that is possible shall. I hope the paving the great court may be done yet, and the Steps up to the Portico, with those on the other side up to the Garden. Moſt of the paving within doors may likwise be done, and I hope all other things to make the eaſt end of the House ready for furniture. I have sent away workmen to begin without a moments loss of time, and shall be after them immediately, but am under the necessity of renewing a requeſt I some time since made to Your Grace, that Mr Travers might receive your order to let me have 400£ more upon account till your Grace's return, the allowance you have thought reasonable may be settled in the proper manner. The death of the poor Vice has made my Money difficulties ſtill greater than ever, so that I moſt earneſtly press Your Grace for this present supply * * *

I shall in a fortnight be able from Blenheim to acquaint your Grace more certainly what may be compased this year, in which no application shall be wanted on my side.

38

[*To* —— ?]

Whitehall Dec^b. ye 27th 1711.

S^r

I here inclose to you the Bill I desir'd tother day you wou'd take a Propper time to shew my Ld Treasurer. It was laſt year put into Mr Secretary St John's hands, by my late Ld Rochester, and my Ld Chamberlain but it being the end of the Session, he thought it too late to offer to the House. My preparing of it, was from an Order of the House of

Lords. If my Ld Treasurer approves of it, as it is, or with any Additions or Alterations he shall think fit to direct, I will Solicite it what I can; but unless it be espous'd by the Court, and recommended to the Queens Servants to take some care of, I doubt the Streets may remain as they are.

I am, S^r

Your humble Servant

J VANBRUGH

39

[*To Lord Treasurer. Oxford.*]

August 3rd—1712

My Lord

M^r. Taylor (Paymaster of the Works at Blenheim) being very Ill, and not likely to recover, is very pressing to have his Accounts pass'd, that no difficultys may be left upon his Family if he should dye. And Mr Bridges of the Ordnance (to whom your Lordship had committed that trust) continuing so indisposed, that he cannot proceed in it, The Duke of Marlborough has directed me, to Apply to your Lordship That you wou'd please to appoint some other Person to inspect and Examine those Accounts; to the End it may Appear, whether the Money Issued for that Work has been Apply'd to it, and to no other Use, as is limited by the Queens Sign Manual.

I am &c

J VANBRUGH

40

[*To the Duke of Marlborough?*]

November the 4—1712

In pursuance to your Graces command, I here give you an Account of what passed with my Lord Treasurer when by your Graces Direction I apply'd to him for money towards carrying on the Building at Blenheim.

Last June was twelve month, by his Lordships order I waited on him at the Treasury, with a State of the Debt; An Estimate of the Future Charge, and an account of what your Grace desires might be carryed on that Year.

My Lord was pleas'd to ask me, If I had well considered the Estimate, so as to leave nothing out.

I said there were many things left out, which I believed your Grace might think fit to do in times at your own Expence but I hoped the Sum I mentioned, might carry the Design as far, as I understood the Queen at first intended shou'd be done on a publick Consideration. I thought my Lord seem'd the better Sattisfied with what I said, finding the Sum necessary to finish the Design, vaſtly less than (as I was told) he had been informed it wou'd be.

He was pleased soon after, to procure the Queen Sign Manual for £20000. And told me, he wou'd give a farther Supply, as soon as possible.

I acquainted the Chief Undertakers, with what had paſt at the Treasury; upon which they went on with the Work, without insiſting, that all the money then Issued, shou'd go in discharge of the Debt which otherwise they would have done.

[Endorsed by Duchess of M.]

Sir John's account of what my Lord Oxford had said to him, upon which he acquainted the undertaker of what had passed in the treasury, upon which incouragement he says, they went on without the Work Mens insiſting upon the money then issued, given in discharge of the debt

[Endorsed.]

This paper shews that the workmen did not take the duke to be pay-maſter. since they carried on the work upon Lord Oxford's assurance of giving more money as soon as he coud & did then direĉt the payment of 20.000£. Paper the 8th.

G. [probably Guidott.]

[Memorandum]   41

. . .ving entry, I have made
mark'd EV.

November ye 10th 1712. Memd: this day, the Duke of Marlborough (upon his Design to travel,) made a new Will, which he executed at St. James's. Mr Cardonel, Mr Cragge and my Self, saw him Sign, seal, declare and publish it, and afterwards Sign'd it as Witnesses in his Presence, with a Codicil. The Duke at the Same time, burn'd his former Will, cancell'd a former Deed, and executed a new one. The Will consiſts of fourteen Sheets, every one of which the Duke sign'd.

J. VANBRUGH

42

[To The Mayor of Woodſtock.]

Whitehall. Jan. 25, 1712–13.

Sir,

Having long had it at heart to see the town of Woodſtock so improved in building and other things, as to bear some proportion with what ſtrangers may reasonably expeĉt to find in a Borough Town, joining to so great a palace as Blenheim; I several times spoke to my Lord Duke about paving the market-place, which he seemed well inclined to, and I believe had done ere now but for the continual *plague and bitter persecution he has most bar-barously been followed with* for two years past. However, upon his going away, I mentioned this thing to him again; and he left such directions with those who take care of his affairs, that I have at last commission to tell you, it will be done, and that I am desired to take some care of it, and to consult with you and the Corporation about the manner and extent of it, which I design to do as soon as I can possibly come down. I desire, if you please, that, in the mean time, you will be considering with the other Gentlemen of any thing necessary to have regard to in it, that, when I come down, all dispatch may be made to begin the work; which, I hope, will not only be to the pleasure and beauty of the town, but prove of good service likewise in respect to your Fairs and Markets. I am, Sir, your most humble servant,   J. VANBRUGH.

P.S. I have lately received some very good hopes, that the Treasury will pay the Blenheim debt; my Lord Duke having offered to advance the money if they will give him only tin-tallies, which will not be payable to him in seven years nor sure then. If it be resolved to pay the debt, I don't doubt but the building will go on again, and my Lord Duke return to inhabit it.

43

[*Anonymous letter to Lord Oxford*]
        (*about Vanbrugh*)   *Y*e 26th *Instant* 1713.

        S*r*
        *A Letter happening accidentally into my hands, Containing the following Lines, I thought it my Duty, out of y*e *Obedience I owe to her Majesty, and respect to the present Ministry, to discover a Person of such trecherous Principles, who altho' being rais'd to such Honor, under her Majesty, yet makes no scruple of railing against the Church's Upholders, and Owns his chiefest Interest lies, in the coming in of the Pretender.*
        *I wou'd have acquainted your Lordship with it before, but that I had not opportunity of securing the Letter, but only reading it; since which time the Person to whom it was sent, hath cut out the Latter Sentence, for fear of a Discovery, Containing the Words, from the Mark to y*e *End of the Letter but the other part I have in which your Lordship may see where it was cut out; if I have said any thing amiss I hope your Lordship will excuse it, as from a Person of Capacity, but a well Wisher to both Church and State—and Y*r *Lordship's most Dutifull Servant*   *J: S.*

        [*Endorsed by Robert Harley, Earl of Oxford:*]
" *Unknown June* 26: 1713. R. *June* 29
    postmarkd Liverpool
    *Concerning M*r *Vanbrugh* ".

44

[*The Letter to his Relation.*]

April ye 2^d 1713.

I don't Know whether you have heard, that I am turn'd out of my place in the Works, for writing a Letter to the Mayor of Woodstock in which I say the Duke of Marlborough has been bitterly and barbarously persecuted, for these two Years past, in which I only meant the Continuall and Daily Libels and Pamphlets which pelted him, but some High-Church Members of Parliament wou'd needs have it, I meant the House of Commons and so have push't the Matter to my being turn'd out, I believe I cou'd have prevented it, if I wou'd have made my Submission to those High-Church Blockheads, but that I wou'd on no terms do.

However, I wou'd not have you Concernd at it, for if the Pretender comes in, I shall gett more by it then they that made it their buisness, or were imploy'd to turn me out.

I am &c.

JOHN VANBRUGH.

45

To Edward Southwell Es^q
  at Kings Weston near Bristol

Castle Howard Oct 23rd 1713.

Sir,

I acquainted you sometime since I had read with much pleasure the letter you enclosed to me wch you had from Mrs Henley. I am since obliged with yours from Kings Weston of the 13th inst, being much pleased with the house being quite covered in so good season, for if the weather is with you as in the North, your walls must have dryed almost as fast as they went up, and there being no great rains to soak them whilst they were open, the house will be dry a year the sooner fort. In my last I told you I wished you would not go up with the chimneys till I was with you on the spot, to make tryall of the heights etc, with boards. I am glad to find you now of the same opinion, tho' you had not yet recd my letter; for I would fain have that part rightly hit off. I likewise think you in the right to clear off the scaffolds, tho' there be more difficulty in getting up the stone for the chimneys.

As to the objections you mention, I can only say I cannot think as they do, tho' it may be I am wrong. As to the door being too little, if an alteration be thought necessary I can show you how to do it; but of these particulars it is better to talk than to write. I hope, however, at last, I shall see you as well pleased as the Lord of this place is; who has now

within this week had a fair tryall of his dwelling, in what he moſt apprehended, which was cold. For, tho' we have now had as bitter ſtorms as
rain and wind can well compose, every room in the house is like an oven,
and in corridors of 200ft long there is not air enough in motion to ſtir
the flame of a candle. I hope to find the same comfort in your Chateau,
when the North Weſt blows his hardeſt; so pray don't think you'll ſtand
in need of a few poor trees to screen you. The poſt will be gone, if I say
anything now, than that I am moſt heartily your humble sert.

J. VANBRUGH.

46

[*To* ——?]

Caſtle Howard Ocʳ 29th 1713

Tis so long dear Sʳ. since I saw you that I shou'd be extreamly glad
you'd let me hear from you. I am but lately got to Lord Carlisles, which
is now so agreeable a being, from the nature of the Place, the Works he
has done, and the manner of his Living, that I shall have much ado to
leave it, till I am forc'd to come to Towne, to take care of several uncom-
fortable things which I fear, will long be Allays to the Pleasures I cou'd
else have some taſt of. I am much pleased here (amongſt other things)
to find Lord Carlisle so thoroughly convinced of the Conveniencys of his
new house, now he has had a years tryall of it: And I am the more pleas'd
with it, because I have now a proof, that the Dutchess of Marlborough
muſt find the same conveniency in Blenheim, if ever She comes to try it
(as I ſtill believe she will in spite of all these black Clouds.) For my Lord
Carlisle was pretty much under the same Apprehensions with her, about
long Passages, High Rooms &c. But he finds what I told him to be true.
That those Passages woud be so far from gathering & drawing wind as
he feared, that a Candle wou'd not flare in them of this he has lately had
the proof, by bitter ſtormy nights in which not one Candle wanted to be
put into a Lanthorn, not even in the Hall, which is as high (tho not indeed
so big) as that at Blenheim. He likewise finds, that all his Rooms, with
moderate fires Are Ovens, And that this Great House, do's not require
above One pound of wax, and two of Tallow Candles a Night to light it,
more than his house at London did Nor in Short, is he at any expence
more, whatsoever than he was in the Remnant of an Old house, but three
housemaids and one Man, to keep the whole house and Offices in perfeƈt
cleanliness, which is done to such a degree, *that the Kitchen*, and all the
Offices and Passages under the Principall floor are as dry as the Drawing
room: And yet there is a great deal of Company, and *very good house-
keeping* So that upon the whole (except the keeping of the New Gardens)
the expence of living in this Great fine house, do's not amount to above

a hundred pounds a year, more than what was Spent in the *Old one*. If you think the knowledge of this, may be of any Satisfaction to my Lady Marlborough, pray tell her what you hear. And if you think it proper, (as from yourself, *I cou'd wish you wou'd say* (what you know to be true) *That whether I am quite* convinced or not, of my having been *so much in* the wrong in my behaviour to her, as she is pleas'd *to think* me, Yet while She does think me so I can't but set the greatest value upon *her Generosity: in urging my Lord Marlborough* in my favour; *I must own to you at the Same time*, That her notion, that I had not done what I did, but upon her declining at Court, has been no Small inducement to me, to expose myself so frankly as I have done, in my Lord Dukes and her particular Cause. for tho', *I cou'd have born she should have thought me a Brute*, I cou'd not endure she shou'd *think me a Rascall.*

I am quite in the Dark about my Lord Dukes being in Flanders. you will much oblige me to tell me if he has any thoughts of coming home which people here say, but I can't believe Another thing they have is, That he was call'd back to Flanders by the Queens command, pray tell me what you think fit, about him, I have writ to him, to tell him some things have fallen in my way to observe, I hope I am mistaken; I won't repeat here what I have writ, because the Letter shall come to you unsealed, you'll favour me in Sending it forward.

I am most heartily your Servt

J. V.

The Archbishop here drinks the Queens health, and her Ministers health, and then says I pray God they are honest.

If you favour me with a Letter pray let me know whether 'tis reckon'd, there may yet be any Roguery about Dunkirk. for I am much Surpris'd at the demolishing it if in earnest.

47

[*To ——?*]

Castle Howard. Nov ye 20th 1713.

I troubled you lately with a Letter relating to the Comedy Stock in Drury Lane. I am since informed you have directed the Present managers to lay before you an Inventory of what was carryed from the Haymarket. I hope they will give you a right one; if they do, you will see, it was the Richest and compleatest Stock, that ever any Company had in England. Consisting of All that was in Lincolns Inn fields (for which I gave £900—). All that was added to it upon the first opening the Haymarket house (which came to a very great Sum) and what was in a most profuse manner added farther, when Mr Swiny brought all the Chief Actors thither from Drury Lane and was Oblig'd to gratify them with whatever they would have. There was besides this (by neglect of those Mr Collier employ'd) a great part of the Opera Stock carryed off. So that, there can be no doubt left, of the Stock being far beyond what ever had been known before upon the Stage. And there was no pretences whatever from those Present Managers to a property in one ragg of it. I give you the trouble of what I now observe to you, doubting whether in Mr Swiny's Absence you may have that exact account in particular which I suppose he could give you. I have an entire Relyance on your Justice, from what I have already found, and for which I shall Always own my Self

Sr Your much oblig'd

And Obed't humble

Servant

J. VANBRUGH.

48

To [the Duke of Marlborough.]

London May 29ᵗʰ 1714

My Lord Duke

I received your Graces commands by the Gentleman who brings you this Letter, to send you an account of what the buildings &c at Blenheim had cost; What was owing and what might be required to finish the design. I don't understand by him that your Grace desires the particulars; but only in general

By the memorial I gave in to the Lord Treasurer the 15ᵗʰ of June 1711. The demand to clear the Debts, and to finish what was always supposed the Queen intended to do; was 87,000£ of which there has since been issued from the Treasury 20,000£. The Debts now are about 42,000£.

So that according to that demand; were the Debts paid, there wou'd remain £25,000 to finish the Building. And I am truly of opinion there wou'd not then rest any thing considerable upon your Grace to do, as the design now stands: Tho many things no doubt might be proposed for farther improvement of the Seat. but very little more wou'd be necessary.

The whole sum that has been received from the Treasury, is 220,000£. so that the whole sum of Money issued, Debts owing and what has been askd from the Queen, amounts to £287,000. A large Sum for a house, but a poor reward for the services that occasioned the Building it.

Mr Strong, the Mason was with me tother day. They can get no sort of Answer from the Treasurer to their last petition. So that having no hopes from him, I find their Council advise them to proceed in their suit against your Grace. Mr Strong on this occasion beg'd I wou'd represent to your Grace with how much reluctance he took this course to prevent the loss of so great a Sum as he Sees he, and his Family are not able to bear. I desired he would consult his council, on that one short, plain but home circumstance of Mr Taylers letter to me, by order of the Treasury. The Queen by that, appearing directly to take the expence upon her; and that, not only by her own expressions; but by the concurrence of her proper ministers (in many matters) the Lords of the Treasury. I told him, I had talk'd of this with several; that they all say, it would infallibly cast the crown, and that altho upon a judgment against the crown, people cou'd not proceed to an execution as in common cases; yet, that I was informed, the crown (for that very reason) ever had paid the money it had been cast for.

Upon this discourse, he promised me to press his council, on this single point of the Letter; of which I have the original by me. But if after all he shou'd not take that course to sue the crown. I humbly offer it to your Graces consideration, whether it might not be adviseable, to put some other of the workmen privately upon it, bearing their charges of the suit, if they would do it otherways.

In my last letter to your Grace, I remember I said, it seem'd to me by peoples dispositions here, that it was high time for a little encouragement from Hanover; which when we since received, by the demand of the writ, I plainly saw, I had not been wrong in my thoughts: For had the Duke immediately followed it; the whole nation had cry'd out to the Court to be friends with him. I dont doubt but it still would do through many more difficultys. but tis not to be conceived how the Jacobites are spirited up, on this accounted for delay; And the Friends to that succession sunk in every thing but resentment at this hard, and (as they think) unkind treatment of them. Those warm honest Gentlemen of the Hanover club at a meeting two nights since, were almost resolv'd to seperate upon it. In a word, one does not know where this thing will go, if something is not quickly done, to give some satisfaction in the Electors present mysterious proceeding. The excuse which came last post, having made things worse and worse; but tis before I am aware I mention this to your Grace, since to be sure you have it in a better light from others; But it lies in my way to hear bitter things said upon it. T'would be very hard we should be yet undone by the Meer Tory Mob, Ignorant, furious country Priests, and Stupid Justices, when all their chiefs of any weight have left them; for by all that I can find, the Squadron that went off, stand very firm as to the grand point. But one odd thing I can acquaint your Grace of amongst them (at least of my Lord Anglesea in particular) that your Grace is held in strong suspicion of having wholy enbark'd in the pretenders interest; and that you are to bring him over. I cannot say that any of them directly believe, but him have nam'd, but I know he is wild enough to credit it, and to be much disturb'd about it. Your Grace will please not to mention from whom you have this, because it comes to me from one his intimates.

(59)

I send with this a Draught of the Obelisk my Lord Carlisle is raising to express his grateful sense as an Englishman, of what he thinks the Nation owe your Grace. it is in all, a hundred Feet high. There is a great deal of the Material prepared, and I have writ this night, to direct the laying the foundations, my Lord Carlisle having given me leave to do so.

I am

Your Graces most humble

and Obedient Servant

J VANBRUGH

The Queen has at last pass'd a Patent (even without my Lord Suffolks concurrence in it) to Mr Anstis for the reversion of Garter. She said she had been under an obligation to me not to consent to it; but my behaviour had been such in writing that Letter to Woodstock, that now she had done with me—That was her expression.

49

To the Duchess of Marlborough.

January 16th 1714/15

Madam

Sir Samuel Garth mentioning something yesterday of Lord Clare with relation to my Lady Harriott, made me reflect, that your Grace might possibly think (by my never saying any thing to you of that matter, since you did me the honour of hinting it to me) I had either forgot or neglected it; but I have done neither.—Tis true that partly by company being in the Way, and partly by his illness when I was most with him, I have not yet had an opportunity of sounding him to the purpose. What I have yet done therefore has been only this. I have brought into discourse, the characters of several Women that I might have a natural occasion to bring in hers, which I have then dwelt a little upon; and in the best manner I cou'd distinguish'd her from the others. This I have taken three or four Occasions to do, without the least appearances of having any view in it, thinking the rightest thing I cou'd do would be to possess him with a good impression of her before I hinted at any thing more. I can give your Grace no farther account of the effects of it, than that he has seemed to allow of the merit I gave her, tho I must own he once express'd it with something joind which I did not like, tho it shew'd he was convinc'd of those fine qualifications I had mentioned, and that was a sort of wish (express'd in a very gentle manner) that her bodily perfections had been up to those I describ'd of her mind and understanding. I said to that, that tho I did not believe she wou'd ever have a beautiful face I cou'd plainly see, it wou'd prove a very agreeable one, which I thought was infinitely more valuable; especially since I saw one thing in hers which wou'd contribute much to the making it so, which was, that we call a good countenance, than which I ever thought no one expression in a face was more engaging. I said further, that her Shape and Figure in general wou'd be perfectly well, and that I wou'd pawne all my Skill (which had us'd to be a good deal employ'd in these kind of observations) that in Two years time, no Woman in Town wou'd be better lik'd. He did not in the least contradict what I said, but allow'd I might very probably be right.

Your Grace may depend upon me that I will neglect nothing I can do in this thing, for I am truly and sincerely of Opinion that if I cou'd be an instrument in bringing it about, I shou'd do my Lord Clare as great a piece of Service as my Lady Harriot.

I am
Your Graces most humble and Obedient Servant
J VANBRUGH

50

To the R^t Honble the Earl of Clare

[*Autumn* 1714 *or early* 1715]
Saturday Night

If I can possibly follow y^r Lordship to Chargate to morrow, I will: & if I can't, I'll be very Sorry.

I will be at home or near it, all Monday afternoon, where if your Lordship pleases to send, I will come & wait upon you wherever you'll command

Your Obedient Servant
VAN

I have given out fresh Instructions today about Lincolns Inn fields, & will Spare no pains, (tho' I make no great bussle) to make that matter move to your Content.

51

To [The Earl of Clare, afterwards Duke of Newcastle.]

Whitehall. Feb. ye 5th 1714/15

When your L'dship comes to pay the Bills, you will see whether there has been above 3 or 4 men a day at Work. They have Appear'd to me a Swarm of Bees, And they have done so much, that I think you may ly in your house the end of this Month if the Upholsterer do's his part. I have given him, Mr Forbes &c a meeting there this morning, and we, have look'd all over. The inner drawing room next the Street, is now

(61)

ready for the Upholsterer, and the next room to it will be ready for him on tuesday. both those Rooms have their New Chimneys But those for the Great eating room and Vestibule, will not be ready to send out of Derbyshire (where they are making) till the end of the Month, so I have directed the Mason to fix two of the Old ones there to serve till the others come. The paving of the Vestibule will be finish'd to night. The floor of the other part of the Room has been done a great While, with Windows, doors &c and the Pillasters are up. So the Painter begins upon it on Monday, and will soon have done. The Hall is paved and has a New Chimney Up.

The left hand eating room, wants nothing but a New Chimney. So the old one must serve for the present the room Next to it is ready, and the Library New floor is doing. Most of the Chimneys are done in the Attick Story, So that the furniture for the Family there, may be put up next week. The Middle room in the Great Appartment above Stairs, will be ready before Mr Vanderbank. but not by the end of this month. The first Great Room I believe will be ready by that time, all but the Chimney piece So the Furniture may be put up, and yr Ldship may use it to pass through to yr Bedchamb : but not to receive Company in, but that I think may be dispenc'd with, as long as all is done below.

I wish you much joy of your Elections, And of a good Parliamt: in generall, for twill be a rare one. And I find our Friends dispos'd to make a good use on't, Hang Whip Pillory &c. I wish they cou'd love one another tho', but they can't; at least, I think they are all resolv'd to hate . The Storm thickens against him daily. but he cocks still, and thrusts his little belly amongst 'em : but I'm affraid they'll give it a Squeeze at last. Jacob Speaks rarely well of Suffolk, And comes to my Levee about the Library we are to go View three or four next week in order to out do 'em all.

I Suppose yr Ldship will take Claremont in your way up. The most usefull Chimney, we have cur'd, others not. But the Dining Room and yr own are well, wch is the main point. I wish every thing there, and every thing every where, just what you wou'd have 'em,

Your most Obedt. Servt

J VANBRUGH

I have promis'd Jacob, to come drink yr health with him to morrow night at Swan Barns; but I shan't keep my word. He desir'd I wou'd tell yr Ldship, he will treat you in Bow Street with a Whiff of the finest Tobacco in the World.

[*To——?*]   52
February 9th 1714/15

Although the enclosed Warrant from My Lord Godolphin it is said waſ to aċt on the Duke of Marlboroughs account I very well remember, that in the beginning of the work at Blenheim, making application to the Duke for his Division in a Purchase of Timber, he told me he would not meddle in any thing of that kind; and on several occasions afterwards explained to me that he had nothing to do in the disposition of the money allotted by the Queen for the Building; but referr'd me to my Lord Treasurer Godolphin.

[*To Jacob Tonson*]   53
Wensday [*Summer,* 1715?]

I have juſt now been with Ld Carlisle, who has named Friday for the Barns Expedition. I have Seen Lady Marlborough Since, and she agrees to it, and will order a Bardge at Whitehall   The Company she names are. Two Ladys besides her Self. Ld Carlisle, Ld Clare, Horace Walpole Dr Samll Garth & Mr Benson

I'm Yrs Faithfully
J. VANBRUGH

54

To the Right Hon. Robert Walpole Esq
at Chelsea.
Oċt. 17*th*, 1715.

The inclosed is the second part of what I troubled you with the other day, which I hope you will think a moſt reasonable application. I have made an eſtimate of your fabrick, which comes to £270; but I have allowed for doing some things in it, in a better manner than perhaps you will think necessary—so I believe it may be done to your mind for £200. But, for your farther satisfaċtion, I desire you will send your clerk of the works to me, and I will explain it so to him, that he may likewise make a calculation, without showing him mine, or telling him what I make the expense to amount to, in the total. And when this is done, we will give each particular article to the respeċtive workmen; and they shall make their eſtimation too—so that you shall know the bottom of it, at laſt; or the Devil shall be in it.

Your moſt humble Architeċt,
J. VANBRUGH.

55

[*To the Duke of Marlborough.*]

Whitehall April 19ᵗʰ 1716

My Lord Duke

Having received a letter from Mʳ Hodges by your Grace's order, about the place of laying the Marble & Timber now to be carried to Blenheim I have writ to Mʳ Joynes accordingly who is ſtill there paying the Country people, but will have done in a week more as Sʳ. Thomas Wheate tells me, who is newly come from thence.

I have acquainted Mʳ. Strong that your Grace does not incline to the laſt proposal he made about his debt &c, upon which I can get no other from him than the firſt ; which was to go on with the Towers upon the foot of the old Contraɛt. Alledging that what remains for him to do in these Towers is the leaſt profitable part and the moſt difficult. I can't deny but there is something in what he pleads, tho' not so much perhaps as he would have it go for, But as he has so great business here in town I'm afraid there will be no bringing him to other terms. Something shou'd be resolv'd on now if your Grace wou'd have the Towers up this Summer.

I have *Proposals for the other masons* work from several Masons, as those of Oxford that work'd formerly at Blenheim; those who built the Duke of Shrewsbury's house & others : Their proposals taking one article with another are not much different : But *their prices are considerably lower than were formerly allowed, partly from the certainty of their pay, and ready money & partly I believe that* they hope they may not be held to that exactness of work. I believe (if your Grace pleases) the beſt way will be to employ several of them ; which will make some emulation.

I have sent Mʳ. Joynes & Bobart among the Quarrys, but do not find there is any likelyhood of having Stone but on the former Terms, Unless (as I lately mentioned to Your Grace) there might be leave to get some from the Duke of Shrewsbury's which would save a great deal of money If your Grace thinks it proper I'll wait upon him from you and see whether he is free to it : I know no objeɛtion but tearing up the ways a little, where the Carts pass through his Grounds, or the danger of the Quarry failing before all be done in his building, As to the firſt the ways muſt be made good again and for the latter, the bulky part of the building is over And I think the Quarry is a very plentifull one.

The house painter has made a great progress and the season has been so dry, that it will soon be time to take up & new lay the floors.

The Chimney pieces are things which take up time & should be put in hand.

(64)

I hope the offering these things to your Grace's thoughts may rather prove some small amusement than a trouble to you, tis at least on that account, this letter comes from
                    Your ever obedient and Most faithfully Servant
                                                    J VANBRUGH

                                56

[*To the Duke of Marlborough.*]
                                                May 25th 1716

    My Lord Duke
        Out of the Several Proposals the Masons have given in, I have collected the Lowest price put to each Article in each Mans proposall, And so made the enclosed Scheme of Prices, to offer to them, which upon the whole, is therefore a good deal Lower than any one of their distinct offers and under what M^r. Strong will come to, by above 20 *p^r C^t*: And the prices at Oxford and other places, are very little if any thing lower; where the Masons are not held to near so good work as will be expected from them at Blenheim—
        I have farther look'd over the Rates my Lord Carlisle pays in Yorkshire; and find them within a Small matter the Same with these, tho' the work is by no means so good, and the Country vastly Cheaper than Oxfordshire: And yet my Lord has, during the whole Course of his Building managed all that part himself, with the greatest care; And tho' he began with Ignorant Masons at Lower Rates, he soon found there was good reason to give more, in order to have his work tollerably done.
        My humble Opinion therefore upon the whole is, That if these who are of the best Masons in England, will undertake the work at Blenheim on the foot of the enclosed Scheme, it woud not be advisable, to let it to any who shou'd even offer to do it something Cheaper were there any such; which I do not know of, or believe there are.   I am
                    Your Graces most humble & most
                            obedient Servant
                                                J VANBRUGH

    Your Grace will please to consider how far the Season is advanced, and that the Masons business is the Slowest and most difficult to drive on.

                            [*Endorsed.*]
    I think there is something material in this concerning the offer Mr Strong made to the D. of M. to take the debt from him & also that he allows that the prices were considerably lower than they were formerly.

57

[*To the Duchess of Marlborough.*]

Whitehall. June 12th 1716

Madam

Though I have no sort of concern (as to myself) to press for any orders relating to Blenheim; I have been thinking since I waited on your Grace, that I shou'd have put you in mind, of the season being so much advanced that unless a speedy resolution be taken, it will be too late to get up the Towers this year, which I remember my Lord Duke express'd an earnest desire might be done, whatever else might be suspended. And indeed, it has been a great misfortune and damage, that end of the House shou'd lye open and expos'd to rains and frost, in the sad manner it has done. There is a great deal of stone upon the ground for that use; as likwise Timber for the roof; And as the masons prices stand *now reduc'd* the charge of the whole will not rise to any mighty matter And the work is of great necessity to be done. The main house being then compleat without doors; shelter'd and Secure from any damage by weather, and the incumbrance of Scaffolding, Stone, Rubble &c remov'd from the Garden side, and before the Gallery which at present makes all *look in a most disagreeable confusion.*

If your Grace thinks it right to proceed on this one part of the work (the others not being press'd by the season of the year) I believe I might set the Workmen upon it without giving my Lord Duke the trouble of my discourse upon it, in his present Indisposition, because the last time he spoke to me of the Blenheim business, he came to an absolute determination on this article of the Towers and the steps up to the portico; and directed me to put them in hand without any farther orders from him on the foot of the Scheme of Prices which your Grace has seen, and which indeed, are as reasonable and low as I ever wou'd desire; And what I never expected to bring the good Masons down to.

I here enclose to your Grace the Contract drawn as you directed; and if you shou'd be of opinion to let this work go on, there will need no other formality of signing at present, than your Grace writing these words at the bottom of it, or something to the same effect.

The Duke of Marlborough is willing, that John Vanbrugh should agree with the Massons and set them to work upon the Towers at Blenheim according to this { *Scheme* / *agreement* } *of Prices and conditions.*

SM.

Your Grace will observe, I have cross'd out the last article, which they very much insisted on, lest they shou'd not afterwards do low work, as well as this, which is not so great a height. And indeed if that should be the case, it wou'd be hard upon them. But I have told them if they do right and honeſtly on their side I wou'd Answer for your Graces doing no hard thing on yours

I am

Your Graces moſt humble

and obedient Servant

J VANBRUGH

The Mason's nam'd in this contraƈt are the two chief Foremen, employ'd by Mr Strong and Bankes during their work at Blenheim. I observ'd them to be incomparable Servants to them, which made me very glad to find them dispos'd to begin work for themselves. And as they are worth but little money yet, they are not in way of living so high as to make great gains necessary for their support. On the contrary, they are saving humble and diligent and purpose by doing something well at Blenheim at low rates, to work themselves into Credit. So that upon the whole, I think it very happy one can engage them. But if your Grace does not think fit to employ them, either now or at all; Mr Strongs man Cash, begs it may not be known he had any thoughts of leaving his maſter to set up for himself.

[*Endorsed*]

Sir John Vanbrughs letter about the building at Blenheim and a copy of my answer June 15th 1716

Sir Johns letter that shews how much he had reduced the prizes; And a Trick in proposing Strong's foreman to do the work, because he thought it dangerous to take lower prizes in his own name.

58

[*To the Duchess of Marlborough.*]

London June 19. 1716

Madam

According to your Graces allowances I have agreed with the Masons, who are immediately going down to Blenheim to begin their Work and I have very great hopes will perform it in the beſt and honeſteſt manner, at leaſt I have as good an opinion of them as I can have of any Workmen.

I cannot see how their proposal for the paving can be a third part dearer than the person my Lord Duke has agreed with, for as I remember he told me at Windsor it was Twenty pence a foot, for work and Materials; and these men's proposals is twelve pence for Work alone which is as I Judge agreeable to the others price, beside I know these men would find Work and materials for 20d. *and do it with the same nicety it has been done by them under their maſters* before, which is much better than what Mr Banks did for your Grace at the Lodge though that is well enough.

I don't remember I ever had any Letter from your Grace from Windsor relating to other works, but you spoke to me once at St James's about the Plaiſterer whose proposals I here enclose.

The Plaiſtering done at Blenheim is all after the Dutch manner which no body is got into the practice of here in England; but it is well worth what it coſts more than our manner there being as much difference as between fine Paper and coarse, besides its being much more laſting.

I likwise here send your Grace the necessary articles for Carpenters work which I have taken from several proposals that is from each of them the loweſt Articles and if those who are good Workmen will take the Work on these terms I believe your Grace may venture to let them be contracted with or if you please to Shew the Articles to any others, you will be farther satisfied whether these rates are higher than they need be. As for those few floors which want new laying I thought it was beſt to do them by the Day and left directions accordingly.

I believe your Grace will not doubt the extreme joy I have to hear of my Lord Dukes growing so much better which I hope will Soon end in a perfect recovery

I am

Your Graces moſt Humble
and Obedient Servant

J VANBRUGH

I don't know whether your Grace has determin'd to employ Mr Joynes at Blenheim, if he is to go it will be necessary he should do it soon, I shall go there as soon as the King is gone.

[*Endorsed*]

Shewing how much he had reduc'd the Prices & a trick about Strong's Foreman.

Mem^m: Sir J.V. sold all the scaffolding when the quarries work was done which put the D of M to a great charge after he took the building upon himself.

This shews the great desire Sir J.V. had for his workmen to do the pavement even at such vaſt low rates for work as he had given.

59

[*To the Duchess of Marlborough.*]

Madam   *Blenheim June 30th—1716*

The letter that your Grace was pleas'd to write me of the 27th, has followed me hither, where I am doing what I can to answer the good opinion your Grace has of my real intentions to do you the beſt services I am able

I have sent for the Plaisterer, to dispatch what is necessary that the Painter may go on, which being no great matter, I have made use of the leave your Grace has given me, to allow him his price for this: When the rest of the House comes to be done you will judge yourself whether it be worth while to continue it or reduce him to the common rates and common work.

The Mason your Grace has set upon the Paving is beginning to work, but does not talk of making such dispatch as I cou'd wish; he reckons to be three weeks, getting to the supping room. The plain paving in *the attick story* shou'd likwise be dispatch'd, for I doubt it won't be right to paint the Wainscot in the Corridour, till that is done.

I believe I shall get the stone for the Steps without doors, cheaper than the Portland by fifty P Cent and by all I can find it is much better.

As your Grace seems very desirous to have the house made habitable as soon as may be, I shou'd put you in mind of the offices which lye Uncover'd in the kitchen court which being the bakehouse Landry, Warehouse, and gate, upon which the cistern must stand from whence all the Water must come to the several parts of the House; it will be impossible to live in it, till these things are done of which the expence is not very great; and your Grace may see in the Estimate my Lord Duke has by him. I should acquaint you farther Madam, that the Masonry of these offices has received very great damage by lying thus open. If you please to have them finish'd I wou'd do them with the most ordinary Oxford stone which both by the material and work will very much lessen the charge; and indeed throughout the whole work to come, I hope to manage that great article of the Masonry, in such a manner as to bring it within near half what it formerly amounted to. I dont mean so much by the Prices (tho that will be considerable) as by sparing in the quantity and making use of cheap sorts of stone in proper places, where the difference wont be distinguished and the strength and duration the same. If your Grace asks, why this was not done formerly; I can only answer, that I have now better experience, for I did as well as I cou'd before, and as well as those I had to assist me cou'd advise.—I have not yet talk'd with the Marble Masons, but shall on Monday, and will then give your Grace a plainer account of their proposals.

The beauty of this place at this time is hardly to be conceived, which all strangers and Passengers will be ten times more sensible of when the house is inhabited than now; for besides the *additional* beauty of the Furniture, they will then comprehend the cast and turn of the House with the conveniencys which they are now quite ignorant of and see all with confusion. I hope (and most heartily wish) the Bath, will so thoroughly reestablish my Lord Duke, that he may enjoy the place in the latter season as he returns, when I hope he will see a great deal done to his satisfaction.

(69)

I believe he will like to know, that Mr Thornhill goes on a pace in the Hall; and has begun with a better Spirit in his paintings than anything I have seen of his doing before. I hope he'll continue it. I know he piques himself upon appearing well at Blenheim. I am

Your Graces most humble and

Obedient Servant

J VANBRUGH

The levelling on both sides the Bridge goes on well

I wish there were permission to do something likwise to the Bridge itself this summer, if it were only to work up the stone that lies there upon the place, which is much in the way and receives great damage by lying upon the ground.

The Kitchen Garden now the trees are in full vigour and full of fruit, is really an astonishing sight. All I ever saw in England or abroad of the kind, are trifles to it

I have look'd over the paper I sent your Grace with the Masons proposals, and find, That all those things the Duke of Marlborough was to provide come within eight pence a foot more for the paving: So that the proposal of these Masons, Cuss and Fletcher, is exactly the same with Palmers; but if he does it well, there's no harm done.

[*Endorsed by the Duchess of M.*]

Sir John Vanbrughs letter where he says the Kitchen Court may be finish'd at a small expence and that the Paving of the Hall was offer'd at the same price by Strongs man as I did infer, which was 12ᵈ pence the Foot I finding stone and that article commonly at 18 or 20 in the Queens accounts I dare say may be computed at four or five shillings by the same man.

60

[*To the Duchess of Marlborough.*]

London July 10 1716

Madam,

I am just returned to Town, and am told by Sir Samuel Garth my Lord Duke comes to the Lodge tomorrow and goes the next day or the day after to the Bath, which makes it impossible for me to wait on him as I design'd the Princes removing to Hampton Court, engaging almost every minute I at present have. I should however give your Grace what satisfaction I can relating to Blenheim, in Answer to the letter you was pleas'd to write me of the 3ᵈ instant. As to the Plaisterer, the Chief part of what he is now to do, is included in the past Account and what is not I think may deserve the differences there is in the price from that of common work; but I desire your Grace will please to observe the differences of a fourth part is only in the Whiting which rises to a small sum; but in the Ceilings which is the great Article it is but a Tenth.

What I meant by painting the Wainscot in the Corridores is That the Wainscot in the Passage Gallery of the Upper Story should not have its last Colouring till the pavement there be laid which is of plain portland, and a good deal of it done. The word Corridore Madam is foreign, and signifys in plain English, no more than a Passage, it is now however generally us'd as an English Word.

The Kitchen court Madam look'd fine and great only from the manner of Building, being all of fine Stone, but there is not one superfluous office. Those which are finish'd are the Kitchen, Scullery Pastry, Dry Larder, Wet Larder, Dairy, Room for the House-keeper, and a common Hall.— Those unfinish'd, are a Bake-house Wash-house Laundry, Necessary Houses, Place to lay fewell in dry and a Drying Yard. With some little low lodgings for inferior maid servants And the Gateway on the top of which is to be placed the great Cistern which receives the Water from the Engine; and serves the House and Gardens.

To compleat all these and pave the Kitchen court stands in the estimate at £2610 as your Grace will see by a Copy of it which I here enclose. And if you think fit, the Masonry of these Offices shou'd now go on (which will receive still much more damage this winter if they lie in the condition they are) there needs no other agreement or signing of Contracts than what is already done with the Masons now at Work, that Contract including every thing I can think of that can happen in these offices. the prices for the coarse stone being specified. So that if your Grace pleases to tell me, you are willing the Walls of the Offices I have mentioned shou'd be got up I dont see you need give yourself or my Lord Duke any farther trouble as to the Masons Article. But I want indeed your Commission to set the Carpenter to work, both for the Roofs of the Towers in the main House, and those of these offices *if they are to go on.*—I acquainted your Grace in my last, That in the propositions I had sent you Nails were included. I must own as far as my knowledge goes, the Rates are as low, as they can be brought, if a tolerable good Workman be employed and they are very little above what the worst work for. I have try'd to get them lower, by all the ways I can think of, but have not succeeded.—I am mighty willing to defer the Greenhouse for a very natural reason which is, I dont love it. As for the Bridge I do love it; but will overcome my passion and not be troublesome about it.

As to the Marble work Sawing was included in the proposals I sent your Grace so that I think the plain work differs little or nothing from what your Grace mentions you have paid. for the little Moulding they call a bead Moulding or staff Moulding is included. As to the rates for other Mouldings I can bring the Masons only to this proposal.

That smaller and greater shall be and allowed one with another.   Thus

Vein'd and White at P Ft Superficial Girt	5^s
Egyptian Black and Yellow and Plymouth at . . .	6^s
Purple	11^s

The freestone to line that which is sawed thin they are to work and fix the Marble to it.—I don't think any thing will be got by making a bargain for every particular design but quite otherwise.   But whether any body will agree for lower rates I can't tell all I have yet try'd are much higher I entirely agree what your Grace says is most reasonable, That the Duke of Marlborough ought to have his work done as low as any body, And I am sure I'll do all I can it may be so.

I am obliged to your Grace for the offer you are pleas'd to make me of the Lodge.   But I thought you had known I was remov'd three Years ago into the old Manor, That is I had remov'd my small household stuff there tho I never put it up.   When your Grace was out of England My Lord Godolphin told me one day he supposed Mr Travers had now no further thoughts about the old Manor and therefore if I lik'd better to lie there than at the House where I was (which properly belong'd to the Baily of the Park) I might remove thither if I wou'd, which I agreed to, and quitted that House accordingly.   This place being near the Works and the Town is much more convenient than any other and very pleasant too, altho in the middle of Rubbish.   I shan't ask your Grace however to be at any expence about it either without or within, not desiring one Inch of Wainscot, and the Walls, Floors, and Roof are firm.   The Hall and Parlour indeed had no floor at all So I pav'd them at my own charge with a Coarse Stone, which cost me under five Pence a foot Stone and Work.   But if your Grace has any reason against my being there I'll remove.

I wish my Lord Duke all the advantage over any body rece'd from the Bath, and am

> Your Graces most
> Humble & obedient Servant
> J VANBRUGH

[Endorsed]

This shews that Sir John owned the Duke of Marlborough should pay as reasonable rates as any body and some artifice about the old Manor House.

61

[To the Duchess of Marlborough.]   *London July* 13th 1716

Madam

I was mightily sorry I cou'd not wait upon your Grace and my Lord Duke Yesterday from Windsor, before you went.   I had the letter your

Grace sent down thither, and find I was not miſtaken, in reflecting, after I had sent you my laſt, that I had mentioned my readiness to remove from the old Manor in so short a way, as might possibly make your Grace imagine, I thought you were displeas'd with my being there; but I really had no such thought; and mean nothing more, than if there might happen to be any reason againſt it. It wou'd be of no consequence or uneasiness to me to remove. I'm obliged however to your Grace for doing me the honour to be so much concern'd about it.—

I have nothing to add now to what I writ laſt but that I find by letters this poſt from Blenheim it will be necessary another remittance of money be speedily made that no sort of ſtop may be made in any thing; tho but for a day, on account of the impertinent ſtorys those Oxford beaſts, are ready to send round the country and are nibbling at already. I know your Graces intention in this point, which makes me take the Liberty to put you in mind of it.

I am to attend the Prince to Hampton court to morrow, where he goes to view the House, diſtribute the Lodgings and direct (I believe) all the unfinish'd rooms to be compleated. This will employ me, the beſt part of the next week; and the moment tis over I design to take Blenheim in my way to Scarborough and Lord Carlisles, having a great mind to try those waters before the Season be over. But when I have your Graces resolutions on the things I mentioned in my laſt I shall leave every thing in such a method at Blenheim that neither time will be loſt, nor any other prejudice happen, by my absence.

> I am
> Your Graces moſt humble
> and obedient servant
> J VANBRUGH

[Endorsed by Duchess of M.]

Mr Edwards shall Send the money.

62

[To the Duchess of Marlborough.]   Blenheim July 27th—1716

Madam

I have received your Graces letters of the 19th and 21st.

Mr Edwards has returned £500 but I believe there will want another remittance soon.

I have sent the Carpenters to work, at the rates I sent your Grace to St Albans which I find lower than the Country Carpenters here offer. But what I have set them upon, is only the roofs and naked flooring; there will be time enough for your Grace to resolve on the rates for boarding.—

I have set the Oxford Masons upon the offices in the Kitchen Court, and do promise your Grace I will have the homely simplicity of the Antient Manor in my conftant thoughts for a guide in what remains to be done, in all the inferior Buildings. And I hope you will in almoft every article of the Eftimate for finishing this great design, find the expence less than is there allow'd. Even that frightful Bridge, will I believe at laft be kindlier look'd upon if it be found (inftead of twelve thousand pounds more) not to coft above three; and I will venture my whole prophetick skill, on this one Point, That if I liv'd to see that extravagant project compleat, I shall have the satisfaction to see your Grace fonder of it, than of any part whatsoever of the House, Gardens or Park: I don't speak of the Magnificence of it, but the agreeableness which I do assure you Madam has had the firft place in my thoughts and contrivance about it: which I have said little of hitherto; because I know it wont be underftood till tis seen; and then every body will say, *t'was the beft money* laid out in the whole design *And if at laft*, there is a house found in that *Bridge your Grace will go and live in it.*

As to the paving above ftairs in the upper Corridore, it may be reserv'd for Winter work when no Masonry can be done without doors, and the Smell of the Painting there will be gone time enough in the Spring. The Plaifterer is at work, and I have said a great deal to him, and he to me about making his work full worth the Price; I am sure he can do it if he will, so if he don't, I shall give him up for the future

The delaying the Marble agreement will be of no great consequence as long as your Grace cannot now think of furnishing till Spring. All I need therefore say of that is, That tis the White Marble that is in general design'd for Chimneys there being but a small Quantity of the Purple, which is for the Saloon.—I don't see any thing more. I have to direct here now, so I design to night or to morrow, to go towards Scarborough, and shall perform your Graces commands to Lord Carlisle, who is pleas'd to write me word, he'll go and ftay with me there, all the time I do.— I intend in my way back to come hither where I should be very happy to find My Lord Duke and will hope I may. I believe I shant be absent above a month. I am

Your Graces moft humble and moft obedient Servant

J VANBRUGH

Here is a great want of somebody in M' Joynes' room ; and will be a greater very soon. Mr Bobart is an extraordinary good servant in his proper ftation, and will be a good check and of great aid to a Clerk of the Works, but no more; and I do assure you Madam, a Work of one quarter what this is, requires a good Clerk; and this requires the beft that can be had: and who is thoroughly skill'd in Architecture as well as in Prices, Measurements and accounts.

In a letter I lately had from the Duke of Newcastle he writes thus
" I wish you all the happiness and success Northwards And pray cast
" an Eye backwards or forwards upon Houghton, which I must think of
" when that great affair of Matrimony is over which I want to talk largely
" with you If you have heard anything lately of it, let me know, for I shall
" come to Town in the Winter with a full resolution to fix somewhere.

If your Grace has any commands for me before I return, be pleased to
direct for me at Castle Howard near York

Mr Travers has play'd no new Tricks that I have heard of.

[Endorsed]

Sir Johns inclination continued to have Mr Joynes employed and something concerning the Duke of Newcastle

A very diverting letter of Sir Johns which only shews the want of a
vast deal to finish that Building.

63

[To the Duchess of Marlborough.]

London Augt. 3^d—1716

Madam

I am much supris'd to find, what I writt to your Grace from Blenheim
has not quite justified me to you, as to what has been done about the
causeway. Since it turns upon a short point of fact My Lord Dukes
giving orders about it, which I do positively affirm he did, and that in
such a manner, as cou'd not possibly be mistaken because it was not upon
a short word or two, but a great deal of plain intelligible talk And that
not in a crowd or hurry, but quietly in a Room alone with only Mr Wise
and I, upon an appointment made us to attend him on the Blenheim affair;
and this when he was very well at least said nothing of being otherwise.
I don't pretend he fix'd any direct Sum, my proposal to him being, not to
go on fast with the work, but to employ a moderate number of men; to
which he agreed and I thought the compleating it in four years at about
900£ a year, was going moderately to work; if I mistook in that sure the
fault was not great Since if it was to be gone on with at all, I might very
naturally think £900 a year was not an immoderate Sum to lay out. But
I think the main point was whether I went on with this to please my own
fancy, without the knowledge and approbation of him who was to pay for
it. If I had done that, I had been much to blame, but since I did not
I hope your Grace will blame me no longer for it.

As to what your Grace says of the design of this Causeway never having
been shewn nor understood. I know no one thing about the building that
was so much consider'd and so cautiously determin'd.—The Duke of

Marlborough your Grace my late Lord Godolphin, The Duke of Shrewsbury, the late Duke of Montague, Sir Christopher Wren and several others
were thoroughly consulted in this matter; and several meetings there were
upon it, at Kensington, Montague House &c, when the Modells were
inspected, and that of Sir Christopher Wren, Stuck full of pins, by which
he pretended to lessen the charge, was quite rejected, and that I propos'd
was resolv'd on, which has never been alter'd since that ever I heard of,
and is the same now pursued.——Besides this my Lord Duke has never
I believe, in ten years time, been once at Blenheim without going to the
brow of the Hill by the Bridge and talking of the Causeway &c Which
I thought he as properly understood as I did. Nor did he ever propose
any alteration in the Design; but only us'd to ask sometimes, if I was sure
of earth to do it, which might be taken from convenient places, which I
always assur'd him there was; and I assur'd him right.

Upon the whole Madam there has been no whimsy or secret in this
matter; but a plain, fair and honest intention to serve you in it, in the
best manner I cou'd.——I have no humour or desires of my own in it, nor
can I see, I have done any thing either on purpose, or by chance, to make
you blame me; which when you *cooly* consider, I believe you will own me
to be true.

As to going on without a contract I can only repeat what I have said
before I did not go on without a contract. The agreement before my
Lord Duke being, that Mr Wise shou'd proceed on his former agreement,
and tis on that foot he is to be paid and no other

As to the computations of the Expence of this and the other works, I
can only say, that they were made with a great deal of pains and care, and
will I believe prove so. I wonder your Grace shoud think they were only
done by random Guess.——

As to the difference between the Estimate which was made of the House
in general and the money it has cost I can give your Grace a very reasonable
account whenever you have a mind to have it.

Your Grace mistakes the article about the Causway Bridge in the
calculation. My Lord Duke has The Masonry of the Bridge standing
there at

	£	s	d
	2643.,	1.,	8
The causway	3500.	0.	0
In all	6143.,	1.,	8

I am so far from disliking the plainness with which your Grace writes,
that I am very glad you do so; there being no other way to a right understanding. But as I have very often seen you *heated* by wrong informations
or misconceptions; and not make any difficulty at owning your *mistake*

when you have found it So I shall be much disappointed, if when I wait upon you at Blenheim, I do not find you very well satisfied with my defence about the Causeway; and in a disposition to believe I neither did intend to promote that work by any trick or indirect means; Or that I ever do intend to conceal any thing from you relating to the works in general. If you do not believe me in this I hope you will Madam when I declare (which I now do) very truly and positively that I will make no secret to you of any thing, and by consequence, if I do muſt be (what by God I am not) a very Lying Rascal.

Here happens to be several very pressing things to be done at St James's againſt the Princess comes to town to Lye in which she keeps me running to and fro between St James's and Hampton court about; but I believe I shall have fix'd all to morrow, so as to be able to wait on my Lord Duke and your Grace at Blenheim on Friday at fartheſt; till when I desire to defer saying any thing more about the Steps   I am

Your Graces moſt obedient
humble Servant

J VANBRUGH

[*Endorsed.*]

A letter of Sir Johns to excuse his having done anything about the Causeway, pretending it was the signed Orders for every thing else, but that was kept a secret.—

A letter, where he says he will never make any secret, of any thing he does in the building to me; and that he muſt be a lying rascal if he does.

64

[*To the Duchess of Marlborough.*]

Caſtle Howard Augt 19th 1716

Madam

I have received the letter that your Grace was pleased to write me of the 9th. I am very glad your Grace is pleased with Mr Southwell's house; it being the sort of Building I endeavour to bring people to, who are disposed to ask my advice or assiſtance: 'tis certain his work has been done cheap and a great deal of it tollerably well: What is now doing at Blenheim is very near (if not quite) at as low rates and will be much better perform'd.

The Stone your Grace mentions near Oxford, is call'd Heddington 'tis a coarse ſtone, but cheaper a great deal than what was generally us'd at Blenheim. I design'd to use no other in the Offices, till I thought of getting the Heythorp ſtone which is ſtill cheaper and better.

The Steps in Mr Southwells Garden are of the same ſtone that is us'd at Blenheim; but it cannot be had anything so cheap. The agreement for them to be delivered into the barge is 6ᵈ a foot running. But the carriage afterwards by water and Land comes to 2 Shillings a foot cubical which is about 18 pence a foot running. Nor cou'd I find t'was possible to get them cheaper any way, for I try'd all; and found to have sent them by water to Oxford, wou'd have been dearer than to come by land directly from Gloucester, which they now do. As to the manner of working them I had given directions before I received your Graces letter, to have them only chizell'd, which they call setting upon the Stroak but they must be better wrought, and set both than Mr Southwells are; some of his steps being abominable. Upon the whole, I think these Steps will do extreamly well and will be a great deal cheaper than Portland. I wish they cou'd be had cheaper still, but I think they can't: for I do assure your Grace there has been no pains or care spared in trying and contriveing to get them at the lowest.

Altho my thoughts of his Grace of Kent are in general by no means to his advantage: yet I cannot think he will ask money for the steps, since he never had any from any body else; and if he were to be paid, as is usual in the best of Quarrys, it wou'd not come to forty shillings for all the stone which will be us'd at Blenheim of that sort.

The Person your Grace desires an account of at Blenheim, is one Jefferson he was there from the beginning at 15 Shillings a week; and did the business of an assistant clerk of the works, in taking an account of all Materials as they come in, which requires a constant attendance from morning to Night But he neither measures the work, nor inspects the execution of it, which is the great Business of a Clerk of the works. I found the man there now, he having been continued in pay by my Lord Duke to take care of the Building &c ever since the work was stop.d. There was besides him, two assistants more, and they had all their hands full. But if my Lord Duke does not go on at above six or eight thousand pounds a year, I believe this one (with Mr Bobart, and a clerk of the works) may do.

The stone that Mr Bobart mentions, that is working up for the offices is a very small quantity, and most of it formerly wrought and Adjusted for that use, tho not sett: it is likewise of small sizes, being scarce any thing but remnants, so not fit for the Tower: I write to him however this post that if they can pick any of it for the use of the Towers they shou'd. The Masons have orders to use no other but the Heythorp in the offices.—
I dont know whether your Grace has not had some mistaken account about what they are doing near the bridge, which is nothing but carting down earth to form the Causeway that must join it. nor is that carry'd on, at any great rate, it being proper to be done by degrees that it may settle the better. They work on both sides the Bridge at a time, that all may rise

together, and have equal settlement, but there is nothing in this that relates to the old Manor; on the contrary, they dig down a great part of the Hill on which it ſtands; and I desire your Grace will believe me that I have no underhand projeċts or fancys of my own to execute, either there, or in any other part of the work, for I have resolv'd, never to give you any diſturbance of that kind.

I am extreamly glad my Lord Duke continues to mend I hope it wont be very long before he thinks of moving to Blenheim, whither I will make all the haſte I can, the Season for the Scarborough Waters, drawing now near a close. I am come from thence, only to ſtay a day with my Lord Carlisle and return again to morrow, it being but Twenty Miles off. The Poſt won't ſtay to let me say any thing now in answer to the other parts of your Graces letter. I am

Your Graces moſt humble
and moſt obedient Servant
J VANBRUGH

[*Endorsed.*]

Sir Johns letter assuring me, that he will give me no more trouble about the Manor House at the same time he was making Walls Slopes and Gardens.—

65

[*To the Duchess of Marlborough.*]

Scarborough Augt 21st—1716

Madam

I answered your Graces letter laſt poſt (of the 9th inſtant) in what related to Blenheim. I can say little more to the other subjeċt, till I see the Duke of Newcaſtle. To whom I design however, in the mean time, amongſt other things to mention something of that, to contribute as much as I can, to the inclining his thoughts ſtill more the way which I really think is beſt for him. And I hope the Duke of Marlborough will be entirely of your Graces opinion. That his money can never be better beſtow'd, than to compass the beſt match in England, for the only Daughter of his next Heir. Tis robbing nobody of it; since in my humble opinion, tis the firſt business either he, or his heir, can have for it: and if Riches are not to be employ'd on such occasions, I know no difference between him that has them and him that has them not.

My Lord Carlisle and the young Ladys give their humble service to your Grace. I read to My Lord what related to Dean Jones, who seems to think Mr Walters takes a little too much upon him, and will not let him dispose of the living. He has writ to my Lord Essex three weeks since, for Mr Jones. For he thinks 'tis right my Lord Essex shou'd name

(79)

the Person.—I can hardly think Mr Walters has such a hank upon him to prevail against my Lord Carlisle. Besides the applications which have been made from your Grace and my Lady Essex. I therefore desire the Dean won't dispair, for I can't but think there's life in't yet. If my lord Essex send a blank presentation I can hardly believe t'will be with leave to Mr Walters to fill it up without my Lord Carlisles concurrence.

I am

Your Graces most humble

and obedient Servant

J VANBRUGH

66

[*To the Duchess of Marlborough.*]

Blenheim Septr. 27th 1716

Madam

I writ to your Grace from hence on Saturday, and hope what I said about the Causeway may have given you some ease. I have since been considering it again both as to the manner of doing it, and the expence; which shall be explain'd to your Grace and my Lord Duke in so intelligible a manner; as I think must leave you in no farther apprehension about it.—

I desir'd your Grace wou'd give yourself the trouble of talking with Mr Townshend (who did Mr Southwells' Masonry) about the working of the Steps in his Garden; and to know what he wou'd work Steps for after the manner I describ'd of the same stone. I have since thought it wou'd do well (that the proposal may be the better understood) to send a small piece ready wrought which your Grace will receive by the Coach if it can be got ready in time; I have try'd several Masons here and thereabouts and dont yet find that any of them will work and set the steps in this manner, under eighteenpence a Foot, superficial.—

By a Letter Mr Bobart has received from Mr Hodges I find tis probable (tho not certain) your Grace may be here on Tuesday. I beg the favour you'll please to let me know at London (where I am now going) if you do leave the Bath so soon—Since if you do I'll be down here again either on Tuesday night or Wednesday morning. I am

Your Graces

most humble and obedient Servant

J VANBRUGH

I have met with Mr Hawksmoor here who has assisted in examining the causeway &c and making a new estimate.

[*To the Duchess of Marlborough.*]   67

London October 18th—1716

Madam

That your Grace might not apprehend there was any thing carrying on at the old Manor against your Orders, I design'd to acquaint you before I came away, that I had set three or four men to work, to do some little necessary things, without which I cou'd not be there; but that they were at my own expence, not desiring to put my Lord Duke to any on my account.—I'm sorry I forgot to apprise your Grace of this, the neglect of it I find had in some measure, the effect I fancy'd it would; tho indeed I formerly did acquaint your Grace that I had done the paving at my own charge; and I'm sorry you coud not as easily believe I wou'd do the rest so; since it is by no means worth my while, to endeavour to put so small an expence indirectly upon my Lord Duke, if by some poor little trick I cou'd do it; I have acquainted your Grace formerly how I came to the Manor; That it was my Lord Godolphins offering it to me, instead of the House I lodged in before, which belong'd to the Baily of the Park. And the beginning of this summer upon my Lord Dukes resolving to go on with the building, I paved the Hall, Parlour Kitchen &c and was now going on with some other things absolutely necessary to make the place just habitable, which I computed upon the whole, wou'd cost me about fourscore Pounds which the rent of a House in the Town, wou'd in a little time have amounted to. This Madam was all my design which if it be agreeable to you, I shall go on with; if not, I beg you'll freely tell me so, for it will be no sort of trouble to me to desist

I am   Your Graces most obedient
humble Servant
J VANBRUGH

[*Endorsed.*]

Sir John Vanbrugh about his paying for all that ridiculous expence at the old Manor House
what he says of Lord Godolphin was not true this is his excuse for making all that expence at the old Manor House without acquainting any body with it

68

[*To the Duchess of Marlborough.*]

Whitehall October 1716

Madam

Your Grace having for some time been uneasy about the stone for steps, apprehending we were in a way of letting my Lord Duke pay more for them than Mr Southwell, or other people had done I writ to him, and his steward both, to get an exact account of the charge of his steps, both Stone Carriage and work; and the account they send me is this

The Steps he has are not from Ross, where my Lord Dukes came from, but out of the Forrest, from whence the Carriage is so easy to Mr Southwells, that he says they must needs cost much more to Gloucester from Ross; and that if they are delivered there for Nine pence halfpenny a foot, he thinks they cannot be dear. Tho' I shou'd here acquaint your Grace that when I writ you, they wou'd come to but Nine pence halfpenny a foot delivered at Gloucester, I computed by what was to be paid by the Ton Weight, and thought they were but six inches thick at which dimension I calculated; but when I came to see those which were sent in, I found they were from seven to near eight Inches thick, which will make them come to between eleven pence and twelve pence a foot running at Gloucester but they are much the better for being thus thick since by this means, they can be notch'd one into another which (besides their weight) contributes mightily to their lying fast and firm.—

Mr Southwell says, his are but 14 Inches broad and from 5 to 6 Inches thick; whereas your Graces are 18 Inches broad, and from 7 to 8 Inches thick. this is a vast difference

As to the workmanship, your Grace in your letter to me on this occasion formerly mentioned his having that done, for three pence a foot running. But he says they cost him between 13 and 14 Pence a foot running; And his are only wrought square, without an Astragal; nor are they let one into another by notches as your Graces are propos'd to be. And if it be true, what Dr Kyrle writes; That, that Forrest Stone is not half so hard as this from Ross (which I have observ'd to be so hard, that every stroke in working fetches fire like a flint) then the rate which Mr Southwell pays for workmanship is dearer than the last offer the Masons made before I came away which was half a Crown a foot running measure, but I shall be glad however to hear they woud come lower still

I hope what I now write will upon the whole satisfy your Grace That no care has been wanting about these steps to have them both good and Cheap I'm sure never more care was taken about any thing. I am

Your Graces most obedient
Humble Servant
J VANBRUGH

[To the Duke of Newcastle.]   69   Greenwich Nov: ye [1716?]

My Lord Duke

I am but just got back, hither, without touching at London, whither I design however to move for good, on Monday next.

I must in the mean time, return your Grace, my very humble & Sincere thanks, for your so Quick dispatch, in your Favour to Jones: who is a most happy Man by it, and begins to think of making his Daughter a Great Fortune, having a Wife, who will hoard up every Penny of the Money.

I have drawn a Design out for a Seat in Esher Church, which I hope will do. Arthur is Coppying it out fair, which when done, I'll send it to the Brigadier. And as Soon as I get to Towne, I'll Speak with Kidwell about reforming the Chimnnys at Claremont. I am Your Graces

most Oblig'd and Obed^t
Servant
J VANBRUGH

I brought up Peter Walters in my Calash.

70

[To the Dutchess of Marlborough.]

6 November 1716

Madam,

When I came to Towne from Blen^h: I rec'd a Letter from the D of N. that he wou'd be in a day or two at Clarem^t: and wanted very much to talk with me. But I having engag'd to Mr W. to follow him into Norfolk, cou'd not ſtay to See him then.

At my return from Mr Walpole wch was Friday laſt, I found an Other Letter from the D. that he was at Clarem^t: and deferr'd returning back to Sussex, till he cou'd See me, So I went downe to him on Monday laſt.

He told me the business he had with me was to know, if any thing more had pass'd on the Subject he had writen to me at Scarborough relating to Lady H. And what discourse might have happen'd wth your Grace, at B. upon it. I told him you had not mention'd one word of it to me. He said that was mighty ſtrange for you had talk'd with Mr Walters about it at the Bath, and writ to him Since, in such a Manner, as had put him upon endeavouring to bring on a direct Negociation. He then told me, That before he cou'd come to a resolution of embarking in any Treaty, he had waited for an Opportunity of discoursing with me once more, upon the Qualitys and Conditions of Lady H. For, That as I know his whole Views in Marriage and that he had hopes of Some Other Satisfaction in it than many people troubled themselves about, I might Judge what a Terrible Disappointment he shou'd be under, if he found himself ty'd for life to a Woman not Capable of being a usefull and faithfull Friend, as well as an Agreeable Companion. That what I had often said to him of Lady H, in that respect, had left a Strong Impression with him; but it being of so high a Consequence to him not to be deceiv'd in this Great point, on which the Happyness of his Life wou'd turn, he had desir'd to discourse with me again upon it in the moſt Serious manner; being of opinion (as he was pleas'd to say) that I cou'd give him a Righter Character of her, than any other Friend or Acquaintance he had. And that he was fully persuaded, That whatever good Wishes I might have for her, as regards to my Lord Marl^b: and his Family, I wou'd be Content with doing her Juſtice, without exceeding in her Character, So as to lead him into an opinion of her Now, which by a Disappointm^t: hereafter (shou'd he marry her) wou'd make him the Unhappyeſt Man in the World. He then desir'd to know in particular What Acc^t: I might have heard of her behaviour at the Bath; and what New Observations I might my Self have made of her at Blen^m: both as to her Temper, Person, Sense, behaviour and many other very nice enquirys. It wou'd be too long to report to your Grace what my Answers were to him: It will be sufficient to Acquaint you, That I think I have left him in a Disposition to prefer her to all Other Women.

When he had done with me on these personal Considerations he call'd Mr Walters (who was there) into the Room. And acquainted him with what had pass'd with your Grace through me, at Severall times, And then Spoke his Sentiments as to Fortune, which Mr Walters intends to give your Grace an Acc^t: of, so I need not.

And now Madam, Your Grace muſt give me leave to end my Letter, with telling you. That if the D of New: was surpris'd to find, You had said so much to Mr Walters at the Bath and nothing to me, on this Subject, at Blenheim I was no less Surpris'd than he, After the honour you had done me, of Opening your firſt thoughts on it to me, And giving me leave to make Severall Steps about it, to his Friends & Relations. As well as to take, such a Part with himself as, you Seem'd to think might probably contribute the moſt towards disposing his Inclinations the way you wish'd them.

I don't say this Madam, to Court being farther employ'd in this matter; for a Matchmakers is a Damn'd Trade, And I never was fond of Meddling with Other Peoples Affairs. But, as in this, on your own Motion, and your own desire, I had taken a good deal of very hearty pains to Serve you, And I think with a View of good Success, I cannot but wonder (tho not be Sorry,) you shou'd not think it right, to continue your Commands, Upon Your Obed^t: humle Servant.

71

[*To the Duchess of Marlborough.*]   *Whitehall November* 8th. 1716

    Madam

When I writ to your Grace on Tuesday laſt I was much at a loss, what cou'd be the ground of your having drop't me in the service I had been endeavouring to do you and your family with the Duke of Newcaſtle,

Upon your own sole motion and desire. But having since been shewn by Mr Richards a large packet of building papers sent him by your Grace, I find the reason was, That you had resolv'd to use me so ill in respect of Blenheim, as must make it Impracticable to employ me in any other Branch of your Service. These Papers Madam are so full of *Far-fetched, Labour'd Accusations, Mistaken Facts, Wrong Inferences, Groundless Jealousies and Strain'd Constructions : That I shou'd put a very great affront upon your under-standing if I suppos'd it possible you cou'd mean any thing in earnest by them ; but to put a Stop to my troubling you any more. You have your end Madam, for I will never trouble you more Unless the Duke of Marlborough recovers so far, to shelter me from such intolerable Treatment.*

I shall in the mean time have only this Concern on his account (for whom I shall ever retain the greatest Veneration) That your Grace having like the Queen thought fit to get rid of a faithfull servant, The Torys will have the pleasure to See your Glassmaker, Moor, make just such an end of the Dukes Building as her Minister Harley did of his Victories for which it was erected.

I am
Your Graces most obedient Ser^t.

J VANBRUGH

If your Grace will give me leave to print your paper I'll do it very exactly; and without any answer or remark *but this short letter tack'd to the tail of them, That the world may know I desir'd they might be published.*

[*Endorsed.*]

a very impertinent letter of Sir Johns for having dropt him as he calls it in the affair of the Duke of Newcastle

To His Grace   72
 The Duke of Newcastle
  at Bishopston
   near Lewis
    in Sussex

London. Nov. ye 10th 1716

My Lord Duke
 I sent your Grace last post, a Coppy of what I had writ to my Lady Marl^b:

I have since I saw you, had a Sight of the Load of Papers she had Sent up to Richards, for a Foundation (tho' a very rotten one) to Quarrell with me. I therefore writ to her, by Thursdays Post, the Letter which I here enclose a Coppy off.

I have this afternoon had one from her, in Answer to that I writ About

(85)

your Grace, In wch she says I have no Cause to Complain of her not Speaking to me and that I shou'd have done it first to her. In short, her Letter is a meer Canter; And by a few words at the latter end About the Building, she shews quite plain, that She was resolv'd to get me out of that, and So judg'd it impossible to concern me any longer in tother affair. I need make no remarks to your Grace Upon this Abominable Womans proceeding Which shall not however lessen my regard to my Lord Duke, nor good Opinion of his Grand Daughter, who I do not think has one grain of this Wicked Womans Temper in her; if I did, I wou'd not advise you to take her, tho' with the Allay of a Million. I am

Your Graces ever faithfull & Obed^t. Servt

J VANBRUGH

The Poor Princess, is most dangerously ill. He has behav'd himself most wondrous well to her, in this bitter time she has had.

Garth and Jacob appointed to meet here this morning to Shew me the Dedication intended to your Grace. which we corrected and Compleated.

73

To His Grace
The Duke of Newcastle
at Bishopston
near Lewis
In Sussex   *Whitehall. Nov ye 15th 1716*

I have rec'd so very kind a Letter from y^r Grace today, I can't forbear thanking you for it to Night, tho' I am in very great haste, and have very little else to say. No doubt but you have heard of the D of Marl^b : being ill again. I Spoke with Lord Bridgwater e'en now, who came from him but yesterday morning. He tells me he is pretty well again; however this sort of Relapse, I doubt portends no good which I am most heartily troubled for. Lord & Lady Godolphin are with him, but will return to morrow, And Since my Lady Dutchess has treated me, both in respect to your Graces concern, and that of Blen^h: in so extraordinary a manner, I think I may freely talk to my Lord Godolphin of the former, and acquaint him with all has past. after which, I will let your Grace know what disposition I find him in.

I here inclose her Letter to me, in Answer to that I wrote her. But pray send it me again. Her recitall of what had past, is pretty near right; But she comes off sadly at last, in saying it was my turn to Speak. for it was nobodys turn to Speak but those who had Something new to say wch I had not, not having Seen y^r Grace but she had; having employ'd Mr Walters to you. Your Grace was in just her Case as to him; And you thought fit to tell me the first moment you saw me, what had past. And so wou'd she have done too, but for the reason I have told her. Which is very plain by her not engaging me to meddle any farther soon after the hopefull Acc^t: I had given her of your disposition. I don't at all believe however, she's Indifferent in the Matter, for she is not a Fool, tho' she's a—Worse thing. But, as in all her other Traffick, so in a husband for her Grand Daughter, she wou'd fain have him good, and Cheap: and she certainly fancys she can wheedle Peter Walters, to play a cunning Knaves part, and bring her business About with you, alone, without meddleing much with your Friends & Relations; for you See she do's not send him to Mr Walpole as she did me, knowing I shou'd certainly go that way, whether she wou'd or not. However; let her good Housewifely projects be what they will, I think it mighty probable this business may Succeed; for I don't doubt but she'll do Something considerable herself and if the Duke is well enough to be treated with, I can scarce think he'll let you Slip, And shou'd he dye, My Lord Godolphin will certainly be in a Condition to do a great deal, And I am confident both he and she, will not be for Sparing their Money on so right an Occasion.

In a Letter the Duchess of Marl^b: writ to me on this Occasion at Scar^b: She exprest herself much dispos'd, to perswade the Duke to part with his money, and was only for Saving her own. So in my Answer I writ thus.

" —and I hope the Duke of Marlborough will be entirely of your
" Graces Opinion; That his money can never be better bestow'd, than
" to compass the best match in England, for the only Daughter of his
" Next Heir, 'Tis robbing nobody of it; Since in my humble Opinion,
" 'tis the first business either he or his Heir can have for it; And if
" Riches are not to be employ'd, on such Occasions; I know no
" difference between him that has them, and him that has them not.

This Letter she writ me Word she read to him, And he Seem'd to take it very right, not shewing any Uneasyness at it. As any thing new happens, your Grace shall know it from
Your truly Obed^t Ser^t:
J VANBRUGH

The Match she says she refus'd was (I have reason to think) Wentworth of the North. The Princess is quite safe.

74

[*To the Duke of Newcastle.*]
Whitehall Nov: ye 27th 1716

I have two Letters from y^r Grace since I writ to you. I went to L^d: Go^n: on Saturday, And by Appointment again on Sunday, when we had time to go over the whole Affair from the Begining. Little particulars I refer to a meeting, I'll only now tell your Grace upon the whole, That I find him personally dispos'd to you, and so desirous of this Alliance, that he frankly says, were the thing in his power, he shou'd not dispute your demands. What Other folks will do he cannot tell how to judge, there being great Uncertaintys in their Resolutions But he is of Opinion, Nobody can help the Birth forward with the Great Lady, but that she muſt be left to her own throws, And we muſt wait a little to See what that will bring forth. They are not yet come to Towne, but will I believe to morrow. And then I am apt to think she will begin to Say something directly to Walters. The Duke is full as well, as he was before this Relapse.

I have not yet had an Opportunity of talking the matter again with Mr Walpole; But I have had some discourse with Lord Townshend upon it. Who is of Opinion, That 'tis beſt to ly by a little, and not seem to her Grace too forward; who very possibly may then come to offer whats reasonable; If not, the Duke of Marlborough's Fate shou'd be waited for. who will probably either grow well enough to be treated with, or not hold out long. in which Case Ld Godolphin will be both Able and willing to end the Matter himself.

As to the Building at Claremt: I am Swearing as much as is necessary to get it cover'd; wch I believe will be out of hand: what neglect has been I can't juſt tell, but however, your Grace need not be in pain of any dreadfull damage to the Work for 'tis not of a kind to receive much; I have been Severall times at Newcaſtle house, wch will soon be ready. I have Stopt Smalwell from Altering the Hall door, till I can fix with your Grace what Stonework shall be Added, for something handsome in that muſt be done. The paving in the Street I have likewise Stopt till the Masons have done, and the rubbish is carryed off; besides, the Manner of doing it muſt be talk'd of, there being no Square Stones to be yet had, that will lye faſt. I am

Your Graces ever faithfull

& Obedt

VAN

The King comes to hold the Sessions, Which will certainly open very near the day Set.

Talking with Smalwell juſt now, I don't know whether the Brigadrs: great zeal for your Graces Service, did not make him think the Bricklayers neglect Something more than it might be.

75

[*To Mr Bobart.*]

London Decr 15th 1716

The agreement with Mr Thornhill was, that all Ornaments shou'd be measur'd as the Historical part, the price being at a Medium on that Account, But I don't see how you can measure any thing that is not painted by him, but only prim'd, If he insists upon it I believe your best way will be, to express it by itself, *but I fear it will make a Quarrell with the Dutchess, which perhaps were better avoided. At least you'll tell him my thoughts of it,* who am

Your real Friend & Servant

J VANBRUGH

Pray do me the favour to know, if the Upholsterer at Oxford will take his things again, allowing him four or (if needs) five pounds. When I have your Answer to this I'll send money to discharge all.

[Endorsed by the Duchess of Marlborough.]

Sir Johns letter to M^r. Bobart where he says that Mr Thornhill the paynter measuring where his pencill has not been may make a quarrel with me which is better avoided & desires he may know that is his opinion.

after this letter Sir John Vanbrugh signd a paper for M^r. Thornell for a thousand pounds all but some odd money for paynting the Hall at Wood-stock, tho except the ovell part of the Ceilling the rest of the work was done at half a Crown a yard, & his estimate to the Duke of Marlborough was to give him Eighteen hundred pounds for the Hall Saloone & Gallery, & the bill signd for the Hall near a thousand pounds was not above the sixth part of the work & this summer I paid out of the Duke of Marlboroughs own money last winter in 1716, I mention this as one proof that I have not made disputes even where there was so much reason to have done it;

76

[*To Lord Godolphin?*]

[1717?]

The Duke of Marlborough being pleased some time since, to let me know by the Duke of Newcastle, he took notice he had never seen me since he came from Blenheim: I was Surprized to find he was not acquainted with the Cause, why I had not continued to wait on him as I us'd to do; And writ him a letter upon it, in which I did not trouble him with particulars, but said I wou'd beg the favour of your Lordship, when you came to town, to speak to him on that Occasion.

And Since your Lordship gives me leave to take this Liberty with you, I will make the trouble as little as I can, both to yourself, and to the Duke of Marlborough, by as short a [word missing] as possible, of what has happened since his Graces return to England, in Two things I have had the honour to be employ'd in for his Service, purely by his own, and my Lady Dutchesses commands, without my applying or seeking for either, or ever having made, any advantage by them, I mean, *The Building at Blenheim And the Match with the Duke of Newcastle.*

As to the former, As soon as the Duke of Marlborough arrived in England, I rec^d. his commands to attend him to Blenheim, where he was pleas'd to tell me, That when the Government took care, *to discharge him* from the claim of the Workmen for the Debt in the Queens time; he intended to finish the Building, at his own Expence, And Accordingly, from that time forwards, he was pleased to give me his Orders, as occasion required, in things preparatory to it; till at laſt, the affair of the Debt being Adjuſted with the Treasury, & own'd *to be the* Queens He gave me directions, to set people actually to Work after having consider'd an Eſtimate, he order'd me to prepare of the Charge, to nish the House, Offices Bridge, and Out Walls, of Courts and Gardens, Which amounted to £54000.

I *Spar'd for no Pains* or Induſtry, to lower the prices of Materials *and Workmanship,* on the reasonableſt consideration, of *Sure and ready Payment.* Which before (as experiments shews) was precarious. I made no Steps without the Dukes knowledge, while he was well: and I made *none without the Dutchess, after he fell Ill.* And was so far I thought from being in her Ill Opinion That even the laſt time I waited on her, and my Lord Duke at Blenheim. (which was laſt Autumn) She Shew'd no sort of *dissatisfaction, on any thing I had done And was pleas'd to express herself to* Mʳ Hawkesmoor (who *saw her after I had taken my leave*) in the moſt Favourable, *and Obliging manner of me ;* and to enjoin *him, to repeat to me,* what she had said to *him.*

Thus I left the Duke and Dutchess at Blenheim But a small time after I arrived in London Brigadʳ. Richards shew'd me a Packet, he had rec^d, from her Grace, In which (without any new matter having happend) She had given herself the trouble, in twenty or thirty Sides of Paper, to draw up a Charge againſt me, beginning, from the time this Building was firſt ordered by the Queen, And concluding upon the Whole, That I had brought the Duke of Marlb: into this Unhappy difficulty Either to leave the thing Unfinishd, And by Consequence, useless to him and his Poſterity; or by finishing it, to diſtress his Fortune, And deprive his Grandchildren of the Provision he inclin'd to make for them.

To this heavy charge, I know I need trouble the Duke of Marlborough with nothing more in my Juſtification than to beg he'll please to recollect;

That I never did any thing without *his Approbation*. And that I never had the Misfortune to be once found fault with him in my life.

As to the Dutchess. I took the Liberty in a Letter I sent her on this occasion, to Say: That finding she was weary of my Service (Unless my Lord Duke recovered enough to take things again, into his own Direction) I wou'd do, as *I saw She desired*, Never trouble her more.

I thought after this, I cou'd not wait upon the Duke, when she was present; And that if I endeavoured to do it, at any other time, she wou'd not like it. There has been no other reason whatever, why I have not continued, to pay my Constant duty to *him*.

The other Service I have mentioned which her Grace thought fit to lay her Commands upon me in was the doing what might be in my Power, towards inclining the Duke of Newcastle to prefer my Lady Harriot Godolphin to all other Women, who were likely to be offer'd him Her Grace was pleased to tell me, on the breaking this matter I was the first body she had ever mention'd it to, And she gave me Commission to open it to the Duke of Newcastles Relations, as well as to himself, which I accordingly did. And gave her from time to time, an Account of what past, And how the Disposition mov'd, towards what she so much desir'd.

Her Grace did not *seem inclind to think* of giving *Such a Fortune. as* shoud be any great inducement *to the Dukes preferring this Match, to others* which might probably be offer'd; But she layd a very great and very just Stress, on the Extraordinary Qualifications And Personal Merits of my Lady Harriot, which She was pleas'd to say, She thought mightily more in my Power to possess him rightly of, than any Other Body she knew; and did not doubt, but I wou'd have that regard to the Duke of Marlborough and *the Advantage of his* Family, as to take this part upon me, and Spare no Pains to make it Successfull. This thing her Grace desired I shou'd do, was so much with my own Inclination; And what I was to Say on the Personal Character of my Lady Harriot as truly my own Opinion of her, that I had no sort of difficulty in resolving to use all the Credit I had with the Duke of Newcastle, to prefer this Match to all others.

His Grace rec'd the first Intimation, with all the regard to the Alliance, that was due to it, And the Hopes of having a Posterity descend from the Duke of Marlborough, had an extraordinary weight with him But I found he had thoughts about marriage, not very usual with men of Great Quality and Fortune especially so Young as he was. He had made more Observations on the bad Education, and wrong manners of the Ladys of the Court and Towne, than one wou'd have expected; And own'd he shou'd think of Marriage with much more Pleasure than he did, if he cou'd find a Woman (fit for him to marry) that had such a turn of Understanding, Temper and Behaviour As might make her a usefull Friend, as well, as an Agreeable Companion, but of Such a One, he Seem'd almost to despair.

I was very glad to find him in this Sentiment Agreed entirely with him in it, And Upon that Foundation, endeavoured for two Years together to convince him, my Lady Harriot Godolphin was happily the very Sort of Woman, he so much desir'd and thought so difficult to find.

The latter end of laſt Summer, he writ to me to Scarborough to tell me; He was come to an Absolute resolution of marrying Somewhere, before the Winter was over; And desired to know, if I had any thing new to Say to him about my Lady Harriot.

Upon this I writ to the Dutchess of Marlborough at the Bath, And Several Letters paſt between her Grace and me on this fresh Occasion, in which she thought fit to express her extream Satisfaction, to find a thing reviv'd she so much desir'd, tho for some time paſt, had retain'd but little hopes of.

Not long after, I waited on Her and the Duke of Marlborough, at Blenheim, But not happening to *be any time alone* with her, And being to See the Duke of Newcaſtle, before there cou'd be any thing new to Speak upon; I did not wonder she said nothing to me of that matter. But when I came to London I was much Surpriz'd to find the Cause of it.

I met with two letters from the Duke of Newcaſtle, expressing a great earneſtness to see me I went immediately to him at Claremont, where he told me his Impatience to see me had been to know, what I might have farther to Say of Lady Harriot; What I had learnt of her Conduct and Behaviour at the Bath what I might have observ'd of her at Blenheim, And In Short That if I knew any thing that cou'd reasonably Abate of the Extraordinary Impression I had given him of her; I wou'd have that regard to the greateſt concern of his Life, Not to hide it from him. For that if he married her, his happyness woud entirely be determined, by her Answering or not answering the Character he had rec^d. of her from me, And upon which he solely depended. That he had therefore forborn *making any Step*, (tho' preſt to it by Mr Walters) that cou'd any way engage him, till he saw me again, And Once for all, rec^d. a Confirmation of the Character so agreeable to his Wishes, I had given him of my Lady Harriot.

As I had nothing to say to him on this Occasion but what was ſtill to her Advantage; he came to an Absolute *Resolution of treating*; and asking me what the Dutchess of Marlborough had said to me at Blenheim about the Fortune, (the Letters at Scarborough having amongſt other things been on that Subject) I told him she had not said a word to me of it, or any *thing Relating* to the matter in general.

The Duke seem'd much surprized to hear me say so, and told me he took it for granted she had let me know what had lately pass'd through Mr Walters, whom she had accidentally fallen acquainted with at the Bath and engaged him in this affair. That he had even press'd him to enter into a direct Treaty, but that he had made *pretences to decline it,* being undetermin'd, till he had Once more had an Opportunity of talking the whole matter *over with me;* especially on what related personaly to my Lady Harriot, having resolv'd to make that his decisive point.

I told him it was very extraordinary, the Dutchess of Marlborough after two Years employing me, And finding I had Succeeded in the very point she judgd me the fittest to serve her in *And by which point almost alone,* she hop'd to *bring this Match about,* shou'd drop me in so very Short a Manner. And that I cou'd conceive no Cause Good or bad for it, Unless she was going to dismiss me from meddling any more with the Building And so judg'd it not proper to employ me any farther in this other part of her Service.

The Duke seem'd inclin'd to hope I might be mistaken in that thought, And so desir'd I wou'd continue to Act in this concern with her: Upon which (calling Mr Walters into the Room) he was pleas'd to relate to him, all that had past through me from the beginning, with the Dutchess of Marlborough, My Lord Townshend, Mr Walpole &c and ended, in desiring we wou'd both join in bringing the matter to a Conclusion, he being now determin'd to treat; And that we wou'd both write to the Dutchess of Marlborough, the next Post.

I writ accordingly, And in the close of my Letter mention'd the Surprise I had been in, to find She had not been pleas'd to continue her Commands to me, in a thing I had taken so much pains to Serve her, And not without Success.

But when I came to London, I heard of the Charge her Grace had thought fit to send up against me, About the building; And so found I had not been mistaken in what I had told the Duke of Newcastle I apprehended might be the Cause of her dropping me in so very easy a manner, in what related to him.

Remarks.

Upon this false assertion of what the Dutchess of Marlborough had said to Mr Hawkesmoor, she met him at Mr. Richard's at Black heath and told him what Sr. John had said as to the Dss. of Marlbs: message by him upon which Mr. Hawkesmoor protested as he had never seen her after Sr. John went away he never said any such thing to him & that it had given him a great deal of trouble very often to see the unreasonable proceedings of Sir John

What he repeats out of his own letter is quite different which may be seen

My Lady Harriot Godolphin had twenty two thousand pounds to her portion, procured by the Dutchess of Marlborough.

To His Grace
The Duke of Newcastle
at Newcastle House.

77

Wednesday. July ye 3^d 1717

My Lord Duke

I attended your Graces coming to the Back ſtairs as you directed me; And Stay'd till half an hour paſt three. I thought Since you did not come, you wou'd like I shou'd shew Mr Bothmer the Paper wth my Answers. which he was very well Satisfied with, but gave me back, to give your Grace. I here enclose it and believe what I set my hand to, will be made good. I am juſt going for a day or two's breath to Greenwich which I ſtand cruelly in need of. The moment I return, I'll wait upon your Grace, I'll only thank you in the mean time for your kind care of your ever truly faithfull & truly Obedient Ser^t   J VANBRUGH

I have waited on Lord Marl^b: so All's well there Pray my Lord Remember to tell him, that what was in the paper relating to your Self & Lady Harriot, is true.

78

[To the Duke of Newcaſtle.]

Bath Oc^t: y_e 9th 1717

My Ld Duke

A Feaver I have been ill handled by, and from which I am but now recovering, has not made me so indifferent to the Misfortunes of Others, not to have been ſtruck in the moſt sensible degree about ten days Since, on the News we had deliver'd to us here for certain of the Dutchess of Newcaſtle being given over. My business now, is only to congratulate Y^r Grace ten Thousand times on the falseness of that Story tho' I find there was enough of it true, to give you a round Allarm. I am extreamly glad to hear Your danger is over, of Losing a Wife, whose place you never can Supply   I am Y^r Graces ever dutiful
& Moſt Obed^t hum^b Sv^t
J VANBRUGH

79

Bath Oĉ^r. ye 14th: 1717

To the Right Honble. the Lords Commissioners of His Majeſtys Treasury.

May it please your Lordships
In Obedience to your Commands signified to me by Mr Kelsall, relating to ye Attorney Gen^{lls}. report, on M^r Anſtis's Petition for a Salary belonging to him as Garter King of Arms.

I believe it will not be necessary to give your Lord^{ps}. ye trouble of a long detail of what has pass'd on this Occasion, But that it will Suffice to aquaint you, That upon an Application to his Maj^{ty}. in Councill from ye Earl of Suffolk, the Lords of ye Cabinet sent for ye Attorney Gen^{ll}. before them, to know why he had not (in pursuance of his Majestys Commands Signified to him by ye Earl of Suffolk ye 22^d of Octr. 1715) prepared a Bill for his Royall Signature, to pass ye Great Seal, containing his Majestys Grant of ye Office of Garter Principall King of Arms to me.

Upon which The Attorney Gen^{ll}. having Obtain'd time from their Lordships to give his Answere Signified to ye Partys concern'd, that it wou'd be necessary for him, to have a hearing of ye whole matter before him, that he might be enabled to make a proper report.

There was accordingly a day set & ye Partys met with their Councill. Some of which not finding themselves Sufficiently prepared; it was put off to another day, when both sides being (in all appearance ready) The Duke of Norfolk was pleased to interpose, and to prevail with ye Attorney to put ye hearing off. without Appointing any other time for it.

The Earl of Suffolk who has all along been very earnest to bring this matter to some Issue, being much Surprised at this Stop, not having had ye least intimation of it, Sent to ye Duke of Norfolk to desire to know ye cause. Upon this, there was a meeting agreed on, between ye Duke of Norfolk my Lord Suffolk, Lord Carlisle and others of ye Family; And ye Duke of Norfolk some time after, let my Lord Suffolk &c^a. know, that he wou'd not meddle any farther in obstructing ye Hearing.

The Partys were then preparing to proceed, when ye Attorneys Indisposition again prevented it, But my Lord Suffolk has given direction to ye Agents employ'd in this matter, to Solicit ye Attorney to appoint a day of hearing, which ye Councill are preparing for accordingly: And I do Assure your L^dships no manner of delay, will be practis'd from my side, it being my most earnest desire to have this dispute determin'd, as soon as possible.

But till it is so, and that ye delay lys entirely on ye opposite side I humbly hope Your Lordships will think it Just & reasonable for ye King to keep his Money in his hands, till he sees whether a Patent granted by himselfe or his Predecessour, determins who is to have ye honour of being his Officer.

All Which is humbly Submitted
to your Lordships great
Wisdom   J VANBRUGH

To his Grace
The Duke of Newcastle

80

Greenwich Dec: ye 21th 1717

My Lord Duke

I was forc'd to come downe here laſt night againſt my good will; for I wou'd fain have Stay'd in Towne till I cou'd have come to my Country morsell (as the Brigadier says) in peace   But the business of this Letter, is to furnish your Graces good Intentions, with one Subſtantiall Argument, if you find occasion for it, wch is: that Yeſterday I look'd over the Bill of my Lord Chetwinds Building, with him himself; And Shew'd him (upon moſt of the Principal Articles) what the King paid more than him. which is so little (making the Allowances for fees and Gratuitys, wch the King's Workmen are forc'd to Allow in the Offices), that it will plainly, appear, from this One examination, (My Lord Chetwinds work being done, at the loweſt rates, paid in the pooreſt houses in Towne) that there is a moſt thorough Care and Strickt management in the Board of Works, And no Sort of ground upon Earth, for the Suggeſtion to the Contrary, And upon this one point (I beg your Grace will frankly say to the King) I desire to have his Favour or Abandon any pretence to it for ever.

If you please to Speak to my Lord Chetwind I believe he will readily confirm what I hear Say.   And So I commit my Cares to your Grace's Friendship, which will ever meet with the utmoſt Acknowledgment, from
Your truly faithfull And moſt Obed^t: Ser^t

J VANBRUGH

'Twas unlucky your Grace was not at the back ſtairs Yeſterday, for Neither King nor Miniſters had one word to say to one an Other: but I thought it was not beſt to break into the Scheem settled, so wou'd not desire Ld Stanhope to go in.

My Ld Sund^d: has told me, when your Grace And Ld Stanhope have Spoke, he'll then talk effectually wth the Dutchess of Munſter.

To his Grace
The Duke of Newcaſtle.

81

Friday One a Clock

I'm Sure your Grace won't easily believe I wou'd invent excuses to keep away from you, But between those two Accursed things of determining the Windsor point, and My Friend Bensons, together with ten Summonses a day I have to Kensington I am not only diveſted of passing one moment to my Satisfaction; but am so disorder'd by the hurry into the Bargain, That I thought 20 times yeſterday, I muſt have dropt dead; My Lord Suffolk is fretted to death too, about Lord Parkers proceeding,

And hearing laſt night, that if the Attorney don't come time enough to make his Report, they will Appoint Mr Curtis to officiate, he has juſt now sent for me, to go with a Letter to the King, to desire he may not be treated in this manner, upon what my Ld Parker alone is pleas'd to call his Opinion; when both the Chancellr, & the Sollicitor have Shewn theirs to be Otherways, But that he may be heard by his Councill at the Cabinet againſt Mr Anſtis's being admitted to perform any part of the office of Garter As my Lord Chancellr advis'd. I am afterwards to follow the Attorney, (who will be in Towne to night) to prevail wth him to make his report in time. And 20 things at Kensington besides all this.

Your Grace will therfore See, tis neither in my power to Attend you as I moſt heartily wish I cou'd, nor to be in a Condition (in the present way I am) to be either entertaining or usefull to you if I cou'd come. But I hope a few days will save me from so much at leaſt of the Plagues I at present ly under That I may be ready to do any thing in the World you will command me who am

Dear Lord Duke
ever your Obedt & much Oblig'd Servt
JV

82

To his Grace
The Duke of Newcaſtle

Sunday Night

Your Grace is ever too good in giving your Self more trouble about me than I can possibly deserve

I wou'd wait upon you to Night to thank You for What you have had of late, but am not yet in time enough to Stir. This Anſtis is a sad thief, and has done juſt as I thought and said he wou'd; And therefore it was I so often reminded my Lord Stanhope, of Obliging him to give Security to the Bishop, to refund the Fees in Case his Patent was set Aside; And the laſt time I saw him at Kensington, (when he came out from the King), he told me time so preſt, there was no preventing his officiating, but for the Fees, he was to do as I desir'd, give Security to refund them. There was then nothing more for my Lord to do, but to write to the Bishop to take that Security, wch the Bishop told me, he wou'd be Sure to do, if he rec'd a Letter from my Lord, as I told him He wou'd. But for fear this Shou'd be forgot, I writ a Letter to my Lord Stanhope that evening to put him in mind of it. I'm sorry it was not done. For if we Vacate his Patent, (As my Councill now Seems very Sanguine in,) this money will all be loſt. As to his present demand of your Grace there can be no harm, if you please to tell him, you can give him no direct Answer, till you return out of Sussex For I have a good deal to say of this matter too long to write.

(97)

I don't however believe my Lord Berkley has paid him, nor that the Other two will. And your Grace may be assur'd, if his Patent be Void he has no more pretence to these Fees than your Coachman has. And therfore the Attorney Gen^{ll} told me tother day, I had done quite right, in getting the Kings Order for his giving Security to refund them. 'Tis very unlucky it was not Signify'd to the Bishop.

As to the tother unlucky affair, I am very far from taking any thing Amiss from my Lord Sunderland about it, for I can easily conceive it done as I have been told it was, And that it was not in his power to hinder it, without Such a sort of Struggle, as I shou'd never have thought reasonable (had I been privy to what was doing) to have engag'd him in. I therfore repeat, I take nothing Amiss from him, and thank him for the offer of his Friendship to me, on any proper Occasion. I am Sure I will never press him to any thing, I can't convince him is so. But I think when I have leave to talk a little to him, of this thing about the Stone, I shall Soon shew him, those who ſtarted the Objeċtion of a Monopoly, either did not at all Underſtand the Case, or else did it. in favour of the Person whose Intreſt it is, to prevent this Lease.

                                        Your Graces ever Oblig'd
                                              & Obed^t
                                              J VANBRUGH

83

[*To the Duke of Newcaſtle.*]

                                                          [*No address*]

I have reason to believe, the King has had such an unfair Account given him secretly of my Management, both of his Houses and Gardens; As muſt make me Appear a very bad Officer in the Employments he has been pleas'd to intruſt me with.

And I am inform'd, This Representation has been follow'd, with an Attempt to have me remov'd from his Service: And that this Attempt, is in a way of Succeeding.

All I beg is, That my Lord Sunderland will please to Obtain his Direction to the Treasury, To examin into the truth of my Conduċt; And to make an Impartial Report to him, how they find it. J VANBRUGH

84

[*To the Duke of Newcastle.*]

                                              Green^h: Mayday
My Lord Duke

I hope all paſt at Windsor, as it Shou'd do. And moſt heartily wish you joy, of your Inſtallation.

I am flead at this time with Bliſters So shall not be Able to come to Towne till the begining of the Week. I have therfore written a Letter

to Mr Benson, (of which I here trouble your Grace with a Coppy.) And beg you will add to all your Goodness, That, of assuring the King, I act the part I have profess'd in my paper deliver'd to him, Of submiting to his Pleasure without murmuring much less, Abating in my Zeal for his Service in my Capacity.   Your Graces ever Oblig'd
& Obed^t Ser^t J VANBRUGH

[To ——?]   85
May day

Your Letter of Saturday I had not till last night, being Out of Towne.

I here Send you the Design, both Plan and Upright for the Addition to the Porche of the Old House but am at a Cruell loss for something as a Clerk of the Works, to explain this And Other things to, as formerly to Smalwell. I Sent for Hopson to me this morning, And he assures me he has sent downe all the hands necessary So I hope all's easy, You'll give my most humble Service to my L^d D, And Lady Dutchess, from faithfully Yours

JV.

To Mr Forbes   86
  at Clarmont
    near Esher
      In Surrey.   *Greenwich. July ye 4*th 1718
Richmond Bagg
  S^r

Kynaston told me, you desir'd to know who the Person was, I design'd to Assign my Lord Dukes Bond to. It is Mrs Smalwell Mother to Smalwell the Joyner; I having an Account depending, with her Deceas'd Husband, (to whom She is Executrix.) which by reason of Quarrels and disputes amongst their family cannot yet be settled; but as I believe there may be about £500. due to them upon the Ballance, I am willing to let them have this Bond, on Acc^t: of so much money; wch can be of no disservice to my Lord Duke, since the time of its' being due, is lengthned to Two Years, instead of one. I did not however make any Step in it, till I had Spoken wth Dr Bowers, and had his opinion and Concurrence in it. But will not do any thing farther, till I hear from you whether you think of any Objections, that may lye to it; which I hope there are not. I am
S^r
Your real humble Servant
J VANBRUGH

If Mr Tonson be wth you pray tell him I was at his house at Barns. yesterday.

I am my Lord Dukes most Obed^t: Servant.

To his Grace   87
    The Duke of Newcastle,
        at Haland in Sussex

Whitehall. Aug^t: ye 7th 1718

My Lord Duke
    After returning your Grace most hearty thanks, for most Sweet
Venison, at the eating of which, Ladys, (amongst other folks) drank your
health; I am to acquaint you, That the Tate a Tate Club reviv'd last night,
at the Hercules Pillars Alehouse, in high Holborn There was Stinking
fish, and Stale cold Lamb for Supper with divers Liquours made of Malt
in an execrable Manner. We drank Your Graces health in them however
(Bumpers) to shew (to one an other) our great regards and respects to you.
And amongst many Material things in our Conversation, it was Nemine
Contradicente agreed, That Your Grace had writ a most Tyranical Letter,
to the Brigadier. And that altho, if he were not a Blockhead, Blockhead-
issime, he might see there was a fund of Love in the bottom of it, Yet it
had so hard an Outside, that a Man of a Moderate Understanding, might
have some Sudden thoughts of hanging himself upon it. In short, he is
of too great importance to our Board, to be parted with till Wednesday
evening at Soonest; Tuesday and Wednesday being days for passing
Monthly Accounts. If he do's not Attend your Grace in 24 hours after,
if you Please to hang him, the Tate a Tate say they have nothing to object.
So much for the Brigadier. As to the Club; one half of it designs to wait
upon you with the Brigadier And the tother half will do it very soon after
if the Devil will let him, who Seems to preside pretty much in his affairs
of late And holds him upon Some difficulty at this Moment. He'll do his
best however to pay his respects to your Grace, on whom he much relys,
for deliverance from all his troubles; And is with true Gratitude
                        Your ever Oblig'd &
                            most Obed^t humble Ser^t
                                J VANBRUGH

                        88
[To the Duke of Newcastle.]
                                August the 30th 1718

    My Lord Duke
        I fully design'd to have waited on Your Grace this day or tomorrow
at Halland; But (besides being more out of Order than ever,) I am Stopt
by Such a Turn of Our Board, as sets us at Our Witts end; And what
the result of it will be, I can't tell. Tho' my Ld Sun^d: has been so good
to me, as to Assure me of the Utmost of his Friendship: And indeed

I am far from having the least doubt of his good Intentions to me. I fear only, those same Letters de Cachet, that Surprise folks every now and then. I wou'd say a great deal to your Grace on this Occasion, were I so happy to be with you. the want of which, I don't look upon as the least of my present Misfortunes But I'm told you will soon be at Hampton Court, which I'm very glad of. In the mean time I most heartily rejoice with you, upon the destruction of the Spanish fleet Let the Torys and the Whigs in friendship with them, be as Angry as they please. Your Grace will See in the Thursdays evening Post, a Letter from Secretary Craggs to Monté Lioné, and his Answer. I'll acquaint you (if you don't know it already,) That What is there in Monté Lioné's Name, was sent to Mr Craggs, who only shew'd it to the King; wheras Lioné hop'd it wou'd have got abroad, but finding it was kept Snug, he form'd this Immaginary Letter from Mr Craggs, & So got them both printed. There will be a Smart Prosecution upon it. Tis reckon'd Lord Stanhope left the Court of Madrid, about three days before the News might arrive of the Ruin of their fleet. Albirone was so stout he wou'd not even consent to a Cessation of Arms I hope he'll Sing another tune now, for all the Torys contrive to make Stocks fall a Little. I once more wish your Grace at Hampton Court who am the most faithfull & Oblig'd of your humble Servants

J VANBRUGH

Ld Marlb: is recover'd. they had given him over. The Treaty is renew'd between the Attorney Genll: & Lady Betty Howard. & I think will be agreed.

To his Grace 89
The Duke of Newcastle
at Newcastle House in
Lincolns Inn Fields

My Lord Duke *Greenwich. Sept: ye 17th 1718*

The inclos'd is the very Petition Mrs Nolan deliver'd to the Regent, and the Answer is written in the Margin, That it shou'd be consider'd. I beg the favour of your Grace, to inclose it in a Letter to the Abbé du Bois, And only Acquaint him, That this Gentlewomans Distress, comes from her having Chang'd her Religion, which has made her Abbandon'd by her Friends; And that you desire he'll give her leave to wait upon him, to inform him farther of the Situation of her Small affairs, in which if he pleases to Aid her, you'll thank him.

Your Graces usual goodness, will excuse this Liberty in Your ever Oblig'd & most Obedt

Sert
J VANBRUGH

90

[*To the Duke of Newcastle.*]

Greenwich. Saturday

I was fully determin'd to wait on your Grace to Night at Claremount, & Attend you to morrow to Hampton Court, But must change that pleasure for the Comfort of a Blister, being cruell bad. I hope on Wednesday I may be Able to do what will be more Agreeable to Your Graces ever most Oblig'd & Obedient

J VANBRUGH

I have a Letter from Lᵈ Carlisle, He says Lady Morpeth is with Child, and Stays wᵗʰ him till Christˢ : He is very pressing with me to come downe, which I shall the more desire to do, that I may obey Yʳ Graces Commands at Nottingham as I go. But I have a sad head at this time, either for Business or Pleasure.

91

[*To the Duke of Newcastle.*]

Greenʰ: Sunday [Sept. 1718]

My Lord Duke

Last night I rec'd the News of poor Lord Suffolks death. My Lord Walden will be at London I believe to morrow Night, And in all probability will desire to be Deputy Marshall as his Father was. The Duke of Norfolk will be prevail'd on by Anstis, to endeavour it may be Lord Berkshire. His Character, yʳ Grace knows full well; And for that of the present Lord Suffolk, I may acquaint you that there is not a more zealous and Determin'd Whig in England. But very warm in his Temper, And 'twere pitty he Shou'd be dissoblig'd at the first Setting out; which I'm much affraid he wou'd be if Lᵈ Berkshire had the preference.

Besides, there is in that office, opportunitys daily, of Obliging Numbers of People which power one wou'd wish, in the hands of One, who will be sure to Oblige the Right Sort. Your Grace will please to Shew my Lord Sunderland what I take the Liberty just to mention, from the hearty wishes I have, that every thing may go in such a way, as to contribute to the Kings Service, for I have no particular Inᵗ: in this thing, worth the Naming; The dispute with Anstis, being now quite out of the Earl Marshals hand, And lying between the Crown and him. I am

Your Graces
most humble & most
Obedᵗ Servant

J VANBRUGH

If my Blisters will do me any good I'll wait on Your Grace very soon.

To his Grace   92
   the Duke of Newcastle.

Thursday Night

  My Lord Duke

    Mᵣ Howard (Uncle to Lᵈ Suffolk) came to me today, to beg I wou'd endeavour to get my Lord up by the Opening of the Session He said my Lord had firmly promis'd him to be up in few days after; but he much desir'd to have him here the first: Which he said he knew I cou'd do more towards, than himself or Any body, for he found I had most Credit with him. Upon which I have writ to him to Night and Send Your Grace a Copy of what I have said, which if you think proper, may be seen by Lord Sunᵈ: Stanhope or who you think fit.

    I shall be glad to find I have writ nothing but what they may approve of: at least I know they'll forgive me, Since they'll believe I do for the best. being most truly theirs, & Your Graces most Obedᵗ humble Servant.

J VANBRUGH

93
[Copy.]

[To the Earl of Suffolk.]

Whitehall Octᵣ. 30ᵗʰ. 1718

  My Lord

    Mᵣ Howard shew'd me to day, the Duke of Norfolks Answer to your Lordship: but I have some reason to believe, that matter is not however to be dispair'd of, I heartily wish Your Lᵈship wou'd resolve to hasten up to Town, Not only as I think it wou'd much Contribute towards the Carrying this point; but as I think likewise, it may prove of service to you perhaps for your whole life; For, give me leave My Lord to offer to your reflection, That there are very sharp eys, on a mans behaviour at his first Appearance upon the publick Stage. And tho' the King can have no ground to doubt your good disposition to his Service, and your Countrys in Generall; Yet the Manner of Your expressing it, will give it a Deeper or a shallower Impression upon him; And by Consequence, turn more or less to your own service and Interest. If his Enymys shou'd make an Atempt the first day the Parliamᵗ: meets. to throw some slurr upon him (as I have reason to conclude they will not fail to do, if they find a strength for it) he cannot but remember with some resentmᵗ:, those who by their Absence expos'd him to it. I therefore take the Liberty, very earnestly to beg Your Lᵈship, That for his Sake your Countrys and Your Own, You will not be away the first day. A warm and generous appearance at Your setting out, will incline the King and every body round him, to favour you in all reasonable things you may hereafter have to Ask; whereas the least Impression, of a Negligence or Lukewarmness, will be very hard to work off, Your L^dship will have the goodness to forgive ye freedome of Advice, since 'tis most truly intended for Your Service, by

Your Lordships most

humble & most obedient

Servant.   JV.

To his Grace   94
   The Duke of Newcastle.

Friday

   My Lord Duke

The Treasury has Order'd the State of the Expences of the Works to be examin'd, And I am doing all I can in the World, to get it done time enough to be laid before the King before he go's; which Sure will give him an Other Notion of my management in that Board than he has at present.

I am likewise preparing a Plain intelligible paper for him, by which he'll see, how the Expence arises to about £33000 p an^m. And by this paper he'll likewise See That if the Contract had gone on with Benson, he had not sav'd him one Shilling; So Vilely did that Gen^t: Impose upon the Treasury, by giving in false Accounts of every thing. I am Your Graces ever Obed^t & most Oblig'd humble Servt

J VANBRUGH

I have writ to Lord Stanhope, to desire he'll Speak to Our new Earl Marshall, Not to let Anstis put any tricks upon me; which he has Already Attempted; in a very Benson like Manner. I have dam'd luck to have two Such Fellows get over me. Pray my Lord, put Lord Stan: in mind of this bit of Friendship.

Lord Lindsay is come to Towne. I'm just going to him.

To his Grace   95
   The Duke of Newcastle
     at Claremont

Friday night late

I am extreamly glad your Grace is pleas'd, with what you find done, And I hope twill be no great Alay to your Contentment (for I am Sure it can be no Prejudice to your Works) that I am not Able to Attend you just at the time you name, tho' I will wait upon you soon enough for any

Service you can have to Comãnd me which Shall be either Sunday Night, or early on monday morning.

I am very proud of my Lady Dutchesses Approbation, And shall ever have a great deal of pleasure in doing any thing that can give her the least Satisfaction And I do assure both her and your Grace, That the dislike I had, to this peice of work in general, has been so far from making me move Idly or Sowerly about it, That I took a Resolution (from the time I found you wou'd not quit it) To try if 'twere not possible to fetch good out of Evill, by the Manner of doing, what I wish'd might never be done.

I rec'd the inclos'd Letter from my Ld Carlisle today.

I am Your Graces ever most Obed^t
& humble Servant
J VANBRUGH

I Apprehend being put more out of humour at this Rascally Board of Works, than ever.

To his Grace   96
   The Duke of Newcastle.

Greenwich. Nov. ye 29th 1718

My Lord Duke

I think I shall dispatch my affaires here on Monday, both Publick and particular; in Order to receive your Graces Commands for Nottingham by the Middle of the Week. But I can go with no Comfort if this Hamp^t: C^t: matter be not Granted or refus'd before I start. I therfore beg, You will with your wonted goodness, get my Lord Sun^d: to defer Speaking no longer, if he has not done it already. As likewise at the Same time, to receive the Kings Orders, for the Letter to the D of Ancaster. that I may take it with me, and make the most on't. Dear Lord Duke forgive Your ever Oblig'd & Obed^t Servt

J VANBRUGH

Mem^d: L'Abbè du Bois.

To his Grace   97
   The Duke of Newcastle in
      Lincolns Inn Fields, London.

Nottingham. Dec. ye 17th 1718

My Lord Duke

Twas horrible a day, as Storms, hail, Snow and the Divil can make it, I have been over your Castle, inside and out: and am glad I have Seen it at the worst. since it has not alter'd my Opinion of it at all: the Rooms being calm and warm, and all Still and quiet within doors. As to the Dehors, I find them capable, of a much better disposition both for me and

(105)

Beauty, than I ever thought on There being not only Space Sufficient for Stables & any other Out Buildings you shou'd ever have a mind to; but you may have as agreable a Castle Garden as you can wish, of near three Acres of ground, And this actually within the Castle Walls. & will lye just under the great Terrass, in a very right manner. The Park, is an extream pretty piece of ground, but is all to be planted. There may be a very Noble pond in it, with small Expence, And the Views from the upper part of it, are right good. The Castle stands more (and in a better manner) distinguish'd from the Towne, than I took it to do: and upon examination of an Old Servant, there, who has liv'd in it fourty Years, I don't find the Chimneys one quarter so faulty as they have been represented. And so upon the whole I think I may most reasonably congratulate your Grace on your being Master of this Noble Dwelling. Which I cannot but think, you will extreamly like when a little us'd to it. At first perhaps, you'll think it Stairs you in the face, wth a pretty Impudent countenance.

In my next letter, I shall be Able to say, what part of the Necessary repairs I think shou'd be put in hand before your Grace comes downe to live here: for at present, I think very little of the Masons Articles (in the Estimate sent you up, Some time Since,) shou'd be meddled with, it being of very great consequence to have them rightly concerted the wants of which I have Seen a sad experience of, in my way hither, and just in such a Case. I mean what has lately been done by the Duke of Rutland in the Outworks of his Castle: where for want of being rightly understood, the whole grace of them is lost: it looks all like pastboard work, and in reality, a great deal of it, is tumbling downe already. Those things will therfore be proper to consider well of when your Grace is here upon the Spot, and not in a hurry: And the execution of them, will not disturb you at all, as at Claremont; Here's space enough to be easy whilst those sort of Works are going on, which will prove an Amusement and entertainment to you. I wou'd therfore by no means advise your Grace, to force a journey hither now; for considering the short stay you can propose to make You will rather find your Self quite confounded, than Able to disgest and Comprehend things so, as to give any usefull directions: Besides; the ways are so execrable and the days so short, that I plainly find, by my own driving, (wch is none of the Slowest) you will Not get hither in less than four days: I therfore hope your Grace will resolve, Only to Order the Painting, Glazing Whitewashing and such things to go on; And leave the rest till I can attend you here in April or May And then; what is done, may be to the purpose. This at least is the Opinion I think I shall be in, when I write to you next post. All I have more to say is

This, That I am Your Graces most truly humble & Obed^t Servant

J VANBRUGH

(106)

98

To [The Duke of Newcastle.]

Castle Howard. Dec. ye 25. 1718

Your Graces Letter to meet you at Nott^m: tomorrow, I found here yesterday. And had been three days, getting from thence to York; through such difficultys as the Stage Coach cou'd not pass, which I left over set and quite disabled upon the way. There has now fallen a Snow up to ones Neck, to mend it, wch may possibly fix me here as long as it did at the Bath this time two Years: wch was no less than five Weeks. In short, tis so bloody Cold, I have almost a mind to Marry to keep myself warm, and if I do, I'm sure it will be a wiser thing than your Grace has done, if you have been at Nottingham. But I believe my second Letter to you, (with Dr Bowers prudent Advice) will have kept you Safe in Lincolns inn fields: from whence I shall desire to receive your Commands at Nottingham in my return to London: designing to Stop as long there, as may be any ways for your Service.

My Lord Carlisle says, if you come to Nottingham now, he believes you will never come there again: but if you stay till Spring, You will perfectly like it, and think you did quite a Right thing in fixing your Northern Seat there. He drinks your Graces health every meal And is as heartily dispos'd to your humble Servant, as any Acquaintance you have in the World; He thinks all the King has been doing is right, and seems to have no Small indignation towards those (Whiggs) who wou'd Obstruct his Measures. I rejoyce with your Grace most heartily, on the destruction of the Earl of Nottinghams Bill. I find many of the Clergy of this Country, dispos'd to be more drunk than ordinary this Christmass, to enable them to bear this Great Affliction with such humility as becomes the Cloath.
I am

> Your Graces ever truly humble
> And truly Obed^t Servant
> And hope the Dutchess of
> Newcastle and Mrs Pelham
> Will give me leave to
> profess my Self the Same
> to them

Pray my Lord tell the Duke of Kingston (& Mr Attorney) That by God I do not contribute to the keeping Ld Carlisle here one Moment. And my Lady Betty her Self, will one of these days I believe do me this justice. But he Swears he will have his Christmass out before he Stirs, tho the World and ten Weddings depended upon it.

I'm very glad I brought Ld Sund^s Letter, it was very well rec'd, and

I did my best to make the most on't. Both Father and Son are good in the Main. The latter will I believe be soon in Towne, and Vote right even in the Occasional Bill. The former has some Sighs and Groans about it. Tho to give him his due, not so much for fear of the Church, as for fear it shou'd not turn to the Kings Service so much as he wishes, and expects. He has however some difficultys upon him, in respect of his Country Intrest which is amongst the High flyers tho' he (with some difficulty) engages them in Elections, to vote for the Low. An Other point with him is, That he Voted with Ld Notting^m last time, and A Man of honour Shou'd not go backward & forward. I pleaded to this, That the matter was neither a point of honour nor Conscience, but purely political & discretional; and that if he consider'd it that way, he wou'd find the Same reason for Voting Against Ld Nott^m: now, that he did for voting with him heretofore: And so upon the whole, I left him I think in a Disposition, either to assist, or oppose very little; this good Bill.

I believe he'll let his Proxy lye for that was what I press'd him most upon, as the easyest to his Tender honour.

99

[*To the Duke of Newcastle.*]

Castle Howard. Jan y^e 4th 17$\underline{18}$
$$19$$

My Lord Duke

By a Letter from London this last post I find your Grace has really been at Nottingham Which my Lord Carlisle and I are both surpris'd at, and both wish you had not; being of opinion it may very probably have given you an Impress^n: of the Place, as may much abate what you hop'd for from it. However, there is this good in it, That you will now be better Able to concert upon the Plans, what may be right to do, in order to making it a more compleat dwelling. I hope your Grace had the last letter I writ to you which was in Answer to that I found from you here at my Arrival. And in which I acquainted you, I wou'd make what stay you shou'd think necessary at Nottingham, in my return; And desir'd I might have your instructions, in what you wou'd have me do there. If your Grace writes to me any time next Week, I desire your Letters may be directed to me, at the George Inn in York, for we shall all go there from home On this day Senight, Stop a day there, and so to Lord Irwins in Our way to Towne, where I shall be very glad to find your Grace, less frightned with the Nottingham Storms and Precipices than I apprehend. At least to encourage you, let me acquaint you, that this Place where I am now, has since I remember been Shiver'd at, when Nam'd for a Winter habitation. And yet, is now so very comfortable a One, that in this Sharp Season, there has not paſt a day, without setting Open Severall times, the door and Windows of the Room My Lord Car: and the Ladys conſtantly use; it has been so much too hot: And all the reſt of the house, is so in proportion. And so may Nottingham Caſtle be made, by the Same care and Methods.

I have a wild ſtrange Acc^t: of the rout my Friend and Superiour Officer, Benson, makes at The Treasury. I find poor Dartignonave scar'd out of his Witts about a Memoriall given in by Campbell and Benson the Young, to decry the Managements of former Boards, and exalt this precious New One. I have no Copy of this honeſt Mem^{ll}: so can say little to it from hence, but that I know of no fault I have committed that a Jurey in Weſt-minſter hall wou'd fine me half a Crown for. And so, having good reason to believe my Lord Sun^d: so much my Friend, that he will never Suffer me to be trickt into a Criminall I am Easy; Let me be but protected from any dark Stroaks in the Kings Closet, and I have nothing to fear To defend me from which, I know I may depend upon Your Graces usual kindness, And I have writ a Short Letter to my Lord Sun^d to beg the Continuance of his. My Lord Carlisle gives your Grace his moſt Sincere humble Service, he conſtantly drinks your health, and looks upon you now as a Neighbour, And hopes there may be a very agreeable correspondence between your Caſtle and his. I believe the Match with the Attorney will be soon adjuſted after the Lady Arrives. I am

Your Graces ever
Moſt Oblig'd & truly
Obed^t Ser^t
J VANBRUGH

We hear Lord Lonsdale has again voted againſt the Court, but don't know in what, for your Grace did not name him about the Proteſtant Bill.

I hear Ld Halifax designs to oppose the Kings intended favour to me, at Hamp^t: Court. which wou'd be a cruell ill Natur'd thing, if he cou'd do it, since to be Sure one wou'd not any way desire to make it a prejudice to him, But Y^r Grace heard what P. Walters said.

100

[*To the Duke of Newcaſtle.*]

York. Jan^y: ye 12th 1718/19

By hearing nothing from your Grace, since your Return from Notting-ham, I much fear I was right, in endeavouring to dissuade you from Seeing it, in Snow and Tempeſts. But considering how your time muſt have been taken up, since you got to Towne, I endeavour to hope the best, and that I may possibly have the honour of a Letter from you this Post.

Lord Carlisle and his Family will be here by and by, I came before them, a day or two. He treats severall of his Friends today at dinner, and afterwards, we all go to pay Our Respects to York, at the Assembly, Where the Ladys will muster Strong on this Occasion Lord Carlisle being the Idol here. And well deserves their Devotions.

To morrow we go on to Lord Irwins. If your Grace has not sent me your Commands Yet, You may still do it, if you please by thursdays post, directed for me at the George in York. After That, if I am to have any Orders from you, they must be sent to Nottingham, where I shall be Some time next week, And very happy if I can be of Any Service, that may please you.

Your Graces ever Oblig'd &

Obed^t Servant

J VANBRUGH

My congratulations are most hearty on all your Parliamentary Successes.

IOI

[*To the Duke of Newcastle.*]

Nottingham Jan^y: y^e 24th 17$\frac{18}{19}$

My Lord Duke

I have been very well pleas'd at my Arrival here to find, you were not so Angry with me but that you wou'd give me leave to make some Attonement, by future Service if I am Able. I have in Order to it, employ'd three days in Viewing every thing you have recommended to me; And tho' I may Appear the less significant to you for the future by owning you have done well without me I will however confess that truth; for I do not See any thing considerable, I wou'd have disputed with you, had I been present at your giving your Orders to the Mayor; And I am very glad I may tell your Grace, I find him in a very good way of executing them, especially in that one thing (of no Small weight with you) dispatch. for there is a very great progress made, And Your Castle will be fit for habitation, Sooner than One cou'd have immagin'd. I need mention nothing in particular of what I have given directions in, (which is little but the manner of doing things already Order'd) Since I shall be so soon in Towne to make my Report to your Grace in Person, I'll therfore say no more now, than to Express my great Satisfaction to hear the Middle of Winter has not discourag'd you, from thinking it practicable to live upon a Precipice a hundred f^t high. For as I have been the Instrument, of Your fixing on this Castle for your Northern Seat, I shou'd have been heartily concern'd to find you dissappointed in it. I have no care now left, but to See the Dutchess of Newcastle as well pleas'd wth it as your Grace is. I hope She won't have the less expectation from my Judgment in Chusing a Seat, from my having chosen a Wife, whose principall Merrit in my Eye, has been some small distant shadow, of those Valuable Qualifications in her, your Grace has formerly with so much pleasure heard me talk of.

The honour she likwise has, of being pretty nearly related to the Dutchess gives me the more hopes I may not have been mistaken. If I am, 'tis better however to make a Blunder towards the end of ones Life, than at the begining of it. But I hope all will be well; it can't at least be worse than most of my Neighbours which every Modest Man, ought to be content wth: And So I'm easy.

I had promiss'd to join Lord Carlisle & his Family two days since at Stamford, but found too much to do here, to keep my word. I hope however to get to Towne before the end of next week, and will immediately wait upon your Grace, whose most humble & most faithfull Servant I shall always be, whether a Married Man or a Batchelour.

J VANBRUGH

Jacob will be frightned out of his Witts And his Religion too, when he hears I'm gone at last. If he is still in France, he'll certainly give himself to God, for fear he shou'd now be ravish'd by a Gentlewoman. I was the last Man left, between him and Ruin.

To Jacob Tonson
in Paris.   102

London. July ye 1st 1719

Here has been so great a Slaughter of your old Friends since you went, I wish those who are left may have share enough in your Affections, to encline you to think of England with any pleasure.

I don't know whether you'll reckon me amongst the first or the last, since I have taken this great Leap in the Dark, Marriage. But tho' you should rate me with the former, I know at least you would be glad to know how 'tis in this (perhaps) your future State: For you have not forgot it ever was agreed, if I fell, you'd tremble. Don't be too much dismay'd however, for, if there be any truth in Married Man, (who I own I have ever esteem'd a very lying creature) I have not yet repented. Thus far, 'tis possible you may believe me; if I offer at more, 'tis like you won't; so I have done. Only this; That I am confirmed (as far as Six months practice goes) my Old Opinion was right; That whatever there was of good or bad in Marriage; it was fitter to end Our Life with, than begin it.

(111)

THE LETTERS

I don't know how to reproach you for not writing to me, Since you might give me my Reproach again; But I have very often enquired at Shakespeare head how you did, and what you did, And more than Once, have found my Self so far from a Slave, that I have dar'd to own I Wish'd my Self with you, for eight and fourty hours: for you must know, whatever evils Marriage may design me; it has not yet lessen'd one grain of my Affections to an old Friend. And as to the Place you are in; I am so far from being disgusted to it, by the treatment I once met with That I think that very thing (at least the Occasion of it) has doubled a Romantick desire, of Seeing it again. In short; I have it so much in my thoughts; that I have talk't even my Gentlewoman into a good disposition of being of the Party if things will fall kindly out for it, next Spring. In the meantime, I hope you'll make a Winter Trip to England; and after being a little pleas'd with some folks, and very weary of others, you'll find your Self ready for a fresh Expedition.

I lately went to make my Ld Cobham a Visit at Stowe. where he is very well, and in very good humour: and much entertain'd with (besides his Wife) the Improvements of his House and Gardens, in which he Spends all he has to Spare. I took Blenheim in my way back, not with any affection, (for I am thoroughly wean'd) but some curiosity, the Dutchess of Marl^b: having taken a Run at last to finish in earnest; which (tho in no good or gracefull manner) She has advanc'd so far; that in less than a Month it will be fit to receive the Duke, who is at Windsor Lodge, 'till 'tis ready for him. He is in point of health, much as usual; and I doubt, not likely ever to grow better. She is likewise in point of vigour as she us'd to be, and not very likely to grow worse.

I din'd yesterday here in Towne, with the Duke of Newcastle; who talk'd very much of you, (as he often do's) and your health and good return was drunk. The Brigadier is at the Old Rate, Storm and Sunshine. He was e'en gone tother day; but the Ladys stood his Friends, and made all up. The Duke has fitted up and furnish'd Nottingham Castle, and designs to go there in August.

I have nothing to say to you of State affairs, the Spirit of that Conversation being all sunk with the Queen. We are so quiet, the whole Regency had fallen asleep, if it had not been for a few Highlanders and Weavers.

I believe my Brother Charles is coming home thorough France; he'll probably Stop a little at Paris, where I hope you'll drink a Chopine together. If you'll let me hear from you, Say what you will, your Letter will be as welcome as ever to Your faithfull Old Friend & Servant

J. VANBRUGH

Claremont

Buildings

103

[*To the Duke of Newcastle.*]

London. July y^e *23*rd *1719*

My Lord Duke

Tho I have not writ sooner to your Grace I neglected nothing in your Service. And as the fixing a Mason, was the thing that press'd most, I sent for Cash from Cannons (where he was at Work) and engag'd him, in Case I shou'd want him. I then explain'd matters with Kidwell: And finding there was really nothing in his declining the Work, but the fear of offending you, by not getting ready in time. I told him he shou'd yet do it if he cou'd find means: Upon which he exerted; got Men proper for his business, and next day, chearfully undertook it.

I had in the Mean time (that none might be lost) prepar'd the Designs, So put his part into his hands And yesterday he was with me, to give me an Account in how good a way he was of Advancing. So that I believe the delay will not be, where I most apprehended But rather in clearing away for the foundations. the account of which I leave to the Brigadier, to whom I must (en passant) do this Justice, that he bestirs himself like a Great Officer, As if he resolv'd to be well with you, whether you will or no.

As for my Self, nothing shall be wanting on my Side, to forward the Work, and to have it as right design'd and well done, as I am capable of, And in Order to it, I shan't fail to go to Claremont, the Moment there is room for the Foundations, And I hope as soon as the Walls are got a little way up, Your Grace may have a mind to run over for a day. I cou'd not be there, to get drunk upon your Birthday, for which I ask pardon; but have eat your Venison here in Towne today with Mr Walters (shou'd have been) &c and wish'd you a long Life, and that you may not repent of laying out more money in Building at Claremont for I shou'd be mighty glad every thing you do, might turn to your Pleasure, without allay: being with very great Sincerety   Your Graces ever
most Oblig'd and Obed^t
humble Servant
J VANBRUGH

I have just now an Account, That a Gentleman newly Arriv'd from Paris, actually Saw Friend Jacob in a Frock.

104

[*To the Duke of Newcastle.*]

Whitehall. Aug^t: *y*^e *6*th *1719*

I rec'd your Graces Commands of the 3^d. Mr Bensons Reign ended next day. But Mr Hewets Patent not being yet past (tho' passing) we have no Board. So that nothing can yet be done about the Gateway, but preparatory. In the mean time I may Observe to your Grace, that I find many people Surpris'd there shou'd be no other Expedient found to make way for Coaches &c, than destroying One of the Greatest Curiositys there is in London as that Gate has ever been esteem'd, and cost a great Sum of money the Building; And so well perform'd, that altho' now above 200 Yrs Old, is as entire as the first day. The Chancellr: of the Excheqr: said much of this to me last night being entirely of Opinion it ought not to be destroy'd, if an other Expedient can be found And there is a very easy one, with Small Expence Which is, To Open the Wall of the Privy Garden, near Lord Rochesters, And turn the Passage thorough a Slip of that wast ground Coming out into the Street again, between Mr Vanhulfio's And the Banquetting house. I know of no Objection to this, And by this Means, Both Lord Stanhope & the Comptroller will be ten times more reliev'd and Accomodated than by pulling the Gate downe. If Your Grace thinks this right, there is time enough to propose it to my Ld Stanhope, Since either this way, or pulling downe the Gate, the end desir'd may be Accomplish'd, in a Months time, whenever tis gone About.

I came to Claremt: on Saturday last, just after Mr Forbes was gone: which I gave yr Grace an Acct: of, in a Letter from thence but by Accident, I find it did not get to London to be put in the Post that Night. I desire to go there again on Sunday to stay two or three days, And I have a Wife, that says She thinks she'll go along with me, Never having Seen that place in Beauty.

I well remember all that was agreed upon in relation to thickness of Walls &c. And 'twas to See that Article of the Walls right, I went on Saturday, the Foundations being then just begun. The Sashes I have directed of the Strongest kind, And yr Grace may depend on me for the rest, for from the time you quite resolv'd you wou'd have this thing done I quite resolv'd to Serve you as well as I cou'd in the doing it.

Jacob is not in a Frock, as was most positivly affirm'd. I here inclose a loving Letter I have from him (the Copy of it) & I can Assure your Grace, the good luck he has had there, in purchasing in the New Company Amounts (if he Sells now) to Ten Thousand pounds proffit to him. This I hear from my Brother; And his Nephew own'd to me yesterday 'twas true; And that he has Advis'd him to Sell.   I am

Your Graces ever most
Obedient Servant
J VANBRUGH

I'm sorry my Project of the Reversion won't do, 'Tis a very hard matter for me to find out any thing, 'till 'tis over late to ask for't; but they know of every thing time enough to help their humble Servants. (without their

Aid) when they are quite determin'd to take care of them. Which is Hewets Case now, and was once before, when Lᵈ Halifax made him Surveyʳ: of the Forreſts, without his ever dreaming of it. I resolve to live in hopes My Lᵈ Sunᵈ: will do the Same by me to help this Pill downe, which is a little Bitter, now I come juſt to the time (and disgrace) of Swallowing it. I don't however Blame any body, nor think them wanting. But 'tis one of the hardeſt pieces of Fortune, that ever fell to anybody. Of which there need be no other proof, than the Report the Auditors have made to the Treasury relating to what they find of the Expences in the Office of Works Which Report Allows what I set forth of having reduc'd the Charge, Above Ten Thousand pounds a Year. One wou'd have thought there needed nothing more, to determine the King, whether I had been an Expensive Officer or a Sparing One.

105

[*To the Duke of Newcaſtle.*]

[*No address*]

Altho it is moſt certain, I have not been faulty, in any one thing that has been Suggeſted to the King againſt me, in respe็t to his Buildings; And that all his prejudice to me in that way, is founded on pure misinformation: Yet Since it may be difficult for those who honour me with their Friendship, to remove the notions he has receiv'd, and to Obtain the Surveyours Place for me, I won't desire, to engage them, in so much trouble upon my Account.

But, as it muſt be a Cruell Reflec๙tion upon me in the World, if, in putting an Other into that Station, I have not some mark of the Kings favour, to Shew, his not being inclin'd to make me his Surveyour, dos not proceed from any General dissatisfa็tion of me I wou'd humbly beg, That he wou'd please to Grant me, What I now have, for Life.

And, that the Person he thinks fit to make Surveyour, may make me some Compensation by money, Which, I have been honeſt enough in my Station, to ſtand very much in need of.

106

[*To the Duke of Newcaſtle.*]

London. Augˡ: yᵉ 11ᵗʰ 1719

Your Graces Letter of yᵉ 9ᵗʰ, I have found at my Return from Claremont. If the Saving of the Gate, muſt Start a New brangle with Boscawen, let it go; else I wou'd give as much money for it, as the making a way thorough the Garden wou'd come to, and so put the King to no expence at all. Besides, the making a way through the Garden, wou'd really be of great use, in the Service intended; the other, will be of Some, but not much. Your Grace Shall have an Acc^t: of the expence you require, as soon as ever we have a Board which will be in a Week.

What I mention'd of my hard luck was far from being meant, any Sort of Complaint either of your Grace, or those Others you Name, who I am entirely Satisfied, do bear me all good will, and do neither Trick me, nor neglect me. There is nothing your Grace has said, in stating my Small affairs, but what is just and true; And I have (in my own thoughts) never once Stated them otherwise So that I have no Other meaning, in what I say about them, but to set forth my ill Fortune by way of a little Vent for ease. But I am not one of those, who drop their Spirits, on every Rebuff: if I had, I had been under ground long ago. I shall therfore go on; in hopes Fortune will one day or other, let those help me, who have a mind to it: And that as I am past over, where my Pretentions are good, And I cou'd be of Use; I may chance to be taken notice of, where my Pretentions Are nothing, And I can be of no Service at all.

I think however at present, I need not trouble your Grace to write any thing to my Ld Sund^d: Nor to read any thing more of this matter, but my most gratefull thanks, for all the kind Expressions of Friendship you have in this last Letter made use of.

I have been two days at Claremont, but not en Famille, a Bit of a Girle popping into the World, three months before its time. And so the business is all to do over again.

I found nothing aMiss at Clarem^t: all going on right, and as fast as is advisable; For I don't think it wou'd be Safe, to have the Walls up to the top, before the Middle of October at Soonest. I design to go there again in a few days, and will keep a Constant eye upon the Advance of the Walls, for there may easily be unlucky Accidents in it, the Length & height being so great; No Cross walls to Steddy it & a mixture of Stone And Brick, which don't Sett equally. But all may be well, with Care Which I will therfore be sure to take, to the best of my Skill. I am

Your Graces most Obed^t
humble Servant
J VANBRUGH

107

To his Grace, the Duke of Newcastle.
    at Haland. near Lewis
        In Sussex   *Augt ye 15th 1719*

This letter is only to acquaint your Grace, wth a Strange affair, if true. That Thornhill has been recommended by Benson, as a properrer Man for Survey^r: of the Works, than Mr Hewet and that there is a Great Struggle for him. I did indeed hear Six weeks ago, That he (Thornhill) was got to be very great with the Dutchess of Marlborough And that his endeavours were to be Survey^r: by letting her find her Account, in work he wou'd do at Blen^h: but I gave no sort of Credit to it. And how to think there can really be any thing in it now, is very hard, And yet I have it from Such hands, that I doubt there's too much mon$\int$trous truth in't. But what part my Ld Sun^d: takes, I don't hear said; tho' I think 'tis impossible he can Suffer such a thing to pass.

Twou'd be a pleasant Joke to the World, to See a Painter made Surveyor of the Works, in Order to Save money; When all the Small knowledge or ta$\int$t they ever have of it, is only in the Great expensive part, As Collumns, Arches, Bass reliefs &c which they ju$\int$t learn enough of, to help fill up their Pictures. But to think, that Such a Volatile Gentleman as Thornhill, Shou'd turn his thoughts & Application to the duty of a Surveyors business, is a Mon$\int$truous project. I'm told, (besides the Dutchess of Marl^b) there's something come from Abroad in favour of it, which is reckon'd the way Benson has work't, And 'tis Supposed is to have money for it himself from Thornhill as well, as to get Some, for Somebody else.

I'm so Sick of this Rhidiculous Story I can write no more on't, nor of any thing else this bout, but Vex'd or pleas'd Shall always continue Your Graces mo$\int$t

Obedient Servant
J VANBRUGH

108

[*To Lord Sunderland? or Stanhope?*]

London. Sep^t: y^e 10th 1719

My Lord

When I troubled y^r L^{d}ship with a Letter the 25th pa$\int$t in relation to Mr Hawksmoors being a Comiss^r: of the Board of Works; I did not know there was ground for any doubt of his being re$\int$tor'd to the Station Mr Benson turn'd him out of, if his Fate was so hard, to dissappoint him of the other.

But having some late reason to apprehend, Mr Hewet (after ten thousand Assurances to me, of his Friendship to him) may endeavour to promote an Acquaintance of his, at his expence: I cannot help being mov'd with a good deal of Resentment, that I shou'd meet with no better a return, to the pains your Lordship knows I have taken, to procure his being Survey^r:

I mu$\int$t therfore beg leave to Apply to your L^{d}ships Friendship and Support on this Occasion, That I may not Appear so low, and Inconsiderate to all about me as I mu$\int$t do, if they See he may treat me, with so little Regard.

(117)

I don't in the least desire to invade or Clip, the Rights of his Office, And therfore do own, when a Clarkship of the Works falls, 'tis in him, to put in another with the Approbation of the Board. And he has accordingly, already Supply'd One Vacancy, with a very Vile Fellow. But this is not the present Case. Here is no Vacancy, but what the King or Treasury shall please to make, by removing those Clarks, Mr Benson (by a trick alone) got in, And who are no ways qualifyed to continue.

I therfore hope, your L'ship will think it wou'd be very hard those Men (Mr Hawksmoor especially) so Unjustly turn'd out by Benson; shou'd have the double Misfortune of being kept out by him who Succeeds him. Especially, when it is consider'd, they were planted there, Not by Sr Christ^: Wren, but by the Kings Express Sign Manual.

If any of them, have forfeited his Favour I shall not become their Advocate. All they ask of me, to Interceed for, is, That if they are Accus'd of any thing; they may have the Common Justice of being heard.

My Lord, the reason I have to fear, Mr Hewet will not Stir to protect them, (that he may have the Introducing of Others) makes me take the Liberty of Saying this Short State of their Case before you, To which, I will only add: That if Mr Hewet sees, I have not Credit enough, to prevail in Such a Point I shall have a very Scurvy time with him: But I hope your Lordship will not let me have that weight to the rest of my ill Fortune.

I most heartily Congratulate y^r Lordship, on the Success of all things Abroad; no body more heartily wishing, you Ease and Happyness at home than   Your ever
Most Obedient humble
Servant
J VANBRUGH

If your L^d ship has reasons unknown to me against a Sign Manual, to restore in general the Clarks turn'd out by Mr Benson; I beg leave to interceed at least for One, who is my Own Clark, and has been employ'd by me, these fifteen Years. His name is Thomas Kynaston. He was Clark of the Works, of the Tower, And Somerset house, And remov'd only to make room for those Mr Benson lik'd better.

I Acquainted Mr Aislaby today, With what I now write to your Lordship, who makes no sort of Objection to it.

To his Grace,   109
  The Duke of Newcastle

Whitehall. Wednesday

Your Grace may be assur'd, it is quite Impossible to Settle every Small thing so, as that the Workmen mayn't have occasion to Ask many Questions: And, their fault is, generally to neglect asking. Dagley is therfore to be Commended for desiring explanation, Which the enclos'd Draught will give him. And he will See, that the Tablet is design'd only to give the Middle break, a few Shillings worth of diſtinction. The Other Windows have all the respect paid them that's due to their Quality, I Speak in a Stile, I reckon he'll like.

Tho' I design to wait on your Grace some where or other to morrow; Yet, leſt I shou'd by any Accident miss you, I'll take this Occasion to Beg, You will let Hewet know, I shew'd You all his Letters. and what I writ to him. And I shou'd be mighty glad, you cou'd find it agreeable to let him See, You think the great Friendship I have practis'd towards him, and the Benefit he receives by it, Shou'd give me a much greater Claim upon him than what I desir'd about a Clark of the Works. He will to this, Answer you in flourishes And Words of no Sincerity, nor indeed, no plain meaning, Which I hope your Grace will let him know, don't pass at all upon you. But unless you tell him so plainly, he'll think they do. for that's always his presumption, that he can wheedle and blind any body. If he says, he Cou'd not have Serv'd Hawksmoor if he wou'd That don't excuse him In the point of friendship or Gratitude to me; because your Grace saw by what he writ, he was resolv'd not to do it tho' he cou'd. Upon the Whole; if he thinks his Shuffling and Cutting, and Professions of friendship to me, pass upon your Grace; he'll think he has me downe, and will venture to Act Yet worse by me, than he has done. But if he Sees, he can neither impose on you nor me He'll perhaps keep his Roguerys a little within Bounds.

I am Your Graces ever Obedient

I'll talk with Kidwell.

J VANBRUGH

To his Grace
The Duke of Newcaſtle.

110

Greenwich. Sunday

I hear your Grace was pleas'd to Storm my Caſtle yeſterday: I hope next time you'll be so Gallant to let me know of your Design, which if I do, I'll endeavour to give you a Warmer Reception.

I can't get to Towne till to morrow night And therfore, leſt poor Hawksmoor shou'd Suffer by my Absence, I beg leave to put his Short Case and Requeſt into your hands now; fearing Somebody or other of the Treasury may chance to Speak early to my Lord Sunderland, for that Small Office of Clark Engrosser, wᶜʰ is but juſt £120 a Year, having no manner of Perquisites attending it. I shall bring the Sides of the Great Room at Claremᵗ: with me, fair Drawn.

Yʳ Graces ever Oblig'd &
Obedient
J VANBRUGH

a Monsr Jacob Tonson,
  chez Monsr Cou{s}telier, Libraire,
    Quay des Augu{s}tins, a Paris.

III

Whitehall, Nov: ye 5th 1719

I rec'd a very welcome and very kind letter from you, some time ago; and was, I do assure you, as heartily pleas'd as any friend you have in the world, with the lucky hit you mention'd in it. The great increase of that good fortune since, is a{s}tonishing to everybody here; and I find some of our keene{s}t men in money matters, who went to Paris two months since, appear {s}till as much at a loss as ever, for a good foundation to this prodigious rise of {s}tock, and say, that those who are allow'd the mo{s}t skillful in things of this nature among{s}t the French, {s}tand only gazers on, but meddle with nothing. I can't however doubt, but you know well what you do, which I mo{s}t truly wish, and that you may bring all your good luck, and all your usual good health, to your ancient seat at Barns, where I shall have much pleasure in talking over your adventures.

I was lately (en famille) downe at Culford, where I cannot say we drank your health, but to your memory; for we believed what the news said of you. I won't say what I cou'd, on the concern I felt on that occasion, le{s}t you shou'd lessen the opinion you always seem'd to have of my sincerity. But this I will assure you, that I have plainly seen, you wou'd not have been dropt as Mainwaring was. I return'd to London, before I knew you were {s}till among{s}t us. I dare say you'll believe the surprise was a pleasing one. I went the next day to Claremont, where you may imagine there was much talk about you: and I do assure you, with no small regard and affection from everybody. Mr Spence was there, who gave us a very agreable and friendly account of you, and joined very heartily with us, in drinking round your health and your return.

I am much oblig'd to your good wishes, in my matrimonial {s}tate; and encourag'd by your opinion that it may possibly do me as much good, as it has mischief to many a one we know, I'll give you however no other account of it till we meet, than that, I have a good humour'd wife, a quiet house, and find myself as much dispos'd to be a friend and servant to a good old acquaintance, as ever.

Yours Entirely,
J. VANBRUGH.

112

[*To the Duke of Newca{s}tle.*]

Whitehall. Nov. y⸳ 23th 1719

My Lord Duke
Having ju{s}t now had an Acc{t}: from the Ma{s}ter of Pauls, that D{r} Thorpe, Prebendary of Canterbury is dead, I have writ to my L{d} Stanhope,

And trouble your Grace with a Copy of my Letter, You having lately told me, you wou'd be so good to Assist in Obtaining Something for a Man who so very well deserves it; for if Such Men pass unregarded, there's Small encouragement for their Pupils, to mind what they say to 'em. And he has now 300 Scholars under his Care, And uses the Same endeavours, as formerly in the Queens time, to give them right Impressions of the Government they ought to stand by.

Your Graces ever Obed^t

What I have writ, is this.

J VANBRUGH

[*To Lord Stanhope.*]   113

My Lord

Tis possible your L^dship may remember I have Several times apply'd to you and my Lord Sun^d: Since the Kings coming to the Crown, in favour of the head Master of Pauls School, Mr Ascough.

And I represented to you, That in the worst of times, he distinguish'd himself in so extraordinary a Manner, for the Service of the Present Establishm^t: That he took constant pains to instruct his Scholars in Right and Sound Principles; Which he labour'd to that degree, As to put them on Certain days in the Year, Upon Publick Exercises, on the Subject of the Protestant Succession in the House of Hanover And the Meritorious Services of the Duke of Marl^b: At which Exercises, Numbers of Persons Need to be Present; and many of the Tory Clergy express'd great Indignation at them.

Several Bishops (now in the best repute) having join'd, by Certificates and Otherwise, in the Character I formerly gave your L^dship and my Ld Sun^d: of this honest deserving Man: you were both pleas'd to promise me, Something shou'd be done for him either by a Dignity or good Living: he, as yet, having neither, tho' above 60 Years Old.

He just now Acquaints me, Dr Thorpe Prebendary of Canterbury, is dead. And begs I wou'd apply to your L^dship in his favour, that he may Succeed him Which I most heartily wish he might, for encouragement of honest Men, in such usefull Stations, as Masters of Great Schools. Your L^dship can say, so much more to your Self on that Subject, than I can offer you, That I need add no more. I am &c

114

[*To Jacob Tonson in Paris.*]

Whitehall. Nov: ye 29th 1719

This is in return to a hearty kind Letter from you, of the 14th Inst: Everything you said in it, was very Agreable to me. But I had one

(121)

Sensible pleasure from the whole, wch no Letter from you, ever gave me before. it was; From Reflecting on the Change, between mourning a Friends Death, and afterwards receiving a Living Epistle from him.

I hear my Ld Burlington is arriv'd, and design (on what you say to his Advantage) to go and wait upon him. I wish you had been enough in Strength, to have accept [*sic*] his offer, of a Place in his Coach; Tho' I suppose your affairs wou'd have oblig'd you, to return again to Paris in a little time. One Seldome hears you nam'd, (since the good fortune that has attended you there) but the Question is Started, How it will opperate upon you, in your way of Living; And various opinions I observe about it What my own has been, you'll hear when you come over; But I observe in your Letter One Strong Symptome of my being right; Since you are so far from forgetting your old Mistriss, Barnes that you intend to Compliment her in the Spring, with £500. for a New Pettycoat. For my part, I think she deserves it, for the Pleasure she has given you And I heartily wish her well, for those she has spar'd me. When I have met with Witty Jokers, I have always Supported her, as I did other agreables. Her Charms don't lye in her Beauty, but her good Conditions. She feels better than She looks, and what she wants in her Eyes, She has in her Commodity. And thence it was, I always found a Tate a Tate more pleasing with you there; than I should have done at Blenheim, had the house been my own tho' without my Lady Marlborough for my Wife. For one may find a great deal of Pleasure, in building a Palace for another; when one shou'd find very little, in living in't ones Self.

I desire to make no such Correction of your Manners as to Stifle one of your Jokes upon Matrimony: for tho' the Chain shou'd happen to hang a little easy about me, (by a sort of Messissippy good fortune); I shall always think of my Neighbours as I us'd to do. And if I shou'd Chance at last, to come in for a share of their dissappointments, I don't know, whether I cou'd not rouze up a Little, give the matter a new turn, and reckon, when my Joke was thrown into the Funds, I had a better Tytle, to a Little merryment upon the Stock, than before. At least, thus I always thought I cou'd do, or I had never Wedd. But more of that, if it comes to the Tryal; I have only now to tell you, My Wife returns your Compliments. She says she's Sorry she has not a Sister for you; but she knows them that have. And if you'll give her Commission, She'll answer for't, to provide at least as well for you, as she has done for me. She desires I'll tell you farther, That I have said so much to her of you, while you were alive, after you were dead, and Since you are alive again, That she knows you well enough, to desire to know you better, and therefore accepts of your dinner at Barnes, and of your promise, to accept of hers at Greenwich where she will treat you with the best of her Good (Yorkshire) Houswifry

& if you will make one at cards as I understand you have often done, with much finer Ladys then I am I give you my word that I will neither cheat nor wrangle. Yr Sernt

Hariot V.

I shew'd Mr Secretary Craggs what you writ to him he returns you his Compliments, and Seems much dispos'd to be your Friend and Servant. His father I have not yet Seen, tho' he is become my Neighbour at Greenwich, having newly bought a house there.

I have yet, only Seen your Nephew for a moment. I shall make all the enquiry I can of purchaces for you and give him notice of them as you desire. Peter Walters tells me of one, which he says a great deal in Commendation of. 'Tis Lady Mohuns Estate, in and about Gerrard Street. £300 a year, in present Possession, and £3500. after a Term of thirteen years the Purchase about £30000. But I don't know, whether you mayn't incline more to a Country Purchace, than a Towne one.

I'm much oblig'd for the advice you give me, to dispose of Some money, where you have Succeeded so well. And 'tis not out of fear, I do not follow it. But to tell you the Truth; I have no money to dispose of. I have been many years at hard Labour, to work thorough the Cruel Difficultys, that HayMarket undertaking involv'd me in; notwithstanding the aid, of a large Subscription Nor are those difficultys, quite at an end yet. Tho' within (I think) a tollerable View.

I have likewise had a very hard Disappointment of not being made Surveyour of the Works; Which I believe you remember, I might have had formerly, but refus'd it, out of Tenderness to Sr Chr: Wren, And I have a farther misfortune, of losing (for I now see little hopes, of ever getting it) near £6000. due to me for many years Service, plague and Trouble, at Blenheim, Which that wicked Woman of Marlb: is so far from paying me, that the Duke being Sued by some of the Workmen for work done there, She has try'd to turn the Debt due to them, upon me. for which I think, she shou'd be hand'd. But I have been so long us'd, to attacks of fortune, of these kinds; and found my Self able to bear up against them, That I think I can do so Still, tho' they cost me Some Oathes and Curses, when I think of them: Which to prevent (it being Sunday) I'll say no more of them now

Since I writ thus far, I have seen your Nephew again, and told him of the Gerrard Street Estate. I find him much concern'd at your Stay, thinking if you were here, you wou'd be better advis'd about the Methods for reestablishing your health, And that it wou'd be easyer for you, to follow them. If that be the Case, COME AWAY. Yours ever

J. VANBRUGH

[*To Jacob Tonson in Paris.*]

Whitehall. Dec: 31ᵗʰ 1719

I have been out of Towne some time, but writ you before I went, to thank you for a very kind and Wellcome Letter, on all Accounts, I had rec'd from you, of the 14th November. I doubt whether you had mine, Your Nephew telling me this morning, you had not mention'd it to him, in those he has lately rec'd from you. There was no business in't however, So if you han't, you have mist nothing, but the Repetition of a few friendly congratulations, and a Line or two of my Wife's, to accept of your invitation to a dinner at Barns when you come over; which I'm glad to find by your Nephew, may probably be in a month.

The Duke of Newcastle is in Sussex for the Christs: I must do him the justice to say, he loves you well enough, to be downe right in some concern; when in your Letters to me, you happen not to mention him; for he really has a great regard to you, in a Serious, as well as merry way; and on the former head, we have very often talk'd of you. The Brigadier has had some terrible Ruffles since you went; But the Ladys are (in Compassion to his Infirmitys) very usefully his Friends, Not but that the Duke, has now and then some small Bowells towards him, but not half what he wants, for his Distempers increase, both in Number and Strength.

The Little Collonel has been some months, in worse disgrace, than ever the Brigadʳ: was, and I don't know whether he'll ever recover his Station again. The Case was, his Breaking out one drunken night at Haland, like Clitus at the Banquet, In short, he attack't his Chief; allow'd him his Virtues but Claw'd him off upon his Vices, of which, he made a Vast over ballance in the account; The Company wou'd have Stopt his Carrier, but in Vain; nor cou'd they pull him from the Table, So his Grace quitted his Stead and not so drunke but he remembered every word next morning, and discharg'd the Colˡ: his house. He has not however, turn'd him out of his Place of Secretary which Employment perhaps, you don't know he ever was in. But the Duke brought it about for him a good while Since, and Sr John Stanley has a Pension instead. I wish I may find means to change my Place in the Board of Works for something else, being very uneasy in it, from the Unparralel'd Ingratitude of the present Surveyʳ, Hewet: who owes his coming in, entirely to me, and that, in so known a manner that he has not the Confidence to deny it to anybody, But he's a Son of a Whore, and I'll trouble you no more about him.

I know no State Matters worth writing, but when you come over, you'll be astonish'd to see, the Low'ring Venom, that hangs in the Countenances of the Male Content Whiggs; The Success of the Foreign Negociations, upon the prosperity of our arms, they cannot bear with common decency;

The Torys Seem good Friends, in Comparison wth them and (in the present juncture) I really believe, are less embitterd Enemys. However, I see no great fear of any extraordinary mischiefs from these ill tim'd broyles, tho' I doubt many good things will be Slipt which are not to be hop'd for in common Reigns. But perhaps the want of them may neither disturb you at Barns, nor your humble Servant at Greenwh. And so let us be easy.

116

[*To Jacob Tonson in Paris.*]

London. Feb. ye 18th 1719/20

Tho' your Nephew tells me, you'll be soon here I take it for granted you may meet with such delays, as may give you time to receive an answer to the last Letter I had from you, Which so pleas'd the Duke of Newcastle, that he took it from me, to shew the Dutchess, Mrs Pelham &c and said he wou'd write three Sides of a Sheet in answer to it, and then give it me to fill up the fourth. He has not however found time to do it yet, but every day says he will.

Our South Sea, is become a Sort of a Young Messissippy, by the stocks rising so vastly; I am however only a looker on, and a Rejoycer, not an Envyer, of other peoples good Fortune. In particular my Brother (who was with you at Paris) who had about £5000 there, which is now near doubled. People in general are much pleas'd with the Parlementary Scheme lately started. But Sr R. Steel is grown such a Malecontent, That he now takes the Ministry directly for his Mark; and treats them (in the House) for some days past in so very frank a manner that they grow quite angry; and 'tis talk'd as if it wou'd not be impossible, to see him very soon expel'd the House. I don't know whether you have heard, he has a month ago work'd a Quarrell So high with my Lord Chamberlain, That a New Licence has been granted to Wilks, Cibber & Booth which they accepting of, and acting under; have Left him with his Patent, but not one Player, and so the Lord Chamberlains Authority over the Playhouse is restor'd, and the Patent ends in a joke. I take hold of this Turn, to call upon those three Gentlemen about the Stock they had of mine, and think they will be willing to come to some tollerable Composition.

The Opera will begin about the 10th of March under the Accademy of Musick. It will be a very good one this year, and a better the next. They having engag'd the best Singers in Italy, at a great Price. Such as I believe will bring the Expences to about twice as much as the Receipts. But the fund Subscribed being about £20000, may probably Support it, till Musick takes such root, as to Subsist with less aid. The King gives a £1000 a year to it.

(125)

Heideggers Masquerades go on with their wonted Success, they are limitted to Six in a year. The 5th is to night, and I am going to it, en famille. Neither my Self, nor my Gentlewoman having been there before. She calls upon me to come away, and Says she can afford me no more time than to present her humble Service to you.

117

[*To the Duke of Newcaſtle.*]

London. Sep^t: ye 15th 1720

I rec'd your Graces Commands about securing Newcaſtle House; with the Account M^r Du Bois sent to you. But if he had been desir'd to take me along with him, he wou'd have found the Diſtemper different from what he took it to be; As I plainly shew'd him yeſterday upon the Spott. And so, we are both of a mind for the Cure, and directions are given to do what is necessary to make all Safe, which will be of Small Expence, and take up little time.

As to the Other works there, I believe they will be compleated in good time, So as your Grace need not be kept longer at Claremont than I suppose you will like to ſtay.

I went with My Lord Carlisle & Lord Morpeth on Sunday laſt, to the Duke of Chandois's Church, and So to dinner wth him. He has very good Musick, And to deal juſtly with his Magnificence, we found Nothing at all in it Ridiculous or Foppish as many people have Represented.

He has done great things since I was there both in Building and Gardening, in which I do Assure you, he has sav'd nothing by not letting me be his Architect; For I had Cutt him out less Expence, And you may be Sure, (I think,) a Better house. His Fronts however, are very fine, and all of Stone. But the inside is of poor Invention.

He talk'd to me of your Graces New Room at Claremont, designing to have Such a One in the New house he Builds in London, tho' he has not yet Seen it you muſt know; but that's Nothing. I have however done all I can to prevent his coming till 'tis quite done; that it may Stair in his face, And knock him downe at Once. To Morrow, Lord Carlisle, Ld Morpeth Ld Rich^d: Sandford, Mr Oldfield my Brother and I, have made a Party to go there. And the Brigadier has engag'd to have a Shoulder of Mutton for us, in the Green Room, wch is juſt done. We shan't fail to drink your Graces and the Ladys healths in (I daresay) the beſt Wine in your Cellar As your very Obedient humble Servants particularly

J VANBRUGH

To Mr Mauduit　　　　　118

   S^r　　　　　　　　　　　　　　　*Nov. y^e* 24th: 1720

    I desire you'll pay the Fees for the Grants to Baker and Neal to my
Wife, who will give you receipts for them from
Your humble Servant
J VANBRUGH

To the Rt Honble　　　　　119
   The Earl of Carlisle
    at Castle Howard near York

   My Lord　　　　　　　　　　*London Feb ye 2d* 1720/21

    I have just now been to wish Mr Walpole joy, of the Kings promising
him to be first Comr: of the Tre^y and Chancellr: of the Excheqr, at the
end of the Sessions. Lord Sund: will then be Secretary of State, and Ld
Stanhope Capt: Genll: That is, I take it for granted it will be so, Since
the King has written a Letter with his own hand to the Duke of Marlb:
with the greatest expressions of kindness & Esteem, to let him know it
will be much for his Service in this Juncture if he gives up that Station.
The Kings writing this Letter, I have only known as a Secret, not yet to
be Spoken of; But that 'tis intended Ld Stanhope shou'd be Capt: Genll:
is talk'd on everywhere. This point of Ld Marlboroughs quitting, has
hung these two days, upon her Graces opposing it Purely I believe for the
money; and so I Suppose she will haggle for a Pention to Support the
poor Old Officer and his Wife.
    What other changes will be, I don't yet know, nor anything more worth
telling your Ldship of this post.
    Her Grace has written a Villainous Letter of me to the Treasury (wch
they don't mind) relating to Blenheim; to Shew 'twas I drew my Lord
Marlb: into that great Expense I have likewise seen an Account She has
given of money I have had She says, for my Reward: Which is false in
every article. I think she once told your Ldship the Same Story.
    I hear she is now Quarrelling with Peter Walters, finding the Suit with
Strong the mason is like to go against her She has played Such tricks in
that affair that her own Lawyers are quite asham'd of the part she puts
them upon, and I believe this day Senight, will go near to give her up.
She now talks she'll bring it into the house of Lords. I wonder her Family
don't agree to Lock her up.
    I hope your Ldship has some Seasonable frost, as we have here at last,
which gives Great Comfort.
I am yr Ldships most Obedt humble Sert
J VANBRUGH

To the Rt Honble   120
   the Earl of Carlisle
    at Castle Howard near York

Feb. ye 7th 1721

Your Ldship will hear by this post, that my Ld Stanhope dyed Suddenly on Sunday. I believe in the present distracted Juncture, the whole Cabinet Counsell wou'd have been a less loss, both to the King and Nation. Not only for his quite Superiour knowledge in all Foreign Affairs, but from the great Credit he had at present at home when few others have any at all. He Stood quite clear in the Eyes of all Partys, in regard to this Devilish Southsea Affair that is like to taint the greatest part of those who were otherwise fit to do business. And has behav'd himself with great Applause in the house of Lords, and with Great Temper now that Peoples Passions who may mean well, and the Artifices of others, who mean the worst of Mischiefs, Seem every day to bring things to the brink of the Utmost confusion, Particularly that, of a difference between the two houses, which at this time, wou'd blow all up.

I need say no more, to incline your Ldship to reflect, how much need there is (and will likely be Still more) of the presence and Aid of those who have Still some Reputation, in this great Scarcity of it; and who have Sence and Temper.

It is not to be conceiv'd, how wild & extravagant the Passions of People (till now quite well Affected) make them talk and act. As if there cou'd be no turn or Change of Government, but what wou'd mend this. And 'tis easy to believe, that those who are dissaffected will not lose this Unforseen Occasion, to thro' all into confusion if possible, and then try what they can make of it. I don't doubt but your Ldship will receive from others, what will confirm this short account I give you of the general Situation. which perhaps may induce you, to think all is enough at Stake to make a troublesome journey reasonable at this time.

I much fear the report of the Secret Comittee won't mend things. I wish something don't then appear against people one wou'd rather it did not. Not so much for their own Sakes (tho' I wish them well) As from the Service they have done, and can still do, the King and his best friends, if they are not disabled from it; wch I have some particular reason to fear more than yet appears abroad. And I believe the P—— knows enough to please him mightily. tho' 'twill gratify his Passions, much more than conduce to his Interest.

Mr Walpole Inspects all the Treasury business tho' he do's not take the direction of it in form till the end of the Sessions.

Secretary Craggs is very ill, His Father is to be examin'd before the Secret Comittee.

To the Rt: Honble: 121
    the Earl of Carlisle
        near York

Feb. 18: 1721

I have two Letters from yr Ldship, and will without delay send you
what you desire.

The King was extreamly shock'd with the News of Ld Stanhopes Death.
he was at Supper with his usual Company when it was brought him, he
rose imediatly and retir'd to his Closet. He has order'd Ld Sunderland
and Mr Walpole to let Lady Stanhope know, he will make her what
amends he can for her Loss, And desires she will let them know what,
and in what manner she would have done, and it shall be comply'd with.

Mr Craggs is another Sensible loss to him tho not to the Same degree.
He holds well however, tho' no doubt Some folks are in expectation these
Stroaks and the disorder of the times may affect him.

By all I can yet learn, I incline to think Ld Sun^d. will not be dropt.
I believe he still has the King, which with the Consideration of his great
Ability in Parliam^t. may probably induce Ld Towns^d: & Mr Walpole to
think it for their own Service to draw with him; especially since the
Publick Cause so much requires a Union. Besides, tis not sure but they
may have Some kind of hold upon him, in these Southsea transactions, by
which they may the less apprehend him, tho he remains in Credit wth the
King, especially if they themselves do him Service in this juncture, wch
some think may be the Case.

Ld Carleton however, is lookt on as his man, if he is made President,
and 'tis plain many others cast their eye towards him; so that I don't at
all see him downe if he gets clear of the South Sea.

at the Same time, whatever the Ks. Sentiments may be of the late comers
in, in regard of the P. I do verily believe, he's Safe enough with them as
to that point, for I believe they are far from having either opinion or
affection that way, from anything they have found in the time of their
being his Counsellors.

The Duke of Rutland has the Smallpox;

Lord Anglesey made a flaming Speech today against the whole Ministry

122

[*To Lord Carlisle.*]

My Lord   *Feb: ye* 20*th* 1720/21

I rec'd the Designs Mr Etty sent me, wch are very well; But I think
any thing of frost work or Rock work, may be more a propo, in some other
parts of the Garden, more retir'd and Solemn; or where there is Water:

and therefore wou'd rather advise a fluted Pillar only and that of the Dorick Order, because it is the Shorteſt in proportion to its height, & in that regard is beſt to Stand alone—I have therefore drawn one, with its finishing on the Top, and its Peideſtal, but 'tis to so large a Scale I can't send it in a Letter—But it shall come with Some things I have to send Mr Etty very Soon of Admll: Delavals.

As to the Obelisks, I believe one may Venture at sight, as I find yr Ldship Inclines. But on farther thought, I am a little fearfull of venturing at any new Stroaks as to their form, in this place, but wou'd rather reserve that Liberty for Single ones, that may be Scatter'd up and down the Woods.

I therefore send your Ldship here, what I wou'd recomend to you for the Parterre if you approve them. The Smalleſt to ſtand, at the 4 Loweſt Angles, and the Largeſt on the higher or inmoſt Angles. The Pillar I propose to ſtand rais'd on a Square bank above the division of the 4 Inmoſt Obelisks, and I think four Vases may be very well plac'd to attend it, at the four Corners, of that Bank, But this shall be farther describ'd with the Pillar, which shall be sent next Week if not Sooner.

The Storm about the Southsea is now near an end, and we are to Expeſt next what good will happen to it from the enquirys that have been made.

I think all are Safe at Court, and My Ld Carteret's (as 'tis taken for Granted) to be Secretary; and Lord Lincolns having the Duke of Rutlands Garter; shows my Lord Sund. Stands on firmer Ground, than people in general fancy'd. Those who are eſteem'd the Duke of Graftons chief Friends, I believe were not a little diſturb'd he had not that Garter, but the Duke of Buckingham dying, that matter is pretty well made up, he being to Succeed him. Upon the whole, I hope they will Agree enough to Aſt pretty well together for the publick Service, and that the Sessions will end, better than moſt folks thought very lately. I am

Your Lordships
moſt Obedt: humble Servant
J. VANBRUGH

My Lady Marlborough has been caſt by the Workmen—the Cause held three days— She's Outragious at it, She accuses the Judges, and says I have forsworn myself. I am told one of them said there was no more in the Cause, but a Rich man on one Side, and a poor man on tother or something to that effeſt.

The denying my Lord Godolphins Aſt bore hard upon them in point of honour.

I shou'd be glad to know, whether 'tis likely your Ldship may come up this Spring, because I am thinking very much in earneſt now, of Waiting upon you early in the Summer with Bag and Baggage. My Wife desires her moſt humble Service to your Ldship, and your Godson can almoſt do so too

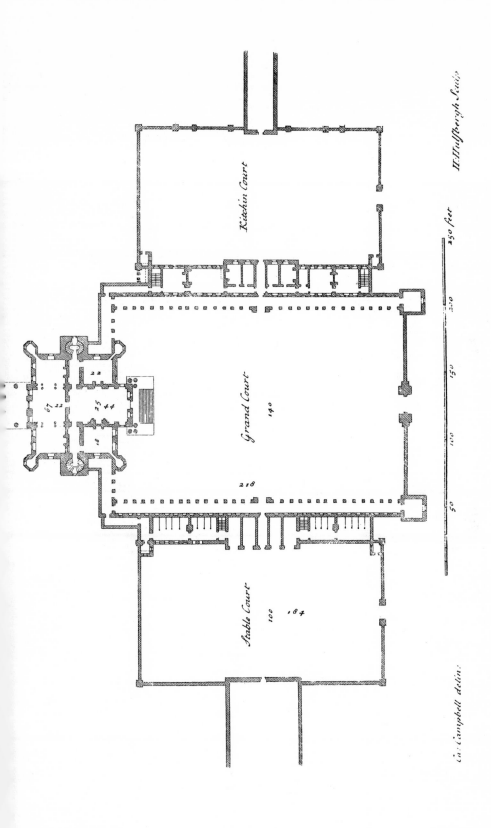

Kitchin Court

Grand Court

140

218

Stable Court

100

184

22

67 22

25 44

18

250 feet

200

150

100

50

Co: Campbell delin:

H.Hulsbergh Sculp:

[To Lord Carlisle.]

My Lord   *Green*: *March ye 25th* 1721

Mr Etty will probably have shewn yr Lordship ere this, a Design I sent him of a Dorick Column for the Parter, which I think will do better only fluted, than with more embellishments. I have made the Piedestal Spread a little more than the Rule, which I think is quite reasonable, and will have a right effect, where a Pillar Stands Single, The Rule being Calculated for Pillars that stand in lines, which alters the Case much. I woud propose this Pillar (if yr Ldship approves of it) to stand elevated upon a Square Bank, at least two foot higher than the upper Division. And I think it might be very handsomely accompany'd, by four Vases upon the four Corners of that Bank.

I am very much affraid of Venturing to Flute the Obelisks: But the Balls upon them, I think will make them Gay, without being Tawdry. The Venturing at one fluted, in a Flower Garden, might be well enough, but I doubt going farther wou'd not be lik'd which I think the Whole Decorations of the Parterre will be extreamly, if rightly and Properly hit off. But I don't dispare of waiting on your Ldship time enough to talk this point over; And I shou'd be I cou'd Spend so much time at Castle Howard, as you are pleas'd to give me leave. But I shall be forc'd to return sooner, than my Inclinations wou'd bring me.

The South Sea is so hatefull a Subject one do's not Love to name it; And yet it do's so interfere with almost every bodys Affairs more or less, that all they have to do, is in some degree govern'd by it. Even I, who have not gain'd at all, Shall probably be a Loser near £2000. I wou'd however fain See an end on't before I come away if I cou'd; for when I know the worst of any thing, I can make my Self tollerably easy. But I am affraid the Parlt: will be forc'd to Sit on a Great While, before they can agree to Settle any thing. And what new work this Knight may Start, if they get him to them, God knows. But I take it for Granted, if he is like to tell them half so much as they have a mind he shou'd do, they'll never have his Company.

As to Ld Sun^{ds}: Case totherday, 'tis certain there was no Sort of proof upon him worth Naming. Scarce enough, even to leave a Suspicion So that the attack has done him Service. And yet, the Clamour runs so high Against allmost any Minister in Power while this Vile mistake was made, That many think a Change wou'd be (or perhaps will be) quite necessary, but where to Change, is the great difficulty. I am

Your Lordships
most Obedt humble Servant
J. VANBRUGH

[*To Lord Carlisle.*]

London April the 22d: 1721

My Lord

'Tis with a moſt Sensible and Sincere concern I condole with your Lordship, on the Loss of my Ld Irwin; If my Lady bears it, better, than I fear there's reason to apprehend, I shall be mighty glad of it, both for her own sake and for your Ldships; who I know have that regard for her, to enter very far, into her afflictions.

I hope however, neither the Publick nor Family misfortunes, will be able much to allay the Taſt you have of reasonable amusemts: Since they are really, our beſt Support in this Life. One may try at Greater things, and one has a Chance, for their Succeeding; but I think we shou'd never lay so much weight upon them, as to fall to the ground, if they are Tript from under us. I will therefore hope, your Ldship is going on with what you intended shou'd be your entertainment this year. I Suppose Mr Etty has shewn you the Draught of the Columns I sent him, which by being fluted, I think will be fine enough. I am adjuſting all my little concerns, as faſt as I can, towards being able to get out of Towne some time next month. I am a little taken up at present, about this Cause of My Lord Marlboroughs, in which her Grace takes a Great deal of Pains to blacken me, since she finds she can do nothing else. The hearing before the Lords, is Appointed for friday next. In the meantime I'm told She is handing about, a Sort of Case (in writing) in which She lays me on. I am but newly come to Towne, and han't yet been able to get a Sight of it. She only sending it to Lords to read, & so getting it back again that I mayn't see it before the Tryal, when I suppose 'twill come out in print. I don't know whether I am rightly inform'd, but I heard it said yeſterday, She had writ to your Ldship, wishing you cou'd be at her Cause. And that she had rec'd an answer in which you said, by what you knew of it already, you doubted if you were you shou'd Vote againſt her. By all I See I believe she'll hardly get any of her own Family to Vote for her. The Judges were mighty clear againſt her, in the Excheqr Court, and if Right won't help her, I fancy affection won't. She's a Vile Woman.

Mr Aislaby is now in a Bad way, the Commons having thrown him into the Directors Bill; which is lookt upon as a sort of a Tack, leſt the Lords shou'd not have paſt it, had it come Single. Mr Walpole took a good deal of Pains to prevent this junction, but to no purpose, what he said, seeming to influence very few. If your Lordship has the Weekly London Journal, you see with what a bitterness the Miniſters are follow'd, and few people Seem much diſturb'd at that paper, tho' I believe it wou'd be hard for them to say, where they Cou'd change to any purpose. My Lord Molesworth is reckon'd the Chief Author of the Journal.

I am

Your Lordships moſt Obedt

humble Servant

J. VANBRUGH

The Dutchesses Cause I hear is put off, to Wednesday senight. The Workmens Spirits are very Low from the fear they are under, that She and her Family, will at leaſt be Able to keep a great many Lords away, who wou'd not Vote for her if they were in the House.

125

[*To Lord Carlisle.*]

London. May ye 5th 1721

My Lord

I am very glad to find by your Ldships Letter of the 29th. Aprll: That neither Publick nor private Rubbs will discourage you from relying on that ground, that has Supported you hitherto. Tis the same sort of Reflection has enabled me to bear up, as I have done, under things that wou'd else infaillibly have knockt me downe. Of which, one (not the leaſt of them) has been this Wicked Dutchess nor has she yet done with me. For having fail'd in her endeavour (in the late Tryall) to throw the Blenheim Debt upon me, wch was infamously labour'd in the Courts, She has now handed a Vile manuscript about in which She abuses me as far as words, (in her way of making use of them) can go. As soon as I had got a Sight of it, which was but on Sunday near Senight, I found I cou'd not avoid Publishing Something to clear my Self; So, as faſt as I cou'd, I huddled up the Paper, I here take leave to enclose to your Lordship, and have sent it about to all the Lords in Towne. as well as given it to the King Prince & Princess.

The Tryall is to be on Monday next.

The Judges who gave the Cause againſt the Duke in the Court of Excheqr:, (and who her Grace abuses soundly in her paper) took Occasion two days Since to declare upon the Bench, That they were extreamly glad there was an appeal to the Lords, That the World might See, how juſt a Decree they had made. I am

Your Lordspˢ moſt

Obedt & humble Sert

J. VANBRUGH

(133)

[*To Lord Carlisle.*]

London May ye 25th 1721

My Lord

I must own when the Cause was put off I thought (as your Lordship did) it wou'd have been dropt; but I was mistaken. It came on, on Tuesday, & was ended yesterday. It went for the Workmen 41. to 25. People talk a little freely of those 25. Especially, the Cause appearing so clear to others, that even the Dukes own Family cou'd not bring themselves to Vote for him, except Lord Bridgewater. My Lord Sund: wou'd not so much as hear the Cause. The Duke of Montague, Duke of Newcastle and Ld Godolphin heard it quite thorough, and then left the House. Among the 25, were, Lord Peterborough, Ld Cadogan, Ld Bristoll, Ld Falmouth, the Bishop of Bangor The Duke of Kingston the Bishop of Salisbury with one or two Bishops more, and to the great wonder of most folks My Ld Chancellr:.

My Lord Cowper & Trevor, were for the Workmen, with almost all the Lords of weight. But scarce any one thought it necessary to Speak a word on that Side nor was there much said on the Dukes—only Ld Peterborough, talk'd Some time.

When the Tryall was over, the Duke of Wharton complain'd to the House of the Paper I had Printed, & was seconded by my Lord Falmouth. It was presently propos'd, by those who were inclin'd to favour me, To defer it till after the Holydays wch was agreed to. I find my Self much Stronger on this occasion, than I cou'd have Imagin'd almost evry Lord in the House showing by Some expression or other, they are not inclin'd to let me Suffer this way. So I make no Apology to her Grace, (as some wou'd persuade me to do) but let the thing take its Fate. Your Ldship perhaps may know (tho' I don't) how the Dutchess of Marlb: comes to engage Lady Betty Lechmere & Lady Mary Howard to keep her Company at these hearings, both in the Court below, and the House of Lords. She Seems to me, to have possest Lady Betty with some opinion of her Cause; but I think not Lady Mary. As to the Inconsistencys her Grace has endeavour'd to shew in my Depositions, for my own part, I can See none, nor do I think anybody else do's; If they had, I believe I shou'd have found the Lords, look with a Cooler Air upon me, Since the Cause is determin'd, than they do; which is so far from Shy, That I don't remember, I ever found on any occasion, so much appearance of their Friendship towards me; And one thing is but too certain, that if I have Stretcht my evidence in favour of the Workmen, it has been to cut my own Throat; for my Lord Marlb: being decreed to pay them, I may be pretty Sure, he will never pay me. wch will be a Loss of £1600.

I am
Your Lordships moſt humble
& obedt Servant
J. VANBRUGH.

[*To Lord Carlisle.*] 127

London June ye 8th 1721

My Lord

I rec'd your Ldships Letter of ye 28th of May and am sorry you shou'd owe any Stroaks of Philosophy to a fit of the Gout. I hope it will prove only a Summer fit, and so be soon over. But I, without the Gout to incline my Philosophy, have every day of my Life Since twenty years old, grown more and more of opinion, that the less one has to do, with what is call'd the World, the more Quiet of mind; and the more Quiet of mind, the more Happyness. All other delights, are but like debauches in Wine; which give three days pain, for three hours pleasure. It has however been my chance, to lead a Life quite againſt my Sentiments hitherto; But I have made a Virtue of Necessity, from Some rebuffs I have met with in this Reign, and lessen'd my concern in things I was tempted before to be busy about which has eas'd me a good deal, and I hope will Still do more.

I think I am got clear of any farther trouble from her Grace and her Law Concerns, only that by the Cause going againſt her, I am cut off from recovering my Pretentions, wch amount to £1660. So much being in arrear to me. But which her Grace to be Sure will never pay me, and I have little View now, of ever obtaining it from the Treasury. Therefore all the good I have from this Decree, is, That I am now safe from being pull'd to pieces by the Workmen.

As to the Complaint made to the House of Lords againſt me I reckon 'tis over. The Dutchess found them so generally well dispos'd to me, on this occasion, That the day Set came, (wch was yeſterday) She went out of Towne, and so did the Duke of Wharton too. My Lord Falmouth was in the House, grumbled much, but did not think fit to Speak aloud, So nobody calling for the order of the day, my Ld Sund: mov'd to adjourn. I hear the Dutchess do's not think of trying her Strength in Weſtr: Hall againſt me; She says, She sees She can have juſtice nowhere.

I hope I shall be able to set out before Midr: day, and tho' I am much oppos'd by wise Women (Mrs Condon amongſt the reſt) in pretending to carry your Ldships Godson such a journey, I resolve to Venture him, for I have a mind to make him as much a Yorkshire man as I can; besides he's so Stout, I think he may travel any where.

I am

Your Lordships most humble

& obedt Servant

J. VANBRUGH

Your Ldship may be assur'd I cou'd have Supported every Fact mention'd in my Paper, the belief of which I found very much inclin'd the Lords to Support me thinking my Case quite a hard one.

[*To Lord Carlisle.*]   128

London July ye 6th: 1721

My Lord

I this Evening set out for York but having a heavy Coach to lug along I design to rest a day or two by the way, at a Friends house, so I shall be upon the Road nine or Ten.

I shall make a very short stay at Coll: Yarburghs, before I wait upon your Lordship at Castle Howard, where I hope I shall find you well in health, and as easy in mind, as an Agreeable Retirement can furnish in these heart aching times.

I was with my Wife, to wait upon my Lady Mary, and to enquire how my Lady Irwin did, when they told us, they were gone two days before for Castle Howard where I hope they are well arriv'd.

I am Your Ldships most humble & obedt Sert

J. VANBRUGH

[*To the Duke of Newcastle.*]   129

Castle Howard. Augt: 8th 1721

I have no other business to trouble your Grace with a Letter upon, but to thank you for your Warrants. The rest, is only to remind you, of my constant Wishes (others wou'd say, Prayers) for your health and happyness wherever I wander. And amongst those good Wishes, One is, that you were here at this time, to See in its Beauty (warm weather too) the most delightfull Place. I ever beheld. Many new Charms open this year, that never appear'd before; And many more will next; that people do not dream of now; If I take in, what a Third will produce, (bar more Southsea Storms) I believe here will be, (beyond all contest,) the Top Seat, and Garden of England. Of the House I say nothing; The others I may commend, because Nature made them; I pretend to no more Merrit in them than a Midwife, who helps to bring a fine Child into the World, out of Bushes Boggs, and Bryars.

(136)

I was at York all laſt Week; A Race every day, and a Ball every night; with as much well look'd Company, as ever I saw got together The Ladies I mean in Chief. As to the Men, the Duke of Wharton was the Top Gallant The Entertainment ending on Friday, He declar'd if the Company wou'd ſtay in Towne one day more, he wou'd treat the Jockeys with a Plate, The Ladys with a Ball, And all together with a Supper. Twas done Accordingly, And my Lady Milner who had all along been his Partner, was now his Queen. When Supper was ended, He invited all the good Company to meet him again that day twelve-month, on the Same Terms; with many decent and good Complimᵗˢ: to the Inhabitants of York and Yorkshire for the Honour they did him, And hop't wou'd do him again. To which they gratefully bow'd, as who wou'd say, Yes. But his Grace, then bethought himself, of one Civil thing more, And Said; That Unless my Lady Milner wou'd Absolutely engage to be there too, he was off, as to the reſt of the Company Upon which She look'd she did not know how, And all went home to Sleep.

He is now here, for two or three days, & we have jok't off the Affair of the House of Lords on both Sides. Here's the House full of Company, which I like better when it's emptyer So am going to morrow to Lumley Caſtle And Delavals. wᶜʰ will take me up a fortnight, I shall then return to York And so here again, if your Grace has any Service to Command.

Your ever Oblig'd & truly
Obedient Servant
J VANBRUGH

My Lord Carlisle desires to send his humble Service to your Grace; And I beg leave to present mine; to the Ladys And Mʳ Pelham.

I hope the Brigadier is got through all his Troubles with Sʳ Thomas. And that he is at ease in body and Mind.

To Brigad Watkins   130
  In Scotland Yard
  Whitehall London.

York. Augᵗ: yᵉ 26ᵗʰ 1721

Cou'd you See how busy I have been, ever Since I writ to you laſt, you wou'd easily forgive my being so long before I did it again. I return'd but laſt night from the North (for here you muſt know we are in the South,) where I have been near three weeks finding a vaſt deal to do, both at Delavals and Lumley Caſtle. Since it is not easy, to go there often, I resolv'd to do all the Service I cou'd while I was there now.

The Admiral is very Gallant in his operations, not being dispos'd to ſtarve the Design at all. So that he is like to have, a very fine Dwelling for himself, now, and his Nephew &c hereafter.

Lumley Caſtle is a Noble thing; and well deserves the Favours Lord Lumley designs to beſtow upon it; In order to which, I ſtay'd there near a Week, to form a General Design for the whole, Which consiſts, in altering the House both for State, Beauty and Convenience, And making the Courts Gardens and Offices Suitable to it; All which I believe may be done, for a Sum, that can never ly very heavy upon the Family. If I had had good weather in this Expedition, I shou'd have been well enough diverted in it; there being many more Valluable and Agreeable things and Places to be Seen, than in the Tame Sneaking South of England.

I am going for three or four days again to Caſtle Howard, where I muſt Spend a Week or ten days, to do what is necessary there. My Lord Carlisle going on with his Works as usual; by which the Seat is wonderfully improv'd this laſt Year. Two Years more, tho' they won't compleat all the Building, will so Beautify the Outworks, of Gardens, Park &c, That I think no Place I ever Saw, will dispute with it, for a Delightfull Dwelling in generall, let the Criticks fish out what particular faults they please in the Architecture. Here are Several Gentlemen in the(se) Parts of the World, that are possess'd w(ith) the Spirit of Building, And Seem dispos'd to do it, in so good a Manner, that were they to eſtablish here a sort of a Board of Works to conduct their Affairs, I do verily believe, they wou'd sooner make Hawksmʳ: a Comissioner of it, than that excellent Architect, Ripley. When I met with his Name, (and Esquire to it) in the News paper; Such a Laugh came upon me, I had like-to have Beshit my Self. Poor Hawksmoor, What a Barbarous Age, have his fine, ingenious Parts fallen into. What wou'd Monsʳ: Colbert in France have given for Such a Man? I don't Speak as to his Architecture alone, but the Aids he cou'd have given him, in almoſt all his brave Designs for the Police. A thing I never expect to hear talk'd of in England, Where the Parts of moſt of the Great men I have Seen or read of, have rarely turn'd to any farther Account, Than getting a Great Deal of Money, and turning it through their Guts into a House of Office, And now I think of eating Pray do me the favour to get a Warrant from his Grace, for an other Buck inſtead of that he sent for a Stag, for I find that will be of no use to me here. the Buck I have had, and very good. The sooner you can send me this, the more you will Oblige, Yours Dear Brigadʳ

J VANBRUGH

131

[*To Lord Carlisle.*]

Whitehall. Nov: ye 16th 1721

My Lord

Tho' 'tis a great while since I left yr Lordship, I am but newly got to Towne, having Stay'd at Several places on the Road, much longer than I design'd. We lug'd the heavy Coach however (and what was in it) well at laſt to Towne, where moſt things have been dissagreeable to me Since I came, especially a new long Bill her Grace has prefer'd in Chancery, againſt every body that was ever concern'd in the Building at Blenheim downe to the pooreſt workman. How much trouble the Roguery of the Law will let her give us, I don't know, but all the mischief they and the Devil can do, She'll pay them for, tho She'll pay nobody else.

I have not yet had time to See almoſt any mortal; So can give your Ldship no acct: of what humour or way people are in, But I Suppose you are near Setting out for London I hope you'll have a good Journey to it, and (for your own Sake) a Quick return from it, for I heartily hate it.

We are a little Cripled in our Opera, by a Letter from Durſtanta; that She is not well, and can't be here this Winter, they go on however and two New Operas are preparing. but Heydegger is much in fear the Bishops won't let his masquerades appear, till the Plague's over. I am told however, the King thinks that no very Stanch reason.

I have Seen some of the Physitians, and askt them how inoculating has really Succeeded, and they assure me, not one Single Person has miscarried, nor that they find any Sort of ground to fear; that those who go thorough the Small Pox that way, will have them again; and one pretty Strong proof they have, by a Young Woman, who ever Since She has had them given her, is employ'd to look after people who get them by the natural course, and yet is not hurt by them.

I am Your Lordships moſt humble &
obedient Servant
J. VANBRUGH

The Torys yeſterday attempted in the House of Lords, to have the Inſtructions for treating the Northern Peace laid before them—There was a pretty long debate upon it, but the worſt Supported, (as I am told,) that has been known, tho' the Duke of Wharton took much pains in it. His chief, (Lord Cowper) voted with the Torys, but did not Speak. the Pupil they say, made quite a poor figure, never yet, having Spoke so ill. They were but 20 on the Division; and a great majority on the other side.

My Wife desires I'll present her moſt humble Service to your Lordship and the Ladys.

To Mr *Joynes*   132
   at the *Pallace*
     at *Kensington.*

Whitehall. Nov. ye 18th 1721

   Mr *Joynes.*

Since I came to Towne, I have Seen the Bill the Duke of Marl^b: has preferr'd in Chancery, against every body concern'd in the Building at Blenheim. I am preparing my Answer, but believe it wou'd be necessary for you Mr Bobart and me, to talk a little together before any of our Answers are given in order to recollect Such facts & passages, as else perhaps we may all make Some mistakes in after so many Years. I therfore wish you cou'd get him (for I don't know where he is) to meet you here on Monday evening about Six a Clock, when I will be Sure to be at home

I am Y^r Servant

J VANBRUGH

[*To the Duke of Newcastle.*]   133

February ye 11th 1721/2

   My Lord Duke

I never was more Surpris'd, at any disagreeable thing, has happen'd to me in my Life; than to find (a day or two ago) your Grace had thrown aside a Small Domestick, of mine, to make way for an other in the Kings Musick.

When I ask'd your Favour for him, I was so far from designing to press you, if I found the least Unwillingness; that if you had not granted it me (as you did) in an easy kind way, at the first word; you had never heard any more of it.

I thought after this, there was no need of my troubling your Grace, with more talk about the matter; especially when I observ'd, you so well remembred, what you had promiss'd; that a year afterwards (on your own movement, without one word from me) you told Coll. Pelham, while I Stood by, I was to have the Second Vacancy And that no mistake might happen, you made him Minute it downe, that moment.

I must own my Lord, I did think I had as much pretention to your Favour & Friendship, as almost any humble Servant you had, And that which made me think so, was, That you us'd to tell me so. How I therfore come to fall so low in your Regards, I can't conceive; because, I am quite sure I have done nothing to forfeit them.

If your Grace has been Solicited, by greater Men than me, for this Small matter, And that your deference to them, has been the Reason for passing me by; I'm sorry there has not been a better; For I am much of Opinion That no Great Man, who was enough your Friend, to entitle him to ask a

(140)

Favour from you; wou'd have press'd you to grant him this, on such Terms Or if he had; I am sure he had given you, a very good reason to refuse him.

As I cou'd not forbear, saying Something to your Grace on this Occasion, And had not a mind to say very much; I rather chose to do it by writing than otherwise; And shall be very glad if your Grace pleases, that we may never have any sort of discourse about it.   I am

Your Graces
most humble and
obed^t: Servant

J VANBRUGH

[*To Lord Carlisle.*]   I 34

London. April ye 6th: 1722

My Lord

I have heard from York, Your Ldship is got well home, which I am very glad of; and heartily congratulate you on your Success at Carlisle.

Here has been a deal of Riotous doings in Several Elections, even of petty officers, as well as members for Parliament; But it must be a great mortification to the Torys to find, that even in this juncture, when so great discontents are Stirring, a Whigg Parliament of no Small majority can be got.   My Ld Townshend and his near Friends seem to think it chiefly owing to the firm declaration in the Kings Speech who he wou'd trust to & Stand by.   And I believe they wou'd have it thought that declaration was very much owing to them—as very possibly it might.

I shall be glad to hear your Ldship is better in respect to your Gout, and that Your Works go on so well, to be an agreeable entertainment to you.

The Publick Divertions here have flourishd as if nobody had left the Towne; the opera in particular, wch confirms me still more that Musick has taken deep root with us.   We don't know yet when the King will go nor do I hear whether a Speaker will be chosen first.   I am

I am,
Your Lordships
most humble &
obedt Servant

J. VANBRUGH

My Wife desires her most humble Service to your Ldship & the Ladys, whom I hope you found well.

(141)

[*To Lord Carlisle.*]   135

London. *April ye 24th* 1722

My Lord

I am mighty glad to find your Ldship grows better, tho' not so fast, as I cou'd most heartily wish. The Duke of Kingston tells me, he thinks you can't avoid another journey up, my Lord Letchmere having declar'd he will act no more in the Young Lady Whartons Trust.

I don't find the Loss of my Ld Sundd: is likely to be much felt in our home affairs; on the Contrary Those who were esteem'd (amongst the Whiggs) his particular Friends, show plainly already, they dont think of listing under any New General on the foot they fought under him; but declare for peace and Unanimity; and in that Strain talk to the King, Saying all they can, to incline him to think, he is Safe and well with Ld Towns^d: & Mr Walpole, and tho' he Seem'd extreamly disturb'd & disconcerted for a day or two, he now grows much easyer, and the Great men are very well pleas'd, with the Disposition they find him every hour more & more in to think the Whiggs will draw together, and that the present Ministry, (whatever has formerly past) will make themselves agreeable to him—What I find of this, is what I thought wou'd be, from the moment I heard my Ld Sund: was dead; for certain he was in a way, of embroiling things much. I fancy, the Whiggs will now incline to try what they can do; without any aid from the Torys, Which will recommend the Ministers more than any thing to the King, as I am well inform'd; it being with much uneasyness, he gave way to some things my Ld Sund: work't him to of that kind, wch my Lord might have felt, had he liv'd longer.

I am

Yr Ldships most obedt Servt

My Ld Scarborough tells me he certainly go's to Lumley Castle the end of May, and has desir'd me to propose some things for him in order to begin his Works there. What I shall be able to do, I don't yet know; but my desires are strongly Northward, especially to Castle Howd;

I was an hour this morning with my Lord Pemk: he is prodigious good to me, and has lately done me the honour of a Visit. Your Lordship is a Vast Favourite with him, he took your Character all to pieces today and put it mighty well together again. I found his Politicks was, that all wou'd now go better.

Tyrril, Gives people a mighty good Acct: of Castle Howd: especially the out Works.

THE LETTERS

[To Lord Carlisle.] 136

London. May ye 5th 1722

My Lord

I don't apprehend any thing amiss, from the Obelisks falling gradually with the ground from North to South as long as those which are on the Same line from East to West stand on the Same Levell; The Case being no more than in a regular plantation up a Hill, where nothing more is endeavour'd or wish'd, than that the Trees may grow of a pretty equal height in regard to one another; but not that the Tops of them shou'd be of one dead level; nor wou'd they be half so beautifull if they cou'd be so, their rising one above another having a much better effect; and so it is in the View of Townes which ly on the Side of Hills, as Constantinople and (in a good degree) London doe, by which means the Towers Steeples and other Eminent Buildings, produce a much finer effect, than if they stood all upon one natural flat; So that I think your Lordship need be in no manner of pain, upon your Obelisks appearing from the farther parts of the Garden, one above another, tho' they really are of equal height—

I am entirely of yr Ldships opinion, that my Ld Sunds death, will prove no loss to the Publick, nor do I find him at all lamented. On the contrary, people now speak freely against the sort of Tory Scheme, he was endeavouring to work the King to, tho' he found mighty difficulty in it, and lost ground by it, wch by what I now hear, might very probably have enabled Mr Walpole in little time, to have blown him quite up; for he took the other point, of standing and falling with the Whiggs, which was not only the Kings own entire opinion, but had been much confirm'd in time past by my Ld Sund: himself. So that to work him off it now, and to bring him to think the Torys cou'd be faithfull to him was what he cou'd not relish, tho' he had been brought a little into it, much against his will, but remain'd very uneasy under it; so that he with pleasure came into that part of his Speech (advis'd to it chiefly by Ld Townsd: & Mr Walpole as I hear) which declar'd who he wou'd rely upon.

It therefore Seems now upon the Whole, as if the Whiggs in the main points, wou'd go pretty well together, and to the Kings liking. Whether the President and Ld Carteret will hold their Stations one knows nothing yet of, only I find it the opinion of many, that it will be hard for the Whigs to act in Confidence with them.

But in the midst of these home affairs, people begin to be much alarm'd from Abroad, there has been a good deal of whispering some time, and now the Sending away, Horace Walpole, Col: Churchill &c and the Kings deferring his Voyage till after the Birthday, with several other Circumstances, increase the talk and fear very much, That there is an alliance form'd or forming, between Spain France & the Czar, which may regard us. Those that muſt know moſt of this at Court, are very Silent but I think don't seem easy. I shou'd not at all wonder (nor be much alarm'd) at the Spaniards hearkening a little to the Acct: no doubt the Jacobites here have given them, of the hopes they had of a Tory Parliamᵗ: and the people of that Stamp shewing themselves much dispos'd on the New Election, to the Pretenders Intereſt. And if some Scheme was form'd to have laid hold of a fair oportunity, 'twas no more than one might well expeꝏ, and that the Spaniards might probably, put a helping hand to it. But in that case, one wou'd think, the neck of it muſt now be broken. I therefore don't like these Symptomes of Something yet to be apprehended, because I have no notion of any thing now being praꝏicable but by a Strong Alliance & an open Warr—Which can't be without France is of the Party and that (in our present want both of money and Credit) might set us cruel hard. People grow into eager expeꝏation of what will come out, and will probably talk one another into greater Apprehentions in a few days, if something don't appear to make them easy. I shall acquaint your Lordship with what I hear and am Your moſt Obedient humble Servant.

To the Rt: Honble   137
    the Earl of Carlisle
      at Caſtle Howard near York

                                London. May ye 10*th* 1722

  My Lord

    Your Ldship will see by the Gazette and other papers, the main that is known of the present affair; all I can tell you farther of it is, That altho' the Miniſters had some Intimation of a Scheme on foot, they neither knew it certain, nor any thing material of it till within this Week. Nor do they yet know, as I am (I think) well inform'd, that the thoughts of attempting the design, is yet over; Only they are easy, as to France or Spain taking any part in it. Having the moſt direꝏ and positive assurances from the Regent, that he can express in words. But they know of more money remitted from hence, than one wou'd imagine, to carry on this Design; & they say, they have already sufficient matter to lay before the Parliament, to obviate any thing that may be Surmis'd, againſt the reality of a deep Design to overset the present Governt:

138

To the R^t. Honble.
The Lords Commiss^rs. of His Maj^ts. Treas^ry

The Memorial of S^r. John Vanbrugh Kn^t.
Surveyour of His Maj^ts. Gardens and Waters.

May it please your Lord^ps.

The great Engine lately erected at Windsor, being of a Power to raise more Water, than the old Pipe that goes up to the Castle will receive, without often bursting and Streining the Engine, To its great damage; it seems absolutely necessary to take up the present Pipe, and to place one of larger bore in the room of it, by which means, there is no doubt, but the Castle will be plentifully Served with Water for the future.

Which is humbly Submitted to Your Lord^ps.

by your most humble and most obedient Servant

J VANBRUGH

Whitehall May 30th. 1722.

139

[To Jacob Tonson in Herefordshire.]

London. June ye 18th 1722

You have regal'd me with the best Sider I ever drank since I was born; but if you had sent me a bit of a Letter along with it, I shou'd have thought it better still; for the more we are pleas'd, the better we are dispos'd to everything that comes in our way.

I can regale you with nothing in return but a short Account of what I was e'en now told by one that knows, of my Lord Marlboroughs Treasure; which exceeds, what the most Extravagant Believer I ever heard guess at it.

The Grand Settlement (which 'twas Suspected her Grace had broken to pieces) stands good. And hands on Immense Wealth to my Lady Godolphin, and her Successors. How much, I can't yet say; but a round Million has been moving about in Loans, as Land Tax &c This the Treasury knew, before he dy'd; and this was exclusive of his Land, his £5000 a Year upon the Post Office, his Mortgages upon many a distrest Estate, His Southsea Stock his Annuitys, which was not Subscrib'd in, and besides, what God Almighty knows of in Foreign Banks. And yet, this Man wou'd neither pay his Workmen their bills nor his Architect his Salary.

(145)

But he has given his Widdow (may a Scotch Ensign get her) £10000. a Year to Spoil Blenheim, her own way. £12000 a Year to keep her Self clean, and go to Law. £2000 a year for ever to Lord Sunderland, and as much to the Dutchess of Montague for Life. £4000 a Year to Lord Ryalton for present maintenance, And to Lord Godolphin, only £5000 jointure, if he outlives my Lady. This laſt is a wretched Article. The reſt of the Heap (for these are but Snipings) go's to Lady Godolphin and so on. She'll have £40000 a Year in present.

I Suppose you don't care a farthing for the Towne, if you did; you'd look into it now and then. I can't blame you however, for you Spend your Life I believe, much as I wou'd do, had I made a good Voyage to the Messissippy. I'll tell you at the Same time that in Spight of all the Misfortunes & losses, that have occasion'd more crying and wailing, than I believe was ever known before; the Opera has been Supported at half a Guinea, Pit and Boxes, and perform'd 62 times this laſt Season. And withall this, the fine Gentlemen of the Buskin in Drury Lane, ride about in their Coaches. The Remnants of Rich, have play'd Something and Somehow, Six times a Week. And Aron Hill has set up a New Playhouse, to come in for a Snack with them in the Haymarket where the french acted

But with all this encouragement from the Towne, not a fresh Poet Appears; they are forc'd to Act round and round upon the Old Stock, though Cibber tells me, 'tis not to be conceiv'd, how many and how bad Plays, are brought to them. Steel however has one to come on at Winter, a Comedy; which they much commend. He tells us he'll make you a Visit in his way to Wales, and Congreve says he'll poke out a letter to you, to thank you for his Syder too.

I am now two Boys Strong in the Nursery but am forbid getting any more this Season for fear of killing my Wife. A Reason; that in Kit Cat days, wou'd have been ſtronger for it, than againſt it: But let her live, for she's Special good, as far as I know of the Matter.

It wou'd be a great Comfort to me; to See you (the only One left) come in at laſt, and pin the Basket. Have a Care of this retir'd Country Life we shall hear of some Herefordshire Nymph, in your Solitary walks; bounce out upon your heart, from Under an Apple Tree and make you one of us; But send it so or not, a married man or a Batchelor, while you and I are in this World, I shall continue, both

Your Friend & humble Servant

J. VANBRUGH

To the Rt Honble;   140
  The Earl of Carlisle
    at Castle Howard near York

London. June ye 19th 1722

  My Lord

     I have only time to night, to acquaint yr Ldship with a few particulars I have learnt of what my Lord Marlborough has left, wch is more than the most Extravagant believers ever nam'd. The Treasury a little before he dy'd found he had a full million, rouling in the Government, on Loans &c, besides his Stocks, his 99 years Annuitys, not Subscrib'd in, His Land, his Posthouse £5000 a year, his Mortgages and God knows what he may have besides in Foreign Banks.

     He has left his Widdow (I wish some Ensign had her) £10000. ayear, to Spoil Blenheim her own way, £12000 ayear more, to keep her Self Clean, and plague folks at Law with, £2000. ayear to Ld Sund: for ever; and as much, to the Dutchess of Montague for life, £8000 ayear to Lord Ryalton for present maintenance, and the Gross of his Wealth (for these are but Snippings) to Lady Godolphin & her Successors according to the Grand Settlement.

     I forgot one Article (a sad one) he has only given Lord Godolphin, a Joynture of £3000 a year if he outlives my Lady. This I fancy was her Graces doings for not Voting for her.

     It having been referr'd to my Ld Godolphin with the other Executors, Clayton & Guidot, to consider about the Dukes funeral and place of burying I have taken the liberty, to mention to my Lord what your Ldship designs at Castle Howard, and has been practic'd by the most polite peoples before Priestcraft got poor Carcasses into their keeping, to make a little money of.

     Sure if ever any Such thing as erecting Monuments in open places was right, it wou'd be so in this Case. But I fancy the Dutchess will prevent his lying near her, tho'/twou'd not make her very melancholy neither.

     The Place I propose, is in Blenheim Park with some plain, but magnificent & durable monument over him. I am

Your Lordships most
obedt humble Servt
J. VANBRUGH

[To Lord Carlisle.]   141

London July ye 19th 1722

  My Lord

     In the last Letter I rec'd from your Ldship you seem to think, the four Obelisks might have been bigger, which 'tis very probable they wou'd not have been the Worse for. however considering how many there are of them, and how near the House; I hope they won't be much objected to, especially when the Pillar is up when it will be Seen, that they are only design'd as a sort of attendants to it. I'm sorry I have so Small hopes of waiting upon your Ldship, and Seeing them this year tho' I sometimes think it may happen to be possible for me, to get downe (tho but for two or three days stay) towards the end of October. I am now going into Dorsetshire, Mr Dodingtons Trustees having met here in Towne, and adjusted all things for executing the Trust, in regard to the Building, which from this time is to go on without any Stop as fast as the Revenue the Southsea has left will allow of, which will be about £1800 a year.

I believe my Lord Godolphin woud have likt very well to have had the Duke of Marlbh: buryed in the Park, with a Very good Monument over him; but the Duke directs in his Will that they shou'd bury him in the Chappell at Blenheim. Here is a Pompous funeral preparing, but curb'd and Crippl'd by her Grace; who will govern it by her fancys, amongst which, there is but one good one, and that is that She'll pay for it.

I don't know whether it won't cost her Ten Thousand pounds. What a Noble monument wou'd that have made, whereas this Idle Show, will be gone in half an hour, and forgot in Two days. The other, wou'd have been a Show, and a Noble one, to many future Ages.

I shew'd the Young Dutchess what your Lordship writ, about so Great a Fortune falling into such Generous hands; which she took mighty well. She says, Covetousness has happen'd to appear to her so very odious in some other people, that she is sometimes frightened, lest she shou'd have seeds in her blood, that may Spring up one time or other. I tell her, now is the time if ever, Since it generally go's along with great Riches.

This Will was made, but in March last; and hurts nobody but her. I don't find however that either She, or my Lord Godolphin have the least disposition to dispute it; and I hope nobody else will; tho' there's a great Temptation to the Duke of Montague, who wou'd come in for three or four hundred thousand pounds, if this Will were set aside; and that the old one be cancell'd, as 'tis said it certainly is tho' I can't believe so great a mistake cou'd be made.

I don't think however, it wou'd be possible to Set this Will aside; Since besides so much as may be pleaded in Support of the Dukes Capacity to make a Will, it recites the former almost thoroughout, and gives the bulk of the Estate where it ought to go, and where all the World knows, the Duke ever intended it. Her Grace has by this Will (for to be Sure that was her doings) made my Lord Blandford Independent of his Father and Mother, Depriv'd her Daughter of the Jewells, and Cater'd bravely for herself I being told yesterday by a good hand, that one of the Executors has said, they know of Six hundred thousand pounds, She had of her own, besides what the Duke has dispos'd of which I have seen vallu'd by way of money and amounts to almoſt £1400000, besides Jewells, Plate, Pictures, Houses & Furniture. So that, at this reckoning, the whole amounts to a great deal above two millions. What my Lord Godolphin enters at present into, is not so much as at firſt was thought; my Lady Dutchess tells me, he finds it to be full £30000 a year however, with which they Seem well content. The Duke has expreſt, an earneſt desire, that an Act of Parliamt: may be obtain'd, to continue this Great Eſtate in his Family; But I find nobody dispos'd to come into it; as indeed I shou'd wonder if they were.

'Tis a great pitty as your Ldship observes, that the Duke made no disposition to publick uses, the want of which Reflects cruelly upon him But that which wounds his Character much more, and will to all ages blaſt it in a great degree, is what now, is freely said, and generally allow'd for truth, that had the Queen liv'd a month longer, he had been Seen to act a Sad part, having made his Peace on the worſt Terms. His Lady, is now look't upon, as a thorough profeſt Jacobite, and her having furnisht money to the Preᵗ: not deny'd by her Family. These are Strange things.

The King is much pleas'd with Kensington and the Easy way of living he is fallen into there. He go's however to Hampton Court the beginning of Next month, and 'tis thought will make some little Tour toward Salisbury and back by Wincheſter & Portsmouth—He is not a bit content with Sr Tho: Hewet in finishing the Rooms at Kensington. I have hopes of his doing something of advantage to me, tho' not as an Architect; which is not a Trade I believe for any body to recommend themselves by at Court. However, I fancy your Lordships Godson will be a Professor that way, for he knows Pillars, & Arches and Round Windows & Square Windows already, whether he finds them in a Book or in the Streets, and is much pleas'd with a House I am building him in the Field at Greenh: it being a Tower of White Bricks, only one Room and a Closet on a floor. He talks every thing, is much given to Rhyming, and has a Great turn to dry joking. What these Seeds may grow to, God knows. they being of a kind, that may do his business, uphill, or downe hill, so perhaps upon the whole, he were as well without them. They serve however to make himself and other people Sport at present. If my Lady Irwin ever has a House under the Cannon of this Caſtle, I shall be glad to see him some amusement to her. I hope She and my Lady Mary are well, which my wife is not but desires her moſt humble Service to them and to your Lordship.

I am yr Ldships moſt obedient Servant

142

[*To the Duke of Newcaſtle.*]

Greenwich. Jany: yᵉ 19ᵗʰ 17$\frac{22}{3}$

I endeavour'd to find your Grace at the House of Lords on Thursday, but miſt you, and cou'd not possibly come to Newcaſtle House before I came out of Towne. I had not however much to say: 'Twas only, that I had Seen my Lord C. and found all was juſt as I had told you. Upon which I thought, it not amiss to tell him I had found your Grace in some uneasyness upon what had paſt on your coming to Visit him, leſt any thing shou'd have been represented wrong, as to your concern, in what had lately happen'd: He seem'd to take very kindly, what I represented to him on that matter as far as it concern'd your Grace with regard to my Lord Lincoln, And said he wou'd send to you, to excuse his not being able to See you, when you did him the honour to design him a Visit. And as to the whole affair, I take him to be in a way of thinking very right of it; at leaſt what I think is so And shall be very glad, if I never find Cause to think otherwise, which I believe I shall not.

On monday I'll return to Towne, and shall be ready to obey any Orders your Grace may have for your moſt humble & Obedient Servant

J VANBRUGH

143

[*To the Duke of Newcaſtle.*]

Greenʰ: July yᵉ 30ᵗʰ 1723

My Lord Duke

I am now very near setting out for the North: I believe I shall get away on Sunday or monday: And have therfore exaſtly fix'd every thing for the Wall and given Billinghurſt Such perfeſt Sketches, for his Inſtructions in carrying up one length or Bay of it to the Top; that I think he cannot miss it. And so at your return, Your Grace may by that Specimen, judge of the reſt.

I have likewise drawn out and sent to the Brigadier, the design for the Garden house, which I think do's mighty well.

I have juſt now a Message from Grimsthorpe, That my Old Friend & Ally the Great Chamberlain is at laſt, gone. I have no particulars how matters are left, But I think the Son he has left, will prove the beſt Soveraign that has Sate upon that Throne, and I hope all reasonable means will be us'd to Cultivate him, for I don't take him to be of an Ungratefull Soyle.

I din'd with Mʳ Walpole at Chelsea on Wednesday laſt, and find him much content with what is doing in Norfolk. I desire your Grace will not let any body hinder you from being so at Claremont because it will be much better for you, as well as for Your moſt Obedient Servant

J VANBRUGH

Happening to meet with Sʳ Richᵈ: Steel tother day at Mʳ Walpoles, in Towne, he Seem'd to me to be, (at leaſt) in the declining way I had heard he was. If it shou'd go otherwise than well with him, Your Grace will give me leave to remind you, of what you told me not long since, of your favourable Intentions towards me, for that Sinecure, The Reversion of which, I now take the Liberty to ask of you.

[*To Forbes?*]   144

Greenwich Augᵗ yᵉ 3ᵈ 1723

Sʳ

I writ to my Lord Duke about a Week since, I desire the Favour of you, to let him know, I am now going for the North, Tuesday, the day I design to set Out; And as I shall make a little Stop at, (and about) Nottingham, I shou'd be Oblig'd to him, if he cou'd Spare me some Venison; wᶜʰ if he do's, I shou'd be glad the Warrant might be sent to Mʳ Pennel by the firſt Poſt: which I'll beg the favour of you, to put him in mind of.   I am

Sʳ Your Assured humble
Servant
J VANBRUGH

145

[*To the Duke of Newcaſtle.*]

Caſtle Howard. Augᵗ 20ᵗʰ 1723

Your Graces very kind Letter, has found me here. And I return you my humble & hearty thanks for it. I have been drinking Waters at Scarborough three or four days, and am to return thither with Lord Carlisle, for a Weeks Swigging more, And soon after that I point towards London. But Shall wait upon his new Grace of Ancaſter in my way, having the honour of an Invitation from him, to consult about his Building; by which I believe he is inclin'd to go on upon the General Design I made for his Father laſt Winter and which was approv'd of by himself.

He certainly has the honeſt heart your Grace says, And I hope will do all that's right. He is not mutinous, but takes more Notice of little things being done, in a kind or Unkind manner, than he Seems to do: And was hurt, by being put to so tedious a Solicitation about that Small business of Oldfields, which to this hour, is ſtill where 'twas. When I come to

(151)

Towne, I will beg of Mr Walpole to Surprise him, with doing something in it, without his knowing he has a thought about it. Tis reduc'd to a Trifle, The Arrear due was £600. But upon some talk he had, between jest and earnest with my Lord Townshend about a Composition for the Widdow, I believe £300. Order'd in the manner I mention, (without any fresh Solicitation) wou'd make all well.

Here has been a great deal of Company of Late, And Lord Halifax, Lady Halifax, Lord Binny and Mr Montague (Westminster) are here still: And profess themselves prodigiously pleas'd. Great improvements have been made Since I was here last, And much greater, we are now setting Out, for Next years Operation. I hope I shall find the Walls at Claremont, as much to my Satisfaction (and your Graces too) as those are here. I find the more my Lord Carlisle sees of them, the more he is pleas'd with them, And I think all that come here, are Surpris'd at their Magnificent Effect.

I am a most humble and Obedient Servant
to your Grace, the Ladys & Mr Pelham.

J VANBRUGH

I am Order'd to make your Grace the Compliments, of My Lord Carlisle And the rest of the Company here.

To Mr Joynes   146
  in the Palace
    Kensington

Greenwich. Nov: ye 11th 1723.
Monday.

Mr Joynes.

I was out of Towne when you writ to me about being examin'd; I shall come to the Board to Morrow Morning, and if necessary will stay in Towne all night, but wou'd gladly Return hither some time on wednesday. So you may send your soliciter to me when you will, during my Stay, or if the matter is not yet pressing, I design to come to Whitehall on Monday next for good. I am

Your humble Ser^t
J VANBRUGH

As to my house, I shou'd be very glad to have Mr Travers for a Tenant, But really, if it has been worth £60. a Y^r hitherto (when the Courts being at Kensington, has been so little for want of the New Rooms being ready for the King's Use,) 'tis easy to imagine it may be worth considerably more, when the King comes to Spend so much of his time there, as I find 'tis taken for granted he will. But thus far I will have regard to M^r

Travers in preference to any Stranger That as I will not now, ask him more, (in View of what I mention) than what I have had while no Court has been there; So if the Court do's come I will not remove him, while he pleases to ſtay Nor raise the Rent upon him, tho' I shou'd be Offer'd more by Another. Which with my Service I desire you will acquaint him with, putting him in mind at the same time, Of the Advantages in this House, by being free from all Parish Dutys, Repairs and the Charge of Water.

I think the House will be clear at Chriſtmass. of which the Servants there will inform you.

[*To Lord Carlisle.*]   147
                                              London. Nov: yᵉ 26th: 1723

    My Lord

I am very sorry to find by my Lady Irwin your Ldship has had so rugged an attack of the Gout; I hope I shall hear soon 'tis quite over.

The Regents Sudden Death, is a great Surprise, and (by the help of some Knaves in Exchange Ally) has frighten'd Some people to dispose of part of their Stocks, which has sunk the Vallue of them pretty much today, but 'tis thought will begin to rise again very Soon. The Duke of Bourbon was design'd by the late Duke of Orleans, to be Prime Miniſtr in his Room very Soon, the Fatigue being too much for him, So he was immediatly Declar'd upon this Accident. I don't find he is eſteem'd a Man of much Parts or Business; a little fickle & much Intereſted; But at the Same time I find all here agree, There is not now one man left in France, in any degree fit to take the Helm into his hand, So low the Great Men run there at present. So that there Seems little Danger at present of any Great Designs being probable, relating to Foreign Affairs, nor have they any tollerable hopes of their Young King proving anything that either the Good or the Bad men of a Nation wou'd wish for, all accounts, both of his parts or Dispositions being bad as may be.

                                   148
[*To the Duke of Newcaſtle.*]
                                      Greenwich. Dec. yᵉ 22ᵗʰ 1723

    My Lord Duke

The Brigadʳ: shew'd me, a Draught Mr Ripley had given in about the Drains, and told me your Grace wanted my thoughts about it.

I desir'd him to tell you, That as there was nothing express't in that Draught, but barely making a large Sewer, I cou'd say nothing to the purpose upon it, without Mr Ripleys telling me his reasons for thinking, that that alone wou'd cure the Diſtemper, Or explaining to me, what (if any thing) he propos'd to do besides.

I brought however the Plan of the present Drains downe with me, and the more I think of the matter, the more I am of Opinion, That the Cure may be made the way I propos'd before, At leaſt, I think it reasonable to try it, Because

1st It may be done in a very little time.

2ly It will coſt a very little money.

3ly It is what muſt be done, tho' a Great Drain shou'd be made; or else that Great Drain will Signify nothing.

What I say, upon my Word my Lord, is in no sort Obſtinately, or peevishly, but purely my thoughts and whether it Succeeds as I expect or not, Sure 'tis reasonable to try this firſt, rather than the other Because.

If this don't do, it will not have coſt you, (I believe) £20

If the tother don't do, it will have coſt you (I believe) £300

I am Your Graces

ever moſt Obedient Ser^t

I writ to Grimsthorp   J VANBRUGH

To his Grace   149
    the Duke of Newcaſtle.

Whitehall. Thursday Night

My Lord Duke

I am juſt return'd from Hamp^t: Court. where every thing in the Princes Rooms will be done as I promis'd, except some little matters in the Chimney, which Signify nothing, not being in the Upholſterers way

I have given all the Orders I can, about the Small matters relating to your Grace. But three or four of the things M^r La Roche desires about the Kitchin and offices, cannot be done at the Kings expence And I know your Grace wou'd not have any of his Orders broken into. They'll coſt you, but a very Small matter, and if you please I'll set men on to do them on your Graces Acc^t And Sorry I am I can do no more. being moſt truly and thoroughly

Your ever Obedient Servant

J VANBRUGH

To his Grace   150
    The Duke of Newcaſtle.

Monday 12 *aClock*

Your Grace will pardon my only telling you, I have Sate two hours with my Lord Carlisle this morning, And find him right to himself and every

body else. I am Oblig'd to go this moment to Greenwich, on some particular business, but shall be back at Night And will endeavour to give
your Grace or my Lord Townshend an Account to morrow, of what has
paſt, which is juſt as I wisht it might be.

Your Graces ever Obed^t
J VANBRUGH

To his Grace   151
    The Duke of Newcaſtle

Tuesday Night

I quite forgot today, a Promise I had made to Shew your Grace the
enclos'd Paper. The Recommendation comes from a True Whig Clergy-
man, a Favourite of the late Duke of Newcaſtles. who lives near Swallow
and to whom Mr Baynes is now Curate. If your Grace is not engag'd,
nor have any body in your thoughts, to whom so Small a living may be
of much Consequence, I beg leave to offer this Man to you; But don't
so far Interest my self in it, to desire you shou'd have any regard to my
Application, if you have the leaſt Inclination, or Occasion to dispose of
this Matter else where.

Y^r Grace's moſt Obed^t
VAN

152

[To the Duke of Newcastle]

Whitehall. Tuesday

I know 'twas from your Graces usuall goodness to me, you wou'd give
me leave to See you this morning, thinking I might have somthing to say
to you, of my own troublesome Affairs; but I have none I need perplex
you with whilſt you have the uneasyness of my Lady Dutchesses Illness
upon you, which few people can be more concern'd at than I am, nor more
heartily wish over, as I hope it will Soon be.

The Model is done, and gone to Kensington, where I hear the King
will View it this morning So I am now going thither.

Your Graces eternally Oblig'd
And ever Obed^t humble Servt
J VANBRUGH

To his Grace   153
    the Duke of Newcaſtle.

Whitehall 5 aClock

Your Grace will not I know be angry with me, (tho' perhaps you may
a little laugh at me,) if I forbear waiting on you today, on Account of the
Diſtemper My Lady Dutchess has the misfortune to be afflicted with.

(155)

For having never had it, and it being of very apt Communication, as well as very mischievous to people at my time of day, I am councill'd not to go in the direct way of it. I am so much out of Order, 'twas with no Small difficulty I went today to Kensington, by appointment from the Vice Chamberlain, who came at last, and told me your Grace desir'd the Model might not be Shewn the King, till you cou'd be there, which wou'd be to morrow noon. I will certainly be there, to receive your Commands, and will always with pleasure Obey them

Your Graces ever most Obed^t

J VANBRUGH

[*To Lord Carlisle.*]   154

Whitehall. Feb. ye 11th 1724

My Lord

Ever since I rec'd your Ldships Letter of the 14th of last month, I have been lay'd up. I am now out of Bed but not downe Stairs, and my head not quite in order to form Designs. I will therfore only say in answer to what your Ldship last mentions, that I believe breaks of five or Six foot might be so order'd to do well; and Shou'd be Square, not round. I will in a little time send a Sketch of that sort; But I still flatter my Self, nothing of this plain or Gothick Sort will be determin'd on at last.

One thing among the rest, I believe will contribute to the changing your Ldships present inclination in this matter is, That I believe, when the Estimates come to be made, The first Design I sent, with the 4 Porticos will be found very near (perhaps quite) as cheap, as any Gothick Tower, that has yet been thought of.

My Lord Morpeth about a month ago, View'd all the Designs I had sent, He declar'd his thoughts utterly against anything but an Italian Building in that Place, and entirely approv'd the first Design.

I am glad I can acquaint your Ldship, that we have prevail'd with my Lord Morpeth, to take under his Conduct the Bill for Reforming the Streets. I finding at last that Mr Walpole was come to think a little Seriously of the matter, as a thing quite fit for the Governmt: to take some care of, concluded, if he engag'd any body of Note to take the Chair He wou'd certainly take care he shou'd be Supported in it; So my Ld Morpeth being nam'd by Mr Frankland and others and Mr Walpole saying nobody wou'd be better, I ask't him whether he wou'd be so good, to Speak to him himself, he said with all his heart. This I immediatly acquainted my Lord with, who seem'd a little unwilling, on a difidence he had of himself, where he shou'd be oblig'd to hold the Chair at a Commitee of the whole House, which he had never yet done. But Mr Walpole having since Spoke to him & every body else pressing him to it, He has at last resolv'd to take all the pains he can, to carry so good a Publick Work thorough, and

has been with me this morning, in order to set the thing in motion immediatly; which I hope and believe he wont fail of being Successfull in; For
I take it for granted, they will Support him.

I am

Your Lordships most humble

and most obedt Servant

J. VANBRUGH

I am glad to hear, your Ldship is got on horseback again, tho' not able
to Walk. I have the new piece of Water much at heart; I hope 'twill do
well but I doubt there's no certain proof till the dry time comes. a Vast
deal of Rain has been this way.

[To Lord Carlisle.] 155

Feb: ye: 18th: 1724

My Lord

I writ to your Ldship the post before I rec'd your Letter of the 9th:
I am not yet abroad, but I think very near it; I am however in a Condition at home, to do some of my Sort of business, and am very glad to
find your Ldship at last incline to the Temple with the four Porticos; I
believe I never mention'd one thing in that Design, that wou'd be of great
Service, in regard to the usefull part of the Room. Which is, That since
the Situation requires it shou'd be open to look out every way, were there
no Porticos, the Sun wou'd Strike in so full, as to make it quite dissagre-
able, whereas these Porticos will keep the Sun almost always out of it, and
yet leave it quite light of the most pleasing kind. And for the Porticos
themselves nothing can be more agreeable than the Seats under them. As
to husbanding the Stone by Rusticks, it might be done; but tho' I am
a very great Lover of Rusticks, I do not think they wou'd by any means
do in this Case the whole turn of the Design being of the more delicate
kind; but another expedient will husband the Stone, better than Rusticks,
and be but what ought to be in this Design, and that is to flute the Pillars,
which do's so much disguise the joints, that one may use almost what
Stones one will. I think a Table fixt in the middle of the Room, wou'd
be right Since there can scarce ever be, occasion to use one in any other
part of it.

As to the Obelisks, I think as your Ldship do's, they are too small,
I believe one may make use of the Stone as it is now wrought from about
the middle downward so that the loss will be the Stone from the middle
upwards; which can however, with very little working, be us'd as ashler
anywhere. But I will consider this matter farther, and give your Ldship
a more certain account.

I remember I made a great blunder, in a letter to your Ldship about

(157)

Six weeks since where I mention'd my Lord Stairs's building in Oxford-shire. But 'tis the Duke of Argyle who has done there what I thought was my Lord. Stairs's. So whether he likes Castle Howard or not, I have nothing to say against any of his operations.

There has dyed of the Small Pox in Paris this last year 14000 people wheras there never dyed in London in the worst years above 3000. This has occasion'd the Physitians at Court there, writing over hither, to Sr Hans Sloan & Mr Amyand the Kings Surgeon (who inoculated the Young Princesses) to know what Success that practice has realy had here—their enquiry has been in regard to the King of France. But the Priesthood presently Stept in, and had the matter sent to the Sorbonne, Whose wisdom and Piety do not think fit to allow of it. I don't hear of any of our Clergy but high Church, who are of opinion with them.

When the King was at Hanover Prince Frederick hinted something to him as if he shou'd not be unwilling to be inoculated if the King thought it right. The King told him, he shou'd not care to direct it, but that he himself had agood opinion of it and the Prince knew how it had Succeeded with his Brother and Sisters. But that he look't upon him to be now of an Age proper to determine such things himself, and so left it to him to think farther of it. The result of which at last is, that here is a Person just arriv'd from the Prince to the King, to desire his Leave that he may be Inoculated, which I Suppose will be agreed to.

The Masquerade flourishes more than ever—Some of the Bishops (from the true Spirit of the Clergy, to meddle in everything) had a mind to attack the King about them, which I believe, he did not like, for he took occasion to declare aloud in the Drawing room that whilst there were Masquerades, he wou'd go to them This, with what the Bishops understood from some Ministers they apply'd to, made them think it might be as well to be quiet.

The Bishop of London however during this, preach'd one very Spiritless Sermon on the Subject which I believe has not lost Heydegger one Single Ticket.

I am Your Lordships
most humble & most
obed^t Servt:

J. VANBRUGH

The Dutchess Dow: of Marlb: has again appeal'd to the house of Lords.

[To Lord Carlisle.]   156

London. March ye 26th: 1724

My Lord

I am very glad your Ldship has determin'd upon the four Porticos. I shall be much dissappointed if that Design don't Succeed well; I'll send

Mr Etty out of hand, what farther Instructions may be necessary for going on with it. As to the inside; I think there need not be any Costly finishing. I wou'd make a Surbase of Wainscote, and then Stucco the Walls quite up to the Cornice. The Ceiling will do very well flat, because it will shape the Room just to a Cube. Or if your Ldship likes it better to show the inside of the Cap, I have no exceptions to it. Whichever way it is done there must be some Compartments in the Plaistering.

I had drawn a rough Sketch of a Design I send your Ldship this Post, before I had your Resolution about altering the Obelisks. I think this will do. I keep to the Proportion of a Dorick Column, which is eight diameters and that is the usual proportion of those in Italy, and succeeds mighty well in two pretty large ones in Mr Dodingtons Garden. I have plac'd one of the present Obelisks by it, drawn to the Same Scale, that your Ldship may See the Great Difference, by adding one foot more to the Diameter.

The rising of the Water in so hopeful a manner, is indeed a Cordial to me; Which tho' I can't say I much want, yet I shou'd have been glad to have found one more in a Postscript, That your Ldship, was not quite sure, you Shou'd not let those loose Stones that ly about the Old House, be rang'd in their Places in the foundations of the New Wing. it cannot be anything like a large article, I fancy, but a very Small one; and wou'd in very Great measure, remove that disagreeable Confusion, and litter, that is a mighty drawback, upon the Beauty of the Court, and North Appearance of the House and what evry body that See the Seat, are sorely hurt with. I shou'd think a hundred pound wou'd do it.

It was resolv'd to place another of the little Turrets, at the angle your Ldship mentions, where the Wall turns up to the intended Temple, and Mr Etty has a Design for it, not much vary'd from the others. But the ground lying so low there, I believe Something higher wou'd do better, So I'll think of another Design—I will likewise send Something for the Walls to butt against, on each side the head of the Lake—Which I doubt can't well be less Bulky, than the Turrets, and therfore may perhaps as well be hollow like them as not.

I dont know what the King will do this Summer, Some fancy, go abroad again, but if one may regard some of the Small German Officers about him, it will be quite otherways Lockman has told me, he thinks he will make a Considerable Progress at home this Year. Which if he do's, is most likely to be Northward. And that is another reason, why I wish those Same Straggling Stones laid to rights.

My Lord Morpeth is often low Spirited about this Paving Bill; and often much Inclin'd to give it up, till another Sessions, thinking the Great Men don't appear in it, as he expected they wou'd. But for my part, I see no rubs or delays, more than what I reckoned upon, from the natural

Course of everything moving in Parliamt: thats worth having; nor do I think Mr Walpole is backward in the thing, tho' he yet has taken little part in it, more than on proper occasions, declaring himself for it. But I think he designs to take a Part to purpose when the Bill is brought in, and comes to be read a Second time. I may be mistaken in this but I can't help reckoning upon it, and therefore have join'd with Mr Strickland, Frankland and others in persuading my Ld Morpeth to go on. Which he do's but I think chiefly in Complaissance to us. But I think nothing is to be carryed of this kind but by Resolution and Pushing on with Vigour. Mr Walpole has now gone so far as to look the Bill over and approve of it. So I hope it will be brought into the House on Saturday. And tho' there Shou'd not be time to get it through this Sessions, I shall be glad to have it lodged in the House, that People may know what it is; and by Consequence that it is not liable to the reflections a Pack of Rogues without doors, cast upon it in order to Stir up the People to come with Clamorous Petitions against it; For this Bill is quite a fair thing, without the least trace of a Bubble or jobb of any kind; and so may bear the light.

I am Your Ldships most
obedt: humble Servt
J. VANBRUGH

I have Mr Ettys Letter
My Lord Walpole is to be marryed
tonight (or is marryed already I
dont know which)

To the Rt Honble   157
  The Earl of Carlisle
    at Castle Howard near York

My Lord   *London. Aprill ye* 11*th:* 1724

I have your Ldships Letter of ye 30th: of March and Mr Ettys since, with the Obelisks. I think the old Plinths may do very well, & I am much mistaken, if the Obelisk thus reveal'd and carv'd, don't please.

I came to Towne but last night; I will get the Design for the Belvedere ready, if possible, to send next Post. I believe four doors will give both Light and View Sufficient, without Windows, and then there will be Space enough for Chairs; the Table I think (as I have mention'd formerly) shou'd stand always fix'd in the Middle of the Room. I have some doubts about the Name of Belvedere, which is generally given to some high Tower; and such a thing will certainly be right to have some time and in Some Place, tho' I can't say I do at present think of one about the Seat, where the View is better than this, But this Building I fancy wou'd more naturally take the Name of Temple which the Situation likewise is very proper for.

I was to wait on Ld Morpeth this morning but did not find him. I am glad to find my opinion confirm'd by that of your Ldship, that it was right for him to bring in the Bill, let its fate be what it wou'd. I hope he will move on Monday for a Second reading, that we may See what kind of objections will rise against it—whether there be time to pass it or no.

What I most apprehend is, that some Simple insignificant Proposal, that will do no manner of good, may be accepted in its room. For something I verily think they will do; but ten to one a Foolish one.

I have met no curious diver into State matters today, to furnish me with any thing worth writing to your Ldship on these Changes By next Post, I shall probably know more.

I am Your Ldships ever truly
obedt Servant
J. VANBRUGH

158

[*To the Duke of Newcastle.*]

Greenwich. July ye 10th 1724

My Lord Duke

I tease your Grace about this Letter to the Arch Bishop, because I am within four days of setting out for Castle Howard, where I shall See the Person I recommend And as I have writ him word long Since what cou'd be done, he'll think odly of me if I am not Able to tell him, it is done.

I'll wait upon your Grace, to receive your Commands for the North before I go, and am

Your ever most Obedient Servt
J VANBRUGH

I have written to Ld Carlisle as my Lord Townshend desir'd me.

159

[*To the Duke of Newcastle.*]

Aug^t: ye 23th; 1724

My Lord Duke

From a hundred miles farther North, I am now got back to the South; —Scarburgh, From whence I am Oblig'd to trouble your Grace, in behalf of the Vicar, my Friend and Kinsman Garencieres, on whose Account you were so good, to write such a Letter, to his Grace of York, as I don't question has produc'd, such an Answer, as I want. Viz: That he will do, whatever your Grace wou'd have him.

Now, it so happens there is a Prebendary of Southwell just deceas'd, by which, there is a Vacancy, worth—Nothing. Yet so it is, We desire, we may have it: because, We are a Youngish Man, of good Bodily Fortitude, and our mind, not so harrass'd by Our Care of Souls, but that we hope we may Out Live, two certain Elderly Persons; which if we do, This same Nothing, may prove worth Something at laſt. In a Word, The Prebend we ask, is but Seaven pounds pr Anm: And will require a Yearly expence of Thirty to do the Duty: But, there is a Good Corps belonging to it, which after the Lives of the Two Persons mention'd, will fall inn And therfore, if your Grace pleases to Ask for it, I will humbly thank you, and my Parson shall heartily pray for you.

It will be necessary in the meantime, to Apprise your Grace, That as Whatever Vacancys happen till the Arch Bp: is inſtall'd, the King has in Stricktness, the disposal of them if he pleases: I believe my Ld Chancellr: muſt be Spoke to, who probably will not take any advantage, from the delay of the Inſtallation, it being intended by the King, a Favour to the Arch Bp: But will I Suppose, referr it to his Grace, In which Case there will I believe be no difficulty. For the Circumſtances of the thing are Such, That None, who have any considerable expeċtations from him (as his Chaplain &c) will ask for it or wou'd accept of it, were it offer'd them. But it Suits our Situation, and therfore I trouble your Grace for it.

I am going to Caſtle Howard in three or four days. I shall Stay there, about a Fortnight, and then look homewards, where I shall be mighty happy, if I find your Grace in all the Health and Happyness ever wisht you. by your moſt Obedt and moſt Oblig'd,

J VANBRUGH

The thing I ask for, is. The Prebend of Southwell, Vacant by the Death of Mr Felton of Nottingham.

I thank your Grace for your Venison, And I have not forgot, Your Seats for Claremont.

160

[*To the Duke of Newcaſtle.*]

Caſtle Howard. Augt ye 28th: 1724

In a Letter I troubled your Grace with, about Spiritual Affairs, I told you I had not forgot the Temporal one, of a Seat for the Water side at Claremont. I had it then by me, rough, and here inclose it, fair. Your Grace remembers it was to be calculated for Brick, not Stone And therfore muſt not expeċt quite a florid thing, but I think t'is a Decent one, and wou'd become the place. However; if it don't please you, it will Serve you to find fault with, till your Obedient humble Servant can Attend you with a Better.

My Lord Carlisle is quite recover'd, and much Your Graces Servant.

To *the Rt: Honble*   161
  The Earl of Carlisle
    at Castle Howard near York

London Nov: ye 21st 1724

  My Lord

I am but newly got to Towne from my Lord Cobhams &c and have been so dissagreeably Hurryed about since I came, that I cou'd not answer sooner what your Ldship writ, about the covering of the round Towers.

I think the Spire that Mr Etty sent will by no means do, a Cap is all that those sort of Towers shou'd have, and I have seen one upon a round Tower on the Walls of Chester, that I thought did extreamly well. I believe it might rise something higher than that I left the Sketch of, but I believe a little help that way will make all right. I therfore here inclose a Draught with the Cap planted quite even with the top of the Battlements, which I am pretty confident will do; I have however sent another with it, which I believe wou'd not be dislikt by many people, but I think the Spiral one will do better, and be more of a piece with the Tower it stands upon.

I don't think any Ornament upon it, better than a Ball, and shou'd incline to it, notwithstanding there are four of them already upon the Obelisks in the Parterre.

As much as I love a Gateway, and by consequence Shou'd be glad to See one up at Castle Howard; I must own, I think the Wing of so much more weight to the Credit of the House, both in regard to the outside and the in, that as far as my Wishes or Opinion may go in the determination, I give them clearly for the Wing. Nay, tho the Consequences shou'd be such as to occasion the finishing the Wall in the front of the Court, where the Gate is design'd in such a manner as may leave it doubtfull, whether a Gate need hereafter be made or no. And Such a Design I have to offer.

I don't yet find Mr Etty wants any farther Instructions for advancing with the Wing, than the Designs he has; if he thinks he do's, and will send his Querys they shall be answer'd. I am
                Your Lordships ever most
                    obedient Servant
                    J. VANBRUGH

I just now read to the Lad, what your Ldship writ of giving him your Blessing tho' he wou'd not Ask it, His answer was, I thank him for sending me his Blessing, and if he sends it me again, I'll pray to god to bless him too.

162

[*To the Earl of Carlisle.*]

London Dec: ye 10*th* 1724

My Lord

A Spiral covering I think will do better than any other Cheap one for the Round Towers, but I cannot think, one so high and Taper as that Mr Etty sent, will do well, for it too much approaches the Spire of a Steeple, and yet is so much lower, as to make a Very ill Spire if it were meant for one. The Spires upon Steeples, are not meant for covering to the Towers they ſtand upon, but as ornaments rais'd upon them, to be seen a great way off. But Towers upon Walls, are Suited to them as part of the Fortifications, and are Suppos'd to be lodgings or Storehouses, and as Such only require a Covering, which may however be in a degree ornamental, but shou'd not look too light and trifling; I am therefore much inclin'd to think, that the Firſt Design, rais'd so high as to show the Whole Cap above the Battlements wou'd be much the Propereſt covering in this Case, and make the beſt figure, with regard to what it belongs considering the whole thing, from the ground to the Ball on the Top.

As to finishing the Front of the Court without a Gateway (at leaſt for the present, and leaving it to future consideration, whether to have any or not) I don't think it wou'd be necessary, (nor indeed proper) to have any opening there, as if an Access to the house in the middle were not to be dispenc'd with. For considering the Approach is Steep, and the House mounted high upon so elevated a Basement, as a Wall of 15ft forms, it may not probably Seem to people, when downe in the low ground, as if it were practicable, without great difficulty, to make the Approach right forward, and therefore might be reasonably dispenc'd with: and properly Supply'd by two Circular sort of Causeways, which on each side shou'd lead by an easy ascent to the Gateways already built. My Lord Cobham is mightyly for this Expedient, and tells me he has seen the very thing done, to a Great Palace in Germany, and had, he thought an Admirable good effect, the plain Wall in the Front looking with a bolder air of Defence than if there had been a Gate through it. If your Ldship, shou'd approve of this way there wou'd be nothing more to do, than to join the Walls from each Side, in a Strait line without any sort of diſtinction or regard to the Middle. I have talk'd of this, to my Lord Morpeth, who (tho' fond of a Gate) approves of it. He seems to wonder your Ldship do's not come up, So I hope for the Happyness of Seeing you here Soon, Twill then I Suppose be time enough to talk and think farther of this Proposition —And there needs nothing more to be said or directed more than has been, to guide Mr Etty in preparing things for the Foundation and Basement of the Wing, if your Ldship determins to go on with it in the Spring.

Here is so much Peace and quietness, both at home and abroad, that I know nothing to entertain your Ldship with, But that Mr Johnston told me he Supt tother night with the King, and told him your Ldship thought you cou'd answer the furnishing him with Game enough, when he shou'd think fit to Honour Windsor again. He said he shou'd be very glad to find you cou'd be as good as your word. They then talkt much of Castle Howard, and Mr Johnston I find set it out to all advantage Giving it a Preference (in taking it all together) to anything he had ever yet met with, consider'd as the Dwelling of a Subject.

I am Your Lordps most humble & most

obedient Servant

J. VANBRUGH

This Girl at Leicester House, is a great Dissappointment, She had very near kill'd her mother. Dr Chamr: lay'd her, and they all agree She cou'd not have liv'd three minutes longer.

163

To the Rt. Honble.
ye. Lords Commrs. of his Majests. Treasury.

May it please your Lords:ps
Your Lordships having Signify'd to me, by a Letter from Mr. Walpole, dated march ye. 26th 1723. That Mr. Wise and Mr. Carpenter having laid before the Treasury Board, an Estimate of the Charge of Planting in ye. Lower Wilderness at Hampton Court, Amounting to £115: 18: 2.

And that the said Mr. Wise and Carpenter being oblig'd by their Contract, to make good at their own cost and Charges, all Plantations that shall at any time happen to dye, I shou'd Examine into that Affair, and make report of it, your Lordps. having had no previous notice or given any Orders for new Works, especially in that part of his Majestys Gardens.

I have Accordingly enquir'd into this Affair, and am oblig'd to represent to your Lordps: That at the very time this Estimate was offer'd to you The Work was Actually done, without so much as my having any knowledge of it, much less giving any Direction for it.

But as to the Charge in making this New Plantation. the Destruction of the Old one, being occasion'd by the overflowing of the Thames, and not any neglect of ye Contractors, your Lordships will please to determine whether it ought to fall upon them or no; Which is humbly Submitted by.

Your most humble and

most obedient Servant

J VANBRUGH

April the 26th. 1725

(165)

THE LETTERS

To the R^t. Honble.
  The Lords of his Majestys Treasury

May it please your Lordships
Having rec^d. a Letter from M^r. Scroop of the 22nd. of April, to signify your Lordships pleasure, relating to a farther supply of Water at y^e. Cockpit, in Case it may be done at little Charge, by laying a new Pipe from y^e. Main near y^e. Gun Houses, I beg leave to acquaint your Lordships, That there having for some time past, been a great Scarcety of Water about Whitehall, occasion'd, partly by y^e. great failure of the Springs in High Park, for want of Rain, and partly by y^e. Proprietors of the new river water, cutting off a branch, which serv'd Whitehall, for many years past, but which they now pretend to have been only upon Courtesy. I have been endeavouring to recover some of the springs about y^e. Mews & S^t. Martins Lane which have been either diverted, or choak'd up, many years ago: and I have so far succeeded in this search, that I believe the Additional quantity of water wch. will now be geather'd from there, will prove Sufficient to supply both y^e. Cockpit, and Whitehall, without any farther Aid. All which is humbly Submitted by your Lords^{ps}. most humble and Obedient Servant

J VANBRUGH

Whitehall
  May 4th 1725

165

[To Jacob Tonson in Herefordshire.]

London Augt: ye 12th 1725

You will perhaps think me a little chang'd (and not for the better) that I shou'd be Six weeks in telling you how kindly I really took the proof of your Remembrance of me, in a Present of your rare good Cider. A Dwelling that produces such Liquor, must mean well to Mankind; I cannot therefore blame you, for passing such a share of your life in it, tho' I cou'd wish it might turn to account in your passing your days Agreeably, that a few of them might be spent at Barns, a Place formerly so pleasing to you and your Friends.

I am now but newly return'd, from a good agreeable Expedition I have been making for Six weeks past; My Lord Carlisle being in Towne with his Daughters, and something better in point of Gout than usual, had a mind in his way back to Castle Howard, to oblige them with a Tour, in which they might see some fine places that wou'd entertain them, I was of the Party and having leave to form the Journey as I wou'd, I carryed them

to Oxford, Seeing several Places by the way, as the Duke of Portlands,
Coll. Tyrrels &c for 'twas agreed, not to Stint them in time a piece of
husbandry, that usually spoils all Journeys of Pleasure. We stay'd in
Oxford (in a Whig Inn) as long as staying was good, and then went on
to Woodstock. This put me in mind, of Our Expedition (in former days)
with poor Lord Essex &c. And had the Same Master of Rowsham, been
at Rowsham now, We shou'd have pleas'd him and our Selves in dining
with him, as We did then.

We Stay'd Two Nights in Woodstock, My Lord and the Ladys, having
a mind to View Blenheim in every part with leisure. But for my own
Share, There was an order to the Servants, under her Graces own hand,
not to let me enter any where. And lest that shou'd not mortify me enough,
She having some how learn'd, that my Wife was of the Company sent an
Express the Night before we came there with orders, if she came with the
Castle Howard Ladys, the Servants shou'd not Suffer her to see either
House, Gardens, or even to enter the Park, which was obey'd accordingly,
and She was forc'd to Sit all day and keep me Company at the Inn.

From hence we went to Ld Cobhams, Seeing Middleton Stony by the
way, and eating a Chearfull Cold Loaf at a very humble Alehouse, I think
the best meal I ever eat, except the first Supper in the Kitchen at Barns.

The Company were so well pleas'd at Stowe, that they stay'd four days,
My Lord Carlisle then went on for Castle Howard, and we Stay'd at Stowe
a Fortnight, a Place now, so Agreeable, that I had much ado to leave it
at all.

You may believe me, when I tell you, you were often talk'd of both
during the Journey, and at Stowe; and our former Kit Cat days, were
remembered with pleasure. We were one night reckoning who was left,
and both Ld Carlisle & Cobham exprest a great desire of having one
meeting next Winter, if you come to Towne, Not as a Club, but old Friends
that have been of a Club, and the best Club, that ever met.

And now I Speak of Chearfull things, it puts me in mind of asking you,
whether there is any truth in what one often hears people say of they
Cyder Countrys; That there is not in any measure So much Spleen and
Vapours, as in other parts of England, which they attribute to the Constant
drinking of Cyder instead of malt Liquors. Nay, they go farther, and say,
That Neither Gravel, Gout nor Cholicks, are known as in other places.
I don't doubt but if there is any thing in this, you have observ'd it. Pray
let me know what your thoughts are of it.

The Duke of Newcastle ask'd me tother day when I heard from you;
He's very much pleas'd with being quite Friends again with you. which
gives the Brigadier some Serious and carefull thoughts. I am Dear Old
Friend, as Sincerely and as heartily Yours as Ever

J. VANBRUGH

[*To Lord Carlisle.*]   166

Greenwich, Sept ye 4th 1725

My Lord

I was very glad to find yr Lordp: had good Diversion at York, and was return'd well to Castle Howard, where I shou'd be extreamly glad I cou'd wait upon you; but I both am at present, and find my Self so likely to be, Clogg'd the rest of this Year, with variety of things I am not at all fond of, that I doubt I must be content to set my heart and thoughts only upon the early part of the next. I shou'd be very glad in the meantime, I cou'd hear of your Lordp: making a Considerable progress, in the Works you proposed to advance this Season, Which tho it is so much Spent, that no great matters can be brought about in whats left of it; yet, as the money allotted for it, is not Spent as well as the time, I hope that will so aid the next years operations, that some very Significant things may appear at the end of it.

I am glad your Ldp likes Mr Popes Inscription My Lord Cobham (who I take to be a very good Judge in such matters,) thinks it as well, as it cou'd possibly be. Every thing proper to be said on the Occasion being express'd in the shortest Compass, and quite in the antique Style and manner. I don't know whether it cou'd have been put into any other English, that wou'd have done better, (He thinks not) but the Expression will not be very familliar to many People especially such, as are no Learnder than I am.

We have had a Week or ten days, of tollerable Harvest weather, now it rains again But I hope in Spight of all this Horrible Season, England will fare better than her neighbours, at least I hear of very little Corn hurt yet.

Mr Hawksmoor is here, and was caught by the Gout a week ago, pretty badly, but has hopes now 'twill go off for this bout. He will send your Ldp the Slates out of hand. I am afraid a Distemper has got hold of me, even worse than the Gout, which is an Asthma; at least I have Strong Symptomes of one. And know well how hard a matter it is to deal with; But if I can't cure that—I will however try once more to cure London Streets, the Speaker Seeming now quite in earnest about it, and desires we will have the Bill ready to bring in, at the opening of the Sessions; So I am preparing every thing I can think of, that may be of Service to Support it.   I am Your Lordships and the Ladys

most obedient humble Servant

J. VANBRUGH

I have given my everlasting Friend the Dutchess of Marlb: Great trouble lately. Having Prevail'd with ye Treasury, to Issue Farther (upon a Privy Seal that Lys for £30000 towards the discharge of the Blenheim Debt, & of wch She has rec'd about £11000) a Sum juſt enough to pay me, being about £1700. And to prevent her Seizing it in Mr Guidotts hands, they sign'd an express order to him that when he rec'd it from the Excheqr, he Shou'd pay it directly to me, Which he has done accordingly.

I don't remember whether I acquainted yr Lordp in my Laſt, that I had made an end of my affairs at the College and rec'd my money £2400. Only there remains Still a Dispute about £300 in Fees, which Mr Anſtis will Cheat me of, if my Lord Sussex will let him. My Parting with that office while I am Living, has made your Ldps Gift of it to me Still the more Valluable, and for which I have therefore the more Acknowledgement to return you

[*To Lord Carlisle.*]   167
Greenwich. Sept ye 11*th* 1725

My Lord

I trouble your Lordp: with this Letter on Mr Hawksmoors Account. Sr Tho: Hewet is dead, and I see no manner of objection now, to the Treasurys reſtoring Mr Hawksr: to what your Ldp plac'd him in, with the Secretaryship you got Annex'd to it.

The difficulty hitherto has been, that the Treasury did not care to break in upon the usual right of the Surveyr, who has the putting in all the Clarks of the Works, when at any time they become Vacant. So that if they had turn'd out the man Sr Tho: put in, he wou'd have put in ſtil another and not Mr Hawksmoor, and so nothing had been got by it.

But now, before a New Surveyr is made, they can reſtore Mr Hawksmoor, without any exception whatever. And it is so very reasonable he shou'd be reſtored, after having been so unreasonably turn'd out; that I can't see it can be refus'd, if your Lordp: pleases to write to Sr Robt: Walpole for him. And besides his own juſt Claim on all accounts, I think he having been placed in the Works by your Ldp when you were in the Treasury muſt give such a weight to your desiring he may be reſtor'd, as can have no denial. I am

Your Lordps moſt humble
And ever obedient Servt
J. VANBRUGH

If your Lp: write soon to Sr Robt: Walpole, you'll please to send your Letter directly to him for I shall not be in Towne to carry it, if you shou'd direct it to me.

The present Clark is a poor mean Country Joyner who never has executed the office since he had it, not being capable. and Sr Ro: Walpole has always reckon'd Sr Tho: Hewet put him in for form, but gave him only a Small allowance out of the Income of the Place, taking the rest to himself, as no doubt was the Case. So there can be no difficulty in sending him home again to his Wife, who keeps an Alehouse in Nottinghamshire Besides he has been lately detected in notorious Crimes that wou'd remove him of Course.

168

[*To Jacob Tonson in Herefordshire.*]

Greenwich, Oct: ye 25*th.* 1725

A Letter, you much obliged me with some time ago, (and which now lys before me) I rec'd just as I was in a hurry, setting out upon a Northern Expedition, I found time however to shew it to the Duke of Newcastle, and he (tho' deep in business) found time to read it, with many expressions of Pleasure. I have not seen him since, (being but just return'd) nor Master Harry neither. But when I do, I will endeavour too please him, as well as his brother, with the Latter part of your Letter, and I do not doubt but he will chearfully accept of the Clubs Invitation, to dine with them one day, or one hundred, if so God pleases. I'm sorry a meeting cou'd not be on the day and at the Place you mention; both I am sure, would be highly agreeable to the Members of it. But they will not so soon be within Call: when they are, we'll try to find some other day of Happy Remembrance.

I have a pleasure in believing, you may have so much Friendship for an old and Intimate Acquaintance, as to take some small part, in the good or Ill that attends them, and therefore it is I'll acquaint you, That through great difficultys and very odd oppositions from very odd folks, I got leave to dispose in earnest, of a Place I got in jest, Clar^x King of Arms, and I sold it well.

Since that; being forc'd into Chancery, by that B.B.B.B. Old B. the Dutchess of Marlb^h: and her getting an Injunction upon me, by her Friend the late Good Chancel^r. who declar'd I never was employ'd by the Duke of Marlb^h: and therefore had no demand upon his Estate, for my Services at Blenheim, I say since my hands were tyed up, from trying by Law to recover my Arrear, I have prevail'd with Sr Rob. Walpole to help me, in a Scheme I propos'd to him, by which I have got my money in Spight of the Huzzys teeth, and that out of a Sum, She expected to receive into her hands towards the discharge of the Blenheim Debts, and of which She resolv'd I shou'd never have a farthing. My carrying this point enrages her much, and the more, because it is of considerable weight in my Small Fortune, which She has heartily endeavour'd so to destroy, as to throw me into an English Bastile to finish my days, as I begun them, in a French one. But I forget that you don't love long Storys, so begging your Pardon for this, I am moſt truly and faithfully Yours, and shall be mighty glad when your affairs and your Inclinations join, to bring you to London.

J. VANBRUGH

[*To Lord Carlisle.*] 169

London. Dec; ye 16th 1725

My Lord

I humbly thank your Lp. for the Warrant you sent me, for a Windsor Doe, which has been Serv'd and prov'd good, tho not over Fat as indeed none are this Season, from the great Rains that have fallen. I am glad I hear of no mischief about your Water under Ray wood So I hope your Dam holds firm.

I never heard till within these three days of your Ldps fall, nor that you had an attack Since of the Gout; which I wish well over. I am sorry to find by a Letter yeſterday from Mr Etty, your Ldp is going on with the Temple inſtead of the Weſt Wing. There are some things in his letter, I am not sure I underſtand especially, what he calls two Square Baſtions at the end of the Wilderness. For I don't know anything by those Names; What I incline to fancy he muſt mean is the New Plantation of Firs to the Southward and the two little Turrets at the Angles to the Parterre. But I can't see there is any need of enlarging them, on account of the Round Baſtions at the Southernmoſt Angles Those being outwards, as Considerable ornaments and diſtinguish'd terminations of the Garden; whereas the Turrets are only as Great Peers, for the two walls which meet there to butt againſt, where they make an inward Angle. But if your Lordp: thinks they are not Considerable enough either in point of finery or Size, in regard to themselves, I will try to make some better Designs. I can't say I like what Mr Etty has sent, nor indeed do I know whether he means the four Little Sort of Turrets at the angles to be additions to what is already built, or the whole to be entirely new. He mentions something about the Niches in the Porticos of the Temple, wch I will answer him upon, and send him the Seſtion he desires.

The Regents had Letters from Hanover laſt night, that the King will set out on Saturday, I wish he don't meet with a piece of ill news on the way, that will trouble him much, Prince William being moſt dangerously ill. He has had a Flux upon him, this month or more, voiding a great deal of blood. Sr Hans Sloan much in Pain about him from the begining, but other advice was hearken'd to, that wou'd not allow him to be in any danger. He was for Some days paſt thought so much better, that Yeſterday the Princess talkd of him without any concern and askt my Wife a great many queſtion how Charles faired with something he had of the kind half a year ago. She went afterwards to the Play, the Prince with her, but when they came home, they found a Sad alarm from a Sudden change to what I think they call a Guile, which people without doors say is certain destruction.

Here is much talk about Towne of Changes amongst the Great. Squabbles at least, and attempts in the way my Ld Letchmere talk'd on the Summer; but I have not yet met with any of those, I can hope to know a little truth from, when I do, your Lp shall have an Account of it, from

Your ever most
Obedient Servant
J. VANBRUGH

My Lord Palmstons house which Joyn'd to the Duke of Kents, did not receive one Shillings damage, nor was it found necessary So much as to remove any goods. This is owing to the advice Mr Hawksmoor & I gave my Lord Ashburnham at the Building of it

To the Rt: Honble: 170
  The Earl of Carlisle
    at Castle Howard near York

London. March the 8th 1725/6

  My Lord

I writ to your Lordp: last Post, and have Since had a letter from Mr Etty; I am glad he is so far prepared towards the Temple. I hope it will get out of the way to an other Work of (I believe) quite as much Consequence to the Value of the Whole.

If your Ldp has a mind to extend the area from a Cube of 20ft to one of 22, it needs have no regard to the Collumns, or other parts of the Architecture, which will all do as they stand at Present.

If I don't mistake, it was proposed to have no Windows or Niches in the Porticos; and indeed I believe they will do at least as well without, but I think there may instead of them, be niches in the inside, which will do very well in Stucco; whether there ever comes any Figures or Vases in them or not.

I don't rightly understand Mr Etty about a Design for the finishing of the Slated Roofs of the two Circular Towers; not knowing whether the Roofs themselves are done, nor in what manner, for several sorts were proposed, but I never heard which your Ldp resolv'd on. If it be only the ornament upon the Point he means, I can think of nothing better than such as are upon the Obelisks in the Parter, nor do I think 'tis worth while

(172)

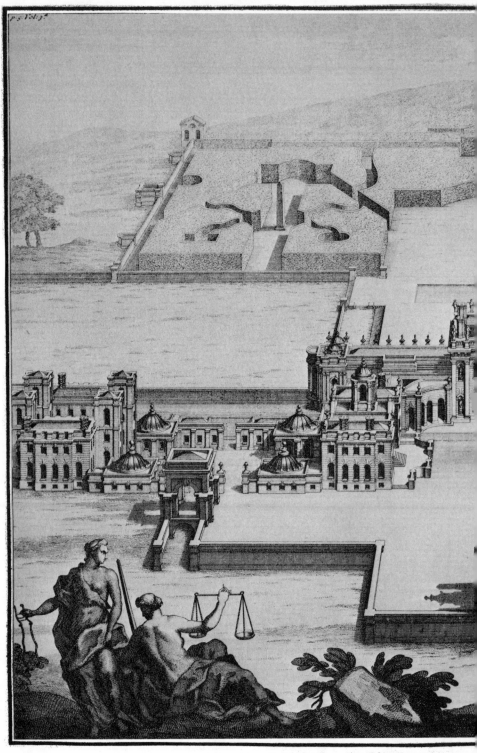

Gu: Campbell Delin:

Castle Howard in Yorkshire the Seat

nourable the Earl of Carlisle &c :

H:Hulsbergh Sculp :

to vary them, unless your Lp: shou'd like to add a Vane or Weathercock upon the Ball.

Your Ldp will no doubt be truly concern'd for the Sudden loss of the Duke of Kingston, who is Succeeded by my Lord Trevor. The Duke was abroad but two days before, tho' not very well; he was to have set out for the Bath as yesterday. I don't yet know directly, what the attack was that carryed him off, people giving Such various accounts of it; But something like the Twisting of the Gutts, I take it to be, by what is said.

I told your Lp in my last, how much I found the Duke of Grafton pleas'd with Castle Howard. I have since Seen my Lord Bathurst, who declares himself quite as much, my Lord Binny do's the Same, and I think my Lord Stairs, but I have not spoke with him himself. They all are vastly Surprised and taken with the Walls and their Towers, which they talk much of. I always thought we were Sure of that Card.

I am Your Lordships
most humble and most
obedt Servant
J. VANBRUGH

APPENDICES

APPENDIX I

I

Sir *John Vanbrugh's* Justification
Of what he depos'd in the
Duke of *Marlborough's* late TRYAL.

In the Answer given in, on the part of his Grace the Duke of *Marlborough* to a Bill preferr'd against him, by some of his Workmen, employ'd in the Building at *Blenheim:* It being thought fit (by those, who since his Grace's Indisposition, have taken upon them the Conduct of his Affairs) to try, if it might not be possible, to make a short end with those People, by (Gallantly) turning the Debt upon me; it was found necessary (and therefore resolved) to declare false, what the late Lord *Godolphin*, has under his honest Hand, in the plainest, fullest, and most express Terms, declared to be true, *viz.*

To ALL TO WHOM these Presents shall come, The Right Honourable SIDNEY Lord Godolphin, Lord High Treasurer of *England*, sendeth Greeting. WHEREAS his Grace *John* Duke of *Marlborough*, hath resolv'd to erect a large Fabrick, for a Mansion House, at *Woodstock* in the County of Oxon. KNOW ye, That I the said *Sidney* Lord *Godolphin*, AT THE REQUEST AND DESIRE of the said Duke of *Marlborough* have constituted and appointed, and do hereby FOR, AND ON THE BEHALF of the said Duke, constitute and

(177)

appoint *John Vanbrugh* Esq; to be Surveyor of all the Works and Build-ings so intended to be erected or made at *Woodſtock* aforesaid; And do hereby Authorise and Impower him the said *John Vanbrugh*, to make and sign Contracts with any Persons for Materials, And also with any Artificers or Workmen to be employ'd about the said Buildings, in each manner as he shall judge proper, for carrying on the said Work, in the beſt and moſt advantageous manner that may be, And likewise to employ such day Labourers and Carriages from time to time, as he shall find necessary for the said Service, and to do all other matters and things, as may be any ways conducive to the effectual Performance of what is directed by the said Duke of Marlborough in relation to the said Works, And I do hereby authorise and require the said John Vanbrugh to lay before me from time to time (in the absence of the said Duke) an Account of his proceedings herein, together with what he shall think necessary to be observ'd, or wherein any further Inſtructions may be wanting. To the end the same may be given accordingly. Dated *June* the 9th. 1705

GODOLPHIN

THIS Warrant however, having at the Tryal in the Court of Exchequer met with a Regard suitable to the great Character of him who sign'd it, it was endeavour'd by his Grace's Council, to lighten the weight of some farther evidence I had been call'd upon to give, by trying to shew some sort of disagreement between what I now depos'd upon Oath, and what I had occasionally writ, in times paſt, on this Subject. And this they labour'd to make out chiefly from a Memorial I once gave into the Treasury for the Duke's Service.

In that Memorial I acted as his Graces Agent, And as I well knew the Queen had in reality engag'd her honour to build the House of *Blenheim* at her own Expence for him, And as I likewise knew, the Treasury was then in hands not extremely well dispos'd towards him. I endeavour'd to do him all the Service I cou'd, by setting the Hiſtory of that matter in the beſt light the truth of Facts wou'd permit: Nor did I think my self at all oblig'd to open any thing that might be turn'd to his disservice, unless I had been close queſtion'd to that end.

But I at the same time took care to say nothing that might not be found consiſtent, with what I shou'd be oblig'd to declare, if (by the Treasury not issuing Money to discharge the Debt) there shou'd afterwards happen any dispute between the Duke and his Workmen, in which I might probably be interogated on both sides, as has now fallen out.

And I think the precaution I took was such as will very fully clear me from any Reflection that can be caſt on my Depositions, which have in the late Tryal been read in Court.

(178)

APPENDIX I

1st. *Objection.*

The first thing they wou'd take hold of in the Memorial I have mention'd, is in the second Paragraph, where they say, 'Tis the Workmens demand for Money (not the Dukes) I pretend to set forth.

Answer.

The expression there used, of the Workmens demand, is none of mine. I only recite the words of the Letter I receiv'd from Mr. *Lowndes,* which call'd for that Memorial.

Nor do I in any part of it pretend to meddle with who the Money should be paid to. I only endeavour to shew the Treasury, That the Queen has engag'd herself to pay for the Building to some body or other.

2d. *Objection.*

In the fifth Paragraph of the Memorial they observe, I say. I was at that time Comptroller of his Majesty's Works, and as such, was order'd to frame a Model of the Intended Building.

Answer.

The Queen having resolv'd to build a House for the Duke of *Marlborough,* at her own Expence, and thinking fit, that the Method for defraying that Expence should be, by issuing Moneys to his Grace, for that end, without Account; The Building was not conducted by her Board of Works, but left to him, to employ such Officers and Workmen as he should see fit.

But his Grace being willing (as was very natural in such a case) to employ our Servants, preferably to others, as far as he thought them qualified for his Service cast his eye upon the Board of Works, where (for Reasons best known to himself) not inclining to engage Sir *Christopher* Wren, her Surveyor, he fix'd upon the next Officer to him, her Comptroller, thinking him (as such) qualified for the Business he was going upon, and so desir'd he would give him his assistance in it. This was what I meant, and what the Treasury must naturally understand, by the Words (as such) Since it was notoriously known to my Lord *Oxford,* Mr. *Lowndes,* and every Clark about him. That by my Patent of Comptroller (alone) I could not intermeddle with this Work of *Blenheim;* but had I acted there as Surveyor for the Queen, I must have had some new Power given me from her, which Power, must likewise have pass'd the Treasury, and that none such ever did pass, was well known there.

3d. *Objection.*

In the twelfth paragraph it is observ'd I say. In pursuance also of her Majeſty's Pleasure, the then Lord High Treasurer did appoint her own Officers, *viz.* My self to be Surveyor of the Works, Mr. *Hawksmoor* to be Assiſtant Surveyor, Mr. *Joynes* and Mr. *Boulter* to be Comptrollers and Clarks of the Works.

Answer.

My Lord *Godolphin* did every thing in this Matter, in pursuance of the Queens Pleasure; Acquainting her from time to time (in the Duke of *Marlborough*'s absence) with all material things he thought proper to direct, to the end nothing might be done but what was agreeable to her, And the Fact I thought was for my Lord *Marlborough*'s Service to insiſt in my Memorial to my Lord *Oxford*, to shew the Queen was appriz'd of all that was done.

Nor cou'd what I there say have any other meaning than what I thus give it, or be taken in any other sense by the Treasury, since (as in the case before) they knew, no Warrant or other Conſtitution whatsoever had gone from thence; which muſt have been, had the Queen's Pleasure meant any thing more, than as I explain it.

4th. *Objection.*

What I have said in this Article Is TRUE, and I have repeated it again upon Oath in Answer to the fifth Interogatory, in my Examination on the Dukes side, before the late Tryal.

But it is likewise TRUE, what I have there said. That when the Duke (on my Application to him, in my own Case) has declin'd giving Order for paying me any Money, I have taken the Liberty to remind him.

That the Money was HIS, and NOT the Queens, That it was HIS, by her Sign Manual, and to be accounted for to NO BODY BUT HIMSELF, and by consequence, could be dispos'd of by NO Authority but HIS OWN.

And that my Lord *Godolphin* had put in that course (I suppose) as the BEST and SAFEST Method for his Service.

This I have often put him in mind of, yet he wou'd neither sign any Order, for the Issuing of Money, nor have the Method alter'd, by which it was issued to him without Account.

If there be something ODD in this, 'tis not from any Inconsiſtencies of mine, What I have said to Facts is TRUE. But why his Grace did not care to CALL the Money his, and yet was willing the Queen and my Lord Treasurer shou'd go on in the same Method of MAKING it his.—I hope I am not to Account for.

APPENDIX I

Upon the whole. Let this Memorial be carried to the utmost that Florid Tongues can wind it; they cannot even pretend to make more of it than this. ·

That out of a more than common Zeal for the Duke of *Marlborough*'s Service (and for which Zeal I dearly paid soon after) I endeavour'd to set his Claim to the Queens Bounty in a Light, that at first View might seem to plead a little stronger for him, than on a closer reflection it would support.

If they who are to plead his Cause at *Westminster*, don't varnish it something more than they (ARE DIRECTED TO) accuse me of having done at the Cockpit; I believe the Person who pays them their Fees, will never think they have serv'd them.

JOHN VANBRUGH

Since I writ the precedent Paper, I heard there was a sort of Case handed privately about, relating to this Blenheim *Affair, in which my Name was pretty much us'd.*

I have at last got a sight of it, and find so much honest Language in it, fair stating of Facts, and right sound Reasoning from them, that one would almost swear it had been writ by a Woman. Some Answer however it shall have.

The late Decree against the Duke of *Marlborough* is said to be chiefly founded on my Warrant from My Lord Treasurer Godolphin. And therefore, to shew the Iniquity of the Decree, the Case sets forth; That my Lord did not know what he did, and that I probably (to some bad end or other) had trick't him into signing this Warrant.

How indifferent soever, that great and good Man might be to his own Interest; 'tis well known he neglected nothing in the Queens, and in his Friends.

Her Present of *Woodstock* to the Duke, and the great Summ of Money she resolv'd should be laid out there for him; made the whole Guift of such weighty Consequence, That if ever my Lord *Godolphin* gave himself a carefull thought in the Dukes Interest, 'tis most certain he would do it then; to the end this large Bounty might prove effectual. And that he did take this care (THIS FRIENDLY CARE) my Paper shall shew the World, tho' that I answer would not.

Take it thus;

I being inform'd, That my Lord *Godolphin* had appointed Mr. *Joynes* to be Clark of the Works at *Blenheim:* Ask'd his Lordship, whether he did not intend I shou'd have some visible Authority likewise, being to act in a Station of much greater Trust? he said certainly I must, and that he wou'd direct a Warrant to be prepar'd out of hand, to constitute me Surveyor with all necessary Powers.

APPENDIX I

Thus it was, and without any other Application Pressing, or Artifice, I came by that Warrant.

That to Mr. *Joynes*, ran thus.

To ALL TO WHOM these Presents shall come, the Right Honourable *Sidney* Lord GODOLPHIN, Lord High Treasurer of *England*, sendeth Greeting. WHEREAS HIS GRACE THE DUKE OF MARLBOROUGH hath resolv'd to erect and make a large Fabrick for a Mansion House with Gardens therunto, at *Woodstock* in the County of *Oxon*. KNOW YE, That I the said *Sidney* Lord *Godolphin* (at the request of the said Duke of *Marlborough*) have nominated, constituted and appointed, and do hereby nominate, constitute and appoint *Henry Joynes* Gent. (in whose ability, faithfullness, and diligence, I do very much confide) to view, examine, and inspect, all the Contracts made or to be made with any Workmen or Artificers relating to the said Building and Gardens, and to admeasure and keep the Accounts thereof; and to see that the said Contracts be duly comply'd with, and to do all other matters and things as he shall judge necessary for the effectual carrying on the said Service: And shall also from time to time (as often as requir'd) exhibit TO THE SAID DUKE OF MARLBOROUGH, or to my self, an account of his Actions and Doings, in pursuance hereof: and shall likewise from time to time, as often as he shall see occasion, make such Remarks or Observations, as he shall think conducive to a most just, fair, and regular management of the said Building and Gardens. Dated this 23d. day of *May*, 1705.

GODOLPHIN

Some time after, my Lord *Godolphin* thought proper to add another Person to Mr. *Joynes*, one Mr. *Boulter* (a Creature of her Graces) and to make them Joint Comptrollers, as well as Clarks of the Works.

And after that again, sign'd another Warrant to empower the Comptrollers to make and sign all Contracts with me. And thus all Contracts were made, and Prices adjusted; and under this Direction, the Building went on above three Years.

At last, Mr. *Boulter* dying, my Lord *Godolphin* sign'd another Warrant, to put one Mr. *Bobart* in his Place, of which here follows a faithfull Copy.

To ALL to whom these Presents shall come, The Right Honourable *Sidney*, Earl of *Godolphin*, Lord High Treasurer of *Great Britain* sendeth Greeting. WHEREAS by an Instrument under my Hand, bearing date the 9th. day of *June*, 1705. I did AT THE REQUEST AND DESIRE of his Grace *John* Duke of *Marlborough*, constitute and appoint *John Vanbrugh* Esq; to be made Surveyor of all the Works and Buildings then intended to be erected or made at *Woodstock* in the County of *Oxon* for the said Duke; and did thereby authorize and impower him the said *John Vanbrugh* to make and sign Contracts with any Persons for Materials, and also with any Artificers or Workmen to be employ'd about the said Buildings, in such manner as he shou'd judge proper for carrying on the said Work, in the best and most advantageous manner that might be: And likewise to employ such day Labourers and Carriages from time to time, as he shou'd find necessary, and to do all other matters and things as might be any ways conducive to the effectual Performance of the said Works. AND WHEREAS by another Instrument under my Hand bearing date the 21st. of *June* 1705. I did at the LIKE INSTANCE AND REQUEST of the said *John* Duke of *Marlborough*, nominate, constitute and appoint *Henry Joynes* and *William Boulter* Gent. to be Joint Comptrollers of the Accounts of the Works, Buildings and Gardens aforesaid, with Authority from time to time, to view, inspect and admeasure all the said Works, Buildings, and Gardens; and to examine all Bargains, Contracts, and Agreements, made or to be made, with any Persons for Materials, or with any Artificers, Workmen, or others, employ'd in or about the same, as by the said several Instruments, relation being thereunto had respectively, more fully and at large doth and may appear; AND WHEREAS by another Instrument under my Hand, bearing date the 29th day of July 1706. I did at the LIKE INSTANCE AND REQUEST of the said Duke of *Marlborough*, direct, That no further Contracts shou'd be made relating to the said Buildings and Gardens, by the said *John Vanbrugh*, but with the Privacy, Consent, and Approbation of the said *Henry Joynes* and *William Boulter*; And that the said Contracts at all times thereafter shou'd be made, sign'd, and joyntly seal'd, by them the said *John Vanbrugh*, *Henry Joynes*, and *William Boulter*. AND WHEREAS the said *William Boulter* is since deceased, and *Tilleman Bobart* Gent. is recommended as a Person very skilfull, able, honest, and industrious; and every way qualified to succeed the said *William Boulter* in the said Trust: Now KNOW YE, That I the said *Sidney* Earl of *Godolphin*, at the INSTANCE AND DESIRE of the said *John* Duke of *Marlborough*, have nominated, constituted and appointed, and do by these Presents, nominate, constitute and appoint him the said *Tilleman Bobart*, joyntly with the said *John Vanbrugh*, and *Henry Joynes*, to do, execute, or perform, or cause to be done, executed and perform'd, all and every the matters and things which the said *William Boulter* joyntly with them the said *John Vanbrugh* and *Henry Joynes*, might or cou'd have done, executed and perform'd, by virtue of the several Instruments above recited, or any of them. And I do hereby further declare, That the aforesaid Constitutions and Appointments, to the said *John Vanbrugh* as Surveyor, and to the said *Henry Joynes* as Comptroller of the said Buildings and Gardens (notwithstanding the decease of the said *William Boulter*) shall be and remain in all other respects, firm,

APPENDIX I

valid, and effectual, to the Intents and purposes therein mention'd and intended. Dated at the Treasury Chambers in Whitehall the 24th day of *September*, 1708.

GODOLPHIN.

And now will any one say, my Lord *Godolphin* was trickt into the Warrant he sign'd to me?

Will any one say, that noble, faithfull Friend to the Duke was thoughtless and negligent in executing the Commission he declared he had charg'd him with?

Will any one be so weak to think (whatsoever they may resolve to say) That in so many Years, and on so many fresh Occasions, to pass Warrants upon Warrants, the Duke never heard what situation, a thing of so near an Affection to him, was in?

Will any one believe, that in so many quiet, fire side, evening Conferences, as happen'd between those two great Lords and her Grace; the manner and method of receiving in, and laying out, those Hundreds of Thousands of Pounds, should never be part of the Amusement? Sure there's some great forgetfullness in this matter.

But I am askt, Why I did not myself, tell my Lord *Marlborough* of this Warrant?

Why truly, because the Warrant told me, he knew it already?

It was however entred with all the rest, in the Books of the Office, where all things were kept in exact Order, for his Grace to see, whenever he shou'd please to inspect them, or direct any body else to do it, as we never question'd but he wou'd, one time or other.

Nor had I ever the least doubt, of my Lord *Godolphin*, constantly acquainting the Duke, when he came home, with what he had done, on his Account, while he was abroad. Especially, in so Material a Point, as that of Money.

And I still less doubted (if possible) of her Graces knowing (even before hand, as well as after,) whatever my Lord *Godolphin* did in that Affair; Nor cou'd I suppose, she wou'd spare her Pains, in reciting it to the Duke, because 'tis well known, She was pleas'd to value no trouble she gave herself, (or other People) in what related to that Building.

Another Question askt me is; Why I did not secure myself, by desiring another Warrant, immediately under the Dukes own Hand?

Had it been possible for me to doubt, the truth of what I already had, under my Lord *Godolphin's*, I shou'd. But I never thought those two Noble Lords upon a foot, of one disclaiming in a Court of Justice, what the other under his Hand, affirm'd to be true.

I readily agree, with what is said in the Case, That my Lord *Godolphin*, was too much my Lord Dukes Friend, to design to Saddle him, with the

(184)

Expence of that Building. AND THEREFORE IT WAS, he put things in that prudent Method for his Service, That the Money to defray the Charge, shou'd be Issued to him, without other Account, than to himself alone.

By this means, Had the Work been driven on no faster, than my Lord *Marlborough* receiv'd Money from the Queen to pay for it; there had been no Debt to the Workmen; nor by Consequence, any Claim upon his Grace.

Now, whether the Workmen, ran thus a head of themselves, or whether they were press'd to it, by any body else. And whether I had Authority, to put them in mind, THAT WHATEVER HAPPEN'D TO THEM, THEY WERE STILL SAFE, I refer to the Decision of the following Letters, which I had the Honour to receive from her Grace.

Nov. the 2d. [1709 Ed.]

" SIR,

" I Receiv'd the favour of your Letter Yesterday at St. *Albans*, I was
" just going into my Coach to come to *Windsor*, and this is the very first
" Opportunity that I cou'd possibly write, and now I am so very ill, that
" I can't do it with my own Hand, which being a very ill one, there needs
" little Apology for that; every word in your Letter concerning the Pay-
" ment of the Carters is reasonable, and if I had known all these particulars
" sooner, I had certainly found out some way To HAVE ORDER'D THE
" MONEY, and you are in the right, for they shou'd be the first People
" paid, for the reasons you give; most of the Undertakers of the Building
" are Substantial Men: AND SINCE NO ACCIDENT THAT COU'D HAPPEN,
" CAN MAKE THEM LOSE THEIR MONEY, they will never let the Work stand
" still, for want of present Payment.

" By what Mr. *Travers* writ to me of his going to *Woodstock*, I believe
" he is there at this time, and I hope he and you together, has found some
" way to prevent, what you apprehend; for the Weather is extreamly
" good, and tho' it is not natural to continue so in *November*, why may
" not it be better then Ordinary, as well as in the other Months so much
" worse? It is extreamly obliging in you to write so warmly, and shew
" so much concern, to make the Building be soon finish'd; the Account
" you give of it is very agreeable, and I desire you won't make such Appli-
" cations between you and I, as you do of the *French* policy to the Work-
" men, nor imply because I have not been able to serve you, while you
" were wanted; that I shou'd be more careless if the business were over;
" for though you have vext me extreamly, in forcing me to things against
" my Inclination; yet I shall always think myself oblig'd to you, and will
" always be endeavouring to be out of your Debt; because I know, that
" what I did not like, as well as what I did approve of, you intended for
" the best, and tho' it is said that in this World there is no perfection,
" you are not the only Architect that thinks 'tis impossible they can err;

" I believe it is the opinion of all that Science, which makes it more reason-
" able for me to forgive you, and I hope you will do the same to your
" humble Servant,

S. MARLBOROUGH

" I did write to you about the Locks before I receiv'd yours, which
" Letter I hope is come safe to you.

Windsor-Lodge, Nov. the 4th. [1709 Ed.]

" I writ to you laſt Poſt, with an Apology of not making use of my
" own Hand according to form; But I think it wou'd be more according
" to reason, to make Speeches when I write so, as to give you more trouble
" than Ordinary to read.

" I am glad to find you have hopes of getting the Stone. I will observe
" your direction about Locks and Hinges when I go to *London;* and I
" give you many thanks, for giving them so particularly. It is a very
" small difference that you mention in Mr. *Kay's* Locks, not worth leaving
" him for, But I am sure all he said to me was very extravagant, and perhaps
" he may be more reasonable upon finding, THAT I WILL EMPLOY ANOTHER.
" I will talk to him again when I come to Town, and if he will put down
" his prices in Writing, and the sizes very exact, and not be unreasonable,
" nor trouble one with a great many words; I have business enough to
" employ him and the Smith that is now at work for me, but some part
" of the Business he muſt lose, and he may thank himself for that.

" I expect my Lord *Marlborough* with the firſt fair Wind; but I know
" nothing of his Intentions of coming to Woodſtock, I believe you may
" govern that as you please, And I think it is not unreasonable for yon
" to conſtrain your self, in ſtaying there upon uncertaintys, when the
" Business does not require it. I will not trouble you to return the Duke
" and Dutchess of *Shrewsburys* Complements, because I fancy by this time
" they are in Town. I am very sincerely your humble Servant,

S. MARLBOROUGH.

St. James's, July the 20th. [1710? Ed.]

" ——Mr. *Travers* has shewn me a Letter concerning Mr. *Parker*, that
" I think sets that matter in a clear light, and has said enough to satisfy
" any reasonable Man, this being only a return of Money, by way of
" Exchange. And Mr. *Parker* has a great convenience by it, AND SAFETY,
" AND RUNS NO RISQUE; ESPECIALLY SINCE THE ASSURANCES HE HAS RE-
" CEIVED FROM MY LORD TREASURER, THAT THE PAYMENTS FOR THE WORKS
" SHALL BE CONTINUED AND COMPLYED WITH, AS BEFORE.
" AND I WILL TAKE CARE, that Mr. *Tayler* shall be enabled to pay to

" Mr. *Parker*'s use here, what Sums he shall advance to the Comptrollers,
" for carrying on the Weekly Payments.
  " There is no Resolution declar'd yet about the Parliament, but many
" believe, *etc.*

I believe I have now said (and produc'd) enough to shew every Body
without a farther Pointer, where the Mystery of this matter lies.
  I don't however for my own Justification say something now, to shew,
That what is in so many Paragraphs pleaded, from the Prices in the Contracts; is as groundless and fallacious as the rest.
  At the beginning of this Work, I one day told the Duke, that the
present Lord *Cobham* had spoke to me of a parcel of Timber he had to
dispose of, and that his demands were so and so: To which he answer'd,
That he could not enter into such particulars, I must transact those Affairs
my self.
  This was all that ever past on that occasion, tho' much is said of it in
the Case.
  And all that ever I thought or understood by what the Duke had said,
was, That the infinite Affairs he had upon him other ways, wou'd not
allow him to negociate such things as those, and that therefore he had
thought fit to entrust me with them.
  And what confirm'd me in this was, That he did go so far as to give
me a general Instruction for my Guide, in relation to the Contracts I was
to make, *viz.* That as on the one hand he would not have extravagant
Prices allow'd, so on the other he desir'd the Workmen might not be so
ground downe as they had been in a particular place he nam'd, and which
he look'd upon as spoil'd by it. But that the Rates might be such as
shou'd have no pretence to the Work not being in Perfection.
  This Instruction I took the utmost care to follow.
  I sent to great variety of Workmen of the same Trade (in different
Countrys, and quite unacquainted with one another) for their Proposals.
  And when by that means I had at last brought the Prices to be moderate
Instead of throwing so great a Work into the hands of a few Undertakers,
I divided it amongst many, three, or four, or five, of each Trade, with
different Rates according to the Performance expected from them.
  This I did, partly to raise an Emulation amongst them, and so have
better Work done, And partly to shew, I had not a design to make advan-
tage by this Building, as was natural for People to think I might.
  The Rates agreed upon in general, (especially to the Masons,) which
were the great Article) were considerably less than what was paid, either
in the Queens Works, or others of any Consideration, about Town.
  And yet, most of the Work done for those Rates, was incomparably
better. So much; That when Mr. *Bridges*, (Surveyor of the Ordnance)

was sent down to inspect the Contracts, and the Performance; He declar'd at his return; He cou'd not conceive how such Work had been done for such Allowances; And made no Objection to any one Article in the Contracts.

And yet the Masons lay under very great difficulties and disadvantages, from the vast numbers of Men, they were forc'd to send for, not only to *London*, but even to the Remotest Countys in the Kingdom: For which they were Oblig'd to pay much greater Wages, than when they have only occasion for a Moderate Number, such as they can procure upon the Spot, without bringing them from their Families, in distant Habitations.

When the Duke of *Marlborough* (since the King's Accession to the Throne) resolv'd to finish the Building. The Masonry was offer'd to Mr. *Strong*, if he would abate of his former Prices, in consideration of more punctual and ready Payment. Which he refusing to do, makes it at least, very probable, those Prices were not out of the way; tho' some of his Workmen (to get themselves into Credit and Business, (having never done anything on their own Account before) did undertake the Work at something lower Rates: On positive Assurance they should never stay for their Money.

It is farther to be observ'd, That all the Contracts had the concurrences of Mr. *Boulter* in whom the Dutchess had so great a Confidence, that he had an Allowance of 400*l.* a Year, which to his dying day he continu'd to think he deserv'd. And yet I never had a difference with him about one single Contract.

One thing more I believe will be allow'd to have it's weight in this great Objection made to the Prices.

The Dutchess of *Marlborough* (who so much complains of them) being pleas'd to build a House at St. *James*'s, and to take the care and direction of it in chief to herself, with Sir *Christopher Wren* as her Deputy Surveyor; she not only employ'd Mr. *Strong*, and another of the *Blenheim* Masons, but paid them much better Prices than what we had allow'd them there. 'Tis true she wou'd have gone to Law with them, but the Duke wou'd not let her.

And I am very much persuaded, were he now in a State of Health, to admit his troubling himself with looking into the present Dispute; He wou'd think the other was much a properer Cause to have shew'd it self in *Westminster-Hall*, than this is to appear in the House of Lords.

I think there need be said no more (tho' a great deal more I cou'd say) to shew the weakness of this poor Plea about the Prices, which is only catching at a Twig to save a sinking Cause.

As to what is said of the Improbability, that the Workmen ever took the Duke to be liable: Since if they had, they wou'd never had been uneasy at the slack payments of the Crown.

This is at the best, but pleading Probability against Facts. For did they not sufficiently shew they look'd upon the Duke to be their Paymaster, when (having seen my Authority by my Lord *Godolphin*, to contract in his name) they wou'd sign no Agreement but what ran accordingly?

Besides, don't my Lady *Marlborough*'s Letters (which by Miracle I kept, and which I here produce) shew, That when they heard Money began to come in slow from Court, and found their Debts were great, they did not care to go on, till MY LORD DUKE gave Assurances by my Lord Treasurer (NOT MY LORD TREASURER BY MY LORD DUKE) that the Payments for the Works shou'd be continued as before.

What they apprehended I think seems very plain.

That as the Queen was really to furnish my Lord Duke with Money to pay for this House, he wou'd be glad to avoid advancing any of his own. By which means if they went on as fast as they were press'd to do, it would run them into giving a greater Credit than some of them cou'd support, and others car'd to do. And this it was that slackned their Vigour, 'till they were acquainted, That my Lord Treasurer had Commission from MY LORD DUKE, to assure Mr. *Parker* the payments shou'd be continued as formerly, and that HER GRACE wou'd take care Mr. *Tayler* (the Paymaster) should be enabled to remit Money accordingly.

Sure there needs no more Words to explain this Point.

All I have more to say to the Paper that has forc'd me to say so much already, is a word in answer to a Cracker let fly at the Tail of it against me, which bursts out thus;

" Upon the whole; if the Dukes conduct be not sufficient to disengage
" him from the Debt, it was impossible for him to have done it by any
" method, but refusing the Queens great Favour. And if at last, the
" Charge run into by Order of the Crown, must lye upon him, yet the
" Infamy of it must lye upon another, who was perhaps the only Architect
" in the World, capable of building such a House; And the only Friend
" in the World capable of contriving to lay the Debt upon one to whom
" he was so highly oblig'd.

I shou'd have thought all Friendship and Obligations out of the Case, where Men are legally call'd upon to declare the Truth upon their Oaths: But since that don't suffice, what follows will.

About two years since, a Gentleman in the Country hearing of a Suit of Law, commencing between the Duke of *Marlborough* and his *Blenheim* Workmen, writ to a Friend of his here in Town, to desire he wou'd let him know, whether I was like to be intrigued any how in the Quarrel, and in general, how my case really was, in regard to the *Blenheim* Affair, in which so great a part of my life had been spent.

APPENDIX I

The answer to the Letter I happening to see, took a Copy of it, and think I cannot write any thing more proper, by way of answer to the Charge above, than to recite it, tho' had it not been for this Charge, I shou'd never have open'd to the World what the following Letter with but too much truth sets forth.

"*SIR*,

"Upon the Building of *Blenheim* being resolv'd on, the Duke of "*Marlborough* was pleas'd to desire Sir *John Vanbrugh's* Assistance in it.

"Sir *John Vanbrugh* accordingly waited upon his Grace down to *Wood-* "*ſtock*, where the Scitation being fix'd, he proceeded by his Graces Order "to think of, and prepare a design to the Building, suitable for that "Scitation, and did prepare such a design as the Duke approv'd of.

"This design was immediately order'd to be put in Execution, the "Queen declaring her intentions, that it shou'd be Built at her Expence, "and Sir *John Vanbrugh* was desir'd by his Grace to take care of it, and "to conduct it in the beſt manner he cou'd, which he accordingly pro- "ceeded in without delay, clearing the Ground, digging the Foundations, "opening a Quarry in *Woodſtock-Park*, &c.

"But the Duke being oblig'd to go for Flanders, on the Publick Service, "directed Sir *John* (in his absence) to apply to the then Lord Treasurer "*Godolphin*, for whatever he shou'd ſtand in need of, which he did from "time to time; And amongſt other things, desir'd he might have some "Authority in writing, for what he was directed by the Duke to transact, "upon which my Lord *Godolphin* gave him the following Conſtitution.

"To all to whom these presents shall come, *etc.*

"Being thus Authoriz'd, Sir *John* proceeded to engage Workmen, make "Contracts, and Buy Materials, and in every thing conform'd himself to "the Inſtructions given him by my Lord *Godolphin* in the Dukes Name.

"And whereas my Lord *Godolphin* was pleas'd to declare to him and "other Officers employ'd in that great Work. That he wou'd by no means "allow of any Perquisites to be made, but that every Body shou'd be well "recompenc'd for their trouble and service in it. Sir *John Vanbrugh* made "no advantages to himself whatsoever; but only rely'd on the Duke of "*Marlborough* to consider him, as he shou'd think he deserv'd.

"In this manner the Work begun and went on, and Sir *John* had the "good fortune to give the Duke such entire Satisfaction, that in so many "Years as it was in hand, he never found fault with one single thing "he did.

"But at length, on the Change of things at Court, the Building was "ſtop'd, and Debt of about 45000*l.* remaining due to the Workmen (of "which about one third has since been paid) they apply'd to the Duke "of *Marlborough* for their Money, which he not being disposed to Pay, a

"Suit is commenc'd against him, in which Sir *John* is made a Party, for
"having Contracted with them on his Graces Account. And in their Bill
"they Pray, That if he had not Authority to Contract with them for the
"Duke, he may himself be oblig'd to Pay the Debt. The Duke in his
"Answer to this Bill, is pleas'd to give up Sir *John Vanbrugh* to defend
"himself as he can, denying that he acted by his Authority.

"This Account is a short, fair, true State of the principal Facts in this
"matter. To which a few Circumstances may properly follow. To shew
"the unparallel'd hard fortune of Sir *John* in his Services to the Duke of
"*Marlborough*.

"Here is the Greatest the Richest and the most powerful favourite that
"was ever known in *England*, has the most valuable present made him
"from the Crown, that was ever made here to any Subject.

"Those who have had the happy Chance to be employ'd by such
"favourites, (especially in their pleasures) and have been so Successful in
"their Services, as to give them entire Satisfaction, have never fail'd of
"making their Fortunes by them.

"Now 'tis well known to all the World, the more than common delight,
"the Duke has from the beginning taken in this Work at *Woodstock*.

"And the Pleasure he had in it, was supported by the design, and the
"performance still answering his Wishes and Expectations.

"And he was pleas'd from time to time, both by Letters and otherwise,
"to express in the strongest and most affectionate Terms. The great
"Sense he had of the Services rendred him by Sir *John Vanbrugh* on this
"occasion, and the resolution he was in, by some manner or other to
"reward him for it.

"Yet such has been his fate. That after Twelve Years employment
"under his Grace, in his Building Service, which consisted, in making the
"designs, having the constant Care and Conduct of their Execution with
"the pains and trust of making Contracts, and passing Bills for near
"300000*l*.

"And after having had the misfortune of being turn'd out of his Place
"of Comptroller of the Works, and losing that of Garter by offending the
"Queen, on the Dukes Account; The state he finds himself in at last
"is this.

"That without one Court favour obtain'd by the Duke for him in this
"long Tract of Years.

"Or any allowance or Present from his Grace ever made him (except a
"Trifle, I believe he wou'd not have him Name.) He has been left to
"work upon his own bottom, at the tedious Treasury; for a Recompence
"for his Services. Where through a tiresome Application of many Years,
"he has to this Hour prevail'd for very little more, than his necessary
"Expences, and instead of any reward from the Duke, finds his Authority

" for acting in his Service disclaim'd, and himself thrown among the Work-
" men, to be torn to peices. For what his Grace possesses and enjoys, in
" the midst of an immence Fortune.

These (and no other) are the Friendships and the Obligations laid by
the Duke of *Marlborough*, upon his Faithful and Zealous Servant,

JCHN VANBRUGH

2

[*To the Lords Comm*ʳˢ *of His Majesties Treasury*]

May it please Your Lord'ᴘˢ

Mʳ. Lowndes having signified to me your Lordᴘˢ. pleasure that I
should prepare and transmit to your Lordships the Ground of the demand
of the Workmen, Which were employd in the building of Blenheim, and
what might be said for Justifying the same.

In Answer to your Lordships Commands, I am necessitated for the
preservation of the Course of the relation or history of this matter, to give
your Lordships an Account not only of matters of fact, in my own privity;
but also of some transactions which Occurr'd in Parliamᵗ. without which
latter, I could not so well Expresse the Ground and foundation of the
demand of the Workmen in that Building.

In the year 1704 the House of Commons Addressed Her Majᵗʸ. to
Consider of some proper means to perpetuate the Memory of the great
Service performed by the Duke of Marlborough; And Her Majᵗʸ. having
in Answer thereto, Signified her Royall Inclinations, a Bill was thereupon
brought in, and an Act passed, enabling Her Majᵗʸ. to grant to the Duke,
the Honor and Mannor of Woodstock, in Consideration of the Eminent
Services by him (before that time) performed for Her Majᵗʸ. and the
Publick, And then a Grant passed under the Great Seale, pursuant to
that Act.

After this, the Arms of the Allies under the Command of the Duke
being blessed with a train of other Successes, Her Majᵗʸ. was pleased to
take his Grace into further favour, And to resolve to build him an House
upon the Mannor of Woodstock, to perpetuate the Memory of these
Services, particularly that of the Great Victory at Blenheim.

At this time I had the honour of being Comptroller of Her Majᵗˢ.
Works, and as such was ordered to frame a Modell of the Designed
Building; and a Modell being framed and compleated was Sett in the
Gallery at Kensington, by the Queens Order, And there left some time,
that She might consider it at Her leisure, both alone and with other people,
and she was pleased to view it thoroughly with the Prince, and to ask all
Questions Necessary for her understanding it perfectly, and She express'd

APPENDIX I

herself extreamly Satisfied with it, and desired to have it dispatcht with all Application, and required no Sort of Alteration in it.

This Modell was preserved at Kensington to Shew that the building exactly pursued it.

The Queen having thus begun the Building at Her Expence: The Lords on their part were desirous to expresse their Sense of the merit of the Duke, and Addressed the Queen to lett them know in what manner it would be most acceptable to Settle the honors and Dignitys of the Duke upon his posterity.

In Answer to which Her Maj^{ty}. was pleased to direct the manner, And to Add, that She thought it would be proper that the Honor and Mannor of Woodstock, and the House of Blenheim, should go along with the Titles.

The Commons on their part addressed Her Maj^{ty}. taking notice, That as Her Maj^{ty}. was at her expence graciously pleased to erect the house of Blenheim, as a Monument of the Dukes glorious Actions, And as the Lords had given rise to a law for continuing his Honor to posterity.

The Commons on their part also declare their ready disposition to enable Her Maj^{ty}. to make some provision for the more Honourable Support of his Dignity to his posterity, which was accordingly done by Act of Parliam^t. In which there is the same expression as in the Commons Addresse relating to the Queens erecting the house at Blenheim, at her own expence.

Her Maj^{ty}. pursuing Her gracious Intentions to erect this Monument as a lasting Mark of her favour, gave Orders to the Lord Treasurer Godolphin by Severall Warrants under Her Sign Manuall to issue monys to John Taylor Gent. to be paid over by him for defraying the Charge of the said Workes, according to such Orders and Directions as he should from time to time receive from Sam^{ll}. Travers Esqr. Her Maj^{ts}. then Survey^r. Gen^{ll}.

In pursuance also of Her Maj^{ts}. pleasure, the then Lord High Treasurer did Appoint her own Officers Viz^t. myself to be Surveyor of the said Works, M^r. Hawksmoor to be Assistant Surveyor, M^r. Joynes and M^r. Bolter to be Comptrollers and Clerks of the Works.

And in this Method the Works were carryed on to a Considerable height; But in the year 1710. The Treasury not issuing money as formerly, the Workmen began to be uneasy and declined giving any further Credit, and then I writ the following Letter to M^r. Harley, then Chancellor of the Excheq^r.

Blenheim Septr. 30th. 1710

S^r.

Although in the Carrying on this Building, It has not been my businesse properly to Sollicite the money for it, but to take care of the Design, the Execution and the Contracts; I hope you will not blame me,

(193)

if looking upon it, much more as an intended Monument of the Queens glory, than a private Habitation for the Duke of Marlborough, I am so much concern'd for it on the former Account, As to represent to you, the extream necessity there is for an immediate Supply, purely to close and terminate what has been Carrying on this Summer, in such a manner as may secure it from receiving vaſt injurys by the Winter Damps and Froſts; for it is so long since any money has been issued for this work, that the Credit is extended beyond even the power of getting in a little lime and bricks, to compleat some things at the very point of finishing, and boards to Cover the other parts that could not be quite got up this Season, I cannot help looking on this Building with the Tendernesse of a Sort of Childe of my owne, and therefore hope you will forgive my troubling you for its preservation.   I am &c.

JOHN VANBRUGH.

Three days after I had sent the above letter, there came an Expresse Order from the Dutchesse of Marlborough to put a Generall Stop to the Building, till money should be orderd from the Treasury to go on with it; And a Stop was put accordingly to it, And then I came away to London and found the following Letter at my house from Mr. Taylour of the Treasury.

Sr.

The Lords Comrs. of Her Majts. Treasury Command me (in the absence of Mr. Lowndes) to acquaint you, That their Lordps. having represented to Her Majty. the Condition that the Building is in at Blenheim as Stated in your Letter to Mr. Travers the 31th paſt, and the great want there is of an immediate Supply of money for it, that so you may not be forced to leave off uncovered and expos'd to the Injurys of the Winter, what is so near a close; Her Majeſty was pleased to say, That altho' the Condition of Her Revenues and the Arrears due to Her Servants and family are such as will not allow at present what may be necessary for carrying on that Work so faſt as She could wish; Yet Her Majty. would by no means have what is so far advanced left in a condition to be injured by the approaching Winter, and therefore Directs; That you do immediately send their Lordps. an account of what money is absolutely necessary for Covering in so much of the said Work as you proposed to finish before Winter, That directions may be given for Supplying the same, in the beſt manner that may be.   I am &c.

J TAYLOUR

Treasury Chambers
    6th. October 1710

APPENDIX I

Upon which I delivered the following Memoriall to the Treasury.

May it please Your Lord^{ps}.

In obedience to Her Maj^{ts}. pleasure signified to me by your Lord^{ps}. Commands, That I should lay before you, what Sume of money may be absolutely necessary for covering in so much of the Building at Blenheim as was proposed to be finished before Winter, I beg leave to represent to your Lordships. That this whole Summer Season happening so much more favourable than usuall, for Carriage of Materialls and raising the Shell of the house; I thought it would be extreamly for the Service of the Building to make an Extraordinary Effort for Covering in (if possible) the whole at once: that therefore I used my endeavours to prevaill with the Workmen and those who furnished the Materialls to give what Credit was possible for them to do, which having occasioned a much greater Arrear, than on the Close of other years, has raised the difficultys your Lordships have been Acquainted with, And which are now so great (the whole work having been at a Stand) that I do not see it will be possible to perform what is absolutely necessary for Securing it from the great mischiefs of the approaching Winter with lesse than an immediate Supply of £8000 which is humbly Submitted to Your Lord^{ps}. by &c

JOHN VANBRUGH

Upon this Memoriall £7000 was Issued, and the Building was covered up till next Summer, when waiting upon my Lord Treasurer, by the Duke of Marlborough's Directions, to know the Queens further pleasure; His Lord^p. was pleasd to order me to lay before him an Estimate of the Debt, and of the future Charge; and an Account of what the Duke desired might be carryed on that Season.

I Waited upon my Lord Treasurer at the Treasury Accordingly, and gave him in writing what he had requir'd of me, upon which he askt me, If I had well considered the Estimate so as to leave nothing out, That I beleived the Duke might think fitt to do in time at his own expence, but I hop'd the sume I had mentioned might carry the Designe as far as I understood the Queen intended should be done on a publick Consideration.

My Lord was pleased to say he would receive the Queens Orders upon what I had represented, and some time after he obtained Her Sign Manuall for £20,000 telling me, that he would looke for a further Supply as soon as possible.

Upon this, a payment was made to the Chiefe Workmen in part of their Demands, and I acquainted them with the Queens resolution communicated to me by the Treasurer, with which encouragement they went on with the building,

APPENDIX I

I hope Y^r Lord^{ps}. will pardon me, if in closing my Answer to the first part of your Lordships Commands, I bring to Your Lordships memory the late transactions in Parliam^t. relating to this Debt at Blenheim, and the intended discharge thereof.

On the 25th. of June 1713 The then Chancell^r. of the Excheq^r. laid before the house of Commons an Estimate of the Debts which were owing to the Severall heads of expence of Her Maj^{ts}. Civill Government, at or about Midsummer 1710. as followeth.

Cofferer of the Houshold	81394
Treasurer of the Chamber	38165
Master of the great Wardrobe	27534
Works and Buildings at Her Maj's Severall Palaces, and other places about	45000
Stables Ext^{ry} over and above what born on the Houshold Establishment, about	10000
Fees and Sallarys payable at the Excheq^r.	10000
Forreign Ministers for Ordinary Entertainment and Extraordinarys about	70000
Pentions and Annuities thereabout	15000
Mr Compton — To Compleat £15000 for french protestants . £7500 — To Compleat other Annuall payments there . 18122	25622
To a Band of Gentlemen Pent^{rs}. a year	6000
For Jewells and plate and presents to forreign Ministers on their return	10000
To the building at Woodstock by Estimation	60000
And for Contingencys of divers natures	23047
	511762 :—

This Estimate of £511762 was refer'd to a Com^{ee}. of the whole house, and a Supply voted for it, which was reported on the 27 June, and being agreed to by the house, a Bill was ordered to be brought in, and read a first time on the 29th. a Second on the 30th. and committed in order to be incorporated into another bill then depending; and no other Estimate on Account of the Debt of the Civill list was provided for, but the Estimate above mentioned, Wherein the Debt due on account of the Building at Blenheim is one expresse Article and part of the £500,000 granted for paying the Debts of the Civill list, After all these proceedings an account was called for of the Debts of the Civill List to Midsum^r 1713. where the Debt of Blenheim remaining due at that time was mentioned only as a demand, but this was called for to no other purpose but to give the house Satisfaction of the State and Condition of the Civill list home to that time. And occasioned no alterations in the Bill for granting the £500,000 wherein this debt was included.

My Lords

As to that other part of your Lord^{ps}. Commands directing me to let your Lordship's know, whether any Account has been made allowed and passed by the Duke of Marlborough of the Expenditure of the money issued for the said building.

I humbly return this Answer thereto.

1. All Contracts with the Workmen and Artificers and for emptions of Materialls were made by me, with the Assistance of M^r. Hawksmoor, M^r. Joynes, and M^r. Bolter.
2. It was M^r. Hawksmores and my duty to see that the Materialls were good, the work well executed, and the building carried on according to the Artificers Contracts, and the Modell and Design of the thing.
3. The Measurement of all the works and reducing the many particulars into Bills Suitable to the rates agreed on, was incumbent on M^r. Joynes and M^r. Bolter.
4. When the bills were thus made up they were reviewed Corrected and reduced as the nature of the thing required by all the above mentioned Officers, & then signd in order for payment.
5. The Bills thus stated and signed were, by the Directions of M^r. Travers, in Conformity to the Queens Sign Manuall, paid by M^r. Taylor.

In this method, and under these Severall Cheques the Works were carried on and Supervised, and the Accounts thereof and of the Expenditure of the moneys issued to that purpose were kept by M^r. Taylor.

In the late Treasurer Oxfords time, M^r. Bridges the Surveyour Gen^{ll}. of the Ordinance was ordered down, and accordingly went to Woodstock and there viewed & considered the Severall Works and examined the Contracts, inspected the Bookes of accounts, and declared his approbation of the Accounts and the prizes and performance of the Works.

But I believe his Grace avoided the Actuall Signing allowing or passing the Accounts of the Expenditure of the money issued for the building partly (as I conceive) because his Grace thought they were kept in an exact and regular manner, and partly to Avoid any Act which might make him personally a Debtor for the Work.

But a few months before the Paymaster M^r. Taylour dyed, M^r. Travers inspected his whole Account, examined his Vouchers, and ordered the Ballance then remaining in his hands (being £835: 16: 7) to be payd over to M^r. Joynes; who has since applyed it, to severall uses relating to the Building, for which he has received Directions from M^r. Travers.

  All which is humbly Submitted by

Your Lordships
most humble and most
Obedient Servant
J VANBRUGH.

3

The Reply of Sir John Vanbrugh on behalf of the Workmen employed in the building of Blenheim, humbly presented to the Kings most excellent Majesty.

  The Lords Commissioners of the Treasury, having been pleased to lay before your Majesty several Objections which occurred to them, against the present Debt to the poor Workmen imployed in the Building of Blenheim, and having therein answered several parts of the Representation, which I delivered to their Lordships for the support of that demand. I think myself bound in duty to the numerous Families whose All is now in Judgment before Your Majesty, humbly to say What may be proper to remove those Objections.

  The First Objection made by their Lordships respect the Words in the Commons Address following Viz^t. That as Your Majesty is at your own Expence, graciously pleased to erect the House of Blenheim as a Monument of his Glorious Actions &c.

Obj- Their Lordships think these Words are in the nature of a Parenthesis, and take notice that they are inserted in the Preamble and recital only of the Act that ensued the address, and that they are not in any of the Enacting Clauses.

Answer In answer to these objections I beg their Lordships to consider, that the Inductive part to the Address or Prayer of the Commons, is Historical; and imports that as Her Majesty was Graciously pleased to build the Duke an House as a monument of his Glorious Actions, And as the Lords had shewn their sense of such distinguishing merit So the Commons on their part, prayed that they might be permitted to express theirs also, and to that end to make a provision for the support of his Dignity.

    The Three Estates of the Kingdom are by this Address described as fully recompensing the Uncommon Services of the Duke. Now to make that part of the Address that describes the Royal Bounty intended by the Queen to be a Parenthesis, is in

(198)

APPENDIX I

My Humble opinion to seclude her Majesty from Her share of the Reward of the Dukes merit, and to deprive Her of the pleasure She then took in concurring with the rest of the Nation in their Munificence to him.

But besides, If it is considered that a Parenthesis may be left out without hurting the Sense of the Words foregoing or following; I cannot but be exceeding concerned; That the Words in question are said to be in the Nature of a Parenthesis, since not only the Words precedent and Subsequent but the prayer of the Address also would be without sense and without Relation too, even to that which was the occasion of the Address, Viz^t. (The Glorious Actions of the Duke) The publication of the Queens pleasure being part of the Induction to the Address, It was therefore necessary to become a part of the Preamble of the Act that was built or founded upon that Address.

But fancy can't suggest a reason to insert the Queens pleasure in the Enacting part of the Act, unless it were to compel the Queen to be pleased to be at the Expence of the Building, which besides the Absurdity contained in such a proposition, would bespeak a Doubt in the Commons of the Queens performing her Word.

As to the following Objections of the Lords of the Treasury

Obj: 1st. That it is not alledged, That any Estimate of the Charge of the Building was laid before Her Majesty.

Obj: 2 That it did not appear to them that there had been any Message sent, or Intimation given by Her Majesty to the House of Commons to inform them that she design'd to erect that Building at her own Expence.

Ans^r. I beg leave to answer that a Model of the Building was made, and viewed by Her Majesty, who was told what the Charge would in the Judgment of the Artificer amount to, and Sir Christopher Wren was sent down for the purpose of taking an Estimate, and made his Report accordingly.

As to the Second Objection I am at a loss what answer to make. For supposing it to be true that the Queen had not given any Intimation of her Design to erect the Building at her own Expence, In this case the Commons must be considered as a number of people concurring in Imagination that the Queen designed to Erect this Building, the strength of which Imagination, must carry them so far, as to attend Her Majesty and tell even the Queen herself what her design was, and the Queen must be thought to believe what the Commons fancy, and all this while no truth in the whole matter.

(199)

But which is more astonishing, this Conception is made a part of a Bill in the House of Commons, is past there, and sent to the Lords, by them read and passed and after all past also by her Majesty, and yet the Queens pleasure has never been intimated to the Commons but taken upon trust only. If this sort of reasoning obtains, the Force and Authority of any Act of Parliament may be easily eluded And the poor Workmen who gave Credit to this public and solemn Declaration of the Queen and Parliament are now to be told that the publication of the Queens pleasure in this manner, was but a Parenthesis and put into the address and the Act of Parliament without any Intimation from her Majesty.

Objn.   The next difficulty that occurs to their Lordships is whether the Commons thought the Sum of 73,000£ issued by Virtue of the Queens Warrants, a considerable present towards such a Work, or whether they looked upon it as an Earnest for her engaging to finish the whole.

Ansr.   To reconcile these Alternative Difficultys, I should think it would be best to put them together as meaning the same thing. A present towards or in part of this work, coupled with the words in the Address, declaring the Queen was to be at the future Expence of the Building, imply an engagement to finish the whole, and is as much as to say The Queen has already bestowed 73000£ towards the Building and is to be at the rest of the Expence.

But if the Lords of the Treasury suppose that the House of Commons meant that the 73000£ was only the present the Queen was to make the Duke on this occasion, it runs them into a manifest Absurdity, for that sum was actually given and the Address they were making speaks of the time to come mentioning that the Queen was to be at the EXPENCE, the one importing the time past and the other futurely, both which must meet together to make good such a Supposition.

Objn.   The next Paragraph which is intended as an Objection being in my poor opinion, the Reverse I need but repeat it as follows.——
" By the Words of the Sign Manual It is directed that the Money
" should be without any Account, Imprest, or other Charge to
" be rendre'd to her Majesty her Heirs or Successors, which is
" a very unusual manner of issuing money when a work is to be
" perfected on Account of the Crown, but is the proper Stile of
" Free Gifts and Bountys.

Ansr.   Does this paragraph mean any thing more than that the Money which the Queen ordered by her Sign Manual, was not for the

Building an house for Herself, but one for the Duke, and that as she had graciously promised to build or give the Duke an House, so she was as good as Her Word, and by her Sign Manual ordered Money to issue for that purpose?

Objⁿ. As to all that is said to distinguish the Earl of Godolphin from the Treasurer and the Queens officers of the Works from being employed immediately by the Queen And as to what is said also that the House was begun by the Duke, and that the Workmen looked upon the Duke as their Debtor

Ans^r. Much might be said in Answer to these Distinctions and Allegations, Yet since the granting of them does very little affect the present Demand, and may Conduce to bring the Question to a short issue, I would therefore admit them to be true And then the matter of Fact will stand thus.

The Queen out of her Royal Bounty resolved to be at the expence of erecting this House, and that the House might be to the satisfaction of the Duke She made him in nature of a supervisor of the expenditure of the Money and of a Superintendent to the Building, which he begins with her Concurrence.

On the other Hand that the Building and the issuing the Queens Money might be to the Satisfaction of the Donor, His Grace made Choice of the Officers which she herself employs on the like Occasion

Now suppose the Workmen from thence and because the House was built for his use, look't upon the Duke to be their Debtor. They look't upon the Crown also to be another Debtor to them, in as much as Her Majesty promised to be at the Expence of it; And there cannot possibly be a doubt that the Queen was answerable for the expence of the building *either to his Grace* or the Workmen at least till She thought fit to put a stop to it.

Objⁿ. As to the discovery That was made of the Queens Ministers design to obtain a supply for the Civil List, and to cast a Reflection on that incomparable Statesman the Earl of Godolphin. The Authors of that Discovery merited well of the Nation, But the relation thereof at large in the Lords representation, has no influence on the present Case except that part of it only which gives an Account that the Earl of Godolphin in his Estimate of the Debts owing by the civil List, makes the Debt on account of Blenheim with several others, amount to but 60000£ together, Whereas the Earl of Oxford in his Estimate makes the Debt Singly on account of Blenheim 60000£ by itself.

Answ^r. From all which, I am not able to infer any thing, Except, That when the One Estimate was made, the Debt on account of Blenheim was less than when the other was made, But the Lords Commissioners will be pleased to remember that both the one and the other Treasurer allowed the Debt (whatever it was) to be a Debt owing by the Civil List, and the last Treasurer promised to Discharge it as soon as possible And yet it can hardly be supposed that the Earl of Oxford had so great a regard and Deference for the High Merit of his Grace the Duke of Marlborough as the now Lords of the Treasury.

Tis true after the late Ministers were discovered in the Injury done to the Earl of Godolphin, they changed that which was before allowed to be a debt on the Civil List, into a claim only but seemed to be the Effect of Anger and was inconsistent with all that passed before and in the milder Construction it might therefore be done because the Debt was then unadjusted. I need not enter into the Construction of the act for raising the 500,000£ for payment of the Debts of the Civil List, nor whether the Debt of Blenheim was therein intended to be provided for, Your Majesty's great penetration will readily determine that matter, And I have been already too tedious and prolix on that head, Nor is it necessary for me to say any thing more or repeat any thing that has been said touching the passing the Accounts relating to the Building, Since it is now made a question Whether the remaining Debt should be paid at all, tho' the Accounts were perfectly settled. But I beg leave to recapitulate so much of my former Representation as tends to evidence the present demand on the Civil List The most of which I humbly conceive is no way answered by the Lords of the Treasury.

1st   The Commons by their Address and the Queen and Parliament by a Solemn Act declared to the Nation that Her Majesty was to be at the Expence of the Building.

2nd   A Model was made, shewn to and approved by her Majesty and reposited in her Palace.

3rd   The Queen not thinking it necessary to make any alterations in the Model required the Building to be dispatched and from time to time issued Money to that purpose by her own Warrants.

4th   Her Majesty directed the House of Blenheim to go along with the Dukes Title which tis presumed she would not have done If She had not in some measure a right to it by being the founder of it.

5th   In an Act which began in the House of Lords in 1706 They took notice of the Building then erecting at Woodstock and settled the same as well as the Manor.

6th　When the Building was stop'd for want of Money issuing out of the Treasury the Queen was inform'd of it; and was pleased to say, That although the Condition of the Revenues and the Arrears due to Her servants and Family were such as would not at that time allow of what might be necessary for carrying on that Work so fast as She could wish, Yet that Her Majesty would by no means have what was so far advanced left in a Condition to be injured by the approaching Winter And therefore directed That I should immediately send an account of what Money was absolutely necessary for covering so much of the said Work as I proposed to finish before Winter that directions might be given for supplying the same in the best manner that might be.—

7th　After this the late Lord Treasurer required an Estimate to be laid before the Treasury of the Debt and future Charge on account of the Building which being accordingly delivered, his Lordship was pleased to say that he would receive the Queens Orders upon what I had represented and some time after He obtained Her Sign Manual for 20,000£ telling me that he would look for a further supply as soon as possible.

8th　In the Estimate of what had been owing for the Queen's Debts at Midsummer 1710 a sum of 6000£ was inserted as so much then owing for the said Building which in the Estimate of what her Majesty owed at Midsummer 1713 was turn'd into a Claim for the reasons above mentioned.

9th　And Lastly the parliament in the 12th Year of the Queens Reign provided 500,000£ for the payment of the Debts of the Civil List of which this of Blenheim (in my poor opinion) is a part.

From all these things I conclude that there never was so much as the appearance of a doubt Whether this Debt of Blenheim was a part of the Civil List Debts till the late Ministers for the reasons above mentioned thought fit to change their Stile and instead of a Debt to call it a Claim And where those Ministers left off their Lordships of the Treasury are pleased to begin, but tis humbly hoped that your Majesty the fountain of Justice and the Guardian of the Rights of the subjects will relieve the Distress of the Numerous Familys of poor Workmen employed in the Building and encrease their prayers for your Majestys long Life & prosperity.

APPENDIX I

To the R^t. Honble.
the Lords Comm^{rs}. of His Majeſtys Treasury

The Memorial of S^r. John Vanbrugh.

Your Memorialiſt begs leave to represent to your Lordships. That in the year 1705. he was appointed by Warrant from the Lord Treasurer Godolphin, to Act as Surveyour for the late Duke of Marlborough, in Designing and Conducting the Building then begun at Blenheim for the said Duke, And did accordingly Act as such, till the Building was ſtop'd in ye year 1712.

That your Memorialiſt during the said time, rec^d. by Order from the Lord Treasurer, out of Money Issu'd by Sign manual toward defraying the expence of that Building, Several Sums upon Account for his charges pains and time employ'd in it.

That when the late M^r. Lowndes, Craggs and Sloper, were in the year 1716, appointed by Privy Seal, to Examine, State, and Allow, the Debts remaining due, to Workmen and others, for Services and Materials at Blenheim before the Building was Stop'd, The Account of your Memorialiſt was examin'd upon a foot approv'd of by the Duke of Marlborough for his allowances and they found there remain'd due to him, the sum of £2463: 10: 9 which Account being Sign'd by them, and Deliver'd to your Memorialiſt; he carry'd it to M^r. Travers, and rec^d. from him, in part of it, £800. out of money remaining of the late Queens Civil Liſt, which had been issu'd by Privy Seal to the said M^r. Travers, to be paid out by him toward the Discharge of the Blenheim Debts, as they shou'd be Stated and allow'd, by the fore-mention'd Commissioners.

That there being afterwards a farther Sum of Money issu'd by Privy Seal into the hands of M^r. Guidott, to be apply'd in the same manner, The Executors of the late Duke of Marlborough apprehending that your Memorialiſt, wou'd claim the remainder of his Debt out of it; preferr'd a Bill in Chancery, To obtain a Perpetual Injunction againſt him, Which was granted, by the late Lord Chancellour, on pretence, That he had not been employ'd in the Works of Blenheim by the Duke of Marlborough, but by the Queen; And therefore, that he had no claim upon the Dukes Eſtate.

Your Memorialiſt being thus barr'd from all means of recovering his Debt by course of Law Againſt the Executors of the Duke, and being adjug'd by this Decree in Chancery, to have been employ'd by the Queen, He humbly makes his application to your Lordships.

That out of the Arrears Arrising from the late Queens Civil Liſt, he may be paid the Remainder of what is due to him, being £1663. 10. 9. As it Stands allow'd, and Sign'd by the Comm^{rs}. appointed in 1716. to pass the Accounts for the Building of Blenheim.

Upon the Parliaments declaring the Blenheim Debt to be the Queens, M^r. Craggs, M^r. Lownds & M^r. Sloper were appointed to State them, which was done Accordingly, And they amounted to £45000. Upon which, £16000 was Issu'd by Privy Seal, to M^r. Travers, directing him to pay it as far as it wou'd go, in discharge of those Debts, as Allow'd by the Comm^{rs}., which was done, And I rec^d. £800 in part of what they had allow'd, and Sign'd, to be due to me.

There was afterwards an other Privy Seal, for £30000 to clear the remainder, which differ'd in nothing from the former; but that the Money was Directed to be paid into the hands of M^r. Guidet instead of M^r. Travers; but to be apply'd as the £16000 had been, £12000 of this thirty, has since been Issu'd to M^r. Guidet, but none of it, has yet been paid out by him, as the Privy Seal Directs.

Qu: Whether the remainder of what is due to me, may not be Order'd out of this money.

J VANBRUGH.

APPENDIX II

Containing letters to the Comptrollers and Clerk of the Works at Blenheim Palace, 1705-6 to 1716. (From MSS. in the British Museum.)

To Mr Bolter,   I
at Alderman Johnson's
at Woodstock, Oxfordshire

Jan: ye 1st 1705 [1705-6?—Ed.]

S^r

I had a Letter from you in which you mention some things relating to Mr Bankes's Work; But you say nothing of the Additional Covering wch I writ to you upon. The flying of the Stone has made a great noise amongst People who are glad of any Occasion to discredit the Work and those who are Concern'd in it. Now, tho' I am satisfy'd the damage is easily repair'd, and what has flown of no Consequence to the Structure in Generall, Yet I shou'd have been glad we had taken such measures as not to give any handle even for a Disadvantageous report, and that I believe had been prevented by a timely Covering. I find Mr Strong is not satisfy'd wth the Covering as it is even now, nay he tells me of some parts that Are not cover'd at all; He says you tould him you had not boards enow; but I fancy there must have been some other reason, because boards enow were to be had, And the River has long been in a Condition to send 'em.

I won't pretend to determine any positive Opinion on this matter till I have been downe, but as far as I can at present See, It Seems as if you thought the Covering Sufficient, tho' Others did not. I'll only say at present, that whatever your thoughts are of it, I'm sure you'll be in the right to do whatever I desire you in this matter, And therfore I once more make it my Request, that you will give such direction, that if any Severe frosts or Rains shou'd happen the remaining part of the Winter the Work may not receive any farther damage by 'em for want of Shelter. 'Tis I that am Answerable for these things as far as the Direction go's, and you & Mr Joynes for the Execution. You never had in your Life to do with any body more easy than you'll find me, & I beg nothing may ever happen to make any dispute between us.

My Lord Duke told me today he wou'd go very suddenly for Woodstock, but he'll first come here to Whitehall to Look over all the Drawing, I Suppose in a Week's time (or if a frost comes sooner) he'll be in Mahon. [?] I have nothing more to say now, but that I am very sincerely

Your Friend & humble Serv

J VANBRUGH

To Mr Boulter
  at Blenheim
    near Woodstock
      In Oxfordshire.   2

                London Jan: y 11ᵗʰ 1706*

S^r

  Sr Richard Temple tells me, he has resolv'd to dispose this next Season of the rest of his Timber and therfore desires to know if there be any farther want at Blenheim. He do's not say anything of raising his Price, tho' he threatned last Year. So I believe we may reckon upon it at the Same. But Mr Barton told me of Some Timber was offer'd to you nearer, and by Consequence wou'd be Cheaper in the Carriage. Pray will you let me know what it is, both as to Price goodness & Quantity, with a Little Abstract at the Same time of what has been us'd, and what is remaining of that we had from S^r R Temple and Mr Holt, That so I may make some Calculation of what will be wanting more in the whole Work. Pray do me the favour to send this as soon as possible, Sr Richard desiring an Answer, that if we want no more he may Agree with Other People who he says are now treating. I believe my Ld Duke won't be downe quite so Soon as he Intended by what he said to me today, So I intend to make you a Short Visit in the mean time, but wou'd first be on or off with Sr Rich^d: Temple. I have nothing more to trouble you with now, So wish you a happy New Year & am   S^r

       Y^r reall Friend
         & Servant
           J. VANBRUGH

  Pray let Mr Joynes know I had his Letter, and the Estimate was in the manner I desir'd it.

  I wish you cou'd send me word what the Glympton Ashler will lye us in, now we*   no more Wall Stones.

  Pray in the Account you Send me of the Timber us'd, let me know what quantity has gone in Mr Wise's Work.

To Mr Boulter
  at Blenheim House
    near Woodstock
      In Oxfordshire   3

S^r

  I had your Answer to the Letter I wrote you for an Acc^t: of the Timber, and believe 200 Trees more will go near to answer Our Wants.

       * Blank in MS.—E$_D$.

My Lord Duke has Spoak to me within these two days to prepare a true State of things to lay before him with what I wou'd propose for this Years execution. I believe in Order to this, and some Other things 'twill be necessary we All meet together here in Towne, and the Sooner the better. I therfore desire you'll think of being here for one Week before M.ʳ Joynes go's downe. M.ʳ Rives will be with you the end of next Week, and may Supply both your Absence for so small a time. 'Twill be necessary in order to lay before My Lord Duke what he desires, that I shou'd have such an Abſtract of the Severall heads of the paſt expence; that I may diſtinguish between what has been Spent upon the Gardens and Other outworks, and that part of the Building that comes within the Eſtimate that was given in about a Year Since. If therfore it be necessary to take Any Memorand.ˢ: from the Books in the Office which M.ʳ Taylor can't give me here; I desire you'll give your Self the trouble of doing it before you come.

I am
Sʳ
Your faithfull
Friend & Servant
J VANBRUGH

To M.ʳ Joynes
  at Blenheim
    near Oxford

4

March yᵉ 6ᵗʰ 1706

Sʳ

If you have with you my Lord Carlisle's Papers, You'll oblige me to draw the Two Fronts, pretty exact they being for the Engraver to work from; As for the Ornaments on the Top, with the Chimneys on the Main Pile, and the Cupola, I'll get M.ʳ Hawksmoor to Add them here, for I believe you have not the laſt Designs of 'em. Pray send 'em as soon as conveniently you can, to

Yʳ reall Friend &
Servant
J VANBRUGH

To M.ʳ Boulter
  at Blenheim

5

London March yᵉ 7ᵗʰ 1706

Sʳ

The Bearer (who accus'd Simons yᵉ Carpenter of some misdemean-ours,) is it Seems Arreſted by him, and forc'd to run away; so is come here to Towne to beg Protection. Now, altho' 'tis very possible this

Accusation againſt Simons had not been made but for some perticular end; and tho' Simons has made some tollerable defence, Yet considering the Appearance of the faċts laid to his charge were true I think 'tis sufficient for him, that we have Allow'd his Defence; but he shou'd by no means be suffer'd to Prosecute this Man; for 'tis certain if he is, we shall never henceforward hear a Word, tho' the Greateſt Roguerys in the World shou'd be committed; wheras if this Man be ſtill employ'd it will keep Simons in awe (who I think there are many reasons to Suspeċt) And on tother Side, it will make Simons have an Eye, to any thing that may be Amiss amongſt the Other Carpenters; So that I think we shou'd take advantage of their quarrells for our Inſtruċtion and at the Same time, suffer neither of them to gain their ends upon the Other. Therfore pray give Simons a check for pushing things so far, and let him know he ought to be Satisfy'd with what we do for his Juſtification, in continuing to Employ him, and not endeavour to terrify Men from giving us Information when they think they see us wrong'd, tho' it may happen there is only the Appearance of it.

There's no more money Order'd yet, tho' we are in daily expeċtation of it. My Lord Duke talks of going about the 20th. And I hope will so Adjuſt things with my Lᵈ Treasurer before he leaves us, that We may begin Our Campaign at leaſt as Soon as he do's his. I Intend to be with you as soon as he's gone, who am

Sʳ
Your reall Friend
& Servant
J VANBRUGH

To Mʳ Boulter
at Alderman Johnsons
at Woodſtock
In Oxfordshire.

6

[*London. Thursday yᵉ* 8ᵗʰ *Novᵇ* 1706?]

Sʳ

I had your Letter. and hope to be with you Very Soon. I juſt now hear a Report. I am much Alarm'd at, that all the Glimpton Stone in the Building flys to peices with the froſt This ill news comes from Oxford, I hope 'tis not true because you Say nothing of it. But pray let me hear from you the truth of this Matter by the firſt Poſt.

Sʳ
Your humble Servᵗ
J VANBRUGH

APPENDIX II

London July ye 10th 1707

S^r

Having had a Meeting here with the Workmen now in Towne, About the Severall Works to be done by them this Season This is to Acquaint you, That the Bricklayers demand,

     1st For Vaulting, 30^s p^r Rod

     2.   For Groins, 6 ft running 6^d

     3.   And that the Measurem^t: may be as is usuall in the Queens Works, Greenwich & most other Buildings, Viz^t: reduced to a Brick & half, but not to any number of Inches.

As to the first, Article, We have our plain Vaulting at Greenwich for 28^s (?) p^r Rod; therefore my Opinion is, not to give more.

For Groins, I believe the Usuall Rate is what they ask, and in Our Work, they must be very curiously done. So I don't know but it may be right to Allow it.

And as to the Method of Measurem^t: I must Confess I meant it as they demand it, when the first Contract was made, And indeed, it is the way we allways practice both in the Queens Works, Greenwich, and Wherever I have been concern'd. And allowing that Measurem^t: Our Contract with them is three Shillings p^r Rod lower than the Directors have ever had it at Greenwich, in the Same kind of Work, tho' they have us'd all kind of means to reduce the Prices of Bricklayers as well as Other Workmen. Besides, considering the Low Work (as in Garden Walls &c) is now past, I believe we must not refuse them in this Point.

I tould you a good while Since the Joyners demands for Shashes. & I remember what we agreed to give them they consented to. But I have now proposed a different Sort of Shash to 'em; which is not only thicker than the Others we design'd, but made in a Manner much more close and lasting. This requires both more Stuff & Labour And the Lowest price I can get 'em to, is 3^s pr f^t. Which however I am of Opinion is more reasonable to give, than the Usuall price for the Usuall Work. I don't know well how to describe this manner to you by Letter; but Mr Hawksmoor is of my Opinion, So if you have no Objection to the price, I'll Order 'em to proceed, for 'tis high time they shou'd be in hand. Thus far I can explain this thing to you; That the Shashes are all Solid, without anything glew'd, And the frames are Oblig'd to be very much larger than usuall & all of Oak. The Shashes are out of 2 Inch and $\frac{1}{2}$ Stuff.

The next thing I have to mention to you, is, the Plumbers. I have a Memorial, (which I here inclose to you,) in which you will see their plea. My Opinion (and Mr Hawksmoor's) is this. That some relief for the future shou'd be given 'em; for I know the Price was run very low, And we have been forc'd to let 'em suffer much by not keeping to Our Contract in point of Payment. However, I have no mind to allow 'em Intrest for the time past; Nor to engage to do so for the time to come; But if you Agree with me, I wou'd help 'em in the Other part of their demand; which is to raise a Shilling in the Price, in consideration of the Long Carriage which if we allow them (vizt: 16^d) we have it still much cheaper than Any body pays here.

I desire you will Show Mr Joynes what I write, & let me have your Answer by next Post without fail because I am going Out of Towne on thursday evening and shou'd give directions to those Men (especially the Plumber) to proceed before I go.

I believe there will be Orders soon, to proceed again Upon the Foundations of the Bridg, but pray let nothing (blanks in MSS.—Ed.) . . . is My Lady Dutchess . . . it. She was pleas'd to write to me, when She sent to (Stop) Upon the Account I gave her of what was intended, because she writ me word, that she found what I said very reasonable, but this being writ to my Ld Duke, she thought 'twas best to obey his Orders; especially Since his Answer cou'd not (at this time a Year) be long aComing. I give you this Acc^t: (myself), but if you find People fancy she is Angry, you may satisfy 'em to the contrary, for there's nothing of it. I have nothing more to say, but that I am

S^r

Your real Friend &
Servant
J VANBRUGH

To Mr Boulter   8
   at Blenheim,
     near Woodstock
      In Oxfordshire.

Hatfield. July ye 25th 1707

S^r

I am got thus far on my way to York, and hope to See you again at Blenheim by this day month at farthest. I had your Letter before I came away. The Sashes I have Suspended till farther Order, The Bricklayers I have Sent downe to you, And I have Order'd the Plumbers to Proceed, for 'tis high time they shou'd be preparing especially Mr Males who has a great deal to Cover this Year. The Prices you mention you us'd to give were I suppose for Casting not Milling, How tho' the price for Milling be much more than for Casting Yet upon the Whole it makes a Cheaper Covering by Near Twenty p^r Cent: for Nine pound a foot mill'd is as strong as 11 or 12 Cast; as I have Seen sufficient Examples. So Upon the Whole, Delays of payment & all things consider'd, I believe we can't be blam'd for allowing a Shilling more, wch is not above 6 p C^t wch we must Allow 'em if we went upon the foot of paying Intrest upon fa ilure of Our Contract.

I find Mr Strong dispairs of getting up both the East Towers, wch I am heartily vex'd at; but I am still more Concern'd to hear him even doubt of quite finishing One. Pray follow him hard; and if Possible don't let him have the pretence of wanting propper Stone. I hope Townesend won't want Spurring but lest he shou'd, pray have an Eye to him, for I much fear his Design may be only to finish the Parapet & Leave the Chimneys & Tower behind, wch must not be on Any Account. I have nothing more to recommend to you now, but heartily wish you well till I see you again, And am

Your reall Friend & Servant

J VANBRUGH

I saw my Lady Dutchess at Windsor last Sunday, She said she wou'd write to me to York if my Ld Duke resolv'd to have the Bridg go on; but I told her a Line to you to tell you my Lord's pleasure in it wou'd be Sufficient, there being full Instructions left to proceed. Pray do me the favour to tell Mr Joynes I just rec'd the Drawings before I came out of Towne; but he'll Oblige me in getting that of the Generall Plan & Upright of my Ld Carlisles, done against I return out of the North As likewise the South Front of Blenheim as it is now determin'd; wch Mr Strong can inform him in.

Mr Hawksmoor gives his humble Service to you.

Pray tell Mr Ryves I had the Venison yesterday and 'twas very Sweet

To Mr Boulter
   at Blenheim
      near Woodstock
         In Oxfordshire

9

London Nov: ye 11th 1707

S^r

I waited this morning on my Ld Duke, who is eager to come downe but will however forbear till the Scaffolds are Struck about the great Pavillion and Quadrant; wch he wou'd therfore have finish'd preferable to every thing. I have writ to Mr Strong this Post to direct all his hands may be employ'd that way that can be, & I desire you'll by some effort or Other get him every Stone he wants for his Cornice or Other part of that work. Both my Ld Duke and Lady Dutchess are in perfect good humour with the Acc^t: I have given 'em of what we have done and are

(213)

doing, And I wou'd fain keep 'em so if possible which nothing will more contribute to, than if I can shortly tell 'em the Work is ready for their Visit.   I intend to come downe very soon to you again, and am

S^r

Your very

faithfull humble

Servant

J VANBRUGH

To Mr Boulter   10
  at Woodſtock
    In Oxfordshire

Lon^d: Nov: ye 18th 1707

S^r

    I rec'd y^r Answer to my laſt And am much concern'd at this Difficulty to get Stone, especially finding my Ld Duke out of patience About it; for this morning, telling him I fear'd it wou'd be three Weeks yet, before the Scaffolds cou'd be Struck about the Great Tower, he was quite peevish upon it, being resolv'd to go downe by that time.   He therfore Order'd me positively, that nothing shou'd be left undone to get that part dispatch'd.   So that whatever extraordinary coſt may be necessary to fetch the Stone in, it muſt not be Spar'd, nor One moments time loſt.   I am

S^r

Your real humble

Servant

J VANBRUGH

To Mr Boulter   11
  at Woodſtock
    In Oxfordshire

London. Dec. ye 18th 1707

S^r

    I desire as soon as this Comes to your hands you'll order the Striking the Shed, and all the Scaffolds about the Great Tower, with the Clearing of every place about the building that can be, both within and without, to Show it to the beſt Advantage; for my Lord Duke comes downe full of Expeĉtation.   I intend to be with you by Sunday Night, and My Ld Duke Sets out on Monday;   I am

S^r

Y^r faithfull

humble Servt

J VANBRUGH

(214)

To Mr Boulter   12
   at Woodstock
     In Oxfordshire

London March ye 29th 1708

S^r

My Lord Duke is gone this Morning for Holland, but will return in a Fortnights time, And then resolves to See Blenheim before he go's to make the Campain. I therfore desire you will press the Masons and Bricklayers now at Work, to make all possible dispatch with the Odd things they have directions to finish, that My Ld Duke may See a Little more done, than was, when he was downe last. These things consist Chiefly in Vaulting the Corridores in Mr Strongs work Vaulting the Kitchin and Under the Collonade in Mr Banks's; And carrying up the Tower over the Gateway in Mr Townsends; I Suppose you go on as vigorously as the Weather will let you in Sinking the Court, for that's a thing my Ld Duke will be pleas'd to See. I'm told Mr Townsend has all the Stone wrought for his Tower as high as the Cornice, I believe he might get it Set in a Fortnight if he pleas'd; pray say all you can to him; and if there comes in any Tainton fit for his Cornice, press him upon that too. He need not fear wanting work the rest of the Summer, I shall cut him Out enough, in the Out Buildings About the Kitchin Court. I hear the Roof is up, on the Old Mannour, Pray Order Schrivens to get it Leaded with Nine pound to the foot. Mr Hawksmoor has a most Cruell fit of the Gout upon him, but I hope will be well enough to come downe with me in Easter week, at wch time I design to See you, who am

S^r
Very faithfull humb:
Servant
J VANBRUGH

I'm much concern'd to hear the ways are so bad you can't make the Teams Stirr.

To Mr Boulter   13
   at Woodstock
     Near Oxford

Aprill ye 1st 1708

S^r

My Lady Dutchesses Servant Ben: was with me this morning, to desire I wou'd put him into Some Employ at Blenheim, telling me that there was Some Changes towards Upon Mr Wises turning out Steven.

I tould him I believ'd he muſt be misinform'd, Since I had rec'd no Letter relating to Any Such thing, which I shou'd certainly have done, if there was Occasion to displace or take in any New Clerks: but if at any time there was an Opportunity, of employing him in any thing he was capable of, And that my Lady Dutchess was willing to part with him, I shou'd be very ready to do it: He is going downe to Blenheim, and will come to you to know if there is occasion for any body of his Qualifications. If there is any thing in what he has heard, I suppose I shall hear from you.

Mr Banks is coming downe, with Inſtructions to employ his Men in preparing what Stone is Upon the ground, for the Out Walls &c behind the Kitchin Wing: I have likewise writ to Mr Townsend, and given him Directions for the Same kind of Work, So I hope they'll soon clear the front of all the Stone that has been thrown aside hitherto. & I shall be very glad to hear there is plenty of New coming in, but the Wet weather which continues here, makes me fear you have the Same. I wish it a quick change & am

Your very humble
Servant
J VANBRUGH

To Mr Boulter   14
   at Blenheim
      near Woodſtock
         In Oxfordshire

Henly. Sunday Aprill ye 25th 1708

Sr

I forgot yeſterday to tell you, that some talk had paſt with Mr Wise About the Work in Levelling the Hill &c. As to that part where the Stone rises, he do's not think it practicable to meddle with it by the Great it being directly a Quarry, and therfore to be wrought as Such by days men; but he Says, as to the Earth that is to Come Out of the Flower Garden in Mr Strongs Work, or the Foundations of the Bridg, he is willing, if we desire it. So he desir'd we wou'd talk about it, and he won't leave such Inſtructions with Mr Bobart, that whatever he Agreed with us for, shou'd ſtand good. If therfore you think it more Advisable to go by the Great, than to employ Our days men, pray know what Bobart demands. I am apt to think the Charge may be near Alike which ever way we go; but perhaps if he do's it, there may be more Expedition. However I leave it to you & am   Sr

Yr
faithfull humb Servt
J VANBRUGH

APPENDIX II

To Mr Boulter
   at Blenheim
      near Woodſtock
         In Oxfordshire

To Mr Boulter
   at Blenheim
      near Woodſtock
         In Oxfordshire

S^r

London. May ye 1st 1708

I rec'd a Letter from you Yeſterday, And am pretty much of your Opinion About Levelling the ground near the House by days men, But when we come to Digg the Foundations of the Bridg, if Mr Bobart has a Mind to that, I believe we may deal with him for't. I hope your Stone comes Now in Apace, And Since there is some Money for the Masons, I hope they'll Double their Forces and drive on Smartly; Especially Mr Strong; for what's to be done by the Others will be easily enough Compass'd.

I had been downe again now my Ld Ryalton is wth you but that I'm Obliged to Stay till my Lady Dutchess has determin'd Severall things in relation to the Joyners Work; I hope however to get downe in ten days at fartheſt: My Lady Dutchess Designs to come About that time, but the Covings in her Bedchamber and My Ld Dukes Rooms shou'd be lath'd that she may the better Underſtand them. I therfore desire you'll get Some Laths in; Not only juſt for that perticular, but the Business in Generall, for I wou'd Set the Plaſterer to Work in the Offices, and in the Upper Rooms of the House as soon as might be.

I think you tould me you had Orderd a Thousand of Chriſt: Deals for Floors. the Sooner they come the better, for I'll Set the Carpenters to Work as soon as I get downe. I have nothing more to say now but that I am

                    S^r
              Your very faithfull
                 humble Servant
                 J VANBRUGH

Pray to me the favour to give my moſt humble Service to my Ld Ryalton; And desire he'll please to Observe the Cap Upon the Great Tower as it is now rais'd: that I may have his Opinion whither 'tis well thus, provided it don't make the Chimnys Smoak: Which can't be thoroughly try'd till the Rooms are glazed, Seal'd & floor'd. So I designe when the Other Tower is Up, to put no Cap on, till this is fully try'd.

To Mr Joynes
  at Blenheim
    near Woodstock
      In Oxfordshire.

S^r   *London. June ye 19th 1708*

I have your Letter of the 16th: And am sorry to find Stone don't come in so fast as it shou'd. I have consider'd all you say on that Matter, And am very loath to come to a higher price than we allow at present; but considering how very far the Season is Advanc'd we have not time to try many experiments without runing a great Risque of Advancing very little this Summer, which wou'd be a Piece of good Husbandry My Ld Duke wou'd never thank us for; If therfore you can find no better Expedient I am of Opinion to Add a Penny a foot for the Great Stones that are Upwards of Thirty ft: but not to Allow any thing more than we do for Smaller, Only this Encouragem^t may be given to those who go to the further Quarrys; That their Bills shall be paid before those who go to the nearest. If you publish this amongst 'em, I believe it may have a good Effect: but in Order to it, I believe it wou'd be right to Speak personally to a good many of the Principall men who have good Teams; And if you can engage a Score of them to ply the Business, You'll soon See the Rest follow their Example.

Mr Wetherhill tells me there are Laths to be had which will do very well, at Oxford, for 17^d a hun^d: If you find they are Cheaper at that price, than we can have 'em if we send 'em Our Selves, buying Cheap Timber of Mr Holt, I believe you had best bespeak a Sufficient Quantity to do the Office Wing, And all that part of the House that is now Cover'd.

Pray call upon the Carpenters to get up the Partitions and let the Bricklayers Work up the Quarters as soon as may be, that they may be dry. I likewise desire Mr Strong will get those Windows in the Attick Story Alter'd out of hand, for those Rooms must be finish'd with all Speed, therfore I wou'd have nothing in the way to hinder the Plaisterer when he has direction to proceed, wch I'll give him very Soon.

I shou'd be glad to hear Mr Banks had near done at the Old Manour. I hope at least all is ready for the Plumber to cover it which I wish he wou'd do out of hand. I hope Mr Bobart go's on briskly with Sinking the ground behind the Kitchin Wing &c Pray let me know About what Number of Men he employs. I hope to be down again in a fortnight at farthest, who am

                                        Y^r Friend & Servt
                                        J VANBRUGH

I hope Mr Townsend has let the Pipes into the Wall, if not, pray call upon him.

If there comes in Bad Stone from Mr Brays Quarrys, I think 'twill be beſt to refuse taking any more from him at All; I hope Mr Strong takes care there comes none but good from those Quarrys where he is concern'd with him.

To Mr Joynes   17
  at Blenheim
    near Woodſtock
      In Oxfordshire.

London. June ye 24th 1708

S^r

    My^t Lady Dutchess is determin'd not to raise the Price for the Carriage of the Stone of any Kind; So that you muſt Acquaint those who go with the Carriages, that there is Positive Orders rather to let the Work ſtand Still than to give any thing more than Six pence a foot, they muſt bring in the Great Stones for that Price as well as the Small Ones. Mr Travers will be downe about Tuesday, but I can't come So Soon. You muſt Advise with him what to do in this Case, I hope the Teams will comply when they See the Order is Absolute.

I am,
Y^r humble Servant
J VANBRUGH

Mr Parker was with me this morning, & Says you writ a Letter to me by laſt Poſt, but I have not rec'd it. I have however order'd 2000. Boards, & some 22. f^t Uffers* to be sent away with Speed.

To Mr Joynes   18
  at Blenheim
    near Woodſtock.
      In Oxfordshire

London. Sep^t: ye 21th 1708

S^r

    My Lady Dutchess designing to be downe the begining of next Week, I desire you'll let the Plaiſterers dispatch her Bedchamber the firſt thing; and let the Two Great Windows that are glaz'd be put up there. And that the Room may look the better, let the Carpenter inſtead of Rough boards, lay downe Some of those they have plain'd, as likewise in her Dressing Room & Closet, But then twill be Necessary to put up a Temporary door between her Bedchamber and the Bowwindowroom to keep people out; as likewise at her Dressing room towards the Back Stair, and at the Weſt end of her Long Closet, that So all the Rooms of her Appart^t:

---

* *Uffers*; timbers suitable for joists, etc.   See N.E.D.—Ed.

(219)

may be enclos'd. Pray desire Mr Strong to get downe all his Scaffolds & Gang ways on the East Front by Saturday, or Monday Night at farthest. And Mr Townsend the Same without fail. The Painter shou'd Prinse the back Side of the Wainscoat that Mr Smallwells men are going to put up in the Room Next My Ld Dukes Tower. But don't let him do any thing to the Rooms in the Office Wing till farther Orders.

Mr Strong and the Carvers, have Directions to dispatch as fast as may be, the four Pinacles for My Ld Dukes Tower, But I desire they will contrive to get up One, upon the South east Angle before My Lady Dutchess comes, wch with the Moddell in Wood will Show what is design'd. pray press this very much 'tis no matter for its being finish'd, if it be little more than Mason'd 'twill do. I don't think of any thing more to say this Post, but that I am

Y^r Friend & Servant
J VANBRUGH

To Mr Joynes   19
  at Blenheim
    near Woodstock
      In Oxfordshire.

London. Sep^t: ye 28th 1708

S^r

I writ to you some time Since; This is now to acquaint you My Lady Dutchess will be downe on friday. pray if the Carvers han't done About Mr Townsends Tower, let the Scaffolds be Struck however. I hope the Plaisterers have done in my Lady Dutchesses Bedchamber. And that All Other things will be in a good posture for her View as was design'd. I hope to be downe on thursday Night who am

Y^r Friend & Servant
J VANBRUGH

To Mr Joynes   20
  at Blenheim
    near Woodstock
      In Oxfordshire.

London. Nov: ye 6th 1708

S^r

Mr Travers came to Towne but last Night I have Seen him today, And he has Adjusted things with Mr Parker, that you need not be at a Stand till money can be had out of the Excheq^r: I have desir'd him to let you pay Mr Wetherhill Thirty pounds now upon Account; which pray let him have as soon as he comes downe.

What you tell me they are doing in Mr Banks's Work is contrary to their direction The Ribbs only shou'd be Ashler, and the rest Brick if there be enough in the Work, also rough Stone; but the Vault shou'd not be turn'd till the Building is Cover'd. nor can I Immagine why they think of doing it Sooner. Mr Townsends Work is to be the Same. And pray See if he can't be finish'd with Stone for the Stools of the Windows of the Kitchin Wing, on the East Side, for I wou'd fain have all done there, And the Sashes in. And pray let That Sash that is up in My Lady Dutchesses Bedchamber, with the Other that came downe Since, be Set up in my Lord Dukes Bedchamber. But give the Plaisterers a Charge not to Break 'em. Mr Hawksmr: has writ About Covering in &c, so I have no more to say now, but that I am Mr Bobart's and Your Friend & Servant

J VANBRUGH

Mr Travers will be with you on Monday

I desire Mr Peisley to make all Speed with the Additions to the Kitchin Clock Tower.

Pray do me the favour to desire Mr Ryves to Send me up a Doe (?) by the Next Carrier, if he can have an Order for it so Soon from Mr Travers.

To Mr Joynes   21
  at Blenheim
    near Woodstock
      In Oxfordshire.

London. Nov: ye 30th 1708

S^r

I have a Letter from Mr Bobart of the 26th and another from you of the 28th. As to Mr Johnsons Limekill, I desire there may be no More Stone dug till you hear from me farther; but if I can prevail with My Lady Dutchess, to let it Stand one year more, I will. I'll wait on her About it in a day or two, And send you her Resolution.

Pray tell Mr Bobart I am glad there's so good a Progress made in things without doors; but I shou'd be glad to know what he do's About the Forrest Trees in the Quarters of the Woodwork I mean as to bringing Lines of 'em every where behind the Hedges, for I take that to be the grand point of all.

Pray to continue to Secure the Work all you can against the Frost, and have an Eye on the Other Side to the Joyners Fires. And now I mention the Joyners, I desire you'll write me word by Next Post, whether there can't be £150. Spar'd out of the 15. you mention, for Mr Smalwell upon Acct: for he shou'd have had Some here & by my neglect miss'd of it.

There will be an other Payment Soon, but he has some Urgent Occasion just at this time, which makes him desire I wou'd get him 150£ if it can be Spar'd.   I am

Sᵣ

Your Friend & Servᵗ

J VANBRUGH

Pray tell Mʳ Ryves I had his Letter, and Shall Speak to my Lady Dutchess.

To Mʳ Joynes   22
    at Blenheim
        near Woodſtock
            In Oxfordshire.

London. Decᵇ: yᵉ 9ᵗʰ 1708

Sʳ

I have yʳˢ of yᵉ 5ᵗʰ : As to this business of Mʳ Johnsons Limekiln, I don't know who 'tis that has moved my Lady Dutchess so much About it, I talk'd to her Upon it tother day, and desir'd that she wou'd at leaſt deferr the pulling it downe, till I had been at Blenheim and was able to give her a farther Account of it She gave me no positive Answer to this; so All I can say to the Matter is, that if she writes any Orders About it, before I come downe, You muſt e'en Obey 'em, tho' I believe she'll let it reſt till I return.

I have hitherto deferr'd coming, partly from my Lᵈ Dukes ſtaying so long Abroad and partly because I wou'd be glad to See My Lady's Tower quite finish'd. Pray write me word in your next when that is like to be, and what height Mʳ Banks and Townsend are got with their Work

I have told Mʳ Smallwell you'll help him to £150. So he'll write to you where he desires to have it pay'd.

I know nothing to hinder my Coming downe in Chriſtmass Week, so desire you'll deferr removing the office till then, for it shou'd now be fix'd in Some place where it may ſtand these Seaven Years.   I am

Yʳ real friend &

Servant

J VANBRUGH

Pray desire Mʳ Ryves to Send up a Doe Next Week

To Mr Joynes   23
  at Woodstock

London. Dec: ye 26th 1708

S^r

The Bearer (Mr Kynaston) who has been for Some Years Past My Cozen* Vanbrughs Clerk, and is Design'd to be employ'd hereafter as Mine, in the Queens Works; comes to Blenheim to See the Manner of Measurements, particularly that of the Masons, in Order to Qualify himself the Better for future business. I therfore desire you'll let him be with you in what Measurements you make during the time my Cozen can Spare him to Stay, which I think is not above ten days. In which you'll Oblige

Y^r
Friend & Servant
J VANBRUGH

I shall certainly be downe this Week.

To Mr Joynes   24
  at Woodstock
    In Oxfordshire
      (readdressed to Mall St. London)

Henderson [Henderskelf?—Ed.]

S^r

I had y^r Letter of ye 3^d And by last Post we sent you full Instructions for Mr Townsend. If he has not already done what he had Designs for, I hope he won't make the want of having these sooner a Pretence for not finishing every thing in the Kitchen Wing this Season. Pray tell him, I do earnestly desire he won't fail in it.

I have heard from My Lady Dutchess, And have a Letter from my Ld Duke; he is mighty desirous to have the Building that is up made habitable. I consulted Mr Strong before I left London, About doing something towards the Great Hall & Salon this Season; but found it was impossible. My Lady Dutchess has since desir'd (this) And that I wou'd send Instructions for it, but I have Acquain(ted) Her 'tis no way to be done this Year, but that we will make (such) Provision in the Winter, as shall raise it very fast in the (Summer). By the talk I had with Mr Strong, I doubt it can't be hoped (to) have both the Great Pavillions compleated this Year. But† . . . let him be very much press'd to finish the Lantern on that towards (?) the Colonade, And to get the Cornish at least up on the Other . . . the Lead may be lay'd and so all kept dry wi . . . Pavillion

---

* *Cousin Vanbrugh*: probably Wm. Vanbrugh, Clerk to the Treasury Chamber.—Ed.
† MS. much defaced.—Ed.

may be ready for furniture with . . . to be done, is the . . . of the Corridores where the Building is cover'd. I Suppose (the) Roof may by this time be up, over the Corridore that runs by (my) Lady Dutchesses Back Stairs; as likewise where it returns towards the Great Hall; if it is, pray let the Bricklayers fall to Vaulting as faſt as they can, both below and Above; Mr Strong is fully inſtruʄted in the Manner of it, And will direʄt 'em.

I don't think they need forbear 'till the Lead is on, tho' I hope the Plumbers are not backwards I'm sure they may easily cover it (before) the Bricklayers can have half done. Pray give my Service (to Mr) Boulter, and tell him I beg he'll do all that is possible, that Mr Strong mayn't have the Pretence of wanting Stone for the Cornish of the Pavillions, for that's what I moſt Apprehend. I shall leave this Place the end of this Week, and Shall be with (you) the Next; for I resolve to dispence with Some places I had promis'd . . . at in my way back, and come direʄt cross the Country to (Blen)heim. I have nothing more to say now, but to thank you (for the) Drawings you sent, And your promise for the rest, I am

Your real friend And Servant

J VANBRUGH

To Mr Joynes   25
   at Blenheim
     near Woodſtock
       In Oxfordshire

London Jan: ye 13th 1708 [1708–9 ?—ED.]

Sr

This unusual Weather has prevented my Coming downe; but as soon as the Ways are tollerable I shall come: I shou'd in the Mean time be glad to know what effeʄts this Sharp froſt may have had Upon the Building, for this will be a thorough tryall.

I writ to Mr Parker some time Since, to desire he'd Order his Barge to receive Some clean Boards from Mr Hopson. I Suppose the Barges have not pass'd Since; As soon as they do, pray Speak to him that they may take in Some Marble at Mr Reynolds's at Fox-hall, which lys ready for 'em. I wish Mr Bobart and your Self a happy New Year & am

Yr Friend & Servant

J VANBRUGH

To Mr Joynes   26
   at Blenheim
     near Woodſtock
       In Oxfordshire   *Feb: ye 10th 1709*

Sr

I rec'd One Letter from you, and an Other from Mr Bobart some time Since: in wch you told me the Damage by the Froſt was but Small.

Mr Banks the Mason was with me Since, And gave me a dismall Account of his Work'd being torn all to peices by the Second Frost, But by yours of the 5th, I find no such thing, So hope he told us wrong. Mr Barton was here yesterday, And I find by him, there is Still a Fortnights work at least for the Mason about My Lady's Tower, wheras I understood by Mr Bobart about Six Weeks Since, that they had then entirely finish'd. Pray let both Mason and Carver make an end with all Speed there, that no Sort of Scaffolding may remain about it; for My Lord Duke will be over very Soon, And as his Stay here will be extreamly Short, I believe he'll go to Blenheim in few days after he arrives.

I had fix'd for yesterday to come downe, but Mr Hawksm: had some business that made me put it off for a Week longer. I shall however be Sure to come very Suddenly, therfore desire you'll let the removing the office rest till then, for wherever we fix it now it must remain severall Years, therfore shou'd not be in the Familys way when they come to Live in the House, which 'tis probable they will the Summer after this. I take it for granted you have no Stone coming in now, tho' I believe you might from Heddington of which we shall use a great quantity this Year, I therfore desire what can be got in may, to employ the Masons the begining of the Season before Other Stone can be had. I am

Your real humble Servant

J VANBRUGH

To Mr Joynes   27
   at Blenheim
     near Woodstock
       In Oxfordshire   London. Feb: ye 17th 1709
  Sr

I have yours of the 13th and am glad to find Mr Bankes's Information was wrong as to his Work being torn. I have spoak to Mr Travers & You shall be Sure to have money out of the First Sum to pay the Carters; tho' I hope there can be No very great Matter owing to 'em.

This return of the Frost has made me put off my coming downe a little longer, but shall be with you as soon as the Weather alters.

Pray give the Inclos'd to Mr Parker, from

Yr Friend & Servant

J VANBRUGH

To Mr Joynes   28
   at Blenheim
     near Woodstock
       In Oxfordshire   London Sept: ye 29th 1709
  Sr

I have a great Complaint against Mr Banks's People, for cutting the large Portland Blocks for paving. while there is Smaller Stuff that will do.

Mr Strong represents this As a most Scandalous Abuse, & Says he is not Able to get it prevented I desire you will look into it, And take effectual Measures, that no Unnecessary Wast may be made of that Stone, which you know costs so dear, and is so hard to come by. Pray let me hear from you how this matter is, with any thing else that may be Necessary to mention to

Y^r Friend & Servant

J VANBRUGH

29

[*No superscription.*—ED.]

London. Dec^b: ye 6th 1709

S^r

   Mr Davis the Glassman was here to enquire after his Bill, which he says Mr Taylor knows nothing of. I thought you had given it him when he was at Blen^h: if you did not, pray send it to him. that Davis may receive some money upon Acc^t.

   I desire you will hasten Andrews with the South Front of the Building, which we spoak to him for. And pray speak to Kit: Cash to send me the Exact demensions that the Bed Chamber next the Gallery will be of; if the Back wall be carry'd up but 18 Inches thick, and the Front Wall Two f^t and half; for I fancy the Joyners have made Some Mistake in the Acc^t: they give me. Or I believe it wou'd not do Amiss; if he sent me the exact plan, of the Anti Room, drawing Room And Bed Chamber of the great East Appartm^t: with the Walls figur'd (as to the thicknesses,) as they now are: And then I can tell what to do in Thining the Walls of the West Appart^{mt}:

I am S^r

Y^r real humble Servt

J VANBRUGH

   Pray do me the favour to let Mr Napier know I have rec'd his Letter, and that he shall hear from me very soon.

To Mr Joynes
   at Blenheim
      near Woodstock
         In Oxfordshire

30

London. Dec^b: ye 18th 1709

S^r

   I have the Plan Kit Cash sent, and believe 'tis right. the South Front is likewise come up but I have not yet Seen it.

   I See you have Order'd the Portland Stone to Oxford, but unless it be got from thence to Blen^h: we shall be much behind hand with the Paving, and have it to do in the Summer when the Masons shou'd be upon other work. I therfore desire you will by any means get it home, And the Marble too if possible And now I Speak of Marble, Mr Reynolds was with me today, and tells me no Barge has yet Call'd for the Black Stones that are design'd for the paving, & wch have layn there at Foxhall these 5 Months. I desire you will take care they may be brought to Oxford without delay, for they will be wanted.

There was to come a Sample of paving from Helinden, pretended to be as white as Portland; 'twas Mr Townsend recommended it; And I think there is some of it at Sr Wm Glin's, by Biceter. Pray get a Small peice and Send it me up to Towne for if it will do inſtead of Portland, 'twill save a great deal of money. I hope the Bladon ſtone comes in, that the paving which is to be of it may be dispatch'd.   I am

Y^r real Friend &
Servant
J VANBRUGH

Pray know of Mr Napier if he rec'd a Letter I writ him near a Week Since, for I have not yet had any Answer from him.

I have juſt now rec'd Mr Peisley with Mr Rowney's Draught. I desire Andrews to proceed upon the North Front, to the Same Scale he has done the South.

To Mr Joynes   31
 at Blenheim
   near Woodſtock
     In Oxfordshire.

London Dec: ye 20th 1709

S^r

I writ to Mr Bobart to Night, but being in haſt forgot to desire he wou'd Speak to Kit Cash and the Carvers to Clear all away that's possible that my Lord Duke may See both North and South Fronts to better Advantage than laſt time. And pray let every place be set to rights as far as possible. I believe he'll set out on Friday tho' he has not yet absolutely fix'd his day.

Leſt Mr Bobarts Letter should Miscarry or be delay'd as it often happens, I'll repeat what it was. which was to desire a good many hands might immediatly be set to Work upon a Place for the Smiths Forge, at the North end of my Garden, a little way from it, towards the brow of the Hill: But don't let any provision be made for the Mens Lodging there, more than juſt a Little hole for One Man, for securing the Iron. Pray let it be done as cheap as possible, for to be Sure it muſt come downe again. My Lord Duke I doubt will be Angry we did not remove the

Smith Sooner, that the Building in which he is, might come downe. 'Twill therfore be right to let him find at least 'tis doing.

If he do's not go till Monday, I'll be downe a day before him; who am
Y^r

real Friend & Servt

J VANBRUGH

To Mr Joynes & Bobart   32
   at Blenheim
     near Woodstock
       In Oxfordshire

April ye 1st 1710

Gentlemen

I had y^r Letter of the 23rd: I'm afraid tho' there be Stone at the Quarrys, it will be late before 'tis got home, both from the badness of the Ways and the late Seeding.

I shou'd be glad to know what sort of Acc^t: it is my Lady Dutchess has had of Iron Work. I have not yet Seen her, but have a discontented Letter from her. I have writ her word I know of none, but that between the Peers on the East Side, which she her Self directed the first time She was downe last Summer, And said she wou'd have it quite plain, that when it was painted of the Grass colour, it might hardly be perceiv'd there was any fence at all.

I desire however there may be a Stop put to it till farther Order. And am
Your Friend & Servant

J VANBRUGH

To Mr Joynes   33
   at Blenheim
     near Woodstock
       In Oxfordshire

London. April ye 29th 1710

S^r

I find it will be a Week still before I can get downe to you; but I shou'd be glad in the mean time to hear what motions there Are towards getting in of Stone. I hope there's a great deal ready in all the Quarrys. Since the Roads must now be tollerable for bringing it in, And I Suppose the Seeding is over. I have heard Nothing from you since I writ about the Cases of Marble & Figures which were sent to Oxford, I shou'd be glad to know whether they are got home to Blenheim yet. With the other Stone which has lain upon the Wharf at Oxford, A great deal of which being for paving, Mr Strongs people might all this while have been employ'd upon it, whilst they had nothing else to do. if it cou'd have been got in. I Speak chiefly of the Portland, for I doubt we muſt Saw a good part of the Large Marble Blocks upon the Spot. And carry 'em away afterwards. I am

Sᵣ

Yᵣ real Friend &
Servant
J VANBRUGH

To Mᵣ *Joynes*   34
   at Blenheim
     near *Woodſtock*
       In *Oxfordshire.*   *London May yᵉ* 6ᵗʰ 1710
  Sᵣ

I had yours of the 30ᵗʰ : And am glad to find by that, and one Letter Since from Mᵣ Travers, that Stone is now like to come in apace; but I muſt likewise desire you'll take Speedy care to get in the Timber we have bought, for the Center of the Bridge shou'd be carry'd on with all convenient Speed.

Mᵣ Strong I Suppose is wᵗʰ you, And will proceed upon the 60 foot between the Main body of the House & the Gallery, till I come downe to give him the Necessary Inſtructions for the Weſt end. The main point is getting in Stone if there be but enough of that, we shan't want Workmen to use it up. I desire particularly you'll look after the Heddington Men, Stone from thence will be of great Service, & Above all, the Hard Stone; without which there's no finishing the low Wall round the great Court.

Neither Mᵣ Hawksmoor nor I can get out of Towne before friday at sooneſt. But there need be no delay for that yet, Since the present Business is nothing but getting in materiall, which I earneſtly recommᵈ: to you & Mᵣ Bobart. & am Your

Friend & Servant
J VANBRUGH

I wish you wou'd make a measuremᵗ: wᵗʰ young Small: when he comes to you.

To Mᵣ *Joynes & Bobart*   35
   at Blenheim
     near *Woodſtock*
       In *Oxfordshire*   *London. June yᵉ* 6ᵗʰ 1710
  Gentlemen,

I have a Letter from each of you; & have written to Night to my Lady Dutchess about Mᵣ Bankes's going on with the Colonade; wᶜʰ I think he may do with very little hindrance to Mᵣ Strongs Work, provided he do's not go on too faſt, but only keep men enow to work up the Collumns and Such other Stone as Mᵣ Strong can Spare. I have likewise Acquainted

My Lady Dutchess, that I have already sent my Ld Duke an exact Draught of the Stone Gallery, wch such description of the Niches as is necessary. I have a Letter from Mr Strong, in which he Complains so much of the want of Scaffolding, that he says the Buildg: will be at a Stand for it, if care is not immediatly taken. This is a Thing that there needs no direction from me for in particular, all such necessarys for Carrying on the Work, being to be provided in Court. And you can judge much better who are upon the place, than I can, what is at any time wanting to that end. I therfore desire you will Immediatly consult with Mr Strong w^t must be had, and Speak to Mr Parker to provide it with all Dispatch. Not forgetting that Mr Banks will likewise want some if he go's on wth the Colonade, And I believe Mr Peisley too at the Bridge. I am

Your very humble Servt
J VANBRUGH

Pray tell Mr Strong, I'll Speak all I can about the Money, that he may not flagg on that Account.

To Mr Joynes   36
   at Blenheim
     near Woodstock
       In Oxfordshire

London June ye 8th 1710

S^r

I writ to you last Post; Chiefly to desire, you wou'd immediatly consider with Mr Strong what Scaffolding wou'd be Necessary for him, and give Mr Parker directions to provide it as Soon as possible; He having writ me word, that his Work will stand for want of it. Pray put him in mind of Coping for the Garden Walls that it may be got in this Summer but he must needs take care it may be sound and good.

Here being a Payment near at hand, Mr Kays desir'd I wou'd write to you to Send up his Bill, Mr Trav^s: not caring to pay more upon Account.

I fancy the Quarrys are almost broke by this time: but they shou'd be press'd to go on still in raising more, for we can never have too much; You will Scarce get a quantity Sufficient I fear of the Square Blew paving, to compleat the G^t: Court, which is a thing shou'd be done if possible. Therfore pray think of it, and press the Men who furnish it, to send in all they can. There is not yet above 700 Yards come in, and I believe the Great Court will take up 3000.

There shou'd likewise be care taken to get in pebbles enow to pitch ten Thous^d: Yards. I reckon to be downe on Tuesday senight, who am

Y^r real Friend &
Servt
J VANBRUGH

To Mʳ Joynes   37
   at Blenheim
      near Woodſtock
         In Oxfordshire

                          London. Sepᵗ. yᵉ 7ᵗʰ 1710

Sʳ

I have a Letter from you, and an other from Mʳ Bobart, with an Accᵗ: of what pas'd with My Lady Dutchess. I think She has given Orders she'll repent of, but be it as she thinks fitt. If she orders the House to be pull'd down, I desire you'll comply wᵗʰ her.

Mʳ Peisley writes me word he cou'd do a great deal this Season to the Bridge if he cou'd have some money; But I can give him no Answer to the purpose on that head yet; there being no Letters come from My Lᵈ Duke in answer to what has been written to him on that Subjeᶜt. I believe the Next Mail we shall know something of his resolution and then I Intend to come immediatly downe to take Measures accordingly. I am
                Yr. faithfull Friend
                   & Servant
                     J VANBRUGH

To Mʳ Joynes   38
   at Blenheim
      near Woodſtock
         In Oxfordshire

                          London. Sepᵗ yᵉ 21ˢᵗ 1710

Sʳ

I have a Letter from Mʳ Strong, in which he complaines of Mʳ Bankes's Cutting out a great deal of Portland Stone for things where it cannot be us'd this Year, which if not Stop'd, will be a hindrance to part of the Winter work in paving &c expeᶜted from him. I desire you will enquire into this Matter, and prevent any application of Portland Stone to Mʳ Bankes's Work, more than is Absolutely necessary in what he wou'd set this Season.

I had been downe with you before now but that I have ſtay'd in daily expeᶜtation of my Lᵈ Dukes direᶜtions about money. He has at laſt order'd that Application shou'd be made to the Treasury, which accordingly is begun; And by what I observe, I believe I may bring you news the begining of next Week, that the Queen resolves to finish the Work at her Expence, and that money will be Issu'd accordingly. I am
                Your assured Friend
                  & Servᵗ
                   J VANBRUGH

To Mr Joynes and Bobart   39
    at Blenheim
        near Woodstock
            In Oxfordshire

                                    London. Oct: ye 10th 1710

    Gentlemen
        I am very glad to find no Mischief has happen'd to the Building,
which I know there was a good deal of reason to apprehend how light
soever My Lady Dutchess might make of it. I writ you word by laſt poſt
I had rec'd a Letter from the Treasury, to Signify the Queens Pleasure in
General for carrying on the Building; And that She wou'd have me lay
before the Lords, how much money might be necessary at this Juncture
to continue the Work till what was intended to be done this Season was
cover'd and Secur'd from the Injurys of the Winter I have accordingly
given inn a Demand today, and hope by Saturdays Poſt I shall be Able
to tell you there is an Order for Some Money I therfore Suppose My
Lady Dutchess has no objection to Mr Strong, Mr Harry Banks And M^r
Peisley's compleating with all Speed what they were upon; The Plumbers
likewise muſt lose no time, and the Carpenters muſt make all Dispatch
in Covering the Grand Arch of the Bridge, and those parts of the Walls
in Mr Strongs Work, that are not Compleat, as the Tower &c. I am
                        Your Friend & Servt
                            J VANBRUGH

                            40
[To Joynes.]
    Mr Vanbrughs. Letter   *[Only superscription.]*
    Oct. 12th 1710

                                    London. Oct: ye 12th 1710

    S^r
        I writ to you and Mr Bobart laſt Poſt, This is to desire, That in
Order to the Eſtimate I expect I shall have occasion to make, you wou'd
farther let me know What Mr Banks Mr Peisleys And Mr Townsends
Bills came to for their Work in the Colonade Kitchen Wing & what has
been Built about the Kitchen Court. And this I shou'd be glad to have
diſtinguish'd in different Articles. Viz^t.

    1 The Colonade by it Self from the Foundation
    2 The Whole Kitchen Wing by it self up to the Tower where
        it rises above the Roof
    3 The Tower from the Roof to the Top
    4 The reſt of the Office Court

                        (232)

I mean only the Measur'd Ashler &c Work in Freestone, not any of the Rubble. And so I understand the Acc^t: you have sent me of the Masons Work in General. if it be otherwise, and that you have included the Rubble, I must desire you to see how much shou'd be deducted out of the £42010: 10: 8 on that Account, for what I want is only the Quantity of Freestone us'd, and what that freestone may have cost in Workmanship.

Pray do me the Favour to send me whatsoever Papers I left in the Right hand Drawer of the Little Table I us'd in my Bedchamber; If you know no body coming up to Towne in 3 or 4 days pray send 'em by the Post. I waited on Mr Harley today, who told me I might depend upon the Treasurys taking care of the Building, they having receiv'd the Queens Directions for it and that they would do what they cou'd at present, and continue to forward it as Money cou'd be Spar'd. I am

Your real Friend & Servt

J VANBRUGH

I have enquir'd at the Treasury just now, and there will be an Order for money to Morrow.

I don't know who will direct the Distribution of it, But if My Lady Dutchess do's it, Upon the List of the Debts you give her, I desire you will make such a demand for the Country People in Generall, that you may be Able to keep two or three hundred pounds in private Bank for Exigencys which She can't foresee. but make no Mention of this to any body.

To Mr Joynes   41
   at Blenheim
    near Woodstock
     In Oxfordshire.

London. Oc^t: ye 19th 1710

S^r

I have y^{rs} of the 15th. And believe I can make shift with the Acc^t: you have sent me; Only I desire you will let me have likewise, an Acc^t: of what the other Building of the Office Court comes to, Eastward of the Kitchin Wing. I mean only as to the Freestone Work.

Davis the Glassman tells me there's a great deal of Glass for the Great Windowes now lying at Oxford, wch will get no good there be sure. Pray see to get it home if possible. there's likewise lead gone for Compleating the Roof.

I have at last got £7000. Order'd, two of wch lys now ready and might have been rec'd two days Since, but here's No body to take Care on't.

Two more will be ready on Monday next; Two the Monday after, and One the Monday after that. Mr Harley has farther told me, that they have now the Queens full Commission to go on with the Work, And that I may depend upon their doing all they can to Advance it.

As to the People in the Mannour house, e'en do as you think Convenient.

I shou'd be glad to hear the Shed over the Great Arch of the Bridge was done, before more wet comes. I hope Mr Peisley will set his Facia there as he design'd. I am

Y^r real Friend & Servt

J VANBRUGH

The Man has brought my Papers.

To Mr Joynes   42
    at Blenheim
        near Woodstock
            In Oxfordshire.

London. Oc^t: ye 25th 1710

S^r

I have a Letter from Mr Travers from the Bath, with all Necessary matters for the money now lying in the Excheq^r being payd into the Hands of Mr Parkers Goldsmith. but it cannot be done till Wensday next; You shall have notice of it the Next day, so that you may Now assure People positivly of money the end of Next Week. I am

Y^r faithfull Friend

& Servt

J VANBRUGH

To Mr Joynes   43
    at Blenheim
        near Woodstock
            In Oxfordshire.

London. Nov: ye 2^d 1710

S^r

I had y^r Letter of ye 26th. Young Mr Peisley told me when he was here, the Rough Arch of the Bridge wou'd be Compleated as indeed 'twas absolutely necessary it shou'd, that it may be equally dry in all parts when the Centers come away. I therfore hope 'tis done.

As to Money, I did my Part, and much more than my part, in Soliciting the Treasury till I got an Order for it; But if there's nobody in Towne to receive it, or that My Lady Dutchess do's not think fitt to let it be sent to you, 'tis not my fault nor shall I give my Self any farther trouble about

it. Pray send up the Copys of Mr Gibbons Bills wch Mr Hawksmoor
writ for. I believe My Ld Duke will be over the end of next Week, and
then I Suppose we shall get to rights again. I am

Y^r real Fr^d & Servt

J VANBRUGH

I desire Mr Ryves to send me up a Doe, if they have begun to Kill
'em yet.

To Mr Joynes   44
    at Blenheim
    near Woodstock
       In Oxfordshire.

London. Jan: ye 9th 1710 [11 ?]

S^r

    Mr Parker tells me you have paid away the whole £5000, which I
am Sorry to hear and hope is a Mistake; for you know we agreed when
you were here, Not to part wth above half of it, that being sufficient for
the Exigencys of the home Carts, Lime men, Brickmakers &c and the
rest being very necessary for other uses which I knew wou'd call for it.
My Ld Duke is very angry at My Lady Dutchesses having meddled at
all with it, & that it has been thus dispos'd of. for I writ to him about it
into Flanders, not doubting but you had reserv'd above £2000 as you
know we resolv'd upon, Notwithstanding what She had said to you: for
the keeping it in your hands was not breaking her order which was only
that you shou'd not apply it to anything else.

    An other thing I desir'd of you was, to make what dispatch might be
with the Measurem^ts: because an Acc^t: of the Debt was expected to be
call'd for, upon my Ld Dukes return. I find severall of the Workmen
very uneasy on this Account; and my Ld Duke is in daily expectation the
Debt will be call'd for. I must therfore desire you will set about this
matter with all Application, and get thorough it as soon as possible.

    My Lord Duke designs to come downe very Suddenly; and that he
may rightly comprehend every thing about the Gallery I desire you will
immediatly set on the Bricklayer to run up the Partition wall in that we
call my Ld Treasurers Appart^t: Kit Cash has the Design and will instruct
him. An other thing I desire may immediatly be gone about (if Mr Barton
be with you, not otherwise) is the striking the Centers under the Great
Arch of the Bridge and pray let them be lay'd so out of the way as not
to confuse the View of the Bridge in any part of it. I wish you and
Mr Bobart a happy new Year, and am

Y^r Friend & Servt

J VANBRUGH

To Mr Joynes   45
    at Blenheim
        near Woodstock
            In Oxfordshire.   *Whitehall. Feb: ye 17th 1710 [11?]*
    S^r

    I have y^{rs} of ye 15th: I shew'd Kit Cash before I came away what work there wou'd be for the Bricklayer this Year; and bad him Speak to Mr Churchhills Man to compute what Number of Bricks wou'd be wanting for it. I desire you will enquire into it, and direct the Bricks to be prepar'd accordingly. My Ld Duke go's in a day or two, And Mr Harley has assur'd me yesterday we shall have money to proceed this year, but w^t the Sum will be, I don't yet know, but he said 'twou'd be Issu'd by weekly Payments. I hope they'll begin soon after my Ld Duke go's.
                         I am
                     Y^r Fr^d & Servt
                         J VANBRUGH

    Pray ask Kitt Cash if the French book of Paladio be not in Mr Strongs Shedd; I thought we had had it in Towne but don't find it.

To Mr Joynes   46
    at Blenheim
        near Woodstock
            In Oxfordshire.   *London March ye 14th 1710 [11?]*
    S^r

    I have yours of the 4th with the Marble Bill enclos'd. As to Boards, Uffers &c I desire Mr Parker will provide them; And that you will see what Quantity may probably be necessary, And give him directions Accordingly. There will a great many be us'd in the Center for the great Arch of the Bridg which must be turn'd this Year: And I must desire in Order to compleating that Work, you will see what we are to hope for, from the Heddington Quarrs. a great deal of that Stone being propper for it. The Hard Stone too, we shall Stand in great need of, for the Low wall round the Great Court, and other uses. I desire you will likewise enquire after the Helmindon Quarry men. for if we have a good Quantity of that it will be of mighty Service; I therfore desire all may be got of it that Can.
    Pray get all the Marble &c home from Oxford as soon as you can; for there will come a great deal more of that kind very soon, which will quite fill up the Wharf. I shall come downe the begining of next Month, who am
                    Your Friend & Servt
                       J VANBRUGH

APPENDIX II

To Mr Joynes   47
  at Blenheim
    near Woodstock
      In Oxfordshire

                      London. March ye 22th 1710 [11 ?]

S^r
    I have been in daily hopes of money being order'd for Blenheim,
wch had been done ere now but for this.* Accident to Mr Harley, he
having Assur'd me that the first time the Queen sate at the Treasury she
wou'd Sign an Order, and that it shou'd be Issu'd by weekly payments.
So as soon as he comes abroad (which I believe won't be long) I don't
doubt but we shall have money, And in the mean time, if Mr Peisley has
a mind to set what stone he has wrought for the Bridge, he may & go on
with working more of that upon the ground, for 'tis resolv'd the Bridge
shall be finish'd this Summer As soon as ever there's money order'd I'll
come downe, who am

                Y^r assured
                    Friend & Servt
                      J VANBRUGH

To Mr Joynes   48
  at Blenheim
    near Woodstock
      In Oxfordshire

                      London. May ye 17th 1711

S^r
    I desire you will make a Step over to the Marble Quarry at Bleching-
ton and take Mr Peisley with you. I want to know the good and bad
Qualitys of that Stone the Sizes of the Blocks which may be rais'd and
the Lowest price. I Believe Sr Thomas Wheat may be Able to inform
you a good deal of it. I wou'd likewise know if it is like to afford a Great
Quantity shou'd it be required. Pray let me have your Answer as soon as
you well can. Mr Harley is not yet Ld Treasurer, and till he is we shan't
be got agoing. How soon that will be I can't tell but be sure the rising
of the Parliament will be the longest.
    I have a Mournfull Letter from Green one of the Heddington men for
£30. to save him from being torn to peices by a Lawyer, but 'tis not in
my power to help him. He desires I'll write to Mr Peisley. All I can say

* Harley was stabbed by de Guiscard March 8th, 1711.

is, that Mr Peisley may tell the Lawyer I'll take care Green shall have this £30. out of the first money that comes for Blenheim, wch to be sure will be very soon. I'm

Y^r Assured friend
& Servt
J VANBRUGH

Pray tell Mr Ryves I rec'd his Letter

To Mr Joynes   49
   at Blenheim
     near Woodstock
       In Oxfordshire.   *London Sep^t: ye 11th 1711*

S^r

I writ to Mr Bobart last Post about setting Men upon the Hill, 'tis a thing no time shou'd be lost in, for 'twill be impossible to work long at it. I forgot to Speak to him and you for my Maids Husband, He is now in the Gardens; at only 7^s a week, He was Sr Thos: Crisps Butler, and not us'd to hard Labour if therfore you find room to employ him in any overseeing part, where his wages may likewise be something Augmented, I desire you will do it.

Kynaston tells me there has yet been nobody with him for the Marble Blocks wch ly in Scotland yard; I remember I writ before I came last downe, to desire you wou'd Immediatly engage the Oxford Barges to call for it. I know there are great Blocks wch they mayn't be willing to take in, Nor do I desire they shou'd, till they are cut, but there are Severall smaller which they can easily deal with, and those shou'd by all means be got to Oxford and so to Blenheim with all Speed; as likewise those of smaller size now at Oxford shou'd be got home, for there will be a good deal of Marble wanted this Winter for Chimney peices, the Salon &c.

You have Mr Reynolds's Bill for Marble deliver'd Since January was twelve months Pray examine it and send it up sign'd that the Money may be had, for He was to have been paid ready money.

Mr Strong tells me there is a check to the Stone coming in, by four or 5 fellows returning without their money; I hope 'twill be retriev'd by the aid has been sent you since I came up for I wou'd fain if possible have Mr Strong get up that South west Tower. I am

Y^r Assur'd Friend &
Servt
J VANBRUGH

They have brought me a Copy of Mr Reynolds's Bill Which I here inclose lest the other shou'd not be wth you.

To Mr Joynes   50
    at Blenheim
       near Woodstock
          In Oxfordshire.   London. Sep^t ye 15th 1711
   S^r

I have your Letter. As to the Kitchen Court, you may forbear till you hear farther but for the Bridge, I have my Lord Dukes express Orders in Writing for carrying it on as far as posible; therefore desire Mr Peisley will proceed upon it with all expedition and that no Directions from Mr Travers to the Contrary may be observ'd. As to the Tower on the Stable Wing its a jest to Mention it. there is not a Stone for it, nor is it a thing can be done in four months time, the expence too I am sure will be near £2000. whereas all that is propos'd to do at the Bridge and Kitchen Court this Year (I mean as to the Masonry) won't come to £600. I shan't be downe again till the week after next. I'll write to Mr Strong about the Stone.

               Y^r Fr^d & Servt
                 J VANBRUGH

Mr Hargraves Wife will send him downe Pelegrims Colour for Priming the Salon. wch he shou'd do.

To Mr Joynes   51
    at Blenheim
       near Woodstock
          In Oxfordshire.   London Sep^t: ye 25th 1711
   S^r

I have rec'd y^{rs} of ye 16th and 22th: with the Marble Bill. I have sent to enquire after the Barge Masters you mention, and when any Marble is put on Board, I'll take care you shall have the Scantlings sent you. I have given directions for 1000 Boards to be sent away with Speed; they must be husbanded all that can be, for they are grown extreamly scarce and dear.

I can say little to the Stone not coming in: Mr Strong writes to assure me 'tis not his fathers or Mr Brays fault. You told me if there was money remitted to pay the Stone Carters half what was due to them you did not doubt but they wou'd fetch in more Stone. but if I understand you right now, they expect the whole: which I fear cannot be had. As to the Letters Mr Travers writ about Stopping the Kitchin Court and Towers of the Bridge, can only repeat that as to that Court it may ly still for the present, but I have my Lord Dukes express commands to carry up the Bridge as far as possible, And therefore do expect that Mr Peisley will regard no

Orders contrary to what he has already from me, unless he has 'em directly from my Lady Dutchess or Lord Ryalton under their own hand. My Ld Ryalton has written to me, that what Orders are to be executed shall come to me to transmit them to the Workmen, and Since I have yet none from him to Stop the Bridge, I desire again that Mr Peisley will push on what I directed with all possible Speed during the good Season. I have nothing more to say now but that I am

Y^r Friend & Servt
J VANBRUGH

To Mr Joynes   52
  at Blenheim
    near Woodstock
      In Oxfordshire.   London. Sep^t: ye 30th 1711
  S^r

I writ in my last all I had to say about your proceedings; I shou'd be glad to hear the Bridge in particular went on without Interruption and with Vigour.

When there is Occasion for any Brass Cocks &c, pray let the Plumber send to Mr Abthorp in Crooked Lane near the Monum^t: I thought to have come downe next week but shall be hindred by the Commission for Building the Churches. I'll get away however as soon as possible. who am Your assured

Friend & Servt
J VANBRUGH

If Mr Bobart has any Latter Peaches & Necktrins, he'd oblige me with one Basket more.

To Mr Joynes   53
  at Woodstock
    near Oxford.   London Oc^t: ye 27th 1711
  S^r

If the Plaisterer has not yet done in the Bow window room, pray let him make all the hast he can. And the Joyners too, in getting their work ready to put up in that room. I shou'd be glad to know what they do in the others of that floor. I hope to get downe the end of next week & am

Y^{rs}
J VANBRUGH

˙Mr Hales's Man Hercules says Mr Schriven the Plumber makes difficulty of doing some little necessary day jobbs, because he is not paid a small bill of about £10.

Here's no news of the bridgemen yet.

APPENDIX II

To Mr Joynes   54
   at Woodſtock
     In Oxfordshire.

London. Nov. ye 13th 1711

S^r

I hear Mr Bridges, of the Ordnance is gone to Blenheim with some sort of Commission, but am not sure whether it be anything farther than what relates to auditing the Accounts, tho' I am told he is desir'd to give his Opinion about the future expence of the Building that is, how much will compleat it. Tho' had he ten times the knowledge in such things that I believe he has, I don't see how he can report any thing to the purpose on that head, without a great deal of talk with me, which I desire you will take Occasion to say as from your Self, if you find any need of it, And let me know what you can of the design of the Journey, if you find there is any thing more in it than Auditing the Accounts. I am Your

Assured Friend &
Servant
J VANBRUGH

To Mr Joynes   55
   at Blenheim
     near Woodſtock
       In Oxfordshire.

London. Nov: ye 22th 1711

S^r

I have had two Letters from you & am glad to find Mr Bridges was so well Satisfy'd. As to George Low, I have already Spoke to Mr Travers since he came to Towne, and won't quit that business, 'till he has my Ld Dukes determination whether he'll pay it himself, or order it to pass in the publick Account. My Lord thought to have set out for Blen^h: yeſterday, but has now put it off for ten days; Pray let Mr Banks's Scaffolds be gone, and all clean'd downe that he may find the Colonade finish'd I hope Kit Cash will likewise get the paving done in the Corridore from the Bow window room, to the Hall. And the Stairs up, that my Lord Duke may go to the Upper Story that way. If the paving be done in the ground floor it shou'd be clean wash'd. I have nothing more now, but to desire you'll send up Mr Gibbons's Bill that he may receive some money, wch I believe he wants, to go on with the Speed requir'd in the Marble Work. I am

Your assured Friend
& Servant
J VANBRUGH

I have agreed with Tyler of Abingdon to carry up all the Marble we have here, on Condition to be paid when he brings his Bill in.

(241)

To Mr Joynes   56
    at Blenheim
       near Woodſtock
          In Oxfordshire.

London. Dec: ye 1st 1711

S^r

I have y^{rs} of ye 20th paſt, and will immediatly give Orders to Mr Hale to Lead the Colonade, so you need send no more after Churchill, who is a very Idle Fellow. I have sign'd Mr Gibbons's Bill and here send you back Smalwells. Both he and Hopson have press'd me hard about the Doors, but I don't think it reasonable to Allow more than 18^s a Y^d Single measure So desire you'll return his Bill and Hopsons made up on that foot. And as soon as you can, that they may receive some money. As to their demand in their next. I don't find my Ld Duke is likely to come downe till Chriſtmas. so have nothing more to say now, but that I am

Y^r assured Friend &
Servt
J VANBRUGH

I desire Mr Ryves to send me up a Doe next Week.

To Mr Joynes   57
    at Blenheim
       near Woodſtock
          In Oxfordshire.

London. Dec^b: ye 3^d 1711

S^r

I desire you'll send me up the Weights of the Copper Balls, both with and without their Bases. as likewise a Coppy of Mr Smiths Bill for them, for I fear he do's not do right by us.

I want too a Copy of Bradleys Bill for the Clock, and shou'd be glad to know if the Weight of the Copper Dial plate &c answer'd what he puts them at.

I sent Smal^s: Bill to you laſt poſt without any Addition or allowances for the Doors, as he & Hopson press'd for. pray let me know in y^r next, whether all their moldings are not measur'd right up and downe, without Girting. I have directed Mr Hales to cover the Collonade with all Speed, so I think you need only write three words to tell Churchill he shou'd not send downe any lead for it. I hope the Mason has done there & clean'd downe; for I believe it won't be long before my Ld Duke comes downe.

I'm Y^rs

JV

When I was at Blen^h: laſt, Mr Warrens man said he wou'd write to his Maſter to take London in his way thither that I might give him directions what to proceed upon: but I hear nothing of him yet. he shou'd write to him again, for the Iron work for the Stairs shou'd go forwards.

To Mr Joynes   58
   at Woodſtock
     In Oxfordshire.

London. Oct: ye 30th 1712

S^r

I writ to you laſt Night to send up an Account out of the Measured Bills of Mr Peisley, Townsend & Banks, what the Expence had been for the Masonry (Workmanship only) in

1. The Kitchin
2. The reſt of that wing up to the Clock Tower
3. The Clock Tower
4. The Other Offices in the Kitchin Court
5. The Bridge.

The Freeſtone work I shou'd have Seperate from the Rubble. This is in Order to an Eſtimate for the other Court on the Stable Side.

I write now again, to desire you will Immediatly come up, and bring these remarks with you; as likewise an Account as near as you can, of what may be due to Workmen for work not yet brought to Account. My Lord Duke requiring with all Speed as near a State of the Debt as we can give him. Pray make no delay, I hope you'll get here on Monday or Tuesday at fartheſt.

I am
Your hum^b Servt
J VANBRUGH

To Mr Joynes   59
   at Woodſtock
     in Oxfordshire.

London May ye 3^d 1715

S^r

I am juſt return'd from the North and find My Lord Duke extremely Uneasy these Bills are not yet fix'd and the Debt exactly ſtated to be Shewn if call'd for. I therefore write by his Order to desire an immediate dispatch may be made, and pray let me know by next post, where abouts you are got in the affair, that I may give him some satisfaction in it. I believe it will be found Necessary, we shou'd Sign all the Books if they are to Appear to any Auditer appointed by the Treasury. And that in Order to it, they muſt be brought up to Towne. I am

Yr Friend & Sert

J VANBRUGH

To Mr Joynes   60
   at Woodſtock
      In Oxfordshire.   *Whitehall May ye 5th 1715*
   Sr

I writ to you laſt poſt, to tell you how reſtless my Ld Duke was, that we had not yet got the Accts: entirely Stated to lay before the Treasury or Parliamt: Mr Wetherhill tells me you want no measurement but Bartons, And that you can't get him to you. I therefore desire you will get somebody at Oxford or else where, to measure his Work wth you and according to that we'll make up his Bill, for the thing muſt not be delay'd a moment longer.

I hope you have examin'd the Copper Balls

I'm Yrs

JV

To Mr Joynes   61
   at Woodſtock
      In Oxfordshire.   *Whitehall May ye 7th 1715*
   Sr

I have yours of ye 5th. I have writ to Mr Barton (who I hear is now at Sr Wm Windhams) to come immediatly to you, As to your coming up, I can only say, That there shou'd not be a day loſt, when you are ready for here is nothing to delay making up the Acct: when you come. My Lord Duke is very Impatient, it not being thought advisable to Stir for money till the Acct: is deliver'd in compleat.

I am glad you find so few errors

Yr humble Sert   JV

To Mr Joynes   62
   at Woodſtock
      in Oxfordshire.

Whitehall. May ye 12th 1715

   Sr

I have yrs of ye 9th. I shall not forget you if any room can be made by Removall of some of the present Clerks, but how that matter will be, is yet not determin'd.

(244)

As to the Blen^m: affair, it is now in motion in the house of Commons And will I believe be determin'd there to morrow, whether it be the Queens Debt or not. So that you shou'd certainly come away, and bring up every thing necessary for compleating the Demand on the Treasury. I told you before, I thought there wou'd be a Necessity for Signing the Books, so they muſt come up. I am Y^r

Friend & Servant

J VANBRUGH

To Mr *Joynes*   63
  at *Woodſtock*
    In *Oxfordshire.*

April ye 5th 1716

S^r

I believe it wou'd not be Amiss, (to gain time) if you talk'd a little with the Severall Quarry Men, of Cornbury & Burford, Heddington &c, to See on what Terms they will furnish Stone having their money paid weekly or Monthly as they please. I forgot to mention this to you, when I was at Woodſtock.

Y^r Friend & Servt

J VANBRUGH

Pray let Mr Peisley take an Account what Quantity of Portland Stone, is us'd in One of the Great Towers, for weathering &c, above the Great Cornice. I don't want to know what workmanship, but how many foot of Stone there may be, the waſt included.

To Mr *Joynes*   59
  at *Woodſtock*
    In *Oxfordshire.*

London. May ye 1st 1716

S^r

I was in hopes you wou'd long e'er this have return'd to Towne, but by what S^r Th^o: Wheat tells me, I Suppose this will find you ſtill at Blenheim, if it do's, I desire you will set the Quarry men to work at Cornbury on the same Terms as formerly unless you can get better, and let them raise what is unbar'd as soon as they can; What I write is by my Lord Duke's direction, in whose name you are to agree wth them And may assure them of their money every Month if they please.

APPENDIX II

Pray let me know what Mr Thornhill do's, my Lord Duke being very desirous he wou'd make what dispatch he can

I am

Y^r Friend & Servt

J VANBRUGH

My Lord Duke wou'd have all the New Stone that comes in lay'd so, as not to be mix'd & confounded with what is upon the ground Already. You may Order Stone from Tainton too, as formerly, but there is no need of pressing to have it in, in such great Quantitys as they us'd to send it. but two or three hundred Tun wou'd do well to be got in, by Midsummer.

Pray let me know when you are like to come up, we want the Kensington Book for March, to Compleat the Quarter.

APPENDIX III

Containing two papers addressed to the Earl of Halifax and to the Commissioners of the Treasury respectively, concerning the administration of the Board of Works. Both dated. (From the Treasury Papers. Record Office.)

I.

To the R^t. Honble. The Earl of Halifax

November the 29th: 1714

My Lord

Upon the general Sentiments your Lordship has been pleas'd to express, in relation to the Board of Works, I beg leave to refer to your farther thoughts, a few heads towards its future Settlement and Reformation; which wou'd Save the King, a very great Sum of Money, in unnecessary and unreasonable Works; and lessen his expence considerably in many Useless or Mischievous Officers.

Perhaps your Lordship may think of Something your Self much more to the purpose, than what I take the Liberty to lay before you; I should therefore only Add, that in whatever Station, you shall think fit to place me, for the execution of the Method you conclude upon; I will do what I can, to be so truely Serviceable to the King in it that he may never blame your Lordship, for being the Instrument of his Favour to me. And I beg your Lordship will believe, I have a most gratefull Sense of your long continued kindness to

Your most humble
and most Obedient Servant
J VANBRUGH

Some Heads for a New Settlement of the Office of Works

1st. That the Offices of Master Mason, Master Carpenter, and all the other Master Workmen, with the Purveyour, and Clark Ingrosser, be Sunk, and their Allowances Saved to the Crown.

2. That for a Check on the Surveyour, in lieu of the Master Mason and Master Carpenter, the Paymaster may be join'd with him and the Comptroller, to make Contracts, pass Bills and Sign the Books.

3. That instead of Seaven Clarks, which at present are employed in the Office of Works, there may be but Two.
Viz^t:
One to sit at the Board as Secretary, to take Minutes, enter Orders, Contracts, Warrants &c. Draw up Reports, Enter

(247)

the Prices in the Office Book as Adjusted by the Board in passing the Bills, and to write out the Book for the Auditor. One other Clark to Assist the Paymaster.

4.   That in all Admeasurements, two Clarks of the Works be Oblig'd to measure together.

5.   That no distinct Office or Officer be continued for Windsor, except a Clark of the Works.

6.   That no work may be done in any private Lodging, at the King's Expence, but necessary repairs, to keep out the Weather, and the Building from falling.

7.   That if any Persons desire to alter or embellish their Lodgings, at their own Expence; They may be Oblig'd to acquaint the Surveyour with it; And not to proceed but by his Permission, or a Warrant from the Lord Chamberlain. And that the Clark of the Works be directed by the Surveyour to take care, that no Such Work vary from what has been consented to, and Allow'd of; which shall be Signified to the said Clark Under the Surveyours hand.

8.   That the Surveyour be carefull to employ no Person as Clark of the Works, who is not duely qualifyed for it, by his Skill in Drawing, Measurements, Workmanship and Materials.

9.   That the Appointments to the Surveyour and Comptroller, be on the foot of a Salary certain without Perquisites of any kind whatsoever.

2.

To the Right Honble. the Lords Commissioners of his Majesty's Treasury.

May it please Your Lordships,

In Obedience to Your Lordship's Commands signifyed to Us by William Lowndes Esqr, the 23th Instant for Perusing the Draught of Orders for the Office of his Majesty's Works Transmitted to Us, and for giving Our Oppinion thereupon, We humbly observe and Propose as follows.

1.   On the first Article for Constituting a Board, We beg Leave to offer to Your Lordships Consideration whether Three may not be sufficient in Regard many of the Commissioners now appointed will be often Absent in the Execution of their other Employments, and We humbly propose that the Surveyor General of the Works, or the Comptroller be allways One, & that the said Surveyor, as such, may be first Named and Preside at the Board, and in his absence the Comptroller.

3.   Three as above proposed, to be sufficient.

4.   Three sufficient, and the Originall Warrants to be Delivered to the Auditors, for Vouchers of the Paymasters Accounts.

5.   Dele, And the Clerk of the house, where the work is to be done.

The Paymaſter desires he may be excused from Soliciting for Warrants; by Reason his whole Time will be taken up in the Execution of his Office and conſtant Attendance at the Board, in the Absence of those Gentlemen who are either Members of Parliament, or have other Important Business. 'Tis therefore Desired this service may be Performed by such of the Writing Clerks, as the Board shall appoint.

The said Paymaſter likewise begs Leave to Represent that having by the Eſtablishment but 20^d p Diem for a Clerk (which is less than any other belonging to the Office Enjoys) no Person of Credit or Ability will serve him on these Terms, so that he has been oblig'd to make an Addition to the present Sallary to the Value of Twenty Pounds p Annum, and therefore humbly Craves the aforesaid Allowance of 20^d may be Encreas't to 30^d p Diem for the future.

8.   Allowance to the Clerks for Travelling, not sufficient.

10.   To the 10th Article We beg Leave to Represent, That, since all Future Contraćts are to be made with the Faireſt Proposer, after Publication, It seems moſt praćticable that it should be left to the Board to Agree with the Undertakers, and all kinds of Artizans either for Work alone or Work and Materials together as shall be found moſt Expedient.

11.   The Maſter Mason and Maſter Carpenter not being of the Board, Their Deputys (if any) seem to come under the head of other Patent Artizans.

17.   Inſtead of the Surveyor making Eſtimates alone he Desires it may be with the Assiſtance and Concurrence of the Board.

18.   The Proposals for Work being left open to all People We beg to be Direćted what service we are to Require from the Patent Artizans.

20.   We humbly propose that the Clerk of the Works of Whitehall, may (as Secretary to the Board) Take minutes—Draw up Reports, Eſtimates and Memorials, Fill up the Blanks left for Prices, in passing the Books, and Cause fair Entrys to be made by the Respećtive Writing Clerks of all Proceedings at the Board.

And We farther Beg Leave to offer the Continuance of a Clerk as formerly but that he may also be oblig'd to make Coppys of such Draughts and Designs, as the Survey^r. shall from time to Time judge proper for his Majeſty's service to the End the same may be kept in Office to have Recourse to on Occation: Together with the Plans, Elevations, and Surveys of all the Royall Pallaces and Gardens, The said Clerk to be Nominated by the Surveyour with Approbation of the Board, and to be Allowed such Travelling Charges as Your

Lordship's shall judge proper when Employed by the Surveyour abroad.

Two Clerks being now appointed to Measure, whereas but One was Required formerly, the Comptroller hopes Your Lords^ps will think that Checque sufficient, provided the Additional Clerk be appointed by him for that service.

We take this Occation humbly to offer to Your Lords^p's Consideration, whether it may not be proper to Incorporate the Office of the Works at Windsor with the Generall Office of the Works at Whitehall and the Payments to be made by the Paymaster Generall.

All which is humbly submitted by

J VANBRUGH

Office of his Maj^ties
Works 31st March 1715

NOTES

p. 3.   London: December 25th 1699. to Charles Montagu 4th Earl of Manchester created Duke of Manchester 1719, at this time Ambassador to the Court of Louis XIV, afterwards ambassador both at Vienna and Venice.

p. 3.   *Jack How;* Vice-Chamberlain to Queen Mary, at this time a Member for Gloucestershire and a thorn in the side of the Whigs. Burnet describes him as " a man of some wit, but of little judgement, and of small principles of religion."

p. 3.   " *Commission againſt Pyrates* "; The affair of Captain Kidd, originally sent out as a Privateer to put down Pirates in the East Indies and himself turned Pirate, was eagerly taken up by the Tories in an attempt to discredit Somers who with Lords Romney (see below) and Bellamont the Governor of Barbadoes had originally financed the adventure.

p. 3.   *Mr Montagu;* Charles, afterwards Earl of Halifax, had just resigned the Treasury after a brilliant tenure of office. He was a great patron of learning and letters and a prodigious collector of epistles dedicatory. Pope satirised him for this last trait under the name of the Buffo.

p. 4.   *Lords Portland and Albemarle;* the earlier and later favourites of William III.

p. 4.   *Lord Romney;* Henry Sidney, Secretary of State 1691–2, then Lord Lieutenant of Ireland, and undistinguished in either office was said to be the only Englishman that William III really liked.

p. 4.   *Mr Newton;* afterwards Sir Isaac Newton.

p. 4.   *Leveridge;* Richard, the celebrated Bass, of Lincoln's Inn, afterwards kept a popular Coffee House in Tavistock St Covent Garden.

p. 4.   *Sir John Philips* of Picton, Bart., M.P. for Pembroke, suc. 1698, died 1736.

p. 4.   *Neal;* Master of the Mint and Groom Porter, the great promoter of Lotteries. See D.N.B.

p. 4.   *Purcell;* Daniel, brother of the great Henry Purcell.

p. 4.   *Fingar;* Gottfried, a court musician under James II and one of the competitors for the music of Semele.

p. 4.   " *Congreves play* " The Way of the World.

p. 4.   *The woman from the Cheshire Cheese;* Mrs. Oldfield (?).

p. 4.   *The Emperors crooked Eunuch Francisco;* Senesino?

p. 4.   *Lady Arglass;* widow of the last Earl who died in 1684. It was an Irish title.

p. 4.   *Lady Dartmouth;* probably the widow of the Jacobite Admiral who died in the Tower in 1690.

p. 4.   *Lady Betty Cromwell;* daughter of Lady Arglass. Luttrell says " an heiress of £2000 a year," afterwards married Edward Southwell (see Note).

p. 4.   *Lord Nottingham's house;* Burleigh on the Hill.

p. 4.   *Duke of Leeds house;* Hornby Castle?

p. 5.   *Duke and Duchess of Leeds;* The celebrated Danby, minister of Charles II was created Duke of Leeds in 1694. His wife was Bridget, daughter of the Earl of Lindsey.

p. 5.   *Lord Carberry;* John Vaughan, a member of the Kitcat; in his youth Pepys said of him " one of the lewdest fellows of the age, worse than Sir Charles Sidly " and Clarendon an old enemy, "a person of as ill a face as fame, his looks and his manner both extreme bad."   He is said to have enriched himself by the sale of his Welsh tenants as slaves to Jamaica; from 1686 to 89 he was President of the Royal Society and was one of the earliest patrons of Dryden.   He died in 1713 and left the largest library of the mystical divines ever collected before that time.

p. 5.   *Mrs Saunders;* this seems too early for Mrs Saunders the actress who did not make her appearance until 1702.

p. 5.   *Henly;* Antony, politician wit and Patron of Letters married Mary, daughter of Perigrine Bertie the Vice Chamberlain of the Household.

p. 6.   Tadcaster. Sunday noon. To the Earl of Carlisle.   The letter should date from 1700 (see Introduction).   Charles 3d Earl of Carlisle was a fellow member of the Kit Cat Club with Vanbrugh and his firm friend throughout the period covered by this correspondence.   His Lordship held a Variety of Offices as Earl Marshall Lieutenant of the Tower Constable of Windsor Castle etc etc and was one of the Regents at the death of Queen Anne and first Lord of the Treasury May to October 1715.

p. 6.   *Lord Burlington;* Charles Boyle 2nd Earl of Burlington died February 1704.

p. 6.   *Hawksmoor;* Nicholas, architect, see Introduction.

p. 6.   *Lanesborough;* The Yorkshire seat of the Burlington family.

p. 7.   London. June 5th 1703. To Jacob Tonson the celebrated publisher and friend of the wits.   Tonson was secretary and leading spirit of the Kit Cat Club; in his later years he was described by Pope as " the perfect image and likeness of Bayles Dictionary: so full of matter, secret history, and wit at almost fourscore."   He died in 1736.

p. 7.   *My brother;* possibly Charles.   See letter, page 112.

p. 7.   *Barne Elmes;* Tonson's country house where Vanbrugh fitted up a room for the Kit Cat Club in which were hung the famous series of portraits.   It is now Ranelagh.

p. 7.   *Sir Godfrey;* Kneller, the portrait painter, was a member of the Kit Cat. Examples of his wit are in Walpole's Anecdotes; it seems to have had a bent towards religious subjects and to have been spoken with a strong German accent (see his defence of the Pretender's legitimacy).   At his country house at Whitton, referred to in this letter and now the College of Military Music, he seems to have divided his time between his painting, the cultivation of flowers, and his duties as a Justice of the Peace, having more regard in his last capacity to Equity than Law.   See Walpole, who quotes Pope—

> " I think Sir Godfrey should decide the suit,
> Who sent the thief (that stole the cash) away
> And punished him that put it in his way."

p. 7.   *Neighbour Burgess;* a farmer who it would seem managed Tonsons garden.

p. 7.   *Duke of Somerset;* Charles Seymour, 6th Duke, was a staunch supporter of the Protestant Succession and a member of the Kit Cat; in the ministerial crises of 1709–10 his policy was " backing and filling " and earned him hard words in the correspondence of the first Duchess of Marlborough. He married as his first wife Lady Ogle, the romantic heiress of the Percy estates. He had a reputation for petty meanness coupled with an extravagant magnificence—he built Petworth—and his pride of birth amounted almost to a mental derangement. Lord Chancellor Cowper says of him " he was a pretender to the greatest courage and steadiness," but almost the only example of these qualities is perhaps his protestation of lifelong devotion and proposal of marriage to Sarah Duchess of Marlborough within a year of the great Dukes death. The Duchess in refusing recommended another Lady in her stead—which advice he took—but it is remarked that his name was erased from all the more abusive passages in her papers after this event.

p. 8. *Lord Essex;* Algernon Capel, 2nd Earl, 1670 to 1710. Described as " a well bred gentleman, brown complexioned and well shaped, but his mouth is always open " and also " the lewdest young man of the town."

p. 8. *Henry St George;* member of a distinguished family of Heralds, son of one Garter King at Arms and brother to another.

p. 8. *Capt Saunders;* afterwards Admiral Sir George Saunders (?).

p. 8. *The Playhouse;* This would seem to be the first mention of the Haymarket scheme. See Introduction, Vol. I and Vol. IV.

p. 8. London July 13th 1703. To Tonson.

p. 8. *Ld Halifax;* see note, p. 3.

p. 8. *Lord Kingston;* Evelyn Pierrepont 5th Earl (1665–1726) created Marquis of Dorchester 1706 and Duke of Kingston and K.G. 1715. The father of Lady Mary Wortley Montagu. He has been described as " a very fine gentleman, of good sense, well bred and a lover of the ladies; . . . makes a good figure, is of a black complexion, well made etc." Lady Mary herself compared him to the lively father of Sir Charles Grandison. He was a member of the Kit Cat into which he once introduced his daughter then a small girl.

p. 9. *My Ld Marshall;* Lord Carlisle.

p. 9. *Gregory King;* see Introduction, Vol. I.

p. 9. *Lady Harriet Vere & Di. Kirk;* these two disreputable ladies seem to have been worthy representatives of two closely allied families of unsavoury reputation since the Restoration. Lady Cowper's lively description of their joint attempt to seduce her husband can hardly be accepted however as unprejudiced. See Diary.

p. 9. John Dormer of Rowsham Oxfordshire.

p. 9. *Dunch;* is described by the D.N.B. as a politician and Bon vivant, he held a great many places and was a member of the Kit Cat.

p. 9. *Lord Grantham;* Henry Nassau-Auverquerque 1st Earl. 1698 to 1754.

p. 9. *Garth;* Sir Samuel, (1661–1718) was a Physician and Poet, a hearty Whig, a member of the Kit Cat and a friend of the wits. His best known poem, the Dispensary, is in support of the medical charity scheme of subsidised dispensaries for the poor (1696). His genial pleasant character is attested by many contemporary writers, including Lady Mary Wortley Montagu who tells a tale of how he ran a race of 200 yards in the Mall against the Duke of Grafton and beat him.

p. 9. *Sir Roger Mosthyn;* 3d Baronet.

p. 9. *Lord Nottingham's daughter;* Lady Essex Finch. Lord Nottingham was the leader of the High Church Tories and had thirty children by his second wife. In 1721 he received the thanks of the University of Oxford for his theological writings.

p. 10. London. July 30th 1703. To Jacob Tonson.

p. 10. *Sir Stephen Fox;* (1627–1716) Paymaster of the Forces. Father of Lord Holland and Grandfather of Charles James Fox. The word " prig " is said to have had a rather different meaning in eighteenth century from our modern word but the following description of Sir Stephen Fox by Evelyn suggests that Sir Stephen had temptations at least to the modern priggishness " In a word, never was man more fortunate than Sir Stephen: he is a handsome person, virtuous and very religious."

p. 10. *Lord Northampton;* married Jane daughter of Sir Stephen Fox.

p. 10. *Lord Cornwallis;* most probably the son of Charles 3d Lord Cornwallis (died 1698) and Sir Stephen Fox's eldest daughter.

p. 10. *Lord Wharton;* Thomas 5th Baron and 1st Marquis (1648–1715) the Arch-Whig, his reputation as a politician and a rake is well known; Swift's criticism though prejudiced is generally allowed to be fairly just: Wharton had no other interests but " Vice and politics, so that bawdy, prophaneness and business fill up his whole conversation." Among the Vices or the business must be counted a passion for Horse-racing to fill out this description.

p. 10. *Dr Sloan;* later Sir Hans Sloan, and Physician to George I. He was a great naturalist and his collections of specimens formed the nucleus of what was to be the British Museum.

p. 10. *Lord Hartford;* eldest son of the Duke of Somerset.

p. 10. *Lady Mary Churchill;* married Lord Monthermer son of the Earl of Montagu, created Duke of Montagu, by Marlboroughs influence in 1704. Lady Mary was not without wit and quarreled violently with her mother.

p. 11. *The Portugal Treaty;* concluded at Lisbon May 16th by Methuen.

p. 11. To Lord Godolphin Nov: 9th 1704. See note, p. 27.

p. 12. *Hill:* Thomas Hill one of the two chief contractors for the fine masons work at Hampton Court. See Wren Society, Vol. IV.

p. 12. *Jackson:* Benjamin Jackson employed as a mason at Hampton Court later about 1701 succeeded Oliver as King's Master Mason.

p. 13. London. July 18th 1707. To the Earl of Manchester then in Venice.

p. 13. *My Lady;* The Earl of Manchester married in 1690 the Honourable Dodington Grevill daughter and co-heiress of Lord Brooke.

p. 14. *Windsor;* the State apartments at Windsor Castle were rebuilt under Charles II by Hugh May one of the more obscure architects of the mid seventeenth century. He is mentioned several times in Evelyn's diary and his only extant works are the chapel at Cornbury House and Eltham Lodge.

p. 14. *My Lady Duchess;* of Marlborough. See elsewhere.

p. 14. *Toulon Expedition;* the allies arrived before Toulon on the 26th of July.

NOTES

p. 15.   London Sept. 9th 1707. To the Earl of Manchester.

p. 15.   *Duke of Devonshire;* William Cavendish 4th Earl and 1st Duke, and builder of Chatsworth was perhaps the greatest Whig noble of his day. He was distinguished alike for the magnificence of his way of living and his astonishing feats of daring among which sustaining a duel against some half dozen adversaries at the Opera House in Paris and dragging a certain fire-eating Colonel Culpepper from the presence of James II by the nose. He had been a member of the Long Parliament and was one of the prime movers of the Revolution. He died on August 18th 1707.

p. 15.   *Sir James Forbes;* Clerk of the Green Cloth. See Le Neve.

p. 16.   *Duke of Richmond;* Charles Lennox first Duke. (1672 to 1723) son of Charles II by Louise de Kerouille.

p. 16.   *Lord Dorchester;* see Kingston note above.

p. 16.   *Toulon and Monsieur Tallard;* The allies retreated from Toulon on August 22nd. Monsieur Talard, Camille d'Hostun Comte de Talard, Marshall of France, negotiated the Partition Treaties with William III and was defeated and captured at the battle of Blenheim. During his captivity he was interned at Nottingham.

p. 16.   London. February 24th 1708. To the Earl of Manchester in Venice.

p. 16.   *My Lord Treasurer;* Godolphin. See note, p. 27.

p. 16.   *Nicolini;* Grimaldi, came over later in the year and had an immense success. In 1711 he performed with great applause in Handel's Rinaldo. His first appearance was at the Haymarket in Pirro e Demetrio by Scarlatti.

p. 17.   *Mr Swiney;* Vanbrugh's partner at the Haymarket. See Introduction, Vol. II. He translated the opera Camilla published in 1706, and several others.

p. 17.   *Mr Bertie;* Perigrine Bertie, son of the Earl of Lindsey and Vice Chamberlain of the Household (?). See above, p. 3 note.

p. 17.   *Valentini;* Urbani, a celebrated soprano, first appeared in 1706 at Drury Lane in Camilla by Bononcini.

p. 17.   London. March 16th 1707. To the Earl of Manchester in Venice.

p. 17.   *Sir George Byng;* Whig Admiral, In Queen Anne's time this distinguished officer never got his due, the Queen being strongly prejudiced against him and his appointment to the Board of Admiralty was the occasion of a bitter struggle. In her successor's time after his great victory at Cape Pessaro (see notes, p. 101) he was raised to the peerage as Viscount Torrington.

p. 18.   *Lord Dorset;* Lionel Sackville, 7th Earl and 1st Duke, was a son of the romantic earl of Dorset, wit and poet and patron of letters. The son lived to hold office under Anne and her three successors and even Swift, who had a grudge against him, spoke well of him.

p. 20.   London. May 11th 1708. To the Earl of Manchester in Venice.

p. 20.   *Vice Chamberlain Coke;* Rt Hon. Thomas Coke of Melbourne, Derbyshire, Vice Chamberlain to Queen Anne and George I. Laid out the gardens of Melbourne with Wise.

p. 20.   *Lord Chamberlain;* Henry de Grey Duke of Kent held this office 1704 to 1710.

p. 21.   *Mrs Tofts;* celebrated English Prima Donna, her successes both musical and amorous were phenomenal, she married Mr Smith the Consul at Venice and retired from the stage but her later years were troubled with insanity.

p. 21.   *Mr Dayrolles;* probably James, diplomatist, represented Great Britain at the Hague 1717–39 (the year of his death) and previous to 1717 at Geneva. A Mr Dayrolles had been in the Bastile with Vanbrugh.

p. 21.   *Margarita;* Francesca Margherita de l'Espina the first celebrated Italian singer to appear in England; she was brought over by a German operatic composer in 1692.

p. 24.   To Manchester July 27th 1708.

p. 24.   *Sir John Coniers;* Virtuoso, Bart. of Horden, suc. 1693, died 1719.

p. 24.   *Duke of Shrewsbury;* Charles Talbot, 1st Duke, son of the infamous Countess of Shrewsbury who assisted at her husband's death, was one of the chief promoters of the Revolution, and a Minister under King William. He had only one eye but a persuasive manner and both Queen Mary and Sarah Duchess of Marlborough are said to have been in love with him. He seems to have been consumptive and was compelled to live for some years in Italy where he married Adelhida Paleotti of whom opinions differ (see Lady Mary Wortley Montagu,) Lady Cowper however had no doubts, " all the world knowing that her Brother (the Marquis Paleotti) had forced the Duke to marry her after an Intrigue together; which made a Lady say, the Duke had been tricked out of the best Marriage (meaning the Duchess of Somerset then Lady Ogle) and into the worst in Christendom." The brother came to England with his sister and lived to be hanged in 1718.

p. 24.   *Lord Bindon;* Henry Howard, afterwards 6th Earl of Suffolk.

p. 25.   *The Vice;* probably Peregrine Bertie, V.C. of the Household.

p. 25.   *Lord Somers;* (1651–1716) the great Whig Lawyer and Lord Chancellor under William. Queen Anne's early dislike of him is said to have quite disappeared under the influence of the ceremonious courtesy and deference with which he always treated her.

p. 25.   *Sir Walter St John;* Grandfather of the celebrated Bolingbroke. See Le Neve.

p. 25.   Bickleswade August 17th 1708 to the Earl of Manchester in Venice.

p. 26.   *Duke of Bedford;* Wriotesley, 2nd Duke 1682–1724.

p. 27.   Blenheim May 31st 1709 to the Lord Treasurer Godolphin. Sidney 1st Earl Godolphin, the great Administrator and finance Minister, Marlbrough's surest ally, has been described as " the silentest and modestest man that was perhaps ever bred in a Court " and Charles II said of him at the outset of his long career that he " was never in the way and never out of the way." Godolphin's great passion was gambling, especially horse-racing, because as he said himself " it delivered him from the obligation to talk much." He was the owner of the " Godolphin Arabian " one of the three horses from which all existing race-horses are descended in direct male line.

p. 34.   Blenheim: July 18th 1709. This letter is possibly to Lord Ryalton Godolphin's son married to Henrietta Churchill afterwards Duchess of Marlborough.

NOTES

p. 37. Blenheim Novr 1st 1709 to the Duchess of Marlborough.

p. 38. *Duke and Duchess of Shrewsbury and their house;* see note above, p. 24. The house was Heythrop designed by Thomas Archer, the builder of St Philip's Birmingham, St John's, Westminster etc. It is interesting in this connection to recall the Duke of Shrewsbury's admiration for Chatsworth (see above) by Talman, as Heythrop shows considerable affinities with Talman's manner. It is however not a very distinguished and indeed rather barbarous piece of Work.

p. 39. London April 28th 1710 to the Duke of Marlborough in the Low Countries.

p. 39. *Dr Newton;* probably Sir Henry (1651–1715) envoy in Tuscany.

p. 40. *Lord Cardigan;* George Brucknel 3d Earl suc. 1703 renounced the Roman Catholic faith and took his seat 1708, died 1732.

p. 40. *Mr Gibbons;* Grinling Gibbons the celebrated wood carver.
The copyist of the Coxe MSS. heads this letter " After mentioning that stone should speedily be provided for the Years work he proceeds "

p. 41. London June 24 1710 to the Duchess of Marlborough.

p. 41. *News of Lord Sunderland;* he was dismissed from Office on the 14th June after a severe struggle between the Queen and the Whig leaders.

p. 43. London Sept 22 1710 to the Duke of Marlborough

p. 43. *Lieut Genl Withers;* Henry Withers, Governor of Sheerness died 1729.

p. 44. Account of Treasury Relations undated

p. 44. *Lord Poulett;* First Lord of the Treasury in the Tory Ministry when that Office was put into Commission after Godolphin's fall.

p. 50. Chargate (?) October 25th 1710 to Mr Mainwaring. Arthur Mainwaring (1668–1712) opened his career as a satirist on the Jacobite side, but becoming friends with Lord Somers and the Marlboroughs he came over to the Whigs and defended Walpole when he was attacked in 1711. After Mainwaring's death in February 1712 a malicious attack on his personal character appeared in the Examiner and Walpole was able to repay the debt he owed by a spirited defence. Mainwaring was a fast friend and regular correspondent of the Duchess of Marlborough.

p. 51. London August 10th 1711 To the Duke of Marlborough

p. 51. *Lord Treasurer;* Robert Harley Earl of Oxford became Lord Treasurer in the May of this year.

p. 51. *The poor Vice;* Perigrine Bertie (?). (See above.)

p. 52. Oxford August 3d 1712 to the Lord Treasurer; Robert Harley Earl of Oxford and Mortimer the Tory leader.

p. 52. November 4th 1712. to the Duke (?) of Marlborough.
The second endorsement to this letter initialed G is possibly by Guidott the Duchesses man of affairs.
Among the Portland MSS. is a letter to Harley from which the following extract may be taken " Your Lordships generosity is much commended at camp for carrying on the building of Blenheim with so much diligence; this is heaping coals of fire on their heads " July 3–14 1711.

p. 53. Memorandum of Duke of Marlboroughs Will.

p. 53. *Mr Cardonel;* Adam de, the Duke of Marlborough's Secretary, was a

NOTES

Member of Parliament and appointed Secretary at War in 1710, but never held the office. He was expelled the House of Commons on a charge of peculation in 1712.

p. 53. *Mr Cragge;* probably the younger Craggs afterwards Secretary of State. See note.

p. 55. Castle Howard; Oct 23 1713 to Edward Southwell, (1671–1730) son of Robert Southwell diplomatist and Irish Landowner, is said to have been educated on the principle " cram into him some Lattin, some Mathematicks, some drawing and some Law—and then let Nature Work." He held various offices as Clerk to the Privy Council and Secretary of State for Ireland. He married Lady Betty Cromwell. See note.

p. 55. *Mrs Henley;* probably wife of Antony Henley. See note.

p. 56. Castle Howard Oct 29th 1713 to Craggs (?).

p. 57. *The Archbishop of York:* John Sharpe elected 1691 died in the February following this letter 1713–14.

p. 58. London May 29th 1714 to the Duke of Marlborough at Antwerp on the Continent.

p. 59. *Hanover Club;* Ambrose Philips the pastoral poet was Secretary at this time.

p. 59. *Lord Anglesea;* Arthur Annesley 5th Earl of Anglesea, leader of the Hanover Tories; he was one of the Lords Justices at the death of Queen Anne but was soon dropped by George I.

p. 60. *Anstis;* John: 1669–1745. Antiquarian, afterwards Garter King at Arms. See Introduction, Vol. I.

p. 60. January 16th 1714–15 to the Duchess of Marlborough.

p. 60. *Lady Harriet;* Godolphin daughter of Henrietta Churchill and Lord Treasurer Godolphin's son Lord Ryalton (see above) who succeeded his father in 1712.

p. 60. *Lord Clare;* Thomas Pelham-Holles created Earl of Clare 19th October 1714 and Duke of Newcastle 11 August 1715 was a firm friend of Vanbrugh. Unhappily the architect did not live to reap the benefit of Newcastle influence during his long tenure of office as Secretary of State 1724–1742 and afterwards.

p. 61. Whitehall, Feb 5 1715, to Lord Clare afterwards Duke of Newcastle The Early part of the letter refers to Newcastle House Lincolns Inn Fields, said to have been built originally by Captain Winde the architect of old Buckingham House.

p. 62. *Vanderbank;* (1694–1739) a popular painter of " Histories and Landscapes." " Had he not been careless and extravagant, says my author, (*Vertue*) he might have made a greater figure than almost any painter this nation has produced; so bold and free was his pencil and so masterly his drawing " Walpole Vol. II. He died of consumption when he was not above 45.

p. 62. *Jacob;* Tonson. Publisher. See Introduction.

p. 63. Wensday to Jacob Tonson. The date of this letter is determined by the revival of the Clare and Newcastle titles in favour of Thomas Pelham.

p. 63. *Horace Walpole;* Horatio Walpole brother of Sir Robert and afterwards Lord Walpole of Woolterton. Horace Walpole the younger has dealt hardly by his Uncle but in spite of his hearty and indeed rather uncouth manners there is reason to suppose that he was a politician and diplomatist of considerable ability.

p. 63. *Benson;* possibly of Bramham, Yorkshire, and afterwards Lord Bingley, but he was a Tory and this may refer to William Benson the Surveyor. See note.

p. 79. Scarborough August 21st 1716. To the Duchess of Marlborough.

p. 79. *Dean Jones;* John, Dean of Bangor inst: 1689 died 1727.

p. 79. *Mr Walters;* Peter, was a Scrivener, in fact a professional matchmaker, and a money Lender. He was called in about the Newcastle marriage (see below) and that between Lord Carlisle's heir and Sunderland's daughter. He was quite a celebrated personage in his day and appears among very distinguished company in Lady Herveys gallery of " Characteristic Pictures." The title of his exhibit was Ruin. Pope also says of him;

> " Whats property, dear Swift, you see it alter,
> From me to you, from you to Peter Walter."

p. 79. *Lord Essex;* 1697 to 1742. William Capel 3d Earl.

p. 83. To the Duchess of Marlborough 6th of November 1716

p. 83. *Mr Walpole;* afterwards Sir Robert.

p. 84. Whitehall Nov 8th 1716 to the Duchess of Marlborough

p. 85. *your Glassmaker Moor;* the following extract from a letter of the Duchess to Mr Jennings in 1714 is the only trace I can find of this character. " Mr Jernas doing his own pictures in the manner you say that are of value, is a sure proof that he believes it a security; but he is I think a great Fopp and conceited in many things; and since you say that you dont understand that matter, I wish you would take an Opportunity of speaking to my Oracle, Mr Moore, for he certainly has very good sense, and I think him very honest and understanding in many trades besides his own. etc."

p. 86. Whitehall Nov 15th 1716 to the Duke of Newcastle.

p. 86. *Lord Bridgewater;* Scroop Egerton, Earl and later Duke of Bridgewater married Elizabeth Churchill 3d daughter of the Duke and Duchess of Marlborough.

p. 87. Whitehall Nov 27th 1716 to the Duke of Newcastle;

p. 88. *The Brigadier;* Brigadier General William Watkins, Keeper of H.M. Private Roads and Conductor and Guide in the Royal Progresses. at £200 per annum.

p. 89. London Dec 15th 1716 to Mr Bobart, one of the Comptrollers at Blenheim. Bobart was probably a member of the family of the well known Keepers of the Physic Garden at Oxford, one of whom manufactured the forged Dragon. See Aubrey.

p. 89. *Mr Thornhill;* afterwards Sir James, (1676–1734) was a very popular fresco painter for the interior decoration of large buildings. He painted the original decorations in the Dome of St Paul's (see curious anecdote in Walpole) the great Hall at Greenwich Hospital, and rooms at Hampton Court and elsewhere. He seems to have been in continual trouble about his fees. Later than this he painted the offices of the South Sea Company, and in the dispute as to fees which followed, it appeared that he only got 25/s a square yard at Blenheim for the Hall This compares badly with the 40/s at St Paul's and at Greenwich. The commissioners arbitrating in yet another dispute concerning the ceilings at Moor Park awarded him £3 per square yard. Walpole says that Thornhill's work at Blenheim is his best, nevertheless he did not continue there and the great Saloon is the work of Laguerre whom the Duchess had already employed at Marlborough House. Laguerre was noted for his modest and unassuming character.

p. 89. To Godolphin in 1717

p. 93. *Lord Townshend;* Charles, 2nd Viscount, (1674 to 1738) Secretary of State 1714–17 and 1721–30.

p. 94. Wednesday July 3d 1717 to the Duke of Newcastle.

p. 94. *Mr Bothmer;* Baron Bothmar George the First's German counsellor. With others of George's German entourage he has been accused of venality " every day some infamous project on foot to get money " in the words of Townshend.

p. 96. Greenwich Dec 21 1717 to the Duke of Newcastle.

p. 96. *Lord Chetwynd;* Walter 1st Viscount; (1678 to 1736) he was Ranger of St James Park & Keeper of the Mall, created Viscount June 1717.

p. 96. *Lord Sunderland;* Charles 3rd Earl (1674–1722) Marlborough's son-in-law; his rather oppressive manner and too aggressive Whiggery had gone far to wreck the party in Queen Anne's time, but thanks to his knowledge of Foreign affairs and his ability to speak German he flourished under George I until the South Sea trouble, and his death. (See below.) Though brilliant and good looking he seems to have been a very unsympathetic character. His vices, his Republicanism, his Gambling, his Bibliophily are unable to soften this impression in face of the united evidence of his contemporaries.

p. 96. *Duchess of Munster;* Ermengarde Melusina von der Schulenberg afterwards Duchess of Kendal. Politically the more important of George's German mistresses.

p. 96. Friday one o'clock. to the Duke of Newcastle.

p. 96. *my friend Benson;* William (1683–1754) succeeded Sir Christopher Wren as Surveyor General, the plum of the architectural profession in 1718. See Introduction, Vol. IV.

p. 96. *Lord Parker;* became Lord Chancellor March 1718. He was afterwards created Lord Macclesfield, (See Introduction in his relation to the Blenheim disputes). He supported the King against the Prince of Wales and his impeachment in later years originated at Leicester House.

p. 97. *Ld Chancellor;* William Cowper, husband of the diarist, so often quoted in these notes.

p. 97. *Solicitor;* General Sir Wm. Thompson: (1678–1739)

p. 97. *Attorney:* General; Nicholas Lechmere, (1675–1727) Solicitor General 1714–18, Attorney General 1718–20, Baron Lechmere 1721. He had been one of the managers against Sacheverel, and his conduct during the Aylesbury Election case, in escaping out of his Chambers by a rope made of the sheets of his bed to avoid being taken into Custody at the order of the House of Commons, is refered to by Lady Cowper as a standing joke in Legal circles. His temper is described as " violent, proud, and impracticable " and Lady Mary Montagu notices his tendency to " flounce." He died of apoplexy while dining at Camden House. See also note.

p. 97. Sunday Night to the Duke of Newcastle.

p. 98. *Lord Berkely*; James 3d Earl and K.G. a distinguished Naval Officer and First Lord of the Admiralty 1718; during the quarrel between George I and his son, Berkely is said to have offered to carry off the Prince of Wales to America and keep him there.

p. 100. August 30th 1718 to the Duke of Newcastle

p. 101. Admiral Sir George Byng destroyed the Spanish fleet off Cape Pessaro on August the 11th. See also note, p. 17.

p. 101. *Count de Monteleone*: Spanish envoy on more than one occasion. When Craggs's genuine letter was published in September we find the town laughing over its faults of style and saying that if only Addison had written it, " he would have given them as thorough a defeat by land as Sir George Byng did by sea " !

p. 101. *Cardinal Alberoni*; chief minister of the King of Spain 1715–19 and the mainstay of the alliance with Sweden against England.

p. 101. Greenwich Sept 17th 1718 to the Duke of Newcastle

p. 101. *Abbé Dubois*; Agent of the Regent Orleans in London.

p. 102. Greenwich Saturday to the Duke of Newcastle August (?) 1718

p. 102. *Lady Morpeth*; Lord Morpeth afterwards 4th Earl of Carlisle married a daughter of Lord Sunderland.

p. 102. Greenwich Sunday to the Duke of Newcastle

p. 102. *Lord Walden*, and Lord Suffolk; Henry 5th Earl of Suffolk died 1st SEPT 1718 his son Lord Walden died 1722.

p. 102. *the Duke of Norfolk*; Thomas 8th Duke being a Roman Catholic exercised his office of Earl Marshal by a deputy the Earl of Suffolk & Bindon.

p. 104. Friday to the Duke of Newcastle

p. 104. *Lord Lindsay*; Peregrine Bertie, title of the son of the Duke of Ancaster.

p. 105. Nottingham Dec 17th 1718, to the Duke of Newcastle

p. 105. *Nottingham Castle*; see Introduction, Vol. IV.

p. 106. *Duke of Rutland's Castle*; Belvoir Castle.

p. 107. Castle Howard Dec 25th 1718

p. 107. The repeal of the Occasional Conformity and Schism Acts passed the House of Commons on December 19th. The Occasional Conformity Act is called Lord Nottingham's Bill as originally being the price paid him by the desparate Whigs in 1711 for his support.

p. 107. *Mr Attorney*; Lechmere married Lady Elizabeth Howard a daughter of Lord Carlisle.

p. 108. Castle Howard Jan ye 4th 1719 to the Duke of Newcastle.

p. 109. *Dartiquenave*; Paymaster of the Board of Works and a man of some reputation as an Epicure.

p. 109. *Campbell*; probably Colin Campbell compiler of Vitruvius Britannicus. See also Introduction, Vol. IV.

NOTES

p. 109. *Benson the Young;* younger brother of William Benson the Surveyor was made Clerk of the Works and Secretary of the Board in place of Hawksmoor. See also Introduction, Vol. IV.

p. 109. *Lord Lonsdale;* Henry Viscount Lonsdale succeeded 1713 and died 1750.

p. 110. Nottingham Jan 24th 1719 to the Duke of Newcastle.

p. 111. Lady Vanbrugh's great aunt the saintly Margaret Blagge, subject of a charming biography by Evelyn, consented to marry, after a nine years courtship, Sidney Godolphin the great minister, and so was grandmother of the Duchess of Newcastle.

p. 111. London July 1st 1719 to Jacob Tonson in Paris.

p. 112. *Romantick desire;* see Introduction, Vol. I.

p. 112. *Lord Cobham;* Sir Richard Temple (1669–1749) created Viscount Cobham 1718, a Whig and a fine soldier, was a good friend to Vanbrugh whom he employed upon his garden buildings at Stowe (see Introduction, Vol. IV) and afterwards raised there a pyramid to his memory.

p. 112. *Highlanders;* General Wightman had defeated and captured the Spaniards at Glen Shiel on June 5th and dispersed their Highland allies.

p. 112. *Weavers;* about this time there were considerable demonstrations on the part of the silk weavers of London in support of the " Callico " Bill a protective measure forbidding the use or wearing of dyed or printed callicos imported from abroad. Several women caught wearing dresses of such material had them stripped off by the mob.

p. 112. *Brother Charles;* (1680–1740) had been in command of the Burford, a ship of 70 guns, with Sir George Byng's fleet at Cape Pessaro (see above). On 14th of February 1719 he had the misfortune to put his ship ashore on the coast of Italy and was fully a month or more getting her off again. He does not seem to have got much further employment afloat after this unfortunate affair. He was elected Member of Parliament for Plymouth in the last year of his life.

p. 113. Whitehall Augt 6th 1719 to the Duke of Newcastle.

p. 113. *Benson's reign ended;* see Introduction, Vol. IV.

p. 113. *Mr Hewet;* afterwards Sir Thomas, had been Surveyor of Woods and Forrests and now succeeded Benson at the Board of Works, probably by the influence of the Duke of Kingston. His wife was an early friend of Lady Mary Montagu.

p. 114. *Tonson's Nephew;* also Jacob, he died 1736 a few months before his more celebrated Uncle, leaving several children, among them another Jacob, and Mary whose son eventually inherited " old " Jacob's letters, among them many of these of Vanbrugh and the splendid series of Kit Cat portraits which his descendants still have.

p. 115. London August 11 1719

p. 115. *Boscawen;* Hugh, Comptroller of H.M. Household became Viscount Falmouth in the following year. See also page 134, where he sides with the Duchess of Marlborough in the House of Lords.

p. 116. August 15th 1719 to the Duke of Newcastle.

p. 116. *Thornhill to be Surveyor;* Walpole mentions the stir among architects at the rumour of Thornhill's intention to undertake that art. He was indeed employed in after years as Surveyor as well as painter at the building of Moor Park from designs by Leoni. The Rev James Dallaway, Walpole's editor, says that he designed and built his own house in Dorset. Judging by an engraving, this house, though much Gothicised later, on one elevation, was a simple but effective design in the then rather old fashioned style of William and Mary. It appears to be of brick with stone quoins and dressings. The whole effect looks very pleasant but definitely in the style of the good country builder rather than the London architect.

p. 117. London Sept 10th 1719 to Lord Sunderland, or Stanhope.

p. 117. *Hawksmoor and Hewett;* In a memorial to Lord Carlisle in 1726 Hawksmoor gives the following details: "When Sir Thomas Hewet was made Surveyor General after the dismission of the said Benson, I had hopes of being restored to some at least of my employment, and Sir John Vanbrugh knowing my hardships endeavoured and was very solicitous for me, and had promises from Sir Thomas Hewet in my favour; but he forgot his obligations to Sir John Vanbrugh and left me to shift for myself."

p. 118. *Mr Aislaby;* John, (1670–1742) Lord of the Admiralty 1710–1714, Treasurer of the Navy 1714–1718, Chancellor of the Exchequer 1718–1721, was ultimately expelled the House of Commons and sent to the Tower for the part he took in the South Sea scheme.

p. 120. Whitehall 5th November 1719 to Jacob Tonson.

p. 120. *Mr Spence;* Joseph (1699–1768) Professor of Poetry at Oxford 1728 and friend of Pope?

p. 120. *Mainwaring;* does this refer to the incident of the Examiner? See note.

p. 121. Whitehall Nov 29th 1719 to Jacob Tonson in Paris.

p. 122. *Lord Burlington;* Richard Boyle 3rd Earl, (1695–1753) the celebrated patron, amateur architect, and connoisseur. See Introduction, Vol. IV.

p. 123. *Mr Secretary Craggs and his father;* James Craggs the younger (1686–1721) was a great favourite of George I and his mistress the Countess Platen. He was Secretary at War 1717 and Secretary of State a year later, he managed the allotments of South Sea Stock for the King's mistresses and was equally envolved in all the other shady parts of that scheme, he had the good fortune to die of Small pox on the day of the presentation of the first report of the enquiry into the Companies affairs in February 1721. His father, also James, a dependent of Sunderland's, was Post Master General and the founder of the family fortunes. He died on the day before he was to appear before the House of Commons, under suspicion of poison.

p. 123. *Lady Mohun;* probably Elizabeth Lawrence, widow of the Lord Mohun who was killed in the doubly fatal duel with the Duke of Hamilton in 1711. By this time she had created a scandal by marrying a very young man Charles Mordaunt.

p. 123. * The part of the letter in Italics is in the handwriting of Lady Vanbrugh.

p. 124. Whitehall Dec 31st 1719 to Jacob Tonson in Paris.

p. 124. Cardinal Alberoni was dismissed on December 5th and Lord Stanhope went to France to concert demands with the French and the Empire. These were agreed upon in January 1720.

p. 125. London Feb 18th 1720 to Jacob Tonson in Paris

p. 125. *Lord Chamberlain;* The Duke of Newcastle.

p. 126. *Heydegger's Masquerades;* John James Heydegger described in the Dunciad as a Swiss, instituted these entertainments which became very fashionable owing to the enthusiasm with which George I took them up. A description is given in a letter of Montagu Bacon's to Lady Mary Montagu. " There was a masquerade on Thursday last at the Haymarket Playhouse. By laying planks over the Pit, they made a continued floor as far as the Boxes, which were blocked up with pieces of fine painting, and two or three of the side Boxes left open for wine and other things. 'Twas of Heidegger's projecting; the price of tickets a guinea and a half, and not only so but they that took them were obliged to subscribe too for the next. . . ." The Bishops looked askance at the masquerades and Lord Chesterfield comments on the " Heat and disorder of the masquerade " in a letter to Mrs Howard. In May 1729 Heydegger and his entertainments were presented by a Grand Jury as nuisances.

p. 126. London Sept 15th 1720 to the Duke of Newcastle

p. 126. *Mr Du Bois;* a fellow member of the Board of works. See Intro., Vol. IV.

p. 126. *Duke of Chandos;* James Brydges created Duke of Chandos in 1719 had been Paymaster General of the Forces. His house at Cannons Middlesex, was a by-word for magnificence in every part, and many of the most expensive painters and sculptors of the day were employed upon it. Dallaway gives 1712 as the date at which it was begun and James of Greenwich as the architect who also built St George's Hanover Square. As to whether Pope intended Cannons as the object of his Satire in the Essay on Taste cannot perhaps be decided, but certainly the poem was addressed to the Earl of Burlington and ridicule of a house by James of Greenwich would come easily to an adherent of the Burlingtonian school such as Pope.

p. 127. London Feb 2nd 1721 to the Earl of Carlisle.
In the middle of the South Sea Crisis, Knight the Cashier (see note, p. 131) had fled the country 23rd of January and Jeckyll's Bill had passed earlier that month.

p. 127. The Duke of Marlborough's resignation followed on a charge of Jacobitism and two desperate appeals on the part of his Duchess to George I through the Duchess of Kendal to which the King returned very cold replies.

p. 128. London February 7th 1721 to the Earl of Carlisle

p. 128. *Lord Stanhope;* created Earl Stanhope 1718 after a distinguished military and diplomatic career in Spain during the war, became Secretary of State in 1714, First Lord of the Treasury 1717, and Secretary of State again 1718 to 21. Lady Mary Montagu cites him as saying that " he imposed on foreign ministers by telling them the naked truth."

p. 128. The suspected people are probably the two Craggses Aislaby and Sunderland, and the Prince's knowledge probably that of the implication of his fathers mistresses.

p. 128. The younger Craggs died Feb 16th and was buried in Westminster Abbey. See note.

p. 129. *Lord Carleton;* Henry Boyle son of the Earl of Orrery, Chancellor of the Exchequer 1702–8, Secretary of State 1708–10, Lord President 1721.

Lady Mary Montagu writes January 1726 " My Lord Carleton has left this transitory world, and disposed of his estate as he did of his time between Lady Clarendon and the Duchess of Queensbury. Jewels of great value he has given, as he did his affections, first to the mother and then to the daughter. He was taken ill in my company at a concert at the Duchess of Marlborough's (Henrietta 2nd Duchess) and died two days afterwards holding the fair Duchess by the hand, and being fed at the same time with a fine fat chicken; thus dying as he had lived in the indulgence of his pleasures."

p. 129.   Feb 20th 1721 to the Earl of Carlisle.

p. 130.   *Lord Carteret;* John, afterwards Earl of Granville, had made his name on an embassy to Sweden and Denmark; his ability to speak German endeared him to George I and his entourage, and he became Secretary of State. His success provoked the jealousy of Townshend and he was eventually shipped off as Lord Lieutenant of Ireland in the midst of the Drapier Letters disturbances.

p. 130.   *Lord Lincoln;* Paymaster General of the Forces 1715–20.

p. 131.   March 25th 1721 Greenwich to the Earl of Carlisle

p. 131.   *Knight;* Robert, Cashier of the South Sea Company fled the country on the 23rd of January 1721 to evade the investigations of the Secret Committee. He lived for some years in Paris where he is described by Lady Irwin in 1730 " Mr Knight lives always here, and is quite metamorphised [*sic*] into a fine gentleman; from being a man of business he is now become a ' gallant homme,' which character just as ill becomes him as a suit of embroidery would a country bumpkin. He keeps a great table, has always a vast deal of company, and being both generous and rich, is much visited and esteemed; amidst all these caresses and plenty he groans for the leeks and garlic of Egypt (if I may use that expression) and is perfectly unhappy he can't breathe the air of dear England."

p. 131.   The Secret Committee charged Lord Sunderland with receiving £50,000 of South Sea Stock without payment. He was acquitted largely by Walpole's influence on 15th of March.

p. 132.   *Lord Irwin;* Richard, 5th Viscount, son-in-law of Lord Carlisle, lost heavily in the South Sea scheme and was constrained to apply for a West Indian Governorship. The expression loss may refer to financial loss or to his departure for Barbadoes.

p. 133.   *Lord Molesworth;* a member of the Secret Committee and one of the most violent prosecutors of the South Sea investigations.

p. 133.   London May 5th 1721 to the Earl of Carlisle. This letter finally establishes the date of the Justification. See Introduction.

p. 134.   London May 25th 1721 to the Earl of Carlisle.

p. 134.   *Lord Peterborough;* Charles Mordaunt, 3d Earl, during Queen Anne's time his military exploits in Spain caused him to be puffed by the Opposition as a second Marlborough but he could not maintain the position they thrust upon him. Horace Walpole credits him with great wit and charm, and we have a curious picture of him some three years later than this letter. " It is a curious sight to see him with his blue ribbon and star, and a cabbage under each arm, or a chicken in his hand, which after he himself has purchased at market, he carries home for his dinner " (Lady Harvey to Mrs Howard).

p. 134. *Lord Cadogan*, Marlborough's old right-hand man who succeeded him as Captain General.

p. 134. *Lord Bristol*; John Harvey created Earl of Bristol 1714, father of the celebrated Sporus.

p. 134. *Lord Falmouth*; see Boscawen above.

p. 134. *The Bishop of Bangor*; Hoadley a latitudinarian, and the protagonist in the Bangorian Controversy, was an intimate friend of the Marlboroughs.

p. 134. *Duke of Kingston*; see above.

p. 134. *Bishop of Salisbury*; William Talbot, nominated 1714, translated to Durham in September of this year.

p. 134. *Lord Cowper*; see above.

p. 134. *Lord Trevor*; Thomas 1st Lord Trevor, Chief Justice of the King's Bench, Lord Privy Seal from 1726 to his death in 1730.

p. 134. *Duke of Wharton*; Philip son of the arch-Whig (see above) amazed the town by his gambling and his gallantries. He became a Jacobite and a convert to the Roman Church and died in a Spanish Monastery in 1731.
" Wharton the scorn and wonder of our days."

p. 134. *Lady Lechmere*; (see also above) Lady Elizabeth Howard daughter of Lord Carlisle and wife of Nicholas Lechmere (see above) was a firm friend of the Duchess Sarah. Lady Lechmere's gambling losses at Bath are noticed by Lady Mary Montagu " —having played away her reputation and fortune, she has poisoned herself. This is the effect of Prudence." The report was false however for she lived to take a second husband Sir Thomas Robinson, a virtuoso of the Burlington group, (see Introduction) and died in 1739.

p. 136. Castle Howard Augt 8th 1721 to the Duke of Newcastle.

p. 137. *Mr Pelham*; 1696 to 1754, Henry was a younger brother of the Duke of Newcastle. He entered Parliament 1718 and was Chancellor of the Exchequer from 1743 to the time of his death.

p. 137. *Sir Thomas*; Hewet the Surveyor. See above.

p. 137. York Augt 26th 1721 to Brigadier Watkins.

p. 137. *Admiral Delaval and his nephew*; George Delaval, as Captain served on Spanish and African coasts, and his nephew Francis Blake Delaval, who succeeded him.

p. 137. *Lumley Castle*; see Introduction, Vol. IV.

p. 138. *Ripley*; Thomas made Surveyor General after Hewet, by the influence of Robert Walpole for whom he carried out Houghton from Campbell's designs. His best known works are the Admiralty (except the screen) and parts of Greenwich Hospital on which Hawksmoor commented: " There is Imperial Mischief (as Alexander says in the play) done to Greenwich Hospital since Sir John died, by whom your Lordship knows well enough; I once thought it would have been a Public Building, but it will sink into a deformed Barrac." Ripley was said to have begun life as a country carpenter.

p. 139.   Whitehall Nov 16 1721 to the Earl of Carlisle

p. 139.   *Inoculation;* Lady Mary Montagu first mentions Inoculation for Small pox and her intention to introduce it in England from Turkey as early as 1717. In the early days of her innovation opposition was very strong: "The faculty rose in arms to a man, foretelling faillure and the most disastrous consequences; the clergy descanted from their pulpits on the impiety of thus seeking to take events out of the hand of Providence; and the common people were taught to hoot at an unnatural mother, who had risked the lives of her own children."

p. 142.   London April 24th 1722 to the Earl of Carlisle.

p. 142.   *Lord Scarborough;* Richard Lumley, 2nd Earl succeeded 1721, had a not undistinguished Political career but was: "apt to melancholy and fits of depression." He committed suicide on the eve of his marriage with the Duchess of Manchester, grand-daughter of the great Duke of Marlborough 1740.

p. 142.   *Colonel Tyrril;* James, after a distinguished military career under Marlborough settled down to complete his father's building scheme at Shotover in which it seems probable that Vanbrugh or Hawksmoor was involved. See Introduction.

p. 142.   *Lord Pembroke;* Thomas 8th Earl.

p. 143.   London May 5th 1722 to the Earl of Carlisle. Note, p. 129.

p. 143.   *The President;* Lord Carleton.   See above.

p. 143.   *Horace Walpole;* afterwards Lord Walpole of Wolterton.   This embassy was a move against Carteret.   The resident ambassador Sir Luke Schwab being his man.

p. 145.   London June 18th 1722 to Jacob Tonson in Herefordshire.

p. 146.   *Cibber;* Colley (1671–1757) son of Caius Gabriel Cibber, sculptor and architect, was made Poet Laureate in 1730 for his plays and celebrated Apology for the Life of Mr Colley Cibber, Comedian.   See Introduction, Vol. I.

p. 147.   London June 19th 1722 to the Earl of Carlisle

p. 147.   *Clayton;* Robert William afterwards Lord Sundon.   Originally a dependent of the Marlboroughs' and, with Guidott, managed the Duke's estate during his residence abroad 1712–14.   Mrs Clayton was a great favourite with the Duchess Sarah who got her made BedChamber Woman to the Princess of Wales; after that the Claytons rise was steady and rapid.

p. 147.   *Guidot;* another member of the Marlboroughs' Court, and trusted by them as a confidant and man of affairs.   Occasional endorsements on the Vanbrugh letters initialed G. are probably his.

p. 147.   London July 19th 1722 to the Earl of Carlisle.

p. 148.   *Mr Doddington;* George Bubb Doddington (1691–1762) afterwards Lord Melcome.   On the strength of his Diary he has been spoken of with self righteous scorn as a "flunkey and a place hunter" but there are indications from among his contemporaries of something different and that he was amusing company. (See Lady Mary Montagu.) He is described, Cumberland, p. 191, "Dodington, lolling in his chair, in perfect apathy and self command, dozing and even snoring at intervals in his lethargic

NOTES

way, broke out every now and then into gleams and flashes of wit and humour."

p. 148. *Lord Blandford;* son of Henrietta Duchess of Marlborough and Lord Godolphin.

p. 150. Greenwich July 30th 1723 to the Duke of Newcastle

p. 150. *the Great Chamberlain;* Duke of Ancaster hereditary holder of that office.

p. 152. *Lord Halifax and Lady Halifax;* George Second Earl, married a daughter of the Earl of Scarborough.

p. 152. *The Duke of Ancaster;* Robert Bertie (1660–1723) formerly Earl of Lindsey, created Duke 1715.

p. 152. *Mr Montagu* (Westminster); Wortley Montagu (?).

p. 152. *Lord Binny;* possibly Benson of Bramham, Yorkshire, who was himself something of an amateur architect.

p. 156. London Feb 11th 1724 to the Earl of Carlisle

p. 156. *The Bill for Reforming the Streets;* This Bill would appear to have come to nothing. It followed on a petition of the citizens of Westminster complaining of the state of the streets. A committee was set up and examined the matter, Vanbrugh making a report which Lord Morpeth brought before the house. It was proposed to set up a Commission to carry out the repaving and administer the money which was to be raised by a " Pound Rate " and a tax on wheeled vehicles and coaches shod with iron.

p. 157. London Feb 18th 1724 to the Earl of Carlisle.

p. 158. *Lord Stair;* the celebrated ambassador of George I in Paris.

p. 158. *The Bishop of London;* Dr Edmund Gibson became Bishop of London in 1720; his denunciations of the Masquerades gave great offence to George I who was devoted to them. Bishop Gibson died in 1748.

p. 158. London March 26th 1724 to the Earl of Carlisle

p. 160. *Lord Walpole;* son of Sir Robert was raised to the Peerage in 1723. He married Margaret Rolle then 14 years of age. This Lady's amours and irreligion became a great scandal in later years. In 1751 she took in second marriage a Mr Shirley of which transaction Lady Mary Montagu writes " she piques herself on not being able to refuse him anything. It has been the way with all her lovers; he is the most creditable of any she ever had; his birth and sense will induce him to behave to her with decency, and it is what she has not been much used to." The poor lady must have been again disappointed for a separation took place at the end of three years.

p. 164. December 10th 1724 to the Earl of Carlisle

p. 165. *Mr Johnston:* probably Mr Johnstone one time Secretary for Scotland: this gentleman posessed a villa at Twickenham the gardens of which were celebrated and at which he entertained lavishly.

p. 165. *Leicester House:* residence of the Prince of Wales.

p. 166. August 12th 1725 to Jacob Tonson.

p. 167. *Col: Tyrril's house:* Shotover Park Oxfordshire in which Vanbrugh and Hawksmoor probably had a hand. See Introduction.

p. 167. *Rowsham;* seat of the Dormers at this time they were members of Pope and Swift's Tory circle.

p. 167.   The Duchess of Marlborough (Sarah) writes to Lord Carlisle to explain this incident, saying she had given orders not to admit Vanbrugh into Blenheim: " I should not do this upon the worthlessness of his character, nor for any abuses in the building occasioned by him, but in the life of the Duke of Marlborough he had the impudence to print a libel both of him and me for which his bones ought to have been broke, but I did not think it worth the trouble of giving any directions about such a fellow who by it added to the contempt everybody had for him before and did not hurt me; besides this his behaviour was so saucy to me both in his letters and everything that he said to me and of me, that one should wonder at any other person after such proceedings should desire to come within my walls etc etc " (from an unpublished MS. at Castle Howard) There is also this curious comment in a letter dated 10th August from William Dowdeswell to Harley 2nd Earl of Oxford and preserved at Welbeck Abbey: " One thing is very remarkable (about Blenheim) the Dutchess has given out a list of persons yt may not see the house, among wm are two of her own daughters and Sir Jo Vanbrugh. It is very hard that these Ladys may not come to see their Mamma, and that ye Dutchman may not visit his own Child, who, however he may appear a meer lump and mishapen to others, may seem beautifull in his eyes that begot him."

p. 168.   Greenwich Sept 4th 1725 to the Earl of Carlisle.

p. 169.   *Lord Sussex;* Talbot Yelverton, created Earl in 1717, afterwards a Deputy Earl Marshal and married to a Pelham.

p. 170.   Greenwich Oct 25th 1725 to Jacob Tonson in Herefordshire.

p. 170.   *Master Harry;* Henry Pelham. See above.

p. 172.   London March 8th 1726 to the Earl of Carlisle.

p. 173.   *Lord Trevor:* succeeded the Duke of Kingston as Lord Privy Seal.

p. 173.   *Duke of Grafton;* 2nd Duke, grandson of Charles II.

p. 173.   *Lord Bathurst;* 1st Lord Bathurst, friend of Pope, Swift, and Burlington. He and Pope laid out the gardens for Mrs Howard, afterwards Lady Suffolk, at Marble Hill Twickenham. See Introduction, Vol. IV.

NOTES TO THE PLATES

Frontispiece : Sir John Vanbrugh after Sir Godfrey Kneller.

Plate I. General Plan of Blenheim Palace ; from *Vitruvius Britannicus*, Vol. I, 1715. " I am at a Loss how to express my Obligation to this worthy Gentleman (Sir John Vanbrugh) for promoting my Labours, in most generously assisting me with his original Drawings, and most carefully correcting the plates as they advanced." (Colin Campbell.)

Plate II. General Plan of Castle Howard ; from *Vitruvius Britannicus*, Vol. I, 1715, " drawn from the originals of the architect and by him most carefully revised." This plan has been transposed in the original printing so that the Office and Stable courts and the wings corresponding to them should be conceived as exchanging their positions. The plan shows a bow window to the cabinet of the Western Suite for which a drawing exists in the British Museum.

Plate III. The Entrance Court, Blenheim Palace ; from a print in the British Museum.

Plate IV. The Old Manor at Woodstock ; from a sepia drawing of about 1700 (?) in the British Museum. The main part of the original palace had been demolished as early as 1617.

Plate V. The Bridge at Blenheim Palace ; from a print in the British Museum. The present appearance of the bridge though very noble lacks the arcades on either side the carriage-way. It seems doubtful if these were ever executed.

Plate VI. Claremont ; this Plate is taken from the decorative border surrounding an engraved plan of about 1750 in the British Museum, and shows the house and outbuildings of Vanbrugh's designing. The plan when compared with that given in *Vitruvius Britannicus*, Vol. III, shows that Kent's alterations to Vanbrugh's lay-out of the gardens were not very drastic, though of course all in the direction of a " judicious wildness."

Plate VII. The North or Entrance Front and Plan of Seaton Delaval ; from *Vitruvius Britannicus*, Vol. III, 1725. The plate gives the front without the wings very nearly as executed, except that the steps were brought further forward of the plinths of the coupled columns, and an elaborately sculptured armorial achievement and trophy was substituted for the lunette in the pediment. There are some discrepancies in the Plan between the Wings as shown and as executed, where they have fine flat bow fronts towards the Office and Stable Courts.

Plate VIII. Perspective view of Castle Howard from the North ; from *Vitruvius Britannicus*, Vol. III, engraved by Hulsbergh. This shows the intended scheme which was never completed. The garden lay-out in the background seems in part imaginary (see Intro. ; p. xxxvii). At each end of the Southern Wings bow windows are indicated, of which that to the East was certainly never executed (see Plan, Plate II). For the arrangement of gates, see pp. xxxvii, 163, 164 ; foundations for the two arched entrances at the sides are said to have been discovered during excavation works some years ago.

THE INDEX

INDEX

INDEX

INDEX

INDEX

INDEX

INDEX

INDEX